Study Guide

Managers and the Legal Environment
Strategies for the 21st Century
FIFTH EDITION

Constance E. Bagley

Harvard Business School

Diane W. Savage

Cooley Godward LLP, Stanford University

Prepared by

Joseph A. Zavaletta

The University of Texas at Brownsville

John C. Jones

The University of Texas at Brownsville

THOMSON

WEST

Australia · Brazil · Canada · Mexico · Singapore · Spain · United Kingdom · United States

THOMSON
WEST

Study Guide to accompany Managers and the Legal Environment: Strategies for the 21st Century, Fifth Edition
Constance E. Bagley and Diane W. Savage

VP/Editorial Director:
Jack W. Calhoun

Publisher:
Rob Dewey

Acquisitions Editor:
Steve Silverstein, Esq.

Senior Developmental Editor:
Jan Lamar

Executive Marketing Manager:
Lisa Lysne

Production Project Manager:
Tamborah E. Moore

Manager of Technology, Editorial:
Vicky True

Technology Project Editor:
Christine Wittmer

Web Coordinator:
Scott Cook

Senior Manufacturing Coordinator:
Charlene Taylor

Printer:
Globus
Minster, OH

Art Director:
Michelle Kunkler

Cover and Internal Designer:
Grannan Graphic Design
Cincinnati, OH

Cover Images:
© Solveig Stibbe/Alamy and Getty
Images, Inc.

Thomson Higher Education
5191 Natorp Boulevard
Mason, OH 45040
USA

Contents

CHAPTER 1
ETHICS, VALUE CREATION, AND RISK MANAGEMENT

Introduction

Ethical decisions are part of every manager's job. A manager's ethics will affect a company's reputation, long-term viability, and the manager's personal sense of worth and accomplishment. Studies and surveys show that ethics affect the short-term bottom line, as well as a company's long-term relationships with customers, suppliers, employees, members of the surrounding community, and other stakeholders. This chapter presents a framework to analyze the interaction of ethics, business, and law. Taking an ecological approach, chapter one presents issues, lessons, and dilemmas faced by managers when considering ethical, legal, and business matters.

I. **LAW AND PUBLIC POLICY.** American law seeks to enhance economic activity, commerce, and for-profit corporations through the pursuit of four key public policy objectives:

   A. **Promoting Economic Growth.** Law protects private property, sets rules to ensure compliance with private contracts, facilitates capital markets, and creates proprietary interests in intellectual property.

   B. **Protecting Workers.** Law protects workers by establishing guidelines for safe working conditions, and sets minimum standards and assurances for contractual and civil rights of employees including workers' compensation regimes.

   C. **Promoting Consumer Welfare.** Law protects consumers by requiring that products are safe when used as intended, encouraging innovation, preventing trusts and price gauging, while punishing fraud.

   D. **Promoting Public Welfare.** Law provides for public welfare by establishing a fair and impartial justice system to resolve commercial disputes, safeguarding the environment, and collecting and spending taxes.

II. **LAW AND STRATEGY**

   A. **Ecological Approach to Business Regulation.**

      1. Porter identifies five forces that determine the attractiveness of an industry: buyer power, supplier power, competitive threats, the availability of substitutes and threats from new market entrants.

1

2.   Good managers incorporate law and the legal regime to increase their industry attractiveness, maximize economic opportunities and minimize financial risks.

B.   **Non Compliance with Law is Not an Option.** Examples of Texaco, Drexel Burnham, TAP Pharmaceuticals, Arthur Anderson, WorldCom and Cendant demonstrate that non-compliance with accounting rules can bring down even multi-million dollar corporations.

C.   **What Should the Firm Do?** Though certain practices might be legal, when firms allow or condone unethical practices, over time, they put the long-term health of the firm at risk. Over time, unethical practices lead to illegal behavior.

> **Case 1.1--*Bammert v. Don's Super Valu, Inc.,*** 646 N.W.2d 365 (Wisc. 2002). Plaintiff, an at-will employee, was terminated in retaliation for the legal and proper actions of her non-employee husband. The Supreme Court of Wisconsin held that although employees *can* recover for wrongful terminations if discharged for their own behavior, which comports with public policy, this rule does not extend to protect the employee for the actions of a spouse. The court refused to create a new public policy exception to the at-will doctrine.

III.   **THE ETHICAL TONE IS SET AT THE TOP.** Consider the pay disparity and wealth gap between CEO and executive compensation compared to that of workers and entry level employees. What message do employees and the public receive when they learn of scandals involving CEO's like Dennis Kozlowski (Tyco), John Rigas (Adelphia), Phil Condit (Boeing) and Dick Grasso (NYSE)?

IV.   **ETHICAL BUSINESS LEADER'S DECISION TREE**
Beyond considerations of shareholder profits, compliance with the law is only a baseline measure of effective managerial action. To ensure success, managers must create a culture of socially responsibility by asking a series of questions:

A.   **Is the Action Legal?**
If the action is illegal or violates the spirit of the law, then clearly the manager must not take the action. Yet not all legal actions are understood as ethical *per se*. See discussion on Saint Thomas Aquinas on law and ethics.

B.   **Would it Maximize Shareholder Value?**
Manager must consider the interests of the shareholders. However, a myopic focus on shareholders can result in unfair treatment of non-shareholders and can harm the bottom line. Due to information transfer via the internet and TV

networks, an increased focus on corporate abuses, environmental harm, and fraud means that when firms do good work, they are rewarded for being good corporate citizens.

C.   **Is the Action Ethical? What is Ethical?**
Managers always employ ethical considerations in their decisionmaking. There are different ways of understanding an ethical decision. The three main ethical frameworks use *teleological*, *deontological*, or comparative justice viewpoints.

1.   Teleological View of Ethics.

- A teleological view is concerned with the consequences or outcomes of decisions. Morality is measured by the effect a decision has on others.
- Utilitarianism, proposed by British philosophers Jeremy Bentham (c. 1748-1832) and John Stuart Mill (c. 1806-1873), is an outcome-based value system that holds an action is ethical if it produces the greatest good for the greatest number.
- This approach is criticized because it tends to reduce the welfare of people to plus and minus signs on a cost-benefit worksheet.

2.   **Deontological View of Ethics.** The deontological view emphasizes the motivation and principle behind an action, not the consequences.

- *Rawlsian* ethics proposes that social interaction should maximize the worst-off in society.
- *Kantian* ethics (named after German philosopher Immanuel Kant (c. 1724-1804)) emphasizes the form of action (not the outcomes) and the reason for choosing said actions.
- Kant argued that "categorical imperatives" are ethical guidelines for behavior.
- An action is ethical, i.e. imperative, if a person would: (a) want everyone to act in this manner (*universalizability*) or accept the action to apply to themselves (*reversibility*).

3.   **Comparative Justice.** Consequences of decisions can be compared between rule-based systems and outcome-oriented (*utilitarian*) frameworks.

- *Distributive* justice focuses on how the burden and benefits of a particular system are distributed among constituents, all the while attempting to maximize the amount of benefits to be divided.
- *Compensatory* justice believes that those who harm others should compensate those same people for the harm done.

- *Retributive* justice emphasizes ways to deter wrongdoers by punishing them instead of simply compensating those they injure.

4. Historical Perspective: Aquinas on Law and Ethics.

- Saint Thomas Aquinas (c. 1225-1274), theologian and philosopher, believed that: Laws could either be just or unjust; Just human laws: (1) are consonant with universal good; (2) can be obeyed; (3) are unambiguous; (4) approved by the community; and (5) universal; and Immoral laws should be disregarded or opposed.

- Modern legal theorists usually separate the dictates of a law and its inherent morality.

- One should distinguish what is legal from what is right as a means to encourage morality through law and the need to reform laws as social mores change.

D. **Actions that Might Maximize Shareholder Value But Would Be Unethical.** The wise manager understands that the long-term benefits of maintaining a good reputation exceed the risks of engaging in short-term, legal, yet unethical behavior.

E. **Actions that Do Not Maximize Shareholder Value But are Ethically Required**. The manager must balance the social responsibility with maximizing shareholder returns.

V. **RESOLVING THE TENSION BETWEEN LONG-TERM AND SHORT-TERM VALUES**

A. **In the Long Term, Good Ethics are Simply Good Business**. Surveys show that major corporations see a positive correlation between financial performance and ethical behavior. Further employees, juries, judges and legislators look to punish corporations that do not make good faith efforts at promoting ethical business practices.

B. **The Tension: Costco, Stride Rite, and IBM**. Companies face real tensions between pleasing employees and their price/earnings ratio. Companies are wont to outsource high-paying jobs as a cost-cutting measure.

C. **Approaches to Reconciling the Tension.** Companies can find varied approaches to resolve tensions between short-term balance sheets and long-term value.

1. Cut employee costs without firing workers.

2. Balance the playing field through international agreements to outlaw bribery practices in foreign countries.

3. Adopt an ethics program to help employees and officers 'walk the walk.' Managers must have a 'moral compass' to guide them when the correct action is not easily apparent.

VI. **SOCIAL RESPONSIBILITY.** Public perception of a company's socially irresponsible or unethical behavior might result in severe financial setbacks, especially where a company's finances depend on retail sales.

A. **Customers and Clients.**

1. Product Safety.
   - Socially responsible businesses place a heavy emphasis on product safety.
   - Instances of well-publicized defects in tires or cars, e.g., Bridgestone/Firestone and Ford have long-lasting effects on public perceptions of product safety.
   - Public sentiment is especially unforgiving when the safety is based on a "cost-benefit" analysis (*i.e.,* GM found it cheaper to pay for human deaths than to recall or redesign the product).

2. Advertising. There are a range of ethical considerations that executives need to consider, what they say in advertisements, whom they target, and public policies surrounding the product and its advertising.

   - Marketing Tobacco and Beer to Children. Parents criticized the use of RJR Nabisco's "Joe Camel" on the grounds that the company targeted children. RJR voluntarily withdrew Joe Camel in 1997. In 1999, the FTC determined that that top alcohol beverage companies were targeting children. The FTC recommended that alcohol companies agree to voluntary restrictions as to limit exposure of minors to their ads.

   - NBC and Liquor Advertising. In 2001, NBC announced a plan to air liquor ads. NBC cancelled the plan after public and Congressional opposition arose.

   - Pfizer and Off-label Drug Promotion. Pfizer paid doctors to market the drug Neurotonin to be used in ways unapproved by the Food and Drug Administration. Pfizer faced criminal charges and paid civil fines of $430 million.

3. **Conflicts of Interest.**

   o **Merrill Lynch and Other Brokerage Firms**. Brokers advised clients to buy low-quality stocks solely to curry favor with Merrill's investment clients. Merrill Lynch paid a $100 million fine to State government for fraudulent trade practices, and a group of brokers paid $1.3 billion to settle similar charges. In 2003 the Securities and Exchange Commission imposed new reporting rules for stock analysts to certify their stock evaluations as accurate and to disclose if they are compensated for their reports.

   o **Citigroup**. From 1996 through 2004, Citigroup made fraudulent financial reports for WorldCom, engaged in predatory lending practices. All told Citigroup paid fines and restitution of nearly $3 billion and set aside reserves of $6.7 billion to pay for lawsuits and fines for financial abuses since 2002.

4. Anticompetitive Tactics: Boeing. Boeing hired former Lockheed officers who helped it win a contract on an U. S. Air Force rocket. The Pentagon indefinitely suspended Boeing from all further rocket contracts, costing Lockheed billions of dollars.

5. Discriminatory Customer Service: Denny's. African-American employees and customers filed civil rights lawsuits for discriminatory treatment and abuse at the hands of Denny's managers and employees. Denny's paid millions of dollars in settlements and the company was cited as one where management either overtly or tacitly advocated racist practices. In 1999 Denny's parent company engaged in a multi-million dollar PR campaign to address public concerns and change its corporate culture. By 2000 a non-profit organization named Denny's as one of the most diverse work places in America.

B. **Employees.**

1. Sweatshops and Child Labor. Public investigation reveals that clothing companies and retailers like Nike and Wal-Mart use child labor, impose harsh work conditions, and pay substandard wages.

2. Danger in the Workplace: McWane, Inc. McWane managers purposefully avoided federal safety standards, had a relatively large number of OSHA violations and targeted whistleblowers for termination.

3. Jobs and Pensions, Bonuses for Layoffs. As Enron collapsed in bankruptcy and executives pocketed hundreds of millions of dollars through stock-option buy-outs, simultaneously evaporating over $3,000 million in employee pensions. AT&T recorded profits of $3,700 million yet eliminated jobs for 9,400 employees, all the while rewarding its CEO with a compensation package of over $18 million.

4. Contingent Workers.

- Large companies are out-sourcing work and replacing full-time employees with temporary workers and independent contractors who are typically paid 35 percent less than regular full-timers.

- Supporters of the contingent worker trend argue that it is necessary to give companies the flexibility to adjust the work force and seasonal labor demands.

- Critics, like Edward Hennessy, CEO of Allied-Signal Inc., assert that the practice saps worker morale, depresses worker productivity and dedication.

5. **Discrimination.** Coca-Cola settled a suit brought by Black employees who noted they were paid less than White counterparts and even White subordinates. Coke also denied Blacks promotions without cause. Texaco lost $1,000 million in market capitalization after the announcement of a class-action suit against it for racial discrimination. Texaco settled the suit for $100 million and established a zero-tolerance policy and took measures to stop racial epithets, taunts and jokes.

C.   **Investors.**

1. Managed Earnings. In an effort to maintain their stock price, many public companies engaged in criminal and fraudulent accounting to show higher earnings.

2. Mutual Fund Scandals. Strong Financial Corp., engaged in high-risk, rapid trades and also made illegal trades after the market closed. Strong's founder, Richard Strong was banned from investment trading for life and paid heavy fines.

D. **Environment.**

1. Shell Oil. Environmental and human rights activists motivated Shell to stop its plan to dump an oil rig in the North Sea and Shell's work with the Nigerian military. Shell adopted a new operations charter emphasizing sustainable development and now reports on the environmental and social affects of their activities.

2. Disposal of Electronics. More than 80 percent of electronics "recycled" in America are simply dumped in countries like China, India, etc. Trash workers in these countries are exposed to severe cancer causing agents. Disposal of electronics poisons ground water with lead and other heavy metals. Recently U.S. computer companies started offering more responsible recycling services.

E. **Communities.**

1. Union Carbide and Bhopal. After a 1984 explosion at a pesticide plant killed 3,000 initially and resulted in the deaths of 11,000 who suffered severe illnesses, Union Carbide settled with the Indian government to pay $470 million. As a result Indians were compensated with only $600 for injuries and $3,000 for each death. In 1999, survivors and victims of the 1984 accident sued Union Carbide and its former CEO, Warren Anderson, in U.S. federal court. Anderson went into hiding to avoid being served. Anderson is also wanted on criminal charges in India by the U.S. government refuses to extradite him.

2. Unocal in Myanmar. Unocal continues to invest in Myanmar (formerly Burma) despite the fact that: (a) a military dictatorship governs Myanmar; (b) in 1997 President Clinton banned all U.S. investment in Myanmar; and (c) in 2004 President Bush declared Myanmar's military government and extraordinary threat and renewed Clinton's ban on trade with Myanmar.

F. **Positive Action.** Despite many examples of corporate misconduct, many companies have undertaken socially responsible moves.

1. Customers and Product Safety. Johnson and Johnson recalled 31 million bottles of Tylenol in 1982 after some pills were laced with cyanide. However the company was slow in warning customers that Tylenol can cause liver damage.

2. Employees.

- After a long student and worker campaign against sweatshops shoe companies like Nike, Reebok, and others have agreed to permit factory visits and audits by the Fair Labor Association. Such a move has encouraged others to improve working conditions overseas.

- Levi Strauss closed 11 U.S. plants but gave employees eight months notice, three weeks salary for every year of service, health insurance and up to $6,000 for job training.

3.   **Environment**. Automakers Honda and Ford have pushed for higher fuel efficiency, created hybrid cars that have lower emissions, and redesigned factories to reduce pollution.

4.   **Community**.

- Dell and Hewlett-Packard have established computer recycling. Dell uses state of the art technology while HP use prison-labor though a subcontractor, Unicor.

- Poultry and Antibiotics. Use of antibiotics in the poultry industry has resulted in the growth of drug-resistant strains of bacteria, injuring human health. Recently the largest companies, Tyson's, Perdue, Foster Farms cut back or eliminated the use of antibiotics.

VII.   SOCIALLY RESPONSIBLE INVESTMENT. Due to public pressure, investors are seeking to promote responsible corporate behavior. The Coalition for Environmentally Responsible Economies (CERES) promulgated investor guidelines that focus on environmental awareness and corporate activities, e.g., preserving natural resources, safely disposing of pollutants, marketing safe products, and reducing environmental risks. Human rights groups and student organizations also lead boycotts and demonstrations against companies that invest in countries with poor human rights records.

VIII.   PROMOTING ETHICAL BEHAVIOR. Managers are role models who set the ethical tone of the corporation and play the most important role in creating an ethical environment.

A.   **Mission Statements**. A company should state its obligation to employees and customers.

B.   **Codes of Ethics and Ethics Training**.

1.   A code of ethics is a means to establish clear guidelines, expectations, and principles of conduct. A code is the surest way to encourage ethical behavior and prevent a crisis before it strikes.

2.   The code of conduct is only as good as the training program utilized to implement the code, re-order corporate culture in support of the values management wishes to impart, and the manner in which employees and management consistently review and consider the code of conduct.

C.   **Oversight.**

1.   Companies often use ethics committees or an ombudsman to investigate complaints, establish guidelines and policies for dealing with infractions or reports of ethics violations.

2.   Social audits are another way to provide oversight of company behavior. Social audits review company performance in sensitive and controversial areas like waste disposal or labor conditions in overseas factories.

D.   **Making It Easier To Blow the Whistle**. Many employees are reluctant to report illegal or unethical behavior to superiors or law enforcement. Despite legal safeguards against management retaliation, many employees suffer after coming out.

IX.   THE LAW AND THE "UNETHICAL."

A.   **Role of Law.** What is the relationship between law and ethics? Ethical guidelines often demand a higher standard of conduct than what the law requires. Often the law sets only a moral minimum. Courts are particularly intolerant of unethical conduct when parties have a trust relationship.

      Case 1.2 –*Meinhart v. Salmon*, 164 N.E. 545 (N.Y. 1928). Meinhard entered a joint venture with Salmon to renovate a hotel. Salmon negotiated another project without informing or including his "partner" Meinhart. Meinhart sued arguing that Salmon had a duty to make Meinhart aware of the new business opportunity and offer Meinhart the right to be a full partner. The court sided with Meinhart and he was granted one-half of the interest and obligations under Salmon's new business venture.

B.   **Law is Dynamic**. Lawmakers and courts adopt onerous regulations when companies fail to meet social standards of ethical conduct. Employers can be held liable for acts of their employees.

1.   *Otis Engineering Corp. v. Clark*, 668 S.W.2d 307 (Tex. 1983). As known to the employer, an employee had a history of drinking alcohol at work. The employer sent the employee home, who killed two women in a car accident. The corporation was liable in that it had a duty to prevent the employee from causing an unreasonable risk of harm to others.

2.   In *Riddle v. Arizona Oncology Services, Inc.*, 924 P.2d 468 (Ariz. Ct. App. 1996), the Arizona Court held that the employer did not breach its duty to an injured 3rd party when an employee drove home from work under the influence of cocaine and crashed injuring others.

3.   Increasingly, managers and corporations are held criminally liable, under the doctrine of "respondeat superior" for the misdeeds of employees.

X.   ADDITIONAL CONSIDERATIONS

A.   **When Ethics Travel**. Managers need to be aware of foreign customs, law, and social practices as to be prepared to balance moral tensions and appreciate cultural differences.

THE RESPONSIBLE MANAGER. Manager's need to exemplify company codes of conduct and ethical standards. Expectations should be written in clear and concise language, distributed, implemented and enforced through training and open dialogue.

INSIDE STORY: ENRON IMPLODES. Enron, a small gas pipeline, that grew, purportedly due to its activity as an energy broker, was revealed in 2001 as having committed a series of illegal accounting moves, fraudulent trades, and schemes to cheat energy consumers. Some of Enron's top officers were charged with felonies and went to prison. After 2001 when Enron filed for bankruptcy, her employees saw their retirement accounts evaporate into nothing and Enron stock, once valued at $90 a share, was worthless.

STUDY QUESTIONS

True-False Questions

__ 1.   An deontological approach to ethics will simply run a cost-benefit analysis of the potential profits earned versus the potential that corporate managers will go to jail if discovered.

__ 2.   The two main schools of ethical thought are teleological and deontological.

__ 3.   Kant's categorical imperative looks to the result of the action, not the form of the action to determine the ethical worth.

___ 4.   The Foreign Corrupt Practices Act prohibits U.S. corporations or citizens from offering any type of gift to a foreign official.

___ 5.   Studies show that ethical standards have no significant impact on a company's "bottom line."

___ 6.   Milton Friedman argues that corporate managers need only be concerned with making profits for the shareholders.

___ 7.   Studies suggest that the greater a manager's compensation, the more likely that he will act unethically.

___ 8.   Promotions always go to managers who put ethical conduct ahead of profitability.

___ 9.   Shareholders who want their companies to utilize socially responsible behavior must, nonetheless, accept sweatshop labor, and corporate malfeasance.

___ 10.   The advertising industry's self-policing has kept federal regulation to a minimum.

___ 11.   The CEO plays the most significant ethical role in instilling ethics in the company.

___ 12.   A corporate code of ethics is best enforced through workshops.

___ 13.   Criminal law, but not civil law, is important in promoting ethical conduct.

___ 14.   A manager can be civilly and criminally liable for the bad acts of a corporation and employees.

___ 15.   Employee drug use at work is a personal matter, irrelevant the corporation's legal liability.

Multiple-Choice Questions

___ 1.   A restaurant donates food to a shelter to feed hungry people. From a teleological view, the most important inquiry is,
   A. "How many hungry people were fed by this action?"
   B. "Why did the restaurant donate the food?"
   C. "Is the action universalizable?"
   D. "Does the utility of the act exceed the futility of the act?"

___ 2.   Which of the following is *not* one of the main categories of the utilitarian framework?

A. Distributive justice.
B. Compensatory justice.
C. Retributive justice.
D. Utilitarianism justice.

___ 3. The OECD Code of Business Conduct includes all of the following *except*
A. acting in accordance with the economic, commercial, and social goals of the host country.
B. abstaining from bribery that seeks favorable treatment from the host country.
C. abstaining from positive contributions to the balance of payments of the host country.
D. protecting the environment of the host country.

___ 4. Corporate compliance with U.S. law on investment, accounting, environmental regulations, corporate gifts:
A. is just another economic consideration like salaries, overhead, and the like.
B. is both an economic and ethical problem.
C. is best left to corporate attorneys to decide.
D. should be detailed in a company code of conduct.

___ 5. Which legal premise was not central to the decision in *Bammert v. Don's Super Value, Inc.*?
A. Courts generally permit companies to fire employees for no reason.
B. Employers may retaliate against employees for the acts of others.
C. All states protect whistle-blowers.
D. On cannot be fired if the reason for their dismissal violates a public policy.

___ 6. Which of the following is *not* a benefit of contingent workers to an employer?
A. Higher employee morale.
B. Lower hourly wage rates.
C. Non-eligibility for employee benefits.
D. Employee drug testing.

___ 7. Generally, which of the following is the *highest* concern by shareholders for their company?
A. Environmental concerns.
B. Safer products.
C. Social and ethical concerns.
D. Higher dividends.

___ 8. Target marketing is allowed only if it:
A. is not racist.
B. is not sexist.
C. involves health concerns.

D. None of the above.

___ 9. With regard to corporate ethics committees, which statement is always false?
A. They are responsible for setting standards for handling employee complaints.
B. Membership often includes executive officers and directors of the company.
C. The Vice President for Ethics investigates employee complaints.
D. Judiciary boards usually decide ethics code violations.

___ 10. Companies usually cite which of the following as the goal(s) of ethics training?

I. Development of general awareness of ethics in business.
II. Zero tolerance for receipt of gifts from suppliers.
III. Attention to practical ethics issues.

A. I and III.
B. I and II.
C. II and III.
D. I, II, and III.

___ 11. A manager can make it easier for whistle blowers by providing all of the following types of support *except:*
A. moral support.
B. financial support.
C. psychological support.
D. free counseling.

___ 12. When deciding on an ethical course of action, companies should first look to the concerns of:
A. Customers and clients
B. U.S. and international law
C. stockholders and public opinion
D. Employees

___ 13. Managers can be held _____ liable for company violations.
A. civilly
B. criminally
C. civilly and criminally
D. civilly but not criminally

___ 14. Managers should emphasize ethical corporate practices because:
A. ethical behavior is always profitable in the long-run.
B. what is ethical is legal.
C. it is a way to generate employee loyalty.

D. it ensures that the corporation will remain free of legal liability.

___ 15. Which of the following is *not* a long-term consequence of white-collar crime?
   A. Lost profits.
   B. Loss of public confidence.
   C. Threat to free enterprise.
   D. Erosion of the moral base of the organization.

Essay Questions

1. Using the Tylenol/Johnson & Johnson case as an example, discuss how a company can use ethics to increase profits.

2. Discussing the Honda and Dell examples, how can a company be more proactively socially responsible?

3. Generally, what should be in a corporate code of ethics?

CHAPTER 2
CONSTITUTIONAL BASES FOR BUSINESS REGULATION

INTRODUCTION

The U.S. Constitution, grants the federal and state governments powers to regulate business and protect the freedom and rights of citizens. This chapter discusses the structure, responsibilities and scope of power of the federal government, and how it impacts the business environment. The chapter discusses federalism and the balance of power between the national and state governments, the Constitution's Commerce Clause, and government protections of individual rights in the business environment.

I.   **STRUCTURE OF GOVERNMENT: Separation of Powers**. The U.S. Constitution divides power between the national and state governments. Further within each level of government, power is divided among three branches, Judicial, Executive, and Legislative. Recent Supreme Court rulings assert that the federal government may only act when given express authority via the Constitution. If there is a conflict between federal and state regulation or law, federal law takes precedence under the doctrine of pre-emption.

    A.   **Judicial Power**. The power of federal courts is found primarily in Article III of the Constitution, which vests judicial power in the Supreme Court of the United States and inferior courts, including Courts of Appeal and District (trial) courts.

        1.   Jurisdiction.

- U.S. District courts must have authority to review the "subject matter" of a case, what is called *subject matter jurisdiction*; and power to rule over the parties, so-called personal jurisdiction.

- *Appellate Jurisdiction*. Article III gives the Supreme Court jurisdiction to hear appeals from lower federal district court decisions involving those subjects and parties described in III.

        2.   Article I Courts. Through its authority under Article I of the Constitution, Congress has established "special courts" with special subject matter jurisdiction, such as the U.S. Tax Courts and Bankruptcy Courts.

        3.   Judicial Review. In the decision of *Marbury v. Madison*, 5 U.S. 1 (1803), the Supreme Court held that federal courts have the power to determine the

constitutionality of the acts of the other two branches of the federal government. The doctrine of judicial review has been followed ever since.

B.   **The Executive Power**. Executive power is found generally in Article II. Power vested in the President, and includes the power and authority to:

> *appoint judges, members of the executive branch, and ambassadors; grant pardons; veto acts of Congress; negotiation treaties; act as "Commander in Chief" of the military; and issue Executive Decrees and Orders that function as law and policy of the United States.*

C.   **The Legislative Power.** Article I, Section 8, of the Constitution enumerates (lists) the primary powers of the Congress, which include:

> *regulating commerce with foreign nations, among the states (the "interstate commerce" clause) and with American Indian nations and tribes; creating and collecting taxes; issuing patents and copyrights; declaring war and raising armies, and passing laws "necessary and proper" to carry out its enumerated (listed) powers.*

D.   **Conflicts between the Branches.**

     1. Though no one is above the law, it understood that the President is immune from criminal prosecution for acts taken as president, unless he is first impeached.

     2. The doctrine of *executive privilege* does not cover acts of the President that occurred *prior* to taking office. *See Clinton v. Jones*, 520 U.S. 681 (1997).

     3. Under the separation of powers doctrine, the President cannot exercise a line-item veto to strike specific provisions of a bill. *Clinton v. City of New York*, 524 U.S. 417 (1998)

II.   **SUPREMACY CLAUSE AND PREEMPTION.** Article VI of the U.S. Constitution declares that the Constitution, laws, and treaties of the United States "shall be the Supreme law of the land." Any federal or state law enacted in violation of the Constitution is void. Any federal law contravening a previous treaty voids that particular part of the treaty. State statutes are pre-empted when such regulations directly conflict with federal law. Review the following examples.

A.   ***Crosby v. National Foreign Trade Council,*** 530 U.S. 363 (2000). The U.S. Supreme struck a Massachusetts law that restricted agencies in Massachusetts from purchasing good or services from companies or individuals doing business in Burma on the grounds that such was pre-empted by a Congressional law that regulated commerce between the U.S. and Burma.

B.   ***Geier v. American Honda Motor Co.,*** 529 U.S. 861 (2000). The U.S. Supreme Court held that federal law pre-empted state product liability lawsuits alleging a failure to equip cars with airbags.

C.   ***Medtronic, Inc., v Lohr***, 518 U.S. 470 (1996; ***Duncan v. Northwest Airlines, Inc.,*** 208 F.3d 1112 (9th Cir. 2000). Though federal law existed regarding the regulation of medical devices and airplane services, federal courts held that state regulations and liability laws were not pre-empted as federal laws did not cover the topic of litigation specifically.

III.   FEDERALISM. Federal power is limited by express provisions and prohibitions in the U.S. Constitution. Typically police powers, matters involving regulation of health, safety and welfare, are reserved to the States.

A.   **Eleventh Amendment.**

    1.   Supports the doctrine of sovereign immunity of the States and shields state governments from lawsuits, save those specifically allowed by the Constitution, e.g. suits pursuant to enforcement of the 14th Amendment.

    2.   In *Alden v. Maine*, 527 U.S. 706 (1999) the Supreme Court held that state probation officers cannot sue their employer (the State of Maine) for overtime pay as mandated by the Fair Labor Standards Act (FLSA). The FLSA was written pursuant to the "commerce clause" of Art I, section 8. But because the 11th Amendment protection of state sovereign immunity applies to all parts of the Constitution preceding it, e.g. Article I, states cannot be sued for money for violating the FLSA.

        Case 2.1--*Nevada Department of Human Resources v. Hibbs*, 538 U.S. 721 (2003). Plaintiff, a state employee sued his employer, the Nevada Dept. of Human Resources, a state government agency in Nevada, for leave as allowed under the Family Medical Leave Act (FMLA). Hibbs wanted 12 weeks unpaid leave to care for his sick wife. Hibbs was initially granted permission, but then a subsequent supervisor ordered him to return to work or be fired. Hibbs refused and was terminated. Hibbs attempted to sue the Nevada state office for violating the federal law. The Supreme Court held that as the FMLA was written pursuant to the 14th Amendment, state governments do not have immunity from suit.

B.   **Dual Sovereignty**. The idea that both the federal and State governments are sovereign. In this case sovereignty means that the federal government cannot intrude and control all activities within a State's territory. However when activity is clearly economic, even if intra-state, the Supreme Court holds that federal regulations take precedence.

         1. *Printz v. United States*, 521 U.S. 898 (1997), the Supreme Court struck down a federal law requiring local sheriffs to run background checks on prospective gun purchasers as an infringement on the 10th Amendment on the grounds that such a law pressed state officials into service for the federal government.

         2. *Reno v. Condon*, 528 U.S. 141 (2000), the Court upheld a federal law prohibiting State governments from disseminating driver's license information without the driver's consent on the grounds that such information is typically used for and within the stream of commerce. Thus within the scope of congressional power under the Commerce Clause.

IV.   **COMMERCE CLAUSE**. The scope and understanding of congressional authority to regulate commerce has evolved. Though Article I, section 8, clause 3 reads: [Congress has the power to] "regulate commerce with foreign Nations, and among the several States and with the Indian tribes" since the 1930s, the clause has been applied to intra-state affairs in labor relations and discrimination with hotels, restaurants, and transport companies.

     A.   Evolving Legal Doctrines.

         1. Though early Supreme Court precedent applied the Commerce Clause to all commerce involving more than one state, *Gibbons v. Ogden*, 22 U.S. 1 (1803), from the 1880s through the mid 1930s, the Supreme Court narrowed the application of the clause holding that activities like mining, farming, and manufacturing could not be regulated by Congress.

         2. From 1937 to 1995 the courts expanded the scope of the Commerce Clause, making federal regulation more and more pervasive in American business from hotels and restaurants to minimum wage and overtime pay requirements, so long as the regulated activity had a "substantial effect" on commerce.

             Case 2.2—*United States v. Morrison*, 529 U.S. 598 (2000). Christy Brzonkala claimed she was raped, assaulted and abused by two Virginia Tech football players, Antonio Morrison and James Crawford. Unable to get redress from the school or local authorities, Brzonkala sued Morrison, Crawford and the university in federal civil court under the federal "Violence Against Women Act" (42 U.S.C. § 13981). The lower courts dismissed the suit holding the law as unconstitutional. The Supreme Court held that VAWA, authorizing suits for tort in federal court, was not a direct regulation of economic commerce. Hence the Supreme Court retracted the expansive dominion of the Commerce Clause in that Congress may no longer regulate any activity, e.g. violence against women, crime, and domestic abuse, simply on the grounds that said activity has a substantial effect on interstate commerce.

B.   LIMITS ON STATE POWERS AND THE DORMANT COMMERCE CLAUSE.

1. While State laws conflicting with federal interstate commerce regulations are generally preempted, even if the Congress has not acted, State acts may be stricken.

2. State regulations shall be upheld if a law: (a) is rationally related to a legitimate end; and (b) does not impose an undue burden on interstate commerce.

3. State laws that attempt to protect in-state producers and or laws that discriminate between out-of-state and intra-state commerce are generally *per se* invalid.

C.   FEDERAL FISCAL POWERS.

1. Though so-called police power is traditionally left to the States and local government, through it taxing and spending powers, Congress can regulate both federal and local activities.

2. The Supreme Court has upheld taxes designed to affect the behavior of businesses as well as those designed to raise revenues.

3. Congress has the power to spend in order to provide for the common defense and general welfare as long as it comports with constitutional limitations.

V.   PROTECTION OF INDIVIDUAL LIBERTIES. The original Constitution and the Bill of Rights guarantee certain individual liberties, rights and protections.

A.   The Constitution

1. In general, States and the Federal government cannot impair obligations of contracts retroactively. See an exception in *Calfarm Insurance Co. v. Deukmejian*, 771 P.2d 1247 (Cal. 1989).

2. The Constitution also bans *ex post facto* laws (laws that punish actions that were not illegal when performed), and prohibits bills of attainder (laws that criminalize known individuals or certain groups for otherwise legal behavior, solely due to their status).

B. **The Bill of Rights**. The first ten amendments to the Constitution, added in 1791, called "the Bill of Rights," enumerate some of the pre-existing liberties and rights of the people and served to announce limits on federal power. Aspects of the Fourth, Fifth, and Sixth Amendments relevant to criminal cases are discussed in Chapter 17.

1. The First Amendment guarantees freedom of religious expression, political speech, press, public assembly and the right to petition the government;

2. The Second Amendment establishes that citizen militias can keep and bear arms;

3. The Third Amendment provides that no soldier shall be quartered in any house, except in a time of war;

4. The Fourth Amendment prohibits unreasonable searches and seizures and that judges shall issue search and arrest warrants only upon probable cause;

5. The Fifth Amendment enumerates rights of criminal defendants regarding grand jury, double jeopardy, and self-incrimination. It also holds that the federal government must ensure due process and provide just compensation when taking private property for public use;

6. The Sixth Amendment guarantees criminal defendants a right to a speedy and public trial, trial by jury trial, the right to an attorney and to confront witnesses;

7. The Seventh Amendment guarantees the right to a jury trial in all civil cases in which the dispute is in excess of $20;

8. The Eighth Amendment prohibits judges from imposing excessive bail or fines. The Amendment also prohibits criminal punishments that are cruel or unusual;

9. The Ninth Amendment guarantees pre-existing and non-enumerated rights as "retained" by the people;

10. The Tenth Amendment reserves authority and rights not otherwise delegated to the federal government nor expressly forbidden to the States, to remain with the States.

C.   **APPLICABILITY TO THE STATES.**

1.   Fourteenth Amendment. The Fourteenth Amendment has three general provisions that are designed to protect individuals: (a) no State shall make or enforce any law which shall abridge the privileges or immunities of citizens of the United States" (the *Privileges and Immunities Clause*); (b) no state shall deprive any person of life, liberty, or property, without due process of law (the *Due Process Clause*); and (c) no State shall deny to "any person the equal protection of the laws" (the *Equal Protection Clause*).

2.   Incorporation Clause. The Supreme Court held that particular provisions of the Bill of Rights apply to States via the Fourteenth Amendment only if said rights and guarantees are fundamental to the American system of law or safeguard essential liberty.

VI.   **FREEDOM OF SPEECH AND THE PRESS**. The Supreme Court does protect all types of speech equally. Political speech receives the highest protection, whereas obscene or slanderous speech is not protected at all. Further freedom of speech and assembly grant groups and individuals the right not to speak or associate. E.g., a Massachusetts law requiring compulsory inclusion of Irish gays in St. Patrick's Day parade was declared unconstitutional, *Hurley v. Irish-American Gay, Lesbian and Bisexual Group of Boston*, 515 U.S. 557 (1995).

A.   **Clear and Present Danger Test.**

1.   Since World War I, the Court has ruled that in wartime, the government may outlaw words when used in given circumstances that create a clear and present danger. *Schenck v. United States*, 249 U.S. 47 (1919).

2.   Speech that produces or is likely to produce imminent lawless or criminal action is not protected. E.g., *Brandenburg v. Ohio*, 395 U.S. 444 (1969); also *Rice v. Paladin Enter., Inc.*, 128 F.3d 233 (4th Cir. 1997)].

B.   **Defamation of Public Figures**. False words that harm someone's reputation are generally not protected speech, *unless* they are said about a public figure by the media, when the speaker has no knowledge that the claims are false or in reckless disregard for the truth. Defamation is discussed further in Chapter 9.

C.   **Obscenity**. Obscene material does not enjoy any protection under the First Amendment. Material is obscene if: it (1) appeals to a perverted interest in sex; (2) has no serious literary, artistic, political, or scientific merit; and (3) is offensive to the average person in the community.

D.   **Academic Research**. Generally professors or researchers are shielded from revealing their research or notes as are journalists. Moreover, if the academics have agreed to non-disclosure agreements they cannot be compelled to reveal their information.

E.   **Pornography and Free Speech on the Internet**. Since 1995 the Congress has passed various laws that criminalized transmission of indecent and pornographic images. The Supreme Court and lower courts have usually struck these laws as overbroad as the laws would purport to ban artistic and literary works. The Courts have upheld two laws tied to the production of child pornography and or limiting minors' access to such images.

F.   **Commercial Speech**

1. Commercial speech (especially advertising) is subject to substantial regulation. The government cannot suppress commercial speech but it can regulate the time, place, and manner of such speech with ordinances that are content-neutral, narrowly tailored to serve a significant governmental interest, and leave open ample alternative channels of communication.

    Case 2.3--*Kasky v. Nike, Inc.*, 27 Cal. 4th 939 (2002). Plaintiff, Marc Kasky sued Nike for false and misleading statements, pursuant to California Business and Professional Code sections 17204, 17535. Nike had taken out ads and made press releases claiming that their employees were paid minimum wage, overtime, fed meals, provided health care, and their working conditions complied with health and safety standards. Nike moved to dismiss arguing that their claims were protected by the First Amendment. The California Supreme Court held that Nike's statements were inherently commercial in nature and thus not entitled to immunity from lawsuit.

2. Liquor and Cigarette Advertising. Federal and State laws designed to curb alcohol ads or compel disclosure have been ruled unconstitutional on the grounds that they either are not rationally related to a government objective or the laws are too restrictive of truthful, nonmisleading statements.

3. Nonspeech Business. States and local government cannot ban commercial activity that also suppresses speech necessary for an economic transaction. *Nordyke v. Santa Clara County*, 110 F.3d 707 (9th Cir 1997).

4. Encryption. Without showing an important government interest, and a law substantially related to the interest, the federal government cannot ban posting computer source codes on the internet. *Junger v. Daley*, 209 F.3d 481 (6th Cir. 2000).

5. International Snapshot. Other nations have greater restrictions on speech and commerce. French law prohibits sale or display of symbols that incite racism. A French court ordered Yahoo! to prevent Internet users in France from accessing auction sites with Nazi paraphernalia.

6. English-Only Laws. Laws that require state or local government to use English only may conflict with freedom of speech protections.

G.   Prior Restraints.

1. Though government may seek to prevent public demonstrations prior to the event with time, place, and manner guidelines, *prior restraints* of speech that prohibit speech in traditionally public areas are strictly scrutinized.

2. Though states and cities may regulate and ban nude dancing and sex-oriented adult businesses, First Amendment protections for the press means that media companies are relatively free from restrictions.

VII.   RIGHT OF ASSOCIATION. The First Amendment guarantees a near absolute right for individuals to associate with whom they please, especially in a political context. E.g., *California Democratic Party et al. v. Jones*, 530 U.S. 567 (2000).

In determining whether a law banning discrimination public accommodations, clubs or non-profit organizations is constitutional, courts balance the state's interest in preventing discrimination against the individuals' right to association. The key issue centers on whether the club or association is a "business establishment" (public accommodation) or a private association. See *Warfield v. Peninsula Golf Country Club*, 896 P.2d 776 (Cal. 1995); and *Boy Scouts of America v. Dale* (2000).

CASE 2.4--*Boy Scouts of America v. Dale*, 530 U.S. 640 (2000). New Jersey state law prohibited discrimination based on sexual orientation in its public accommodations. Dale was an openly gay scout master. The Boy Scouts sought to revoke Dale's BSA membership. The Supreme Court held the BSA was primarily an expressive association and hence the Boy Scouts had the right to deny an association with any person based upon that person's point of view.

VIII. **FREEDOM OF RELIGION**. The Constitution, through the First and Fourteenth Amendments, prohibits the government from establishing a state religion or from interfering in the Free Exercise of religion.

    A. ***Jimmy Swaggart Ministries v. Board of Equalization***, 493 U.S. 378 (1990), the Supreme Court held that a general sales tax on sales of religious materials was not an infringement on the free exercise of religion as the tax was applied neutrally to sales regardless of the nature of the seller or purchaser.

    B. ***Mitchell. v. Helms***, 530 U.S. 1296 (2000), along the idea of neutrality, government may provide books and other materials to private, religious schools, just as the State supports non-religious schools.

    C. ***Tucker v. Calif. Dep't of Education***, 97 F.3d 1204 (9th Cir. 1996), as a matter of neutrality and allowing individuals their freedom of exercise of religion yet not encouraging one religion over another, the Ninth Circuit federal appeals court held that the State of California could not impose a near total ban of religious iconography from the workplace in state offices.

IX. **DUE PROCESS**. Under the 5th and 14th Amendments the federal and state governments must ensure due process to persons facing the loss of "life, liberty or property." The courts have determined that due process includes both *procedural* and *substantive* aspects.

    A. **Procedural Due Process**. The government must provide adequate notice and fair hearings. Generally, criminal defendants, over civil defendants, are afforded greater due process because of the possibility of imprisonment or death

    B. **Substantive Due Process**. Substantive due process analysis usually considers what fundamental rights and liberties must be protected or may be curbed, e.g. free speech, freedom of religion and association, freedom of contract, marriage rights, the right to travel and privacy.

        1. Economic Regulation. From roughly 1897 to 1937 the Supreme Court rejected efforts of state governments to restrict out-of state competition or interfere with labor contracts. Since 1938, so long as the State government can show some rational basis for a law in that it purports to improve the health, safety and welfare, law may have incidental effects on economic activity and the freedom to contract.

2. Protection of Fundamental Rights. Laws that interfere with or limit fundamental rights (e.g., marriage, child-rearing) will be held unconstitutional, unless the law can be shown to promote a compelling state interest. For example, a person can always refuse life-sustaining medical treatment, *Cruzan v. Director, Missouri Dep't of Health*, 497 U.S. 261 (1990).

3. Limits on Punitive Damage Awards. The Supreme Court has held that punitive damage awards in civil tort actions cannot be so excessive as to violate the defendant's substantive due process. Further, tort defendants must always have an opportunity to challenge jury awards. *Honda Motor Co. v. Oberg*, 512 U.S. 415 (1994).

> **Case 2.5. *State Farm Mutual Automobile Ins. Co., v. Campbell, et al.*,** 538 U.S. 408 (2003). State Farm insured Campbell, who lived in Utah. Campbell was responsible for an accident and ordered to pay over $185,000 in damages. State Farm, which had originally refused to settle with the injured parties, also refused to cover the judgment. Ultimately State Farm did pay the full amount of the judgment to the parties, but Campbell sued State Farm for fraud. Evidence was shown at trial that State Farm had a practice of capping its payouts – regardless of the language of their policies and committed fraud outside Utah. A jury awarded Campbell $2.6 million in compensatory and $145 million in punitive damages. The trial judge lowered the award to $1 million and $25 million respectively. The Utah Supreme Court reinstated the punitive award of $145 million. The U.S. Supreme Court found the punitive amount excessive (neither reasonable nor proportionate to the harm caused) given that the largest fine for fraud under Utah's criminal law was only $10,000.

X. COMPENSATION FOR TAKINGS.

A. **Eminent Domain and Just Compensation**. Normally the government cannot take private land for public use (e.g., to construct a highway, build a park, expand an airport) without compensating the owner at fair market price. The process by which the government seizes such territory is called *eminent domain*.

B. **Takings via Mere Government Regulations**

1. If a local zoning ordinance is too severe or excessive, the owner may claim inverse condemnation and be entitled to just compensation. *Nollan v. California Coastal Commission*, 483 U.S. 825 (1987). *See* Chapters 18 and19 for further discussion on land use and environmental issues.

2. *Eastern Enterprises v. Apfel*, 524 U.S. 498 (1998). A federal law that required payments from mining companies was ruled an unconstitutional taking as enforced against Eastern Enterprises which had stopped its mining operations in 1987.

XI.   EQUAL PROTECTION. The 14th Amendment reads that no state shall "deny to any person within its jurisdiction the equal protection of the laws." The Supreme Court has read this language into the 5th Amendment as to apply to the federal government. In general, equal protection law centers around types and levels of discrimination within government and industry.

A.   **Establishing Discrimination.** Laws may be challenged as violative of equal protection in three ways: (1) facially as the law explicitly enumerates groups or classes of people; (2) as applied, when the law is facially neutral but as a practice treats groups differently; and (3) in effect even if the law and its application are neutral towards groups.

B.   **Validity Of Discrimination**. The Supreme Court has established three legal tests to determine if a law violates the equal protection clause of the Constitution.

1. *Rational Basis Test*. If a statute involves economic regulation or social welfare (e.g., welfare payments, housing, school funding, and government employment), the Court will apply a "*rational basis*" test and frequently uphold the statute so long as the law seeks to advance a legitimate government objective.

2. *Strict Scrutiny Test*. If a statute involves interferes with a fundamental right such as privacy or speech, or creates a "suspect class" (such as race), the Court will apply the "*strict scrutiny*" test and uphold the statute only if it serves a compelling state interest and is narrowly tailored to achieve that interest.

3. *Substantially Related Test*. If a statute distinguishes people along lines of gender, or age (a quasi-suspect class), the Court will uphold the statute only if it is substantially related to an important governmental interest.

C.   **Racial Discrimination**. Since 1954, with *Brown v. Board of Education* 347 U.S. 483 (1954), the Supreme Court has ruled that a State cannot compel racial segregation as such violates the equal protection clause. Applying this rule to government contracts and affirmative action policies has been controversial.

1. In *Adarand Constructors v. Pena* (1995), the Supreme Court ruled that all racial classifications are subject to strict scrutiny. Further government

regulations can only consider race or create *benign* racial classifications so long as there is a rational basis for doing so.

2. "Diversity" considerations in university admissions policies are also subject to strict scrutiny.

> **Case 2.6--*Grutter v. Bollinger***, 539 U.S. 306 (2003). The University of Michigan's highly rated law school used a number of variables in deciding whom to admit. Using a 150 point scale, applicants received points for their undergraduate GPA, LSAT scores, if they were a resident of Michigan, economic class, race, and other factors. The Supreme Court upheld the Michigan policy of seeking ethnic diversity within its law school student body but held that admissions officers could not use race to allot a specific number of points to under-represented groups (Blacks, Latinos, and American Indians). Rather admissions officers could use race as a consideration in whether to admit a particular student. On the same day, the Court held that Michigan could not use an identical system to determine admissions for undergraduate students. See *Gratz v. Bollinger*, 539 U.S. 244 (2003).

D.   Other Forms of Discrimination.

1. **Gender**. In *United States v. Virginia* (1996), the Supreme Court ruled that the Virginia Military Academy, an all-male, state-supported military college, violated the Equal Protection Clause by excluding women. The Court held that classifications based on gender must (i) serve important governmental objectives, (ii) be substantially related to achieving those objectives, and (iii) rest on an "exceedingly persuasive justification." Gender discrimination is discussed further in Chapter 15.

2. **Aliens**. Non citizens are not entitled to all the constitutional guarantees afforded to citizens. Statutes that discriminate against aliens, save those tied to state employment, are usually subject to strict scrutiny.

XII.   RIGHT TO JURY TRIAL. The Seventh Amendment provides that "[i]n Suits at common law, where the value in controversy shall exceed twenty dollars, the right of trial by jury shall be preserved." Suits at common law (in contrast to suit in equity) are lawsuits where a plaintiff seeks to enforce a legal right and win a money judgment. Suits in equity seek enforcement of contracts or injunctions. The Supreme Court has not applied the Seventh Amendment to the state courts or state claims brought in federal court. See 257 F.3d 235 (2d Cir. 2001).

XIII. EXTRAS

A.   **The Initiative Process**. Twenty-four states allow the initiative process by which citizens may propose laws and have them adopted via state-wide referendum.

B.   **Preserving Constitutional Rights**. Though the Constitution speaks directly to the Federal and State governments, its purposes tied to granting and ensuring equal treatment of all citizens, if not persons, also extends to private business.

C.   **Effects of Politics on Supreme Court Appointments.** Presidential nominations to the U.S. Supreme Court, and lower courts, are a highly political process and have long-lasting effects on policy and law. Due to recent political battles between Presidents and the U.S. Senate, more often nominees have written few judicial opinions and few law review articles which would expound upon the jurist's view of a given principle in law.

STUDY QUESTIONS

True-False Questions

__ 1.   Without a grant of authority from the Constitution, a federal government action is always unconstitutional.

__ 2.   The Dormant Commerce Clause gives state governments the power to regulate nearly any business activity, regardless of the impact on interstate commerce.

__ 3.   The Supremacy Clause of Article VI states that federal law always takes precedence over state law.

__ 4.   The President must sign and enforce all laws passed by Congress.

__ 5.   Through executive privilege, the President remains above the law.

__ 6.   State sovereign immunity is absolute and one cannot sue a state without its permission.

__ 7.   Under the Family and Medical Leave Act, private employers must grant employees up to 12 weeks unpaid leave to care for a newborn, but the law does not apply to people who work for State government agencies.

__ 8.   Based on the Supreme Court decisions in *Lopez* and *Morrison*, Congress can now regulate any activity so long as there is a link to commerce.

___ 9. When determining a tax law's constitutionality, courts must consider the purpose of the tax.

___ 10. States must guarantee every citizen all the liberties, rights, and protections listed in the Bill of Rights.

___ 11. The Supreme Court has held that the government generally cannot regulate individual, political or commercial speech.

___ 12. Substantive Due Process means only that government must provide reasonable procedures and fair practices in hearings and trials.

___ 13. For-profit and non-profit organizations cannot discriminate against members or patrons on account of race or religion, but may refuse service or membership to others based on political values.

___ 14. State governments and the federal government have the power of eminent domain.

___ 15. Using a strict scrutiny test, courts will uphold laws so long as they further a compelling governmental interest.

Multiple-Choice Questions

___ 1. What Constitutional Articles gave Congress the authority to establish federal courts?

   I.   Article I
   II. Article II
   III. Article III

   A. I
   B. III
   C. I and III
   D. I, II, and III

___ 2. Which of the following is *not* an Article I court?
   A. United States Tax Court.
   B. United States District Court.
   C. United States Bankruptcy Court.
   D. all of the courts of the District of Columbia.

__ 3. Which of the following is *not* a power of Congress?
     A. Coining money.
     B. Establishing post offices.
     C. Declaring war.
     D. Granting pardons.

__ 4. Which case established that executive privilege does *not* protect the president during the term of office from civil litigation over events that occurred before he took office?
     A. *Marbury v. Madison.*
     B. *Clinton v. Jones.*
     C. *United States v. Nixon.*
     D. *Ford v. Carter.*

__ 5. In which case did the Court limit Congressional efforts to regulate non commercial activity?
     A. *United States v. Lopez.*
     B. *Clinton v. Jones.*
     C. *United States v. Nixon.*
     D. *Katzenbach v. McClung.*

__ 6. State regulation affecting interstate commerce will be upheld if the regulation is:

     I. Rationally related to a legitimate state end.
     II. Not creating an undue burden on interstate commerce.
     III. Important to the state and causes little or no federal regulation problems.

     A. I, II, and III
     B. I and II
     C. I only
     D. II and III

__ 7. Article I, Section 10 of the Constitution specifically prohibits a state from:
     A. Passing *ex post facto* laws.
     B. Passing Bills of Attainder.
     C. Impairing the obligation of existing contracts.
     D. Legislating all of the above.

__ 8. Which right is *not* found in the First Amendment?
     A. Freedom of speech.
     B. Freedom to bear arms.
     C. Freedom of the press.
     D. Freedom of religion.

__ 9. Which of the following is *not* found in the 5th Amendment?
   A. The necessity of grand jury indictments.
   B. The double jeopardy clause.
   C. The right against self-incrimination.
   D. The right to a speedy trial.

__ 10. To establish discrimination using equal protection grounds, the plaintiff can show the statute discriminates in all of the following ways *except:*
   A. on the face of the statute.
   B. in its purpose.
   C. in its subjective intent.
   D. in its application.

__ 11. All racial classifications are subject to the _____ test.
   A. Strict scrutiny.
   B. Substantially related.
   C. Rational basis.
   D. Equivalency.

__ 12. Which of the following is *not* subjected to the intermediate-level, substantially related, test?
   A. Alienage.
   B. Socio-economic class.
   C. Gender.
   D. Illegitimacy.

__ 13. Which of the following is a protected form of speech?
   A. Bribery.
   B. Perjury.
   C. Solicitation of prostitution.
   D. None of the above.

__ 14. The Communication Decency Act was:
   A. overruled by the Supreme Court.
   B. passed to outlaw nudity on the Internet.
   C. applied only to personal web pages.
   D. none of the above.

___ 15. The First Amendment clauses involving religion are the:

    I.   Freedom and Restoration Clause
    II. Establishment Clause
    III. Free Exercise Clause

A. III
B. I and II
C. II and III
D. I, II, and III

Essay Questions

1.   How did the Supreme Court use cases and the Commerce Clause to help enforce and promote the Civil Rights Act?

2.   Why is the freedom of speech not unlimited in a democracy?

3.   How can Congress regulate speech on the internet when cyberspace includes transnational transactions?

CHAPTER 3
COURTS, SOURCES OF LAW, AND LITIGATION

INTRODUCTION

In our litigious legal environment, managers must understand the structure and processes of the judicial system to be prepared, as necessary, to protect their rights and their companies. This chapter discusses the structure of the federal and state court systems, sources of law, and the litigation process.

I. HOW TO READ A CASE CITATION

A. Citation Information

When a court decides a case, the court writes an opinion, which is published in one or more *reporters*—collections of court opinions. The citation of a case (the *cite*) includes the following information in this order: the Plaintiff's name, the Defendant's name (both *italicized* or <u>underlined</u>), the Volume number and Title of the reporter in which the case is reported, the Page Number at which the case opinion begins, the Court that decided the case (if the court is not indicated, it is understood to be the state supreme court or the U.S. Supreme Court, depending on the reporter in which the case appears), and the Year in which the case was decided.

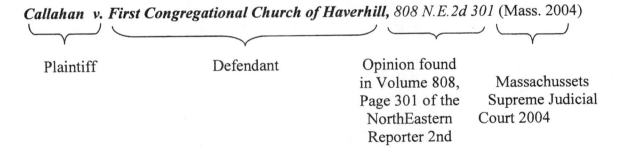

Callahan v. First Congregational Church of Haverhill, 808 N.E.2d 301 (Mass. 2004)

Plaintiff   Defendant   Opinion found in Volume 808, Page 301 of the NorthEastern Reporter 2nd   Massachussets Supreme Judicial Court 2004

B. Multiple Citations. Some cases are in more than one reporter.

1. Example: *Walkovszky v. Carlton*, 18 N.Y.2d 414, 276 N.Y.S.2d 585, 223 N.E.2d 6 (N.Y. 1966) is found in multiple reporters: volume 18 of the second series of New York Reports, volume 276 of the second series of the New York Supplement, and volume 223 of the second series of the North Eastern Reports.

2.   On appeal, the "plaintiff" is appellant or *petitioner* (the loser of the trial) v. appellee or *respondent* (the winner). Therefore, if the defendant lost at the trial level and appealed the decision to a higher court, the name of the defendant (now the appellant) would appear first in the case citation.

II.   **The U.S. and State Court Systems.** The United States has two co-existing judicial systems, federal and state.

A.   **Federal Court Jurisdiction.** As granted by the U.S. Constitution and federal law, federal courts have jurisdiction over federal questions, diversity, and suits in which the United States is a party.

1.   A federal question exists when the lawsuit concerns federal law, e.g., a right asserted under the U.S. Constitution or a federal statute. There is no minimum monetary requirement for lawsuits involving a federal question.

2.   Diversity jurisdiction exists when a lawsuit is between citizens (or a corporation) of two different states and the amount in controversy, exclusive of interest and all costs, exceeds $75,000.

- Under the *Erie Doctrine*, typically the State law of the forum will govern the dispute.

- To determine if a case maybe be held in federal court due to "diversity" the courts must determine the "citizenship" of each party. Courts look where a business is headquartered, where it files tax returns, or has shareholder meetings. As well courts note where the company engages in business.

3.   Federal courts have jurisdiction over suits when the United States government, or an officer or agency thereof, is a plaintiff or defendant. There is no minimum monetary requirement for lawsuits where the United States is a party.

B.   **Federal Courts.** The federal court system has District Courts, appellate courts, specialized courts (e.g., U.S. Tax Courts and Patent Courts), and a Supreme Court. Federal judges are nominated by the President and confirmed by the U.S. Senate. Federal judges have a lifetime appointment.

1.   U.S. District Courts are divided into 94 districts across the U.S. and her territories. District Courts are trial courts.

2.   U.S. Courts of Appeal. Appellate courts review district court rulings and administrative agencies. Usually a panel of three judges reviews the case. If the losing side wishes, they may appeal from the three-judge panel and request a review from the entire court (*en banc*).

3.   Specialized Federal Courts. Bankruptcy, tax and other courts have jurisdiction to rule on only specific issues or topics as determined by Congress.

4.   U.S. Supreme Court. The high Court reviews appeals cases from lower federal courts and appeals from State Supreme Courts. The Court generally has discretion to review a lower court ruling. When at least four agree to hear a case the Court grants a *writ of certiorari*.

5.   Standing. Parties or persons can only sue if they have "standing" that suffer from a real case or controversy (or can articulate some interest in the case or a law) and have a legal remedy available to them.

> **Case 3.1 –*National Credit Union Administration v. First National Bank & Trust Company*,** 522 U.S. 479 (1998). Commercial banks had standing to challenge a rule by the federal National Credit Union Administration (NCUA), which regulated credit unions Though private banks were not members of credit unions, the Supreme Court allowed them to sue the NCUA because the Federal Credit Union Act affected a "zone of interest" of the banks.

C.   **State Courts** handle the majority of legal disputes in the United States. The court systems of each state are created and governed by the constitution of that state. State courts decide criminal matters, civil suits, and other specialized legal disputes.

1.   State Trial courts handle things like minor traffic offenses and multi-billion dollar tobacco litigation. Most states have small-claims courts that allow persons to represent themselves in matters involving a limited sum of money, usually up to $5,000.

2.   State Appellate Courts, like their federal counterparts, hear appeals from lower trial courts and can affirm, reverse, or vacate and remand any final decision of a lower court.

3.   State Supreme Courts are the courts of highest judicial authority in that state. Most states have one supreme court that hears all cases; however, in

Texas the Court of Criminal Appeals hears all criminal appeals and the Texas Supreme Court hears all civil appeals.

III. **PERSONAL JURISDICTION.** State courts must have personal (*in personam*) jurisdiction, or legal authority, over the parties of the property (*in rem*) involved in the case. The federal government established in rem jurisdiction for cases regarding URL domain names when *in personam* jurisdiction is unavailable.

    A. **Minimum Contacts**. State courts acquire personal jurisdiction over out-of-state defendants through "long-arm" statutes when defendants have "minimum contacts" with the state. Minimum contacts occur when the defendant engages in practically any business in the state, including phone calls, mail, or causing tortious injury in the state.

    B. **View from Cyberspace—Personal Jurisdiction on the World Wide Web**. Federal courts find that personal jurisdiction is properly exercised in proportion to the nature and quality of the commercial activity conducted on the internet. Courts typically decline jurisdiction when the website is "passive" and the defendant merely posts information. Courts will find "minimum contact" jurisdiction over an out-of-state defendant with an interactive website that engages in business transactions in the forum state. In foreign countries with lesser protections for advertising, courts will claim jurisdiction over businesses using the internet to post information.

IV. **CHOICE OF LAW, CHOICE OF FORUM AND THE DOCTRINE OF *FORUM CONVENIENS*.** What law applies when parties are from different states or distinct nations?

    A. **Choice of Law**. In diversity cases, generally the law of the state having the most contacts to the litigants or most interest to the litigation will be applied.

    B. **Contracts**. Sometimes a state court will look to where a relevant contract was signed, regardless of the citizenship of the parties. Parties may also agree contractually to resolve various disputes in a given forum under a set of laws of a particular state.

    C. ***Forum non conveniens***. Defendants may request a specific court on the grounds that the jurisdiction chosen by the plaintiff poses a hardship.

        Case 3.2--*Dawdy v. Union Pacific RR Co.*, 797 N.E.2d 687 (Ill 2003). Dawdy's truck was hit by a truck driver employed by Union Pacific in Macoupin County, Illinois. Dawdy filed suit in Madison County. Union Pacific filed a motion to change the forum to Macoupin. Though lawyers for both sides were closer to Madison County and the defendant did business there, the Illinois

Supreme Court held for Union Pacific given the proximity to witnesses and the ability to view the site of the accident. The dissent claimed that moving cases to a different forum should only occur under exceptional circumstances.

V.   SOURCES OF LAW. In order to decide how to rule on a case, courts look to federal and state constitutions, statutes, regulations, and common law (previous court rulings).

A.   **Constitutions.** Courts are often required to interpret constitutional provisions, especially claims to implicit or non-explicit rights or liberties.

Case 3.3--*Board of Education of ISD #92 of Pottawatomie County v. Earls*, 536 U.S. 822 (2002). The local school district adopted a rule requiring all students to submit to drug testing as a condition to participation in sports programs. The Supreme Court held that the search was not unreasonable, and hence the policy did not violate the Fourth Amendment.

B.   **Statutes and Regulations.**

1.   Federal statutes are found in the *United States Code* (U.S.C.) and cover a wide-range of topics, e.g., food and drugs, patents, labor relations, civil rights. State legislatures also adopt complementary and overlapping laws on employment, marriage and divorce, property, wills and probate, corporations and the like.

2.   Congress established regulations to govern the day to day activities of federal agencies like the IRS, Department of Transportation, Federal Communications Commission, Securities and Exchange Commission. These rules are found in the *Code of Federal Regulations* (CFR). See further discussion of administrative law in Chapter 6.

C.   **Common Law.** Settled legal principles and case law, made by judges, serve as the foundation for topics in contract law, agency, and torts – areas where the Constitution or statutes do not guide judges.

D.   *Stare Decisis* is a doctrine in law used to guide judicial decisions.

1.   Lower courts are bound to follow a decision of a superior court, and ultimately, the U.S. Supreme Court.

2.   Once a court resolves a particular issue, other courts addressing a similar legal problem will generally follow that decision. However, "peer" courts (e.g., different state trial court or different federal courts of appeal) are not

required to follow others. Federal courts interpreting state law must follow that state's courts holdings.

3. The U.S. Supreme Court rarely overrules its previous opinions, e.g. *Planned Parenthood of SE Pa. v. Casey*, 505 U.S. 833 (1992) largely followed *Roe v. Wade*, 410 U.S. 113 (1973), though it has when social circumstances and attitudes change. Contrast *Plessy v. Ferguson*, 163 U.S. 537 (1896) with *Brown v. Board of Education*, 347 U.S. 483 (1954), on the topic of racial segregation.

> **Case 3.4--*Lawrence and Gardner v. Texas***, 539 U.S. 558 (2003). Texas state law criminalized same-sex sodomy between consenting adults, but allowed opposite-sex sodomy. Previously the Supreme Court held that "there is no right to engage in homosexual sodomy" *Bowers v. Hardwick*, 478 U.S. 186 (1986). In *Lawrence* the Court held that *Bowers* was wrongly decided, noting that most states and nations have legalized homosexual activity, and that the government was bound to protect individual liberty, including private adult sexual activity.

E. **Restatements.** Many common law principles have been collected into *restatements* by legal scholars, attorneys, and judges. Restatements summarize and explain various areas of law, such as torts, contracts, property, and trusts. Restatements are persuasive, but do not bind judges to make particular decisions.

VI. **CIVIL PROCEDURE** includes and refers to the methods, procedures, and practices that govern civil lawsuits from start to finish. Specific rules address every requirement, from filing deadlines, how to provide parties notice, and request documents. States have their own rules, and federal district courts may adopt local rules.

A. **Pleadings in Federal Courts.** Federal district courts are bound by the Federal Rules of Civil Procedure (FRCP) and Courts of Appeal follow the Federal Rules of Appellate Procedure (FRAP). Pleadings include the Complaint, Summons and Answer.

PLEADINGS

Complaint → Summons → Answer

1. Complaint. The suit begins with the plaintiff filing a complaint. The complaint briefly states the facts, explains how the court has jurisdiction, and the legal basis for the remedy or relief requested.

2. Summons. After the complaint is filed, the clerk of the court sends a summons which, along with a copy of the complaint, is served upon the defendant.

3. Answer. The defendant's answer usually denies the allegations in the complaint. The answer can also set forth affirmative defenses, explaining the defendant's action was justified. The answer may also initiate a claim against the plaintiff, a counterclaim. If the defendant does not file an answer within the time required, a default judgment may be entered for the plaintiff.

B. Pre-Trial Activity.

1. Motion to Dismiss. Defendants typically bring motions to dismiss the complaint on the grounds that the court has no jurisdiction or the plaintiff has failed to state a claim upon which the court can grant relief.

2. Summary Judgment. If there are no disputed factual assertions, either side may request a favorable judgment based on the pleadings and or additional affidavits and documents. Summary judgments are rarely granted, but when done, almost always for the defense.

3. Pre-Trial Conference. Allows each side and the court to coordinate the completion of discovery, scheduling of witnesses, consideration of amendments to the original pleadings, and discussion of settlement in lieu of trial.

C. Trial. American trials follow a standard format, selection of a jury (if applicable), opening statements, presentation by the plaintiff and rebuttal by the defense. After all the evidence, motions for a directed verdict, closing arguments, jury instructions, and verdict.

TRIAL

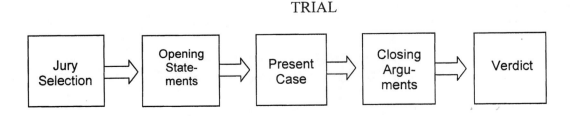

1.   Jury Selection. Attorneys (or parties) are allowed to question and interview potential jurors and strike one from the jury pool on the grounds that the individual juror is unfit or biased. No juror may be stricken on account of their race, ethnicity, or gender.

2.   Presentation of the Case. Parties proceed with opening statements. Plaintiff always goes first in trial because he or she has the burden of proof.
   - When a party asks his own witness a question, the witness is undergoing "direct examination."
   - When a party asks the opposing side's witness a question, the witness is being "cross examined."

3.   Motion for a Directed Verdict.
   - At the conclusion of the plaintiff's case, the defense may request that the judge enter a verdict in the defense's favor.
   - The judge must then assume all the facts alleged by the plaintiff are true, and if such allegations do not support the plaintiff's claim, a judge will rule in favor of the defense.
   - The same process may occur after the defense presents counter-claims or affirmative defenses.
   - Assuming the court denies all motions to dismiss, the parties give their closing arguments to the jury, after which the judge instructs the jurors on the law of the case.

4.   Jury Verdict. After hearing all the evidence and receipt of instructions from the judge a jury deliberate in private and renders a verdict. In federal court jury verdicts must be unanimous, not all state courts follow this rule.

D. Post-Trial Motions.

1.   JNOV. Losing parties may request that the judge set aside the jury's verdict and render a judgment notwithstanding the verdict (a judgment *non obstante verdicto* or JNOV). Judges only grant such given the facts, the rule of law and on the theory that "no reasonable jury" could have made the particular verdict now overruled.

2.   New trial. Judges may grant a motion for a new trial in the event that serious error occurred during the course of the trial or jury deliberations.

3.   Appeal. Losing parties may appeal trial court verdicts, but appellate courts primarily review rulings of law like directed verdicts and procedure

(e.g. jury instructions), and even jury awards. Appellate courts do not reconsider evidence or facts, but whether evidence was properly admitted or rejected.

VII.   **DISCOVERY.** Discovery is the formal process by which parties collect and learn of evidence that all parties will prosecute or defend claims.

A.   **Objects of discovery** include depositions (sworn usually oral questions of a witness), interrogatories (written questions to the parties), and requests for production of documents, which include not only tangible items such as medical records, but also intangible evidence such as computer files and e-mail.

B.   **Purpose and Drawbacks.**

1.   Discovery helps to prevent "trial by ambush" and reveals the strengths and weaknesses of the case and facilitates settlement by the parties.

2.   Courts can order discovery, turning over of documents or evidence, may issue sanctions for failure to comply with a party's legitimate requests (e.g. Wal-Mart), or "quash" a request for discovery.

3.   Discovery can be costly and time consuming, hence Congress has taken action to prevent "fishing expeditions."

VIII.   **ATTORNEY-CLIENT AND OTHER PRIVILEGES AND THE ATTORNEY WORK-PRODUCT DOCTRINE.** Generally any person with relevant information can be required to testify in depositions or at trial. However specific "privileges" protect communications between attorneys and clients.

A.   **Attorney-Client Privilege.**

1.   Definition. Attorney-Client privilege belongs to the client who seeks legal advice and protects those communications that are intended to be confidential, only revealed between the client and the attorney.

2.   Limits. Privilege does not protect client communications that are made to further a crime or illegal act. 66 U.S.L.W. 1112 (Aug 19, 1997). As well the communications must be between a client and their attorney regarding legal advice. See United States v. Frederick, 182 F.3d 496 (7th Cir. 1999).

3.   Corporate Clients. What element of the corporation is the attorney's client? In *Upjohn Co. v. United States*, 449 U.S. 383 (1981) the Court created a "subject-matter" test to determine what communications are

privileged. Any employee-counsel communication is protected if the subject matter of the communication relates to the employee's duties and the communication is made at the direction of a corporate superior.

B. **Attorney-Client Privilege Under Siege.**

  1. Sarbanes-Oxley demands that attorneys report financial malfeasance to their superiors, CEO or ultimately the Board of Directors.

  2. The Securities and Exchange Commission requires attorneys to make noisy withdrawals when attorneys learn that their employers fail to correct SEC violations.

  3. American Bar Association model rules of professional conduct direct attorneys to report "up the ladder" and permit breaches of confidence to prevent serious financial harm.

  4. The U.S. Department of Justice demands that companies waive attorney-client privilege, when seeking sentencing reductions.

C. **Attorney Work Product Doctrine**. Protects information an attorney prepares in anticipation of litigation, including private memoranda and thoughts of the attorney about a legal matters. Work-product doctrine, broader than attorney-client privilege, protects discovery that is not protected by the attorney-client privilege. *National Education Training Group, Inc., v. SkillSoft Corp.*, 1999 WL 378337 (S.D.N.Y. June 9, 1999).

D. **Other Privileges**. Beyond attorney-client privilege, there are priest-penitent privilege and the doctor-patient privilege. The Fifth Amendment grants the accused the right to refrain from self incrimination in criminal proceedings. Court recognize a privilege for corporate self-critical analysis. *Tice v. American Airlines, Inc.*, 192 F.R.D. 270 (N.D. Ill. 2000).

IX. **CLASS ACTIONS.**

A. **Certification**. If a company's conduct or product affected or affects many people in a common way, courts may certify a class action lawsuit. Recent class-action suits include asbestos, silicone-breast-implants, and anti-tobacco litigation.

B. Individuals may **opt out** of the class and pursue private or separate action.

C.   **Defendant Concerns**. Defendant-companies see class action suits as a "strategic management tool" as they can reduce or limit the damages, lower litigation costs by consolidating all claims in one court, and even limit long-term liability.

D.   *Amchem Products Inc. v. Windson*, 521 U.S. 591 (1997). Class-actions pose difficulties in certifying a class and settlement.

   1.   With asbestos litigation it might be difficult to determine the actual size of the class. There might not be enough commonality among the plaintiffs and it might not be possible for one attorney or firm to represent them.

   2.   Settlements must be approved by courts. Because slightly different classes of plaintiffs might have widely different claims or need for varied forms of relief, hence Courts are to examine class certification more carefully.

X.   LITIGATION STRATEGIES FOR PLAINTIFFS.

   A.   THE DECISION TO SUE.

      1.   When planning to file a lawsuit, the plaintiff must consider alternatives to suit, which legal claim is most likely to succeed, in which court to file, the likelihood of recovery, and the effects of possible negative publicity.

      2.   Frivolous or under-investigated suits can result in legal sanction, namely the court may order the plaintiff to pay attorney's fees for the defense.

   B.   **The Decision to Settle.** Over 90% of all civil suits settle before trial. Frequently it is most cost-effective to negotiate via an arbitrator or mediator as to avoid the costs of discovery and evidence collection.

   C.   **Pre-Trial Preparation.**

      1.   The company should select personnel to act as contacts for the attorneys and undertake a "cost-benefit" budget for the expenses of litigation.

      2.   Executives and employees that will be involved with the lawsuit preparation should not handle public relations and should develop a "document retention strategy."

      3.   No employee should discuss the suit with family or friends.

Political Perspective: Should the United States Adopt the British Rule that the Loser Pays the Winner's Attorney's Fess? Advocates claim the rule will decrease the likelihood of frivolous suits and encourage alternatives to law suit. Critics note that such a system, as is the case in Britain, will discourage citizen groups, consumers and workers from challenging corporate giants.

XI. **LITIGATION STRATEGIES FOR DEFENDANTS.**

    A. **Respond to Complaints**. A defendant company should never disregard the summons and complaint. The company should consult counsel, plan a defense strategy, and follow it.

    B. **Internal Preparation**. Factual and legal preparation should be done promptly, so that important evidence—such as the memory of key witnesses—is not lost.

    C. **Understand the Plaintiff**. If the plaintiff felt it necessary to sue, perhaps their complaint is legitimate. Defendant should consider the possibility of a settlement. Sometimes an apology—while legally risky—is better than a legal defense.

    D. **Prepare for Trial**. If the suit cannot be settled, then the defendant should proceed yet be wary of bad faith tactics.

XII. **DOCUMENT RETENTION AND DESTRUCTION.** When a company is a defendant in a lawsuit, company documents, including computer files, may be used to prove liability in court. Court rules and federal law punish intentional destruction of documents, e-mails, and memos. A good policy can reduce corporate liability, protect trade secrets and reduce litigation costs.

    A. **Designing a Policy**.

        1. Though federal and state regulations require companies to retain certain records, documents that a company is not required to retain for any business or legal purpose should be eliminated at routine intervals, according to company policy.

        2. Private and confidential records should be safeguarded, and destroyed as soon as possible to avoid liability.

        3. Too often employees treat electronic communications (e-mail and instant messages) as informal, yet they are often filled with significant or damaging information. Companies must develop codes to regulate and control e-mail and their destruction.

B.   **Necessary Elements of a Document-Retention Program**. Legal and acceptable document-retention (destruction) programs must be planned, regular, and systematic. *Zubulake v. UBS Warburg LLC*, 216 F.R.D. 280 (S.D.N.Y. 2004). Companies should conduct regular audits and destroy corporate documents in the "ordinary course of business" (not selectively), but must cease any destruction upon notice of a lawsuit. *Carlucci v. Piper Aircraft Corp.*, 102 F.R.D. 472 (S.D. Fla. 1984).

XIII. EXTRAS.

A.   **The Responsible Manager: Reducing Litigation Costs**. Responsible corporate managers find ways to reduce or eliminate litigation costs before they arise or reduce them once a lawsuit it filed. Managers optimize corporate health by finding ways to resolve conflict rather than leaving it to the lawyers who are trained to be adversarial and overcome an opponent.

B.   **Inside Story**: Arthur Andersen and Frank Quattrone Shred Their Credibility.

1.   Accounting firm Arthur Andersen admitted publicly that it destroyed a significant amount of correspondence and records with Enron. Without access to its documents, Arthur Andersen had little defense against allegations of intentional fraud in its audits of Enron.

2.   After Frank Quattrone, a technology banker, learned of an impending SEC investigation and impending subpoenas for e-mails, he informed employees to delete past messages. Quattrone was ultimately sentenced to 18 months in prison for perjury.

STUDY QUESTIONS

True-False Questions

___ 1.   The appellant and the respondent are the same party in the original lawsuit.

___ 2.   Federal courts are courts of limited subject matter jurisdiction.

___ 3.   Corporations can reduce conflicts in diversity suits by using contracts that compel parties to agree to accept the law and procedural rules of a particular state regardless of where the lawsuit is filed.

___ 4. Federal courts only consider the location of corporate headquarters when considering diversity status.

___ 5. At least six Supreme Court Justices must be present to hear a case.

___ 6. The Supreme Court must hear every case that is appealed to it.

___ 7. State courts handle most of the lawsuits in the United States.

___ 8. Because the United States Constitution does not expressly contain a right to privacy, no court can protect individual rights to privacy.

___ 9. State courts issue regulations to guide policies and practices of federal agencies.

___ 10. *Stare decisis* only means that previous Supreme Court decisions must *always* be followed.

___ 11. Restatements provide judges and attorneys with summaries of principles of law.

___ 12. If a defendant receives the summons and complaint and fails to respond and file an answer, no legal action can be taken.

___ 13. As statements under oath that can be used as evidence in court, depositions and interrogatories are, in effect, the same thing.

___ 14. The attorney-client privilege limits the types of evidence that can be produced at trial.

___ 15. The work product privilege protects all documents in an attorney's client file.

Multiple-Choice Questions

___ 1. Typically, federal courts are courts of _____ subject matter jurisdiction, and state courts are courts of _____ subject matter jurisdiction.
    A. general; limited.
    B. limited; general.
    C. general; general.
    D. limited; limited.

___ 2. Federal courts derive their legal power to hear civil cases from all but which of the following?
A. diversity jurisdiction
B. federal question jurisdiction
C. cases when the United States is a party
D. state constitutions

___ 3. Which of the following is *not* a test used by federal courts to determine a principal place of business for a multi-state business?
A. Total Activity Test.
B. Nerve Center Test.
C. Shareholder Site Test.
D. Place of Operations Test.

___ 4. A trademark lawsuit is proper in:
A. Federal court.
B. State court.
C. Federal court if the plaintiff sues in good faith for more than $50,000.
D. In either state or federal court.

___ 5. Which of the following is *not* a primary function of a court of appeals?
A. Review trial court decisions.
B. Review important evidence during a trial.
C. Review decisions of certain administrative agencies.
D. Issue writs to lower courts and litigants.

___ 6. Personal jurisdictional in state court may be based on _____ jurisdiction.

I. *In rem.*
II. *In personam.*
III. *In banc.*

A. I or II.
B. I only.
C. I, II, or III.
D. II or III.

___ 7. Which of the following would be a sufficient nexus for a nonresident defendant to have with a court?
A. Be sued in the court's jurisdiction.
B. Own property in the court's jurisdiction.
C. Do business in the court's jurisdiction.
D. All of the above.

___ 8. Which of the following is *not* a typical state court of limited jurisdiction?
A. Small Claims Court.
B. Juvenile Court.
C. County Court.
D. Traffic Court.

___ 9. Chief Justice Rehnquist explicitly stated that *Roe v. Wade* was wrongly decided, and should be overturned, in which case?
A. *Plessey v. Ferguson.*
B. *Griswold v. Connecticut.*
C. *Planned Parenthood v. Casey.*
D. *Ginsburg v. Lewinsky.*

___ 10. The complaint makes allegations of all of the following *except:*
A. The facts of the case giving rise to the dispute.
B. The legal theory for relief.
C. An in-depth description of the allegations.
D. The prayer for relief.

___ 11. If the defendant does not file an answer within the required time period, a _____ judgment may be entered for the plaintiff.
A. Defense.
B. Default.
C. Pleadings.
D. Cross-claim.

___ 12. The attorney-client privilege belongs to the:
I. Attorney.
II. Client.

A. I
B. II
C. I or II
D. I and II

___ 13. Which of the following statements is false concerning the attorney-client privilege in a corporate setting?
A. The privilege applies to legal and business advice from an attorney.
B. Communications with the attorney should be from senior management.
C. All files and documentation should be confidentially maintained.
D. Requests for legal advice from a company should be in writing.

__ 14. Class-action lawsuits are discouraged or not certified by courts if:
   A. Plaintiffs suffer different types of injuries from the same product.
   B. No single lawyer or firm can represent all plaintiffs adequately.
   C. A future group of people will suffer the same injuries, yet are not informed of the lawsuit.
   D. None of the above.

__ 15. Which situation would most likely be settled?
   A. A case with ambiguous legal issues.
   B. A case that would be a large recovery if the plaintiff wins, and not much harm if the plaintiff loses.
   C. An honest dispute.
   D. A case when one side acted unreasonably.

Essay Questions

1.   Why should bias be less in federal court for diversity cases?

2.   Why do federal judges have lifetime tenure?

3.   Why should an attorney take a deposition of a witness when the witness will be at trial?

Chapter 4
ALTERNATIVE DISPUTE RESOLUTION

Introduction

What are the alternatives for dispute resolution in businesses? This chapter presents some non-litigation alternatives that managers have: negotiation, mediation, and arbitration, hybrids such as mini-trials, med-arb, and summary jury trials. This chapter discusses fundamental legal aspects for resolution of business disputes, and presents strategies for managers to stay out of court. The chapter concludes with a review of how the law compares ADR to litigation.

I.   **THINKING ABOUT ALTERNATIVE DISPUTE RESOLUTION (ADR).** Managers must know the company's needs and constraints before selecting a mechanism to confront or avoid litigation. Managers must note the best decision; consider the company's public image and confidentiality; and, in some cases, account for liabilities of business partners. The following six questions can help managers plot a course of action:

   A.   **How are disputants represented**? Will parties have lawyers, advocates or represent themselves?

   B.   **Who makes the final decision**? Judges, attorneys, a company representative, a neutral party?

   C.   **How are facts found, and standards of judgment set**? Do participant present facts, will the arbiter do an investigation?

   D.   **What is the source of the standard for resolution**? Are there set rules, according to legal standards, will the parties establish the standard?

   E.   **How will the decision be enforced**? Will the resolution create a legal contract?

   F.   **Who will pay for the dispute resolution procedure**?

II. **VARIETIES OF ADR.** Three fundamental varieties of ADR are: negotiation, mediation, and arbitration. In addition, managers have more options: mini-trial, med-arb, arb-med, and summary trials.

   A.   **Negotiation** is simply the give-and-take that people engage in solve disputes. Different types of negotiations serve a company's different needs e.g., transactional negotiations, dispute resolutions, distributive or zero-sum negotiations, and integrative or variable-sum negotiations.

1. Planning and Preparation. Managers must asses their Best Alternative to a Negotiated Alternative (BATNA). Establish the company's interests and rank the importance of each issue to be negotiated.

   - Negotiation Preparation. Analyze the nature of the conflict, specify goals and objectives, understand the opponent and the particular circumstances

   - Common Negotiation Mistakes. Pursuing a course of action to justify an earlier decision, failure to recognize the opponent's desires, irrational considerations tied to the anchor price, failure to reframe the issue, ignoring relevant data, hubris.

2. Liability for Failed Negotiations. Within the U.S. typically there is no legal liability for failure to finalize a contract after a series of negotiations. In other jurisdictions, the rules are the opposite.

   > Case 4.1—D. *James Wan Kim Min v. Mitsui Bussan K.K.*, Toyko High Court (1987). Parties entered into a joint venture for logging in Indonesia. After negotiations, Mitsui agreed to loan pay Min $4 million for the right to log, but later refused. Though the parties never concluded a contract, the Japanese court held that as negotiations give rise to an expectation, Min was entitled to recover damages as Mitsui violated principles of good faith and trust.

B. **Mediation**. Mediation occurs when parties choose an impartial person, a mediator, to help the parties to resolve a dispute. Mediation allows for mutually acceptable settlements and is suggested by judges and lawyers as an alternative for litigation. It is faster, costs less, less adversarial and private.

   1. History. The mediation process is not new. Mediation has been present for many centuries. Historically, the mediation process shows that parties are more satisfied with the outcome.

   2. Selecting a Mediator.
      - In the 1980s, the Society of Professionals in Dispute Resolution formed a commission to establish criteria by which mediators ought be accepted. Mediators should be knowledgeable of the process, understand the parties' needs and interests, screen out unresolvable issues, help parties reach their own informed choices.

- The CPR Institute for Dispute Resolution offers Panels of Distinguished Neutrals to help people resolve their differences.

3.   Confidentiality. As go-betweens, mediators do not favor one party, but must maintain protect the confidence of the parties. Many states extend legal privilege to mediators. Federal courts are more willing to extend such privilege as well.

4.   When to Use Mediation. If parties wish to seek an alternative for litigation and settle a dispute in good faith, mediation is worthwhile otherwise mediation can be a waste of time. Mediation is advisable in an unsettled area of law and when parties wish to avoid publicity.

5.   Mediation Process. Each party is supposed to help construct a solution to the dispute, but generally mediators provide a set of ground rules to govern the process.

6.   Dangers. There are limited procedural protections for parties in mediation. Primarily unequal parties do not bargain equally or with rights that would be guaranteed under law. Mediation might generate unintended consequences affecting future business dealings.

Viewpoint from Cyberspace: ADR for Online Disputes. With heavy commercial traffic on the internet, businesses and consumers must find ways to resolve transactional conflicts. European, UN-based, and American governmental organizations have approved or suggested regulations to administer ADR for online transactions.

C.   **Arbitration**. a process whereby parties present their disagreement to an independent third party, an arbitrator, who renders a final (usually) binding decision. Like mediation, arbitration is quick, less costly, and usually private.

1.   Arbitration Process, similar to a trial, it is adversarial and has three phases:

- Pre-hearing. Parties submit documents, statements, and briefs.
- Hearing. Like a trial, parties present evidence, yet the rules of evidence are relaxed.
- Post-hearing. The arbitrator issues a decision.

2.   Choice of Arbitrator. An arbitrator is either chosen by the parties or a third-party, such as the AAA. An arbitrator with the necessary knowledge to handle the level and type of the disputed issue should be chosen.

3. Arbitration Clauses. Generally parties contract to use binding arbitration in the event of a dispute. Parties arbitrate specific issues. Arbitration clauses are important at an international level when parties come from different nations as a means to avoid litigation in foreign legal systems.

4. Judicial Enforcement. Most states have incorporated laws to conform to the Uniform Arbitration Act. Congress also passed and the Supreme Court has upheld the Federal Arbitration Act. *Southland Corp. v. Keating*, 465 U.S. 1 (1984).

- Arbitration of Statutory Claims. The Supreme Court has upheld contracts where parties agree to have to resolve rights before an arbiter instead of a court. *Rodriguez de Quijas v. Shearson/American Express, Inc.*, 490 U.S. 477 (1989); *Doctor's Assoc., Inc. v. Casarotto*, 517 U.S. 681 (1996).

- Arbitration of Employment Disputes. Employers may compel their employees to resolve disputes in arbitration instead of taking claims to court. *Circuit City Stores, Inc., v. Adams*, 532 U.S. 105 (2001).

  Case 4.2—*Circuit City Stores, Inc., v. Adams*, 532 U.S. 105 (2001). Saint Clair Adams applied for and accepted a job a Circuit City. As a condition of employment, Adams signed an agreement to go to arbitration to resolve any labor dispute. Two years later, Adams filed an employment discrimination suit, but Circuit City looked to dismiss and force Adams into arbitration. The Supreme Court upheld the contract due the Federal Arbitration Act (FAA) which applies to most labor contracts.

- Unconscionable Arbitration Agreements. Generally in law, courts will not enforce "unconscionable" contracts – those where the weaker party has little or no bargaining power yet agrees to that which is irrational.

  Case 4.3--*Circuit City Stores, Inc., v. Adams*, 279 F.3d 889 (9th Cir. 2002). On remand from the Supreme Court, the Ninth Circuit Court of Appeals declared, as allowed by the FAA, (arbitration clauses may be held void if they violate state law on contracts) that Circuit City's demand that its employees submit to arbitration was an unenforceable adhesion contract.

5. **Judicial Review of Awards**. The FAA lists four circumstances for which an arbitration award may be set aside by a court:

- The award was a product of corruption, fraud, or undue means;
- the arbitrator was demonstrably impartial or corrupt;
- the arbitrator engaged in misconduct, e.g., refused to hear pertinent evidence; and
- the arbitrator exceeded their powers, or executed them so poorly that a final award on the issue put to arbitration was not made.

Case 4.4--*Green Tree Financial Corp. v. Bazzle*, 539 U.S. 444 (2003). The central question before the court was whether the arbitrator exceeded his power in certifying a class of plaintiffs, though the contract in question was silent on this topic. The court understood that the arbitrator was only following the edict of a South Carolina district court and remanded the case to the arbitrator to decide if the contract would allow "class arbitration."

III.   **HYBRIDS**. There are hybrid forms of ADR available to find the solution to the disputed issues, such as med-arb, mini-trials and summary jury trials.

A.   **Med-Arb**. Med-arb is a combination of the procedures of mediation and arbitration. Med-arb uses the same process, and uses the same person as the mediator and arbitrator, either by agreement or binding decision.

B.   **Arb-Med**. Parties using arbitration/mediation go first to an arbitrator, who decides without notifying the parties while they attempt to resolve their dispute through mediation. If mediation fails, the arbitrator's award is unsealed.

C.   **Mini-Trial**. In a mini-trial, lawyers conduct discovery for a limited period, then exchange legal briefs or memoranda of law. Lawyers present the dispute to a neutral third party, often an attorney or a judge. After the mini-trial, managers of the businesses in dispute meet directly, without lawyers, to resolve the conflict. However, if the process fails (like with arb-med), the third party issues a non-binding opinion.

D.   **Summary Jury Trial**. A summary jury trial enables disputants to present their case. Because parties present a case before a real jury, which renders a non-binding decision, parties can assess how decisionmakers might decide a real trial (thus encouraging settlement).

E.   **Collaborative Law and Other Techniques**.

1.   Collaborative law looks to combine mediation and negotiation in an efficient manner. Typical negotiations with lawyers and parties cost far less than regular trials.

2.   Ombudspersons (ombudsman is also gender neutral) also serve as channels to resolve conflicts and let parties air concerns before they escalate.

IV.   **OTHER LAWS FAVORING SETTLEMENT OVER LITIGATION**. Government has created statutes to strengthen ADR methods of operation, as the processes are cost-saving and outside traditional court channels. The judicial system promotes alternatives to litigation in a variety of ways.

A.   **Pretrial Conferences**. Pretrial conferences are designed to encourage parties to settle the conflict without a trial.

B.   **Liberal Discovery**. Both parties are exposed to the all data pertaining to the disputed issue, in an attempt to eliminate asymmetric information between the parties.

C.   **Rejected-Offer Sanctions**. If one party refuses to accept a favorable settlement before the trial for capricious and unrealistic reasons, they may be penalized.

D.   **Negotiation as Evidence of Fault**. The federal rules of evidence, encourage negotiation, by limiting the introduction of negotiations as evidence in a trial. However some information included in negotiations can be introduced.

E.   **Tortious Dispute Resolution**. Managers are not immune from judicial action solely because their company pursues ADR. Managers and companies might still be liable in tort for causing injury to a person or property.

V.   **THE RESPONSIBLE MANAGER: STAYING OUT OF COURT**. Litigation is perhaps the worst thing that can happen to a company due to the effect on the company's financial and public positions. Managers should seek ways to stay out of court. Legal problems are part of business so managers should develop and implement an alternative dispute resolution program.

VI.   **INSIDE STORY**: Arbitrating the Dot-Com Bust. At the end of the 20th century, many lawsuits were brought against brokers by those who lost money investing in dot-com companies. One mechanism designed to facilitate such claims is the National Association of Securities Dealers (NASD). Because the NASD typically offers no explanation for its rulings, and doe not release figures on its awards, it has been subject to criticism.

STUDY QUESTIONS

True-False Questions

___ 1. The Biblical story of King Solomon is an example of ADR.

___ 2. Negotiation is, by definition, always forward-looking.

___ 3. In *Circuit City Stores, Inc. v. Adams* the Supreme Court upheld the arbitration clause in the employment contract.

___ 4. At the core of any dispute is the realization that the parties are vying for the same thing, and the result must be a zero-sum game.

___ 5. Arbitration is a process whereby parties present their disagreement to an independent third party who renders a final (usually) binding decision.

___ 6. Mediation is a facilitated negotiation.

___ 7. A mediator can help parties reach a consensus even if a party is acting unreasonably.

___ 8. It is possible for mediation to diffuse difficult interpersonal tensions.

___ 9. One factor that favors mediation over litigation is the legal uncertainty of litigation.

___ 10. Like mediation, arbitration is binding and enforceable in court.

___ 11. Due to its adversarial nature, an arbitration hearing is more tightly structured than mediation.

___ 12. The binding arbitration awards without explanation cannot be challenged in court.

___ 13. Arbitration clauses are almost essential in international contracts.

___ 14. The EEOC opposes mandatory arbitration of racial and sexual discrimination claims.

___ 15. Arb-med process force parties to accept arbitration, if mediation fails.

Multiple-Choice Questions

___ 1. _____ is *not* a basic type of ADR.
   A. Negotiation.
   B. Mediation.
   C. Assessment.
   D. Arbitration.

___ 2. In _____ negotiations, mutual gains are possible as parties trade lower-valued resources for higher-valued ones.
   A. Integrative.
   B. Distributive.
   C. Transactional.
   D. Dispute.

___ 3. Before beginning negotiations, a manager should do all of the following *except:*
   A. Analyze the nature of the dispute.
   B. Ask what the opponent's objectives are.
   C. Outline the scope of the negotiation.
   D. Understand the particular negotiation situation.

___ 4. Common structural barriers include:

   I. Conflicts of interest.
   II. Symmetric information.
   III. Political constraints.

   A. I and II.
   B. II and III.
   C. I, II, and III.
   D. I and III.

___ 5. Psychological barriers include all but which of the following?
   A. Reactive devaluation.
   B. Divergent construals.
   C. Psychological dissonance.
   D. Loss avoidance.

___ 6. Common negotiation mistakes include all of the following *except:*
   A. Assuming that what is good for you is necessarily bad for your opponent.
   B. Pursuing a negotiated course of action to justify an earlier decision.
   C. Placing too much confidence in your opponent's judgment.
   D. Being affected by readily available information and ignoring other less accessible data.

__ 7. Qualified mediators should be able to all of the following *except:*
   A. Help parties assess their alternatives.
   B. Decide the issues of the dispute.
   C. Earn trust and maintain acceptability.
   D. Help parties invent creative options.

__ 8. Lawsuits require the disclosure of information that parties may want to keep secret. Which of the following situations would cause the least problems for privacy concerns?
   A. Trademark infringement.
   B. Client lists.
   C. Trade secrets.
   D. Internal training documents.

__ 9. Which of the following is *not* a ground rule from the American Mediation Council?
   A. The process is voluntary.
   B. Each party cannot withdraw at any time after mediation has begun.
   C. The process is nonbinding.
   D. The mediator shall be neutral and objective.

__ 10. The Supreme Court has upheld arbitration agreements under which Acts?

   I.   The Sherman Act.
   II. RICO.
   III. The Securities Exchange Act of 1934.

   A. I and III.
   B. I only.
   C. II and III.
   D. I, II, and III.

__ 11. Which of the following is *not* a circumstance in which an arbitration award may be set aside by a court under the Federal Arbitration Act?
   A. The award was obtained by fraud.
   B. The arbitrator was not impartial.
   C. The arbitrator acted within the scope of his or her duty.
   D. The arbitrator refused to postpone the hearing when just cause was given.

__ 12. A court should overturn an arbitration award when the decision:
   A. Violates public policy.
   B. Was arbitrary.
   C. Was capricious.
   D. All of the above.

__ 13. _____ is when parties in a dispute put their case before a real jury for a nonbinding decision.
   A. A mini-trial.
   B. A summary jury trial.
   C. Med-arb.
   D. Arb-med.

__ 14. According the Federal Rules of Civil Procedure, a defendant can offer to settle no less than ____ days before trial.
   A. 10.
   B. 7.
   C. 30.
   D. 60.

__ 15. Which ADR method decides which party or parties pay for the method prior to commencement?
   A. Mediation.
   B. Negotiation.
   C. Arbitration.
   D. Litigation.

Essay Questions

1. What are the best arguments to support the idea that a mediator's decisions and work products should remain confidential.

2. Why is arbitration usually binding?

3. Compare and contrast mediation and arbitration.

4. What role should the Internet have in mediating online disputes?

Chapter 5
AGENCY

Introduction

Agency is the most pervasive legal relationship in the business world. In an agency relationship the *agent* acts for or represents the *principal*. The principal delegates some of all power to the agent. The agent manages the assigned task and exercises discretion. The agency relationship may be created by express or implied agreement or by law. Without agency, corporations could not function. This chapter defines and discusses central principles of agency law. It describes different methods by which an agency relationship can be formed. The chapter identifies types of agency relationships and the consequences that flow therefrom. It examines the duties agents owe principals, and an agent's authority to enter into agreements that bind the principal. Finally, the chapter discusses the extent to which a principal may be liable for the tortious or illegal conduct of an agent.

I. **FORMATION OF AN AGENCY RELATIONSHIP.** An agency relationship can be formed by an agreement, oral or written, between parties. If an agent signs an agreement on behalf of the principal, the agreement is enforceable against the principal. Agency can also be implied based on the conduct of the principal, even if there is no formal agreement. There are other ways of forming an agency relationship without an agreement, e.g., agency by *ratification* or by *estoppel*.

II. **TYPES OF AGENCY RELATIONSHIPS.**

    A. **Employee.** The employer-employee relationship, also known as master-servant relationship, is the most common type of agency. An employer has the right to control an employee, and an employee may bind an employer to a contract.

    B. **Independent Contractor.** An independent contractor, e.g., a plumber or electrician working for a house builder, or a lawyer working for a client, are not employees of the principal. The principal lacks control over the agent.

III. **DISTINGUISHING BETWEEN EMPLOYEES AND INDEPENDENT CONTRACTORS.**

    A. **Distinctions** between employees and independent contractors are tied specific legal obligations.

        1. Employers are generally liable for employee torts, must pay taxes and provide benefit plans on behalf of employees.

2. Independent contractors are generally liable for their own torts, and responsible to deduct or pay income, social security, unemployment and self-employment taxes.

B. **No Bright Line Test**. Courts consider many factors in order to characterize the agent as an employee or independent contractor:

1. Employer's control over details of work.
2. occupation of agent
3. Level of supervision
4. Degree of skill required for agent
5. Who provides tools and workspace
6. Length of time worker is engaged
7. Method of payment
8. Whether agent offers services to the public

IV. **FIDUCIARY DUTY**. As fiduciaries, agents have certain responsibilities to the principal.

A. **Loyalty**. The fiduciary must act for the sole benefit of the principal.

B. **Obedience**. The fiduciary must obey all reasonable and legal orders.

C. **Care**. The fiduciary must avoid mistakes, and tortious conduct.

> **Case 5.1--*Feddeman & Co. v. Langan Associates***, 530 S.E.2d 668 (Va. 2000).
> Former employees of Feddeman & Co, left the firm and joined Langan Associates, after merger-buy out talks broke down. In effect, the former FC employees, who owed a duty of loyalty to FC, simply devastated the existence of FC and the financial position of their employer through an organized walk out.

> **Case 5.2--*Green v. H & R Block***, 735 A.2d 1039 (Md. 1999).
> H&R Block, a tax preparer, was paid by Green and others to fill out federal income tax forms. H&R Block created a scheme by which they were enriched and exacted indirect fees from their clients, for those clients who were entitled to a refund. Because H&R Block did not inform their clients of the schemes, they failed to act with the utmost fidelity to the principal, rather sought to enrich themselves in a manner that was in conflict with the interests of their clients.

V. **AGENT'S ABILITY TO BIND THE PRINCIPAL TO CONTRACTS ENTERED INTO BY THE AGENT**. Agents can bind the principal in a number of ways.

A.   **Actual Authority**.

　　1.   **Express Authority**. An agent has express authority to bind the principal when the relationship is created orally or in writing. An agent has express authority if they believe the principal authorized their actions.

　　2.   **Implied Authority**. An agent with express authority to bind the principal also has implied authority, given a reasonable basis to engage in particular conduct.

View from Cyberspace: Intelligent Agents and Click-Wrap Agreements. Intelligent agents are semi-autonomous computer programs. A prominent feature of electronic commerce is the "click-wrap" agreement, where users assent to a contract by clicking an acceptance box. At the urging of MicroSoft Congress passed the Electronic Signatures in Global and National Commerce Act which recognizes the validity of contracts executed by "electronic agents" (computer programs).

B.   **Apparent Authority**. An agent has apparent authority to bind the principal when a third party reasonably believes that an agent has authority to act, based on a third party's reasonable belief that the principal authorized the agent.

　　Case 5.3--*Powell v. MVE Holdings, Inc.*, 626 N.W.2d 451 (Minn. Ct. App. 2001). The CEO of MVE Holdings, David O'Halleran negotiated a termination and buyout package with Powell. There was a dispute over the price MVE would pay for Powell's stock. The legal question centered on whether O'Halleran had the authority to commit MVE to a contact to buy Powell's stock. The Court held that Powell had a reasonable belief that O'Halleran acted as the agent of MVE as was empowered to bind the principal.

C.   **Ratification**. The principal's approval of a prior unauthorized act by an agent binds the principal to a legal contract.

D.   **Undisclosed Principal**. An agent may conceal the principal's identity. Though a third party does not know the agent is working for the principal, the principal is bound to the contract.

VI.   **LIABILITY FOR TORTS OF AGENTS**. Torts, civil injuries, may serve as grounds for a lawsuit against the principal under the concept of *respondeat superior* (vicarious liability) when an employer/principal is responsible for acts or omissions of its agent.

A. **Scope of Employment**: Generally principals are only responsible for the torts of their agent when the injury occurs within the course and scope of employment. Liability is based on a factual analysis:

   1. Did the employee have the employer's authorization to act?
   2. To what extent were the employer's interests advanced?
   3. Did the employer provide the instrumentality that caused the injury?
   4. Did the employer have reason to know that the employee would perform the act?

   Case 5.4--*Riley v. Standard Oil Co. Of New York*, 132 N.E. 97 (N.Y. 1921). Riley was hit and injured by a Standard Oil truck driven by Million. Million had been instructed to drive the truck from a mill to a freight yard and back. On the way back, Million detoured to visit his sister's house, about four blocks out of the way. The court held that Million was driving a truck within the scope of his duty, so Standard Oil was liable.

B. **Liability for Torts Outside the Scope of Employment**. Under certain circumstances an employer may be liable for the agent's torts, even outside the scope of employment. Various factors are considered to determine the principal's liability:

   1. Did the employer intend the employee's conduct or its consequences?
   2. Did the employee's rank in the company make them the employer's alter ego?
   3. Can the employee's action be attributable to the employer's own negligence or recklessness?
   4. Did the employee use apparent authority to act or to speak on behalf of the employer, and was there reliance upon that apparent authority?
   5. Was the employee aided in accomplishing the tort by the existence of the agency relationship?

   Case 5.5--*Pennsylvania State Police v. Suders*, 124 S.Ct. 2342 (2004). Nancy Suders worked as a police communications operator. Three supervisors harassed Suders sexually and created a hostile workplace. After she complained they retaliated, ultimately arresting her and forcing her to resign. Though a trial court dismissed the suit against PSP, the U.S. Supreme Court held that a jury should be allowed to decide whether the employer was responsible for the acts of those who abused Suders.

C. **Torts of Independent Contractors**. The doctrine of *respondeat superior* establishes a liability scheme that applies only to actions of *employees*. A principal may be liable for the torts of independent contractors involving highly dangerous acts or non-delegable duties, when a contractor's actions are within the scope of employment.

VII.   **LIABILITY OF THE PRINCIPAL FOR VIOLATIONS OF LAW BY THE AGENT.** A company can be held vicariously liable for violation of the law by an employee, even if a manager tells the employee not to violate the law.

> **Case 5.6--*Del Amora v. Metro Ford Sales & Service*,** 206 F.Supp.2d 947 (N.D. Ill. 2002). Del Amora was in the process of getting divorced. His wife's brother, Jesus Roman worked for Metro Ford. Through his position at Metro Ford, Roman sought and collected credit report information about Del Amora. Del Amora sued Metro Ford for violation of the Fair Credit Reporting Act (FCRA). Though Metro Ford did not authorize Roman to learn about Del Amora's credit, because Roman was only able to get such records due to his position, Metro Ford was in the best position to screen and train employees as to prevent violations of FCRA.

VIII.   **RESPONSIBLE MANAGER: WORKING WITH AGENTS.** The manager-employee relationship requires loyalty and trust. A manager must be able to avoid legal situations that would damage a company's economic status and reputation. The position of a manager as a fiduciary should uphold the best interest of the company and set policies to reduce legal liability. On a whole, a responsible manager must understand the legal environment in which the operations take place.

IX.   **INSIDE STORY: WHEN "TEMPORARY" WORKERS ARE EMPLOYEES.** The litigation arose from the hiring of people as freelancers. MicroSoft hired employees as "independent contractors" continually. These employees wanted benefits, including the right to buy company stock, but were denied. The IRS held they were employees and demanded that MicroSoft pay payroll taxes, unemployment, and employer withholding taxes, and MircoSoft agreed. The Ninth Circuit Court of Appeals ruled that independent contractors and long-time temporary employees at MicroSoft, who worked at least half time or five months a year, had become common-law employees which enabled employees to recover damages and entitled them to compensation for their exclusion from the Employee Stock Purchase Program. *Vizcaino v. Microsoft*, 173 F.3d 713 (9th Cir. 1999)

STUDY QUESTIONS

True-False Questions

___ 1.   Agency agreements must be written.

__ 2. An agency agreement can be implied from conduct.

__ 3. After a principal accepts the benefits of the actions of another person (an agent), the principal has ratified their agency.

__ 4. The most common type of agency relationship is the real estate agent.

__ 5. The person hiring an independent contractor bargains only for the results of their labor.

__ 6. An independent contractor cannot be an agent.

__ 7. Generally, employers are liable for the torts of their employees and independent contractors.

__ 8. For payroll reasons, an employer may be able to hire an independent contractor for less cost than hiring an employee to perform the same task.

__ 9. If an employment status is stated in the employment contract, then based on court decisions, that status determines the relationship.

__ 10. Loyalty and profitability are the hallmarks of a fiduciary relationship.

__ 11. An agent has the duty to act with utmost care while an agent.

__ 12. An undisclosed principal can be contractually bound to a third party.

__ 13. Express authority is one way a manager can determine whether or not an officer has implied authority to execute an agreement for the company.

__ 14. An officer of a company does not have the unilateral authority to bind the corporation to sell or purchase shares of its own stock.

__ 15. Ratification, unlike authorization, must be given expressly.

Multiple-Choice Questions

__ 1. Agency relationships can be formed without previous agreement by:

       I. Ratification.
       II. Estoppel.
       III. Subsequent agreement.

A. I, II, and III.
B. I and II.
C. II and III.
D. I and III.

___ 2. The employer-employee relationship is mainly characterized by the right to _____ the employee.
A. Pay.
B. Control.
C. Suspend.
D. Reclassify.

___ 3. The employee may bind the principal contractually under the theory of _____ authority.

I. Actual.
II. Accidental.
III. Apparent.

A. I only.
B. III only.
C. I, II, or III.
D. I or III.

___ 4. A contractor hires an electrician as a subcontractor. In this case the electrician is:
A. An employee.
B. An independent contractor.
C. A principal.
D. None of the above.

___ 5. The employer is *not* obligated to deduct _____ for independent contractors.
A. Federal income taxes.
B. Payroll taxes .
C. Unemployment taxes.
D. All of the above.

___ 6. Which of the following is *not* a factor in determining the status of a worker?
A. What degree of skill does the work require?
B. Does the employer provide the tools with which to work?
C. What time of year is the worker employed?
D. Is the worker paid hourly or by the job?

___ 7. An agency relationship is created by:

    I. Express contract.
    II. Implied contract.
    III. Law.

    A. I, II, or III.
    B. I or II.
    C. II or III.
    D. I or III.

___ 8. Which of the following is *not* a fiduciary?
    A. An officer.
    B. A director.
    C. A minority shareholder.
    D. An agent.

___ 9. Express authority may be given by the principal's:
    A. Words.
    B. Acts.
    C. Neither A nor B.
    D. Both A and B.

___ 10. If an agent is told to buy a van for transporting children for no more than $35,000, the agent has implied authority to:
    A. Select the make and model of the van.
    B. Negotiate the price of the van.
    C. Finalize the sale.
    D. All of the above.

___ 11. Ratification can be:

    I. Expressed in writing.
    II. Implied in writing.
    III. Expressed by spoken words.

    A. I only.
    B. I and II only.
    C. I and III only.
    D. All of the above.

___ 12. An agent may legally conceal the principal's _____.
   A. Name.
   B. Identity.
   C. Existence.
   D. All of the above

___ 13. The principal will be bound to any contract entered into by an agent with _____ authority.
   A. ratified
   B. apparent
   C. actual
   D. undisclosed

___ 14. If an agent acts within the scope of authority of employment, the employer is liable for the agent's tortious conduct under the doctrine of:
   A. *Nunc pro tunc.*
   B. *Respondeat superior.*
   C. *Pro se superior.*
   D. *De minimis non curat lex.*

___ 15. If the principal has to pay damages to a third party because of an agent's tortious conduct, the principal has the right to demand:
   A. Reimbursement from the agent.
   B. Reimbursement from the third party.
   C. Further assurances from the third party.
   D. All of the above.

Essay Questions

1. Why is it probably cheaper to hire an independent contractor than an employee for the same job?

2. Compare and contrast actual and apparent authority.

3. Why are principals usually not liable for the torts of independent contractors?

4. What precautions should companies make to prevent liability for the conduct of an electronic agent that automatically executes a electronic contract?

CHAPTER 6
ADMINISTRATIVE LAW

INTRODUCTION

This chapter examines the role of administrative agencies in the legal environment, how they function, exercise power, and carry out procedures on a daily basis.

CHAPTER OUTLINE

I.   **HOW ADMINISTRATIVE AGENCIES ACT**. Administrative agencies operate primarily in four basic ways: making the rules, conducting formal adjudications, taking informal discretionary actions, and conducting investigations.

   A.   **Making the Rules**. State legislatures and Congress frequently pass authority to administrative agencies to carry out oversight and regulation, under certain principles and guidelines. Promulgation of rules and regulations requires notice to the public, evaluation, and adoption.

   1.   Notice to the Public. First an agency must give public notice of its proposal, and allow time for written public comment to the proposal.

   2.   Evaluation. Once an agency evaluates public comment, it may change the proposed rule, and re-publish the revised rule for public comment once again.

   3.   Adoption. Finally an agency adopts the new rule formally by publishing it in the *Federal Register*, and the Code of Federal Regulations.

   Case 6.1--*U.S. Chamber of Commerce v. U.S. Department of Labor*, 174 F.3d 206 (D.C. Cir. 1999). The Occupational Safety and Health Administration (OSHA), part of the Department of Labor, issued a directive (the Directive) establishing a program to address worker safety at dangerous workplaces. The Directive set up a procedure whereby dangerous workplaces would be placed on a "primary inspection list" and subjected to inspection. The Chamber of Commerce challenged the Directive for failure to provide public notice and an opportunity for public comment. As OSHA failed to do so, the court vacated the Directive because it was neither a mere procedural rule nor a policy statement.

   B.   **Conducting Formal Adjudications**. Congress allows administrative hearings to expedite conflicts and legal questions about government practices and procedures.

Through administrative hearings, with discovery and evidence under oath, an administrative law judge, makes rulings that may be appealed to a court.

Historical Perspective: From Revolutionary War Vets to the Environment. America's first administrative agencies were established in the 1790s. Throughout the history of the United States, Congress has used the power of legislation and delegation to create agencies to deal with social and economic crises.

C. **Taking Informal Discretionary Actions**. Informal discretionary actions include contracts, planning, and negotiations. Often problems must be solved by practical decision-making, inappropriate for slower-paced court litigation.

D. **Conducting Investigations**. Agencies may conduct investigations over their areas of authority. Agencies use subpoenas, interviews, searches, etc., in relation to both civil and criminal suits.

II. ADMINISTRATIVE AGENCIES AND THE CONSTITUTION. Constitutional issues of separation of powers and proper delegation of authority, as well as the limits imposed by the Bill of Rights arise in the context of administrative actions.

A. **Separation of Powers and the Patriot Act.**

1. The Constitution provides for three branches of the federal government: legislative, executive, and judicial, but administrative agencies (part of the executive branch) both create rules and issue judgments raising concerns about improper usurpations of power. See *Humphrey's Ex'r v. United States*, 295 U.S. 602 (1935); *INS v. Chadha*, 462 U.S. 919 (1983).

2. The USA Patriot Act grants more power to the Executive branch. Section 215 commands a judge to issue an order to authorize a search when requested by government, hence granting judicial power to executive agencies.

B. **Delegation of Authority**. Legislatures may delegate some of their authority to administrative agencies. However Congressional guidance or policy and standards must be clear. *Whitman v. Am. Trucking Ass'n, Inc.*, 531 U.S. 457 (2001).

C. **Limits Imposed by the Bill of Rights**. The Bill of Rights regulates agency operations.

1. Self-Incrimination. Under the Fifth Amendment, a person or company may refuse to answer questions or render evidence that would subject them to criminal prosecution.

2. Probable Cause. Administrative agencies do not need probable cause to begin investigations that a person or company has violated a law or regulation.

3. Search and Seizure. In the administrative context, agencies can search and inspect property and records without restriction.

4. Right to Jury Trial extends only to cases for which a right to trial by jury existed at common law, prior to the adoption of the Constitution, hence there is no constitutional right to a jury trial in a formal administrative hearing.

III. **PRINCIPLES OF ADMINISTRATIVE LAW.**

A. **Choice of Approach**. In the absence of congressional direction, an agency can promulgate general rules or act on a case by case basis.

B. **Authority to Act**. Personnel or officers in the executive branch may only affect decisions and rules if they have actual authority. The government cannot be bound by those agents who attempt to exceed their legislative or rule-based authority.

IV. **JUDICIAL REVIEW AND AGENCY ACTIONS.** Generally, agencies have discretion to act, and courts may not review such discretionary decisions and actions. Non-discretionary acts are reviewable, but courts are often deferential to the agency.

A. **Review of Rule Making and Informal Discretionary Actions**. Courts usually permit agency moves unless such are *arbitrary and* capricious. However courts will not permit agency regulations inconsistent with statutes or not expressly delegated by Congress. See e.g., *Ragsdale v. Wolverine World Wide*, 535 U.S. 81 (2002); *Food and Drug Administration v. Brown & Williamson Tobacco Corp.*, 529 U.S. 120 (2000).

B. **Review of Factual Findings**. Courts use the *substantial evidence* standard to review factual findings to determine whether the evidence in the record supports an agency's conclusion. Courts will defer to an agency's reasonable determinations of the facts. See *Consol. Edison Co. v. NLRB*, 305 U.S. 197 (1938).

C.   **Review of Statutory Interpretations**. Courts generally defer to an agency's construction (or interpretation) of relevant statutes.

> **Case 6.2--*Cellular Telecommunications & Internet Association v. Federal Communications Commission*, 330 F.3d 502 (D.C. Cir. 2003).** In 1996 the FCC promulgated rules requiring cell phone companies to implement "phone number portability." Cell phone companies petitioned the FCC to forbear from enforcing the rule. The Telecommunications Act listed specific provisions as to when and if the FCC could forebear. The court held that the FCC was authorized to understand the rule on forbearance as it reasonably understood and fairly implemented.

D.   **Review of Procedures**. Absent compelling circumstances, agencies may establish their own procedures. Courts require agencies to follow guidelines for Due Process as demanded by the Constitution.

E.   **No right to Probe the Mental Processes of the Agency**. Courts cannot revoke or block agency actions due to the motivation of bureaucrats. Courts may only consider the authority to act, agency right of discretion, and rational basis for action.

F.   **Timing of Review**. Two judicial doctrines are designed to prevent premature transfer of cases from the administrative arena to judicial courts.

> **1.**   Exhaustion of Administrative Remedies. Parties that do not like agency rules or policies must usually pursue all of the possible remedies and redress within the agency prior to filing court pleadings. Note exception in *Harline v. Drug Enforcement Administration*, 148 F.3d 1199 (10th Cir. 1998). If parties do not raise all complaints in administrative hearings, a judicial court may rule that such claims have been waived (lost). See *Sims v. Apfel*, 530 U.S. 103 (2000).

> **2.**   Ripeness. Courts will not decide hypothetical questions, rather only address actual cases and controversies. Thus courts refuse to hear challenged to proposed administrative rules until both promulgated and after such imposition causes a hardship.

G.   **Standing to Sue**. One may only sue if:

> **1.**   They have suffered or are likely to suffer a particular, concrete and actual **injury**;

2. The injury is **tied to the action** challenged; and

3. It must be likely that **redress** will remedy or prevent the injury. See *Lujan v. Defenders of Wildlife*, 504 U.S. 555 (1992).

   Case 6.3--*Baur v. Veneman*, 352 F.3d 625 (2d Cir. 2003). Baur, a citizen, beef eater, was concerned that the head of the U.S. Department of Agriculture, Ann Veneman, established a policy to allow "downed" cattle to come to market for human consumption. Because government documents supported Baur's assertion that he, and millions of others, might suffer ill-health from eating such cattle, he was granted standing and allowed to sue the USDA and block the policy.

V. **DECISION-MAKING POWER AGENCIES.** Certain principles limit and guide the regulatory power of administrative agencies.

   A. **Only Delegated Powers.** Administrative agencies are allowed to do what Congress allows.

   B. **Obligation to Follow Own Rules.** Administrative agencies are required to follow their own rules and regulations, *e.g., Service v. Dulles*, 354 U.S. 363 (1957).

   C. **Explanation of Decisions.** Administrative agencies must explain the basis for any decisions and show how they considered all relevant matters.

VI. **FINDING AN AGENCY'S OWN RULES.** Though documents like the *Federal Register* and the *Code of Federal Regulations* provide guidance about administrative agencies, particular internal rules are not necessarily codified in one source.

VII. **OBTAINING DOCUMENTS FROM AN AGENCY.**

   A. The Freedom of Information Act (FOIA) authorizes any one to request records of the federal government.

   B. Not all government documents are available to the public, such as: diplomatic communiqués, personnel files, military and national security files, etc.

   C. Private companies may shield documents later obtained by the federal government by labeling them as privileged and confidential.

GLOBAL VIEW: THE BRITISH FINANCIAL SERVICES AUTHORITY: In contrast with the U.S. system of government collection of financial records in banking, securities, commodities and insurance, the British rely on a private system. The practice functions as a quasi-governmental records collection service. However the British practice is distinct from the American experience in that it maintains anonymity from public scrutiny not directly allowed or demanded by the British government.

VIII. IN BRIEF: SEVEN BASIC STEPS FOR WORKING SUCCESSFULLY WITN AN ADMINISTRATIVE AGENCY.

    A. Identify agency standards and rules.

    B. Identify the agency's formal structure.

    C. Determine the facts before the agency.

    D. Identify interests and those involved in decision-making.

    E. Adopt a strategy.

    F. Eliminate adverse effects on interested parties.

    G. Get involved in the administrative process – stay involved.

IX. THE RESPONSIBLE MANAGER: Working with Administrative Agencies. Managers must deal with regulatory agencies at the state and federal level. By following the "seven steps" managers can be successful.

X. INSIDE STORY: REGULATION OF VOICE OVER INTERNET PROTOCOL PHONE SERVICE. Voice over Internet Protocol (VOIP) transmits voice signals via the internet. VOIP does not fit neatly into the regulatory scheme of the Telecommunications Act of 1996. The FCC ultimately adopted rules to regulate VOIP which need not follow standard phone company local access and long-distance rules which previously had to provide band-width to competitors.

STUDY QUESTIONS

True-False Questions

___ 1. The process that administrative agencies use to adopt rules is identical to the legislative process.

__ 2. Agencies formally adopt rules by publishing them in the Federal Register.

__ 3. Federal officials may decide to adopt nearly any procedural rule within their jurisdiction.

__ 4. The governments attempt to reach a consensus of major groups affected by new regulations is known as "re-neg."

__ 5. Formal adjudications typically involve a pre-hearing discovery phase.

__ 6. Administrative adjudications are virtually identical to courtroom trials.

__ 7. An administrative agency's decision in a formal adjudication can be appealed to a judicial court.

__ 8. In regards to their informal discretionary actions, administrative agencies must still show that they followed written procedures.

__ 9. Administrative agencies must grant jury trials to those who bring complaints and demand a hearing before an ALJ.

__ 10. Because administrative agencies craft their own rules, the Constitution does not apply to them.

__ 11. Staff in administrative agencies have legal authority to act so long as they have apparent authority.

__ 12. Courts use a substantial evidence standard to review factual findings of agencies in formal adjudications.

__ 13. The Supreme Court has relaxed the definition of standing to permit individuals to sue federal agencies in court.

__ 14. As a general rule, courts will not review an administrative action until administrative remedies have been exhausted.

__ 15. The ripeness doctrine is specifically excluded from the administrative process.

Multiple-Choice Questions

__ 1. Which of the following are primary ways in which agencies function?

      I.   Making rules.

       II.   Informal discretionary actions.
       III.   Formal adjudications.
       IV.   Conducting investigations.

     A. I, II, III, and IV.
     B. I, III, and IV.
     C. I, II, and IV.
     D. II, III, and IV.

__ 2.   _____ is *not* a necessary step in the agency rule making process.
     A. Notice.
     B. Evaluation.
     C. Qualification.
     D. Adoption.

__ 3.   Newly adopted rules by agencies are first published in the:
     A. Code of Federal Regulations.
     B. *Federal Register*.
     C. *United States Law Week*.
     D. *Wall Street Journal*.

__ 4.   In formal agency adjudications, the presiding official is entitled to do all but:
     A. Administer oaths.
     B. Rule on offers of proof.
     C. Take depositions.
     D. Decide the case at hand.

__ 5.   Which of the following is *not* one of the things that a trial and an agency formal adjudication have in common?
     A. Evidence presented.
     B. Direct examination.
     C. Cross-examination.
     D. Juries.

__ 6.   Typically, a court reviewing an administrative agency's ruling uses:
     A. Evidence in the record.
     B. Attorney's briefs.
     C. Supreme Court precedent.
     D. *De novo* law.

__ 7. Which of the following is *not* characterized by informal discretionary action of an administrative agency?
A. Adjudication of worker's compensation claims.
B. Filing class action lawsuits.
C. Issuance of welfare benefits.
D. Filing Social Security claims.

__ 8. An agency may file:
A. Administrative suits seeking civil assessments.
B. Suit for civil penalties.
C. Suit for criminal penalties.
D. All of the above

__ 9. The doctrine raised in court cases by an agency's exercise of authority is the _____ doctrine.
A. Due process.
B. Delegation of authority.
C. Separation of powers.
D. Separation of state.

__ 10. Which Constitutional protections have been eroded when applied to agencies?
A. Self-incrimination.
B. Search and seizure.
C. Jury trials.
D. All of the above.

__ 11. Courts will uphold an agency's rule making and informal discretionary actions unless they are:
A. Arbitrary and capricious.
B. Per se invalid.
C. Lacking a preponderance of the evidence.
D. Incorrect beyond a reasonable doubt.

__ 12. Which doctrine(s) prevent the premature transfer of administrative agency actions to court?

I.   Exhaustion of administrative remedies.
II.   *Res judicata.*
III. Ripeness.

A. I and II.
B. I and III.

    C. II and III.

    D. I, II, and III.

__ 13. Which statement is *false* concerning the ripeness doctrine?

    A. Courts will not hear a case until it is ready to be decided.

    B. Ripeness frequently arises in pre-enforcement reviews.

    C. The general rule is that judicial review is proper when the impact of the action is direct on the appellant, indirect on society in general, and immediate on both to make the review appropriate.

    D. none of the above

__ 14. Agency action contrary to or in excess of its delegated authority is:

    A. Void.

    B. Valid.

    C. Voidable.

    D. Unenforceable.

__ 15. The Freedom of Information Act specifically exempts all of the following information in the government's possession, *except:*

    A. Confidential commercial and financial information.

    B. Records relating to all personnel rules and practices.

    C. Information compiled for law enforcement purposes.

    D. Geological information concerning wells.

Essay Questions

1. How are administrative agencies beneficial with regards to social justice and ethics?

2. Why are there no jury trials allowed in agency proceedings?

3. What are the benefits and limitations of the relative autonomy of administrative agencies (and the lack of judicial oversight)?

CHAPTER 7
CONTRACTS

INTRODUCTION

Contracts are essential to business. A contract is an agreement, between two or more competent parties, that courts will enforce. Depending on the state, the legality of contracts is determined by statute, Article 2 of the Uniform Commercial Code (UCC), the Restatement (Second) of Contracts and or common law. This chapter discusses, analyzes, and examines all elements of contracts and the laws that make them enforceable.

I. **BASIC REQUIREMENTS OF A CONTRACT**. Contracts are promises, oral or in writing. A valid contract has four elements: agreement, consideration, capacity, and legality. If the contract was made with fraud, duress, or misrepresentation, courts may refuse to enforce it. As **agreements**, valid contracts require an offer and acceptance

II. **OFFER**. An *offer* is a manifestation of willingness to enter into a bargain. An offer is effective if (1) the *offeror* intends to be bound, (2) the terms are reasonably definite, and (3) the offer is communicated to an *offeree*.

   A. **Intention**. Offers made in jest or the heat of anger do not show a sincere intention to be bound. Advertisements are generally not offers, but invitations to negotiate.

   B. **Definiteness**. Essential terms (price, subject matter, duration of the contract, and manner of payment) are not left open.

   C. **Communication**. The offeror must communicate the offer to the offeree.

   D. **Termination of Offer**—an offer can be terminated two ways:

      1. Termination by Operation of Law. An offer is terminated when the time for acceptance elapses, or after a reasonable period of time; or

      2. Termination by Action of the Parties. The offeror can *revoke* at any time before the offeree accepts. An offer is also terminated when rejected. A *counteroffer* is a rejection of the original offer (a rejection).

   E. **Irrevocable Offers** arise in two circumstances: with an option contract; and if an offeree has relied on an offer their detriment.

1. Option Contracts. The offeror agrees to hold an offer open for a period of time in exchange for consideration. E.g., a company might agree to wait ten days to fill the position of manager while the person offered the job decides whether to accept, in exchange for $200 from offeree (consideration).

2. Detrimental Reliance occurs when the offeree changes their position because of their justifiable reliance on the offer.

III. ACCEPTANCE is a response by the offeree indicating willingness to enter into the proposed agreement. (Both offer and acceptance can be oral, written, or implied by conduct).

A. **Mode of Acceptance**. The offeror is the "master of the offer" with sole power to specify the means of acceptance.

B. **Mirror Image Rule**. Traditionally contract formation required that acceptance be identical to the offer. If not, no contract has been formed.

C. **Intent to Be Bound**. In general, to determine the enforceability of contracts, courts examine (a) the intent of the parties to be bound, and (b) the definiteness of the terms of the agreement. See Inside Story of *Pennzoil v. Texaco*, *infra*.

IV. CONSIDERATION. Contracts are exchanges of something of value (*consideration*), e.g., money, an object, a promise, a service, forbearance or assignment. A promise to do something illegal is not valid consideration. A promise to fulfill a pre-existing obligation is not consideration.

A. **Adequacy of Consideration**. Generally, courts will not scrutinize the value of the consideration (the fairness) of a contract.

B. **Bilateral and Unilateral Contracts**. Consideration can be either a promise to act or performance of the act itself. A *bilateral contract* is a promise in exchange of another promise. A *unilateral contract* is a promise given in exchange for an act.

C. **Mutuality of Obligation in Bilateral Contracts**. In a bilateral contract both parties are obligated to perform their side of the bargain.

D. **Illusory Promises**. An illusory promise confers neither benefit on the promisee (creditor) nor subjects the promisor (debtor) to a detriment, hence is unenforceable. Sometimes parties mischaracterize a unilateral contract as an illusory promise.

Case 7.1--*Dahl v. HEM Pharmaceuticals Corp.*, 7 F.3d 1399 (9th Cir. 1993). HEM Pharmaceuticals designed a new drug, Ampligen. Dahl and the other patients signed consent forms warning of the experimental nature of Ampligen and possible side effects. Patients were free to withdraw from the clinical trial at any time, but if they completed the study they could receive Ampligen for a year, at no charge. At the end of the study, HEM refused to provide Ampligen to patients for free. The court held that patient participation in the drug trial created a unilateral contract and ordered HEM to provide Ampligen to participants who wanted it.

E.   **Conditional Promises**. Contracts may include conditional promises, of which there are three types:

　　1.   Conditions precedent must be satisfied before performance under a contract is due.

　　2.   Conditions concurrent occur when the mutual duties of performance are to take place simultaneously.

　　3.   Conditions subsequent operate to terminate an existing contractual obligation if a specific condition occurs.

F.   **Requirements and Output Contracts**. In a ***requirements contract***, the buyer agrees to buy all of its requirements of a specified commodity. In an ***output contract***, the buyer promises to buy all the output that the seller produces.

V.   CAPACITY.

A.   Persons entering into contract must have the ability to understand the nature and effect of an agreement. Minors and mentally incompetent persons lack legal capacity. Contracts are *voidable* if one party lacks capacity. However, minors and mentally incompetent persons may be held liable for contracts for necessaries, e.g., food, clothing, and shelter.

B.   Contracts made by incompetent persons may be *void*, *voidable* (at the option of the incompetent person), or *valid*.

VI.   LEGALITY.
Contracts must have a legal purpose. Contracts that are contrary to a statute or public policy are illegal and generally considered void.

A.   **Licensing Statutes**. If a party fails to have a required state license, the other party to the contract does not have to fulfill its side of the bargain (i.e. pay for services).

B.   **Other Contracts Contrary to Statute**. Some statutes expressly make a contract illegal, *e.g.*, prostitution, price-fixing agreements, bribes, such contracts are void.

VII.   PROMISSORY ESTOPPEL (or *detrimental reliance*) provides an exception to the requirement of consideration if four requirements are met:

     A.   **Promise**. There must be a promise; a statement of future intent to act or make a promise is not sufficient;

     B.   **Justifiable Reliance**. The promise must cause the promisee to take an action that he or she would not have otherwise taken;

     C.   **Foreseeability**. The action taken in reliance on the promise must be reasonably foreseeable by the promissory; and

     D.   **Injustice**. A promise that has been reasonably relied on will give rise to judicial relief only if the failure to do so would cause an injustice.

         Case 7.2--*Pop's Cones, Inc. v. Resorts International Hotel, Inc.*, 704 A.2d 1321 (N.J. 1998). Pop's was a franchisee of TCBY. The president of Pop's met with an agent of Resorts Int'l Hotel (RHI) about moving its location and leasing a property from RHI. Pop's let its old lease expire in anticipation of moving into an RHI property. Later RHI withdrew its offer to Pop's. Pop's sued to compel RHI to allow Pop's to rent space from RHI. The New Jersey Court held that as Pop's relied on the promises of RHI, and suffered, i.e. lost its previous store location, that RHI was bound to a contract.

VIII.   UNCONSCIONABILITY. A contract is *unconscionable* if it is oppressive or fundamentally unfair.

     A.   **Procedural Element** of an unconscionable contract lies in oppression and surprise. *Oppression* arises from unequal bargaining power preventing real negotiation or meaningful choice for one party. *Surprise* arises when the terms of the contract are physically hidden or stated in convoluted terms.

     B.   **Substantive Element**. A contract may manifest substantive unconscionability if it is "overly harsh" or produces a "one-sided" result.

     C.   **Releases** are conditions that purport to relieve one party from liability for injuries suffered by the person using the facility. The trend is to honor these agreements.

         Case 7.3--*Schmidt v. United States*, 912 P.2d 871 (Okla. 1996). Elizabeth Schmidt went horse riding on a military base as signed an agreement promising to forbear from suit against the United States. While riding Schmidt was thrown and injured, and sued the ultimate employer, the United States. Though the U.S. moved for summary judgment, the Oklahoma Supreme Court held that the case must go to trial. Though Schmidt signed a release, such would not be honored if the defendant committed an intentional, willful or fraudulent act or gross and wanton negligence.

Historical Perspective: Unconscionability and Freedom of Contract. Individuals are supposed to have freedom to contract as a means to promote market efficiency. The idea also means that generally courts will not impose their judgment on what is a fair bargain between parties. Still sometimes parties do not have equal bargaining power or information. Thus when the legislature has not set guidelines to govern a particular contract, courts will review contracts as a matter of fairness and public policy. If a court deems that a contract does not manifest an equal exchange, it can be void as unconscionable.

IX.   GENUINENESS OF ASSENT. A court will refuse to enforce a contract if one or both of the parties did not genuinely assent to the terms of the contract, even if otherwise there is evidence of a valid contract with consideration.

    A.   **Fraud**. A contract is voidable if tainted with fraud.

        1.   Fraud in the factum is the misrepresentation or untruth about a *material* fact of the contract.

        2.   Fraud in the inducement occurs when a party makes a false statement (or fails to disclose information) as to persuade the other to enter into an agreement.

        3.   Promissory Fraud is manifest when a party promises, yet has no intention of satisfying the promise.

    B.   **Duress**. A contract is also voidable if one party was forced to enter into it through fear created by wrongful or illegal acts or threats (see also undue influence). Economic duress is usually not enough to invalidate a contract.

    C.   **Ambiguity**. If the terms of a contract are subject to differing interpretations, courts might construe the ambiguity against the party who drafted the agreement or as justice requires.

    D.   **Mistake of Fact**. A mistake of fact might make a contract voidable. A court's willingness to void a contract based on mistake depends heavily on particular circumstances. Court look at three factors to determine mistake:

1. Substantiality of the Mistake. A court is more likely to void the contract when the mistake has a material effect on one of the parties. See *Raffles v. Wichelhaus*, 159 Eng. Rep. 375 (Exch. 1864), contract void for mutual mistake.

2. Allocation of the Risks. If one party accepts a risk (of a mistake or misunderstanding) that party must bear the consequence. However when dealing with merchants, lay people cannot be understood to assume the risk.

3. Timing. The party alleging a mistake of fact must give prompt notice when the mistake is discovered.

E. **Mistake of Judgment (or Value)** occurs when parties make erroneous assessments about some aspect of the bargain. Such a mistake is not a valid defense to void enforcement of the contract. *Bissell Homecare, Inc. v. Oreck Corp.*, 243 F.3d 563 (Fed. Cir. 2000).

X. STATUTE OF FRAUDS. Certain types of contracts, while valid if merely oral, must be put in writing to become legally *enforceable*.

A. **Transactions Subject to the Statute of Frauds** include:

1. A contract for the transfer of any interest in real property (such as a deed, lease, or option to buy);

2. A promise to pay the debt of another person;

3. An agreement that by its terms cannot be performed within 12 months (starting from the time the contract is signed); and

4. A prenuptial agreement.

View from Cyberspace: Electronic Contracts under UETA and the E-Sign Act. As of May 2004, 40 states adopted the Uniform Electronic Transactions Act (UETA). The UETA explains how and when electronic contracts are enforceable. The essential element necessary to determine the validity of an electronic signature is whether the person intended the process or mark provided to act as a signature and whether it can be attributed to that person. The provisions of the federal E-Sign Act are similar to the UETA. The E-Sign Act has mandatory provisions for interstate and foreign e-commerce. Notice, UETA and the E-Sign Act do not cover all agreements and types of contracts.

XI. **THE PAROL EVIDENCE RULE.** When there is a written contract that the parties intended would encompass the entire agreement, parol (spoken) evidence of prior or contemporaneous statements will not be permitted to alter or void the contract, unless the written contract is ambiguous, or unless the parol evidence is used to show mistake, fraud or duress.

XII. **CHANGED CIRCUMSTANCES.** Contracts can provide for a variety of future events so that the parties involved can allocate the risks of different outcomes. These include impossibility, impracticability, and frustration of purpose.

    A. **Impossibility.** If the subject matter of a contract is destroyed, the parties are discharged from their contractual obligations.

    B. **Impracticability** when performance is possible but commercially impractical, a party can breach. However as a rule, impracticability is difficult to prove.

> **Case 7.4--*Norcon Powers Partners, L.P. v. Niagara Mohawk Power Corp.*,** 705 N.E.2d 656 (N.Y. 1998). In 1989, Norcon, an independent power producer, entered into a contract with Niagara Mohawk Power Corporation, a public utility provider, whereby Niagara agreed to purchase electricity from Norcon's Pennsylvania facility, for twenty-five years. There were three pricing periods under the contract. Concerned that Norcon would be unable to satisfy, Niagara demanded that Norcon provide assurance that it would perform all of its future obligations. Norcon sued Niagara, seeking a declaration that Niagara had no contractual right to demand such assurance. The Court held that the doctrine of adequate assurance of future performance (as in U.C.C. Section 2-609) should be incorporated into New York common law and applied to long-term commercial contracts.

    C. **Frustration of Purpose** occurs when performance is possible, but new circumstances make the contract useless to one or both of the parties. The defense of frustration requires that the event which created the frustration was not the party's fault and not considered in the original contract.

    D. **Contracts with the Government and the Sovereign Acts Doctrine.** When a party's performance is made illegal or impossible because of a new law, the contract is usually discharged and damages are not awarded. Under the sovereign acts doctrine, the government generally cannot be held liable for breach of contract due to legislative or executive acts. However see an exception in *United States v. Winstar*, 518 U.S. 839 (1996).

XIII. **CONTRACT MODIFICATION**. Traditionally, contract law does not allow a contract to be modified for only one party. A *novation*, substitution of one of the old parties, creates a new contract, can effect the desired change. As well both parties may agree to terminate a contract.

XIV. **DISCHARGE OF CONTRACT**. Commonly, discharge occurs when both parties have fully performed their obligations. What happens when either party has not fully performed?

    A. **Material Breach**. If one party fails to perform, e.g., not performing a service after receiving payment, that party commits a *material breach* of the contract. Such breach discharges the other party from its obligations and provides grounds to sue for damages.

    B. **Anticipatory Repudiation**. If party A knows ahead of time (before performance is due) that party B will breach the contract, A may commit an *anticipatory repudiation*. Such repudiation is treated as a material breach. By treating an anticipatory repudiation as a breach, party A can avoid having to wait until an actual breach before taking action.

    C. **Mutual Rescission** occurs when both parties agree to terminate the contract. A mutual rescission is itself a contract (with a valid offer, acceptance, and consideration).

    D. **Novation**. If party A prefers to retain the original contract, a third party may be substituted for one of the original parties, B. The third party will assume B's rights and responsibilities. All parties must agree to the substitution.

    E. **Accord and Satisfaction**. An *accord* is formed when the creditor accepts the debtor's offer to settle the dispute for an amount less than amount due. Such *satisfaction* discharges the debt.

    F. **Change of Circumstances and Law**. Impossibility, impracticability, frustration or changes in law may discharge the contractual obligations of both parties.

XV. **DUTY OF GOOD FAITH AND FAIR DEALING**. Every contract contains an implied covenant of good faith and fair dealing in its performance. The implied covenant imposes a duty on each party to refrain from any action that will deprive the other party of the benefits of the agreement.

XVI. **THIRD-PARTY BENEFICIARIES**. At times, one who is not a party to a contract may enforce a contract. A third-party beneficiary cannot sue to enforce the contract unless the contracting parties intended to benefit the third party.

    A. **Creditor (Intended) Beneficiary**. If the promisee entered into the contract in order to discharge a duty he or she owed the third party, then the third party is a *creditor beneficiary* and has the right to enforce the contract between the promissor and promisee.

B. **Donee Beneficiary**. A *donee beneficiary* is created when the promisee does not owe an obligation to the third party, but rather wishes to confer a gift.

XVII. REMEDIES. If one party breaches, the other party is entitled to monetary damages or specific performance. Damages give the plaintiff the benefit of the bargain or put the plaintiff in the position the party would have been, had the contract been performed.

  A. **Expectation Damages.**

  1. Compensatory Damages give the plaintiff the benefit of the bargain, putting plaintiff in the cash position she would have been had the contract been fulfilled.

  2. Consequential Damages. Compensate plaintiff for losses that occur as a result of the breach. Consequential damages must be reasonably foreseeable (by the breaching party) and certain. See *Hadley v. Baxendale*, 156 Eng. Rep. 145 (1854); *Stove & Mfg. Co. v. Am. Ry. Express Co.*, 51 S.W.2d 572 (Mo. App. Ct 1932).

  3. Incidental Damages are those less and relative minor damages incurred by a non-breaching party, e.g., charges, expenses, commissions, costs of transportation, etc.

  4. Mitigation of Damages. When party A breaches a contract, party B has a duty to mitigate (or lessen) the amount of damages that flow from the breach.

  B. **Reliance Damages** compensate the plaintiff for any expenditures made in reliance of a contract that was subsequently breached. Reliance damages return it to the position it was in before the contract was formed.

  C. **Restitution and *Quantum Meruit***. Restitution is similar to reliance damages, but examines what the other party has gained from the transaction. Restitution is ordered under the theory of *quantum meruit* if the breaching party has received a benefit for which it has not paid.

  Case 7.5--*Glendale Federal Bank, FSB v. United States*, 239 F.3d 1374 (Fed. Cir. 2001). GFB entered into a merger with First Federal Savings and Loan of Broward County, Florida (First Federal). At the time of the merger, liabilities of First Federal exceeded the market value of the assets by $734 million. Pursuant to its contract with the government, GFB was permitted to treat First Federal's negative net worth as goodwill for regulatory capital purposes. Eight years into the contract, Congress passed the Financial Institutions Reform, Recovery and Enforcement Act (FIRREA). FIRREA required Goodwill to accelerate its amortization schedule. FIRREA also established new capital requirements. Glendale failed to meet the new requirements, and forced to engineer a massive recapitalization. Glendale filed suit for damages. The court had to decide as to what form of relief expectancy, reliance or restitution, GFB was entitled. Glendale was entitled to recover restitution damages and "non-overlapping reliance damages" for a total of $908,498,000 in damages.

D.   **Liquidated Damages**. Parties may agree to pay damages to the other in case of a wrongful breach. Courts will not enforce penalties, or clauses that provide for damages that are substantially higher than the losses.

E.   **Specific Performance and Injunctive Relief**. A court may order the breaching party to complete the contract as promised when (1) the goods are unique (e.g., an antique car or a painting); (2) the subject of the contract is land; or (3) the amount of the loss is so uncertain that there is no fair way to calculate damages.

XVIII. **PRECONTRACTUAL LIABILITY**. Under traditional contract law, the offeror is free to back out and revoke an offer at any time before the offer is accepted (i.e. before a contract is made). Courts typically impose a duty to negotiate in good faith (see *Markov v. ABC Transfer & Storage Co.*, 457 P.2d 535 (Wash. 1969)), especially if a letter of intent between two parties specifically includes the duty. In narrow circumstances, American courts impose precontractual liability on theories of misrepresentation, promissory estoppel or restitution.

Case 7.6--*Copeland v. Baskin Robbins*, **117 Cal. Rptr. 2d 875 (Cal. Ct. App. 2002)**. Baskin Robbins planned to close its factory in the City of Vernon. Copeland sought to buy the factory, conditioned on Baskin Robbins agreement to purchase Copeland's ice cream. Baskin Robbins ultimately stopped negotiations and did not agree to Copeland's terms. Copeland sued that he had lost expected profits. The California courts held that Copeland had no legal remedy for Baskin Robbins negotiated in good faith and could not be held liable for Copeland's "expected" profits that would have been realized if the parties reached an accord.

XIX. **MERGERS AND ACQUISITIONS.**

A.   **Generally**. A corporation can acquire control of another (the *target*) by merger. Mergers cannot be completed until the shareholders approve.

B.   **Agreements**. Mergers and acquisitions are usually governed by detailed acquisition agreements containing:

1.   Representations and warranties about the entity being sold;

2.   Covenants, which are promises to do or refrain from doing something; and

3.   Conditions that must occur to close, or consummate, the transaction (or events that will terminate one party's obligation to close).

XX.   **INTERNATIONAL SNAPSHOT**. Though most English speaking nations use common law principles to interpret and form contract law, non-English speaking nations use civil law (statutes). Whereas American courts may impose economic liability for breaches on theories of misrepresentation, promissory estoppel or restitution, civil law countries of France, Germany, the Netherlands, and Japan, have different rules and remedies. The European Union is working to adopt a uniform law on contracts. To head off legal problems, managers are advised to include choice of law and choice of forum clauses in contracts.

XXI.   **RESPONSIBLE MANAGER: Acting in Good Faith and Dealing Fairly**. It is preferable to put the terms of an agreement in writing. It is best to hash out any ambiguities at the negotiation stage while parties are on good terms. Positions tend to polarize once the agreement is signed. Managers should avoid signing letters of intent unless they intend to be bound by the terms. Astute managers realize that contract drafting and negotiation can provide opportunities to strengthen business relationships and to protect key assets.

XXII.   **INSIDE STORY**: ***Pennzoil v. Texaco***. In 1983 Pennzoil and the Getty Oil Company negotiated a merger, had a series of meetings, and even press releases. Texaco, however, made a subsequent offer to Getty and Getty accepted. Pennzoil sued Texaco for tortious interference with a contract. Getty asserted that it had never signed a memorandum of agreement and made a counteroffer to Pennzoil, that Getty later withdrew, so that Getty could accept an offer from Texaco. A Texas jury sided for Pennzoil and award it over $10 billion. Though the judgment was upheld on appeal, Texaco filed for bankruptcy and settled with Pennzoil for $3 billion.

STUDY QUESTIONS

True-False Questions

__ 1.   A valid contract requires an offer and an acceptance resulting in agreement between two parties.

___ 2. Offers made in jest are generally not offers because a reasonable person could assume such an offer lacks the intention to contract.

___ 3. Most advertisements are treated as offers.

___ 4. A counter offer is a rejection of the initial offer.

___ 5. An option contract is an irrevocable offer, but a firm offer is not.

___ 6. An offer that states that you can accept only by e-mail is invalid.

___ 7. Alice offers to sell Bob her car for $10,000. Bob says he will buy it for $10,000 if Alice paints it. This offer and acceptance satisfies the mirror image rule.

___ 8. There are three basic types of conditions that can be added to contracts: antecedent, precedent, and subsequent.

___ 9. A wanted poster is an example of a unilateral contract.

___ 10. In a requirements contract, it would allowable for a buyer to double the amount needed under the contract.

___ 11. All contracts made by a person adjudged incompetent are voidable contracts.

___ 12. Courts usually refuse to enforce unconscionable contract terms.

___ 13. Fraud makes a contract voidable.

___ 14. Many courts would allow the sale of property at say 50% of the market-value even if the owner had to sell to avoid bankruptcy.

___ 15. An oral contract covered by the statute of frauds is still a valid contract.

Multiple-Choice Questions

___ 1. Which of the following is *not* a required element of a valid contract?
   A. Mutual agreement.
   B. Consideration.
   C. Capacity.
   D. Illegality.

___ 2. Which of the following statements is false concerning an offer?
   A. The offeror makes the offer.

B. The offeror has the intent to make the offer.
C. The terms of the offer are definite.
D. The offer is communicated to the offeror.

__ 3. Which of the following is an offer?
A. A statement that is secretly not an offer, but objectively sounds like an offer.
B. An offer made in obvious jest.
C. An offer made in anger.
D. All of the above

__ 4. Which of the following is *not* considered an essential contract term?
A. Price.
B. Subject matter.
C. Duration of the contract.
D. None of the above.

__ 5. The UCC allows an open or reasonable _____ if the parties clearly have the intent to contract.
A. Quantity.
B. Price.
C. Delivery date.
D. Subject matter.

__ 6. Which of the following terminates an offer by operation of law?

   I.   Death.
   II. Revocation.
   III. Rejection.
   IV. Destruction of the subject matter

A. I, II, and III.
B. II and III.
C. I and IV.
D. I, II, III, and IV.

__ 7. Adam offers to sell his car to Barbara for $8,000. Before Barbara can accept, Adam revokes his offer. Adam's revocation was _____:
A. Valid.
B. Void.
C. Voidable.
D. unenforceable.

__ 8. Which of the following is valid consideration?
A. A promise to complete the contract.
B. A promise not to kill you.

C. Moral or social consideration.
D. None of the above.

__ 9. Jessica promises to buy all the widgets Grace produces in 1999, if Jessica wishes to do so. This promise is _____:
A. Valid.
B. Illusory.
C. Voidable.
D. Void.

__ 10. Wade promises to buy Paul's business for $500,000 if the highway in front of Paul's business is widened before March 1, 1999. This is an example of a _____ condition.
A. Subsequent.
B. Concurrent.
C. Precedent.
D. Antecedent.

__ 11. Knowingly lying to get someone to sign a contract is known as: _____.
A. Duress.
B. Mistake.
C. Fraud.
D. Undue influence.

__ 12. Which of the following is *not* a traditional justification for requiring a contract to be in writing?
A. Avoids fraudulent claims that an oral contract was made.
B. Avoids fraudulent claims regarding the terms of the contract.
C. Encourages contracts to be in writing.
D. Psychological effect that oral contracts are inferior to written contracts.

__ 13. Which of the following is *not* governed by the statute of frauds?
A. Transfer of an interest in real property.
B. Promise to a debt.
C. Agreement which by its terms cannot be performed in one year.
D. Prenuptial agreement.

__ 14. _____ occurs when performance is possible, but changed circumstances have made the contract useless to one or all of the parties.
A. Frustration of purpose.
B. Impossibility.
C. Impracticability.
D. Frustration.

___ 15. Fred lists his wife, Wilma, as his life insurance beneficiary. What type of beneficiary is Wilma?
   A. A creditor.
   B. A spousal beneficiary.
   C. A donee.
   D. An incidental beneficiary.

Essay Questions

1. Why must an offer be communicated?

2. Courts normally do not inquire about the adequacy of value of consideration in a contract. Why not?

3. Why must an injured party mitigate his or her damages?

CHAPTER 8
SALES AND E-COMMERCE

INTRODUCTION

Virtually all commercial enterprises are the purchase or sale of goods. While most international sales are governed by the Convention on Contracts for the International Sale of Goods, sales of goods in the United States are governed by Article 2 of the Uniform Commercial Code (UCC). Many provisions of the UCC, however, can be changed through express agreement. When the UCC is silent on a subject, common-law contract provisions described in Chapter 7 usually apply. The chapter also discusses the laws of e-commerce.

I. **WHEN DOES ARTICLE 2 OF THE UCC APPLY?** The UCC is a model code that only applies to contracts for the sale of goods. The UCC defines *goods* as "all things (including specially manufactured goods) which are movable (not land or fixtures) at the time of identification to the contract for sale." The UCC does not apply to computer programs and software (see the UCITA). Further the UCC regulates sales by both merchants and non-merchants. The UCC defines a merchant as "a person who deals in goods of the kind or otherwise by his occupation holds himself out as having knowledge or skill peculiar to the practices or goods involved in the transaction."

II. **CONTRACT FORMATION.** Under the UCC, a contract is enforceable if parties intend to be bound, though terms are left open for later agreement. If a dispute arises over a missing term, the court may use UCC "gap-fillers."

   A. **Offer**. The term is not defined by the UCC. Under the UCC, neither an invitation for bids nor a price quotation is an offer.

   B. **Acceptance**. The UCC does not define *acceptance*, but acceptance may contain terms additional to or different from those in the offer. This is different from the mirror-image rule.

   > **Case 8.1--*Specht v. Netscape*, 306 F.3d 17 (2d Cir. 2002). Netscape made "free" software available on their website, but included a licensing agreement. Specht challenged adherence to the licensing agreement on the grounds that Netscape's contract violated federal law and was not conspicuous. The appeals court sided for Specht and held the arbitration clause in the agreement was not binding.

   C. **Consideration**. Contracts ordinarily must have consideration to be enforceable. An offer signed by a merchant that indicates the offer will be kept open is a *firm offer* and is not revocable for lack of consideration.

III.   **BATTLE OF THE FORMS**. The UCC effectively abolishes the mirror-image rule. It is not necessary for an offer and acceptance to match exactly. Also, adding to, or modifying terms in the offer does not make created a counteroffer, as it would under common law.

     A.   **Definite Response**. A definite and timely assent to an offer constitutes an acceptance. The crucial inquiry is whether the parties intended to close a deal.

     B.   **Conditional Response**. If the offeree wants to make a counteroffer, rather than an acceptance, she should state clearly that the acceptance is conditioned.

     C.   **Acceptance with Missing Terms**. When the parties ship, receive, and pay for goods without first agreeing on all material terms, UCC § 2-207(3) provides that the terms of the contract are those on which the parties agree in writing.

     D.   **Acceptance with Additional Terms**. If either party is *not* a merchant, additional terms are construed as proposals and do not become part of the contract. If all parties are merchants, additional provisions automatically become part of the contract, unless:

        1. The offer expressly limits acceptance to the terms in the offer;

        2. The new terms materially alter the original offer; or

        3. The party making the original offer notifies the other, within a reasonable time, that it objects to the new terms.

     E.   **Acceptance with Different Terms**. Different terms neither defeat the acceptance nor impede the formation of the contract. However there are questions as to whether different terms become part of the contract because UCC §2-207 does not address the question.

        Case 8.2--*Richardson v. Union Carbine Industrial Gases, Inc*. 790 A.2d 962 (N.J. Super. 2002). Richardson, an employee at Hoeganaes, was injured at work by a furnace explosion. Richardson sued, among others, Rage Engineering, which provided a system purchased by Hoeganaes. In their negotiation to complete their contract, both Rage and Hoeganaes included boilerplate contracts purporting to demand indemnification as a condition. Rage argued that they were not responsible for Richardson's injuries, as Hoeganaes indemnified Rage. The court found that as the boilerplate contracts negated the other, the parties had not agreed to that aspect of the contract, hence Richardson could sue Rage.

     F.   **Proposed Revisions to Section 2-207**. To clarify contracts the UCC could be modified to declare that different terms could become part of a contract between merchants; additional terms could be ignored or treated as separate offers; opposing terms could "knock out" each other and UCC gap-fillers could be put in their place.

IV.   **STATUTE OF FRAUDS**. Section 2-201 of the UCC is a *statute of frauds*. 2-201 provides that a contract for the sale of goods for at least $500 is unenforceable unless it is at least partly in writing: (1) there must be some writing evidencing the sale of goods; (2) the writing must be signed by the party against whom enforcement is sought; and (3) the writing *must* specify the quantity of goods.

A.   **Some Writing**. In a UCC contract, the writing need only detail the quantity of goods to be sold to make an enforceable contract unless:

1.   The goods were specially manufactured for the buyer and not suitable for resale to others in the ordinary course of the seller's business;

2.   The defendant admits in a judicial proceeding that there was an agreement; or

3.   Payment for the goods was made and accepted or the goods were received and accepted.

B.   **Signature**. The writing must be signed by the party against whom enforcement is sought, unless the sale is between merchants, and:

1.   A confirmation of the contract has been received;

2.   The party receiving it has reason to know its contents; and

3.   That party has not made a written objection within ten days after the confirmation was received.

C.   **E-Sign Act and Uniform Electronic Transactions Act**. The federal E-Sign Act states that "a signature, contract, or other record relating to such transaction may not be denied ... solely because it is in electronic form." Under the E-Sign Act and UETA, almost any mark or process intended to sign an electronic contract (including a "click-through" process) constitutes a valid electronic signature. Current proposals for the UCC include ***digital signatures*** and would supersede the E-Sign Act.

V.   **DUTY OF GOOD FAITH UNDER THE UCC**. The UCC imposes an obligation of good faith in contract performance and enforcement.

VI.   **WARRANTIES.** The UCC's warranty provisions note attributes of goods under: express warranty, implied warranty of merchantability, and implied warranty of fitness for a particular purpose.

Historical Perspective: From Medieval Guilds To Online Arbitration. As the middle ages of Europe led to development of private guilds and commissions designed to establish and enforce local regulations, so too as e-commerce generated private systems of regulation.

A.   **Express Warranty**. An express warranty is an explicit guarantee by the seller that the goods will have certain qualities. Buyers must also rely on the seller's declarations. However, if a seller is merely *puffing* she has not made a warranty.

> **Case 8.3--*Connor, Inc. v. Proto-Grind, Inc.*, 761 So.2d 426 (Fla. App. 2000).** Doug Connor, president of Connor, Inc., was interested in purchasing a commercial grinding machine made by Proto-Grind, Inc., "the Proto-Grind 1200." Proto-Grind's brochure described the machine as the "toughest grinder on the market" and that the machine could grind timber, stumps, and railroad ties into mulch. Connor witnessed a demonstration where a large log was reduced to mulch. During the demonstration, he spoke to the president of Proto Grind, and explained he wanted a machine that would grind palmettos, palm trees, oak trees, etc. Proto Grind assured Connor that the 1200 was capable. Connor signed a sales contract which provided for a two-week trial period during which time he could use the machine and purchase it only if satisfied. After the machine experienced problems, Protos waived the first installment payment of $5,500 extended the trial period. Connor accepted. Protos failed to fix the 1200 and Conner sued for breach of express warranties that: (1) the machine would grind organic materials effectively; (2) the 1200 would be free from defects for six months; and (3) Proto-Grind would fix the machine. Proto-Grind won a directed verdict on the grounds that Connor waived the express warranty in exchange for elimination of the first installment payment. The appeals court reversed and remanded for trial holding that a finder of fact could reasonably conclude the oral promises made were more than puffing, that Connor relied on the affirmations, and that because a product deficiency was not cured, Proto-Grind breached this express warranty.

B.   **Obligations for Statements to Remote Purchasers**. The general rule holds that the warranty is only a guarantee from seller to buyer and no one else may sue for a violation of a warranty. Proposed changes to the UCC would allow remote purchasers to sue for breaches of warranties and require remedial promises.

C.   **Implied Warranty of Merchantability** guarantees that goods are reasonably fit for the general purpose for which they are sold, properly packaged and labeled.

The warranty applies to all goods sold by *merchants* in the normal course of business.

1.   Under UCC § 314(2) goods must:

- Pass without objection in the trade under the contract description;
- Be fit for the ordinary purposes for which such goods are used;
- Be within the variations permitted by the agreement and be of even kind, quality, and quantity within each unit and among all units involved;
- Be adequately contained, packaged, and labeled as the agreement may require; and
- Conform to the promises or affirmations of fact made on the container or label, if any.

2.   Reasonable Expectations. The key issue in determining merchantability is whether the goods do what a reasonable person would expect of them. See *Lescs v. William R. Hughes, Inc.*, 168 F.3d 482 (4th Cir. 1999).

D.   Implied Warranty of Fitness for a Particular Purpose guarantees that the goods are fit for the particular purpose the seller recommended and applies to merchants and non-merchants alike. A "particular purpose" means the purpose peculiar to the buyer or the buyer's business.

1.   The warranty is implied *only* if four elements are present:
- The buyer had a particular purpose for the goods;
- The seller knew or had reason to know of that purpose;
- The buyer relied on the seller's expertise; and
- The seller knew or had reason to know of the buyer's reliance.

2.   **Reliance**. Though the implied warranty usually arises when the seller is a merchant with some level of skill or judgment, it is not restricted to such circumstances. To prove that the buyer did not rely on the seller's expertise, the seller must show that:

- The buyer's expertise was equal to or superior to that of the seller;
- The buyer relied on the skill and judgment of persons hired by the buyer; or
- The buyer supplied the seller with detailed specifications or designs for the seller was to follow.

E.   Limiting Liability (and recovery for a breach of warranty).

1.   The seller can avoid responsibility for the quality of the goods under any of these warranties by:

   - Not making any express warranties;
   - Disclaiming any warranties of quality making the buyer aware of disclaimers such as "AS IS";
   - Refraining from professing expertise with respect to the goods and leaving the selection to the buyer.

2.   Recovery for Breach of Warranty. To recover for breach of warranty, a buyer must prove that:

   - The seller made an express or implied warranty;
   - The goods were defective at the time of the sale;
   - The loss or injury was caused by the defect rather than the buyer's negligent or inappropriate use of the goods; and
   - The seller has no affirmative defenses.

VII.   **MAGNUSON-MOSS WARRANTY ACT (MMWA)** protects consumers against deception in warranties. Consumers have the right to sue a manufacturer or retailer for failing to comply with the act or the terms of a written or implied warranty arising from the act. A *full warranty* gives the consumer the right to free repair or replacement of a defective product.

VIII.   **RIGHT TO REJECT NONCONFORMING GOODS.** A buyer has the right to reject nonconforming goods. The rejection must be made within a reasonable time after the goods are delivered.

VIEW FROM CYBERSPACE: Taxing E-Commerce. Presently Congress has prohibited tax on internet access and e-commerce. Since *Quill v. North Dakota*, 504 U.S. 298 (1992), companies are not required to collect sales taxes on interstate internet sales. A study in 2000 estimated that states lost $525 million in potential revenue via internet transactions.

INTERNATIONAL SNAPSHOT. Since July 2003, a European Union directive (B2C) levies a tax on goods and services sold within the EU. As well companies outside the EU are required to levy the value-added tax (VAT). There is a question as to whether the EU rule can be compelled against U.S. companies.

Case 8.4—*Moore & Moore General Contractors, Inc. v. Basepoint, Inc.*, 485 S.E.2d 131 (Va. 1997). Moore & Moore was the contractor for a Red Lobster restaurant. Plans for the cabinets called for "melamine" cabinets; it is unclear what that term means. Basepoint was a subcontractor and delivered particle-board cabinets instead of sturdier plywood cabinets. Moore & Moore's representatives inspected the cabinets and accepted the goods. When the inspector for the restaurant saw the particle board cabinets, he ordered them replaced. Moore & Moore then rejected the cabinets and demanded that Basepoint deliver new cabinets within one week. Basepoint notified Moore & Moore that they could not meet that deadline. Moore & Moore bought cabinets elsewhere and refused to pay Basepoint. Basepoint sued Moore & Moore for delivery of the particle-board cabinets. Moore & Moore counter-sued for the labor and materials needed to remove and replace Basepoint's cabinets. The trial court ruled for Basepoint. The Virginia Supreme Court affirmed the decision on the grounds that under the UCC, although Moore & Moore had the right to reject the particle-board cabinets, as it installed them, Moore & Moore made a complete acceptance and waived its remedies for recovery.

IX. **ALLOCATION OF RISK OF LOSS.** In the absence of an agreement to the contrary, the UCC places the risk of loss on the party controlling the goods at the time loss occurs. The UCC allows the buyer and seller to negotiate liability for risk of loss.

   A. **Goods Shipped by Carrier.** When goods are shipped by carrier, the risk of loss passes to the buyer under one of two conditions:

      1. At the time the goods are properly delivered to the carrier, if the contract does not require delivery at a particular destination; or

      2. At the time the carrier tenders the goods to the buyer at the specified destination.

   B. **Goods Held by Independent Warehouse.** The risk of loss passes to the buyer when the buyer receives the document entitling it to pick up the goods.

   C. **All Other Cases.** If goods are neither shipped by carrier nor held by an independent warehouse, the allocation of the risk of loss in transit depends on whether the seller is a merchant.

      1. *If the seller is a merchant,* the risk of loss passes to the buyer only when the buyer receives physical possession of the goods.

      2. *If the seller is not a merchant,* the risk passes to the buyer when tender of delivery is made.

         Case 8.5--*Lynch Imports, LTD. v. Frey*, 558 N.E.2d 484 (Ill. App. Ct. 1990). Buyers purchased a car from seller for $8,706. The sales form had additions that guaranteed the buyers' satisfaction. Buyers financed $4,000 and paid the rest by check. The agreement noted that the buyers would take possession of the car, then return it that the seller would install an air conditioner. When the buyers returned the car, they were informed that the car had been previously damaged. Upon learning that, buyers refused to take possession of the car, refused to get financing for the balance of the car payment, and stopped payment on the check given to seller. The seller sued the buyer for breach in that the buyer had accepted the car by taking possession. The legal question centered on whether the buyers' initial possession was a full acceptance. Under the UCC buyers may retain the right for deferred acceptance, especially if the parties' contract so notes.

X.   **UNCONSCIONABILITY**. If a contract is so unfair as to "shock the conscience" of the court, a judge may negate the offending terms or the entire contract. Under common law unconscionability can be either procedural or substantive.

     A.   **Procedural Unconscionability**. A contract is procedurally unconscionable when one party is induced to enter a contract without having any meaningful choice, a "take it or leave it" contract (also known as an *adhesion contract)*.

     B.   **Substantive Unconscionability**. A contract is substantively unconscionable if its terms are unduly harsh or oppressive or unreasonably favorable to one side.

         Case 8.6--*Jasphy v. Osinsky*, 834 A.2d 426 (N.J. 2003). Jasphy brought three mink coats to be cleaned and stored. The cleaning company demanded Jasphy sign a release of liability. The next day the coats were lost in a fire, which was the fault of the cleaning company. After Jasphy sued, the furrier filed a motion to dismiss, which was denied. Because the contract was boilerplate, Jasphy was not a merchant, and had less bargaining power she could not be held to the strict language of the contract.

XI.   **COMMERCIAL IMPRACTICABILITY UNDER THE UCC**. Under the UCC a failure to perform is not a breach if performance is made impractical by an event unforeseen by the contract. A party seeking discharge must show three things:

     A.   **Underlying Condition**. There must be a failure of an underlying condition of the contract, that is, a condition that was not included in the parties' bargain; and

     B.   **Unforeseen Contingency**. A seller seeking discharge must prove that the contingency that prevents performance was both unforeseen and unforeseeable; and

     C.   **Impracticable Performance**. The party must prove that the performance was impracticable due to a marked increase in costs of the transaction – over 100%.

IN BRIEF
COMPARISON OF UCC, COMMON LAW, UCITA, AND CISG

	Scope	Battle of the Forms	Warranties	Statute of Frauds
UCC	Sale of goods	Contract even if acceptance has additional or different terms	1. Implied warranties of merchantability and fitness for a particular purpose 2. Any express warranties made	Sales of $500 or more
Common Law	Provision of services Contracts for sale of land or securities Loan agreements	Mirror-image rule	Any express warranties made	Transfer of real estate Contract can't be performed within one year Prenuptial agreement Agreement to pay debt of another
UCITA	Computer information (including software, computer games, and online access)	Contract even if acceptance has additional or different terms, unless acceptance materially alters the offer	Warranty of noninterference and non-infringement Implied warranties of merchantability of computer program, informational content, fitness for licensee's particular purpose, and fitness for system integration Any express warranties made	Contracts for $5,000 or more
CISG	Sale of goods by merchants in different countries unless parties opt out	In practice, mirror-image rule	1. Implied warranties of merchantability and fitness for a particular use 2. Any express warranties made	None

XII.   **DAMAGES.** The UCC tries to put the non-breaching party in the same position it would have been in if the contract had been performed. This is usually done through award of monetary damages.

A. **Seller's Remedies.**

1. Buyer Breach. The measure of damages is the difference between the market price at the time and place for delivery and the unpaid contract price, minus any expenses saved because of the buyer's breach.

2. Measure of Damages. In the alternative, if this measure of damages is inadequate to put the seller in as good a position as performance would have, then the seller is entitled to recover the profit it would have made from buyer's performance.

B. **Buyer's Remedies**

1. Seller Breach. If a seller breaches, the buyer may cancel the contract and recover as much of the price as has been paid and then either:

    - *Cover*, buy goods elsewhere and be reimbursed for the extra cost of the substitute goods; or
    - Recover damages for non-delivery.

2. Buyer's Remedies.

    - If buyer elects to cover it must do so in good faith and in a reasonable time period.
    - If buyer elects damages, the measure of damages is the difference between the market price at the time the buyer learned of the breach and the contract price.
    - The buyer may also recover consequential damages.

XIII. **SPECIFIC PERFORMANCE**. If the promised goods are unique, then a court may order the seller to deliver them for monetary compensation will not be adequate to remedy the loss suffered by the buyer.

XIV. **GLOBAL VIEW: THE CONVENTION ON CONTRACTS FOR THE INTERNATIONAL SALE OF GOODS**. The international sale of goods is outside of the scope of UCC Article 2. Today, the signatories to the CISG account for nearly two-thirds of the world's imports and exports.

A. **Scope of Convention**. CISG applies to oral and written sales contracts between parties within signatory countries, unless the parties have expressly opted out of CISG. Generally, CISG does not apply to goods bought for personal use, stocks, negotiable instruments, money, or ships and other marine vessels.

B.   **Offer and Acceptance**. Under the CISG an offer is effective when it reaches the offeree, and it may be withdrawn if the withdrawal reaches the offeree before or at the same time the offer arrives. A contract is concluded at the moment acceptance becomes effective. Custom and course of dealing between the parties is also considered.

C.   **Battle of the Forms**. Under CISG, a reply that contains additional terms or other modifications is a *rejection* of the offer and constitutes a counteroffer.

D.   **Good Faith**. CISG promotes "the observance of good faith in international trade."

E.   **Implied Warranties**. CISG holds sellers liable for implied warranties of merchantability and fitness for particular use and for any express warranties they make.

XV.   **THE RESPONSIBLE MANAGER: Operating under Varying Legal Regimes**. Any manager who enters into contracts should know which body of law will govern the transaction. The manager should determine whether the transaction is governed by Article 2 of the UCC, the common-law rules concerning contracts, CISG, or UCITA. Article 2 applies only to the sale of goods, not services or land. CISG will apply to most international sales of goods, unless the parties affirmatively opt out of its provisions. In states that have enacted the Uniform Computer Information Transaction Act, UCITA governs contracts to license or buy software, computer programs, multi-media products, computer games, and online access. In sum a good manager always obtains legal advice to resolve any doubt as to which body of law controls in a particular situation.

STUDY QUESTIONS

True-False Questions

___ 1.   Under both common law and the UCC, a contract is enforceable only if all necessary terms are expressed at the time of contracting.

___ 2.   The UCC defines "offer" as an objective proposal with definite, certain terms that is capable of being accepted by the offeree.

___ 3.   For acceptance, the UCC follows the common-law "mirror-image" rule.

___ 4.   The new UCC Article 2B will effective eliminate the distinction between goods and services for software transactions.

___ 5. Under the UCC, a firm offer is irrevocable without consideration.

___ 6. Under the UCC, if the original contract had to be written to satisfy the statute of frauds, then any agreement to modify that contract must be written to be enforceable.

___ 7. The UCC has expressly abolished the "mirror-image" rule.

___ 8. Under the UCC, when an acceptance contains different terms from the offer, those different terms neither defeat nor impede the formation of the contract.

___ 9. The UCC requires that all contracts for the sale of goods for $5,000 or more must be in writing to be enforceable.

___ 10. The UCC writing requirement allows that the price, time and place of payment or delivery, the general quality of the goods, or any particular warranties may all be omitted.

___ 11. Generally, the only term that must be written in a UCC contract is the quantity term.

___ 12. According to UCC Section 2-313(2), "puffing" is the unlawful warranty of the quality of goods.

___ 13. The implied warranty of merchantability applies to all goods sold in the normal course of business.

___ 14. Fungible goods include stocks and insurance policies.

___ 15. "As is" and "with all faults" are examples of express warranties.

Multiple-Choice Questions

___ 1. Under the UCC, the most important item for a contract is the:
   A. Quantity.
   B. Quality.
   C. Price.
   D. Intent to contract.

___ 2. Which of the following is an offer?
   A. Price quote.
   B. Sales proposal subject to approval.
   C. Newspaper ad.
   D. None of the above.

__ 3. Fred offers to sell Barney Fred's car for $1,000. According to the UCC, Barney can accept by:
   A. Any reasonable means.
   B. Letter only.
   C. Saying so, but only in person.
   D. No method.

__ 4. Which of the following is *not* in the UCITA?
   A. Issues arising from electronic data interchange.
   B. Enforceability of shrink-wrap and click-wrap licenses.
   C. Express and implied warranties for hardware and related services.
   D. Conduct constituting acceptance of offers.

__ 5. A firm offer is:
   A. Found at common law.
   B. Valid without consideration.
   C. Voidable.
   D. Effective for one year.

__ 6. Which of the following would be a counteroffer rather than an acceptance?
   A. "This acceptance is conditional on offeror's acceptance of all additional terms."
   B. "This acceptance is subject to the conditions stated herein."
   C. "Acceptance is expressly limited to the condition of purchase on the reverse side of this document."
   D. None of the above.

__ 7. If both parties are merchants, additional provisions in the acceptance automatically become part of the contract, unless the:

   I.   Offer expressly limits the acceptance to the terms of the offer.
   II. New terms materially alter the original offer.
   III. Offeror notifies the offeree that the offeror objects to the new terms.

   A. I or II
   B. II or III
   C. I, II, or III
   D. I or III

__ 8. If no quantity is specified, the contract is unenforceable, unless all of the following exist *except:*
   A. The goods are a hybrid of goods and services.
   B. Payment for the goods was made and accepted.
   C. Delivery of the goods was made and accepted.
   D. The goods were specially manufactured, not readily resalable, goods.

___ 9.   A car dealer states that a car will go 100 mph. The buyer responds that she never drives above 70 mph. The buyer returns the car because it fails to achieve 100 mph. *If* there is a warranty here, which of the following is the buyer going to have to prove to be successful?

   I.   The statement related to the car.
   II. The buyer relied on the statement.
   III. The statement was in writing.

   A. I, II, and III.
   B. I and II.
   C. II and III.
   D. I and III.

___ 10. To be merchantable under UCC, goods must:
   A. Be fit for the ordinary purposes for which the goods are used.
   B. Be adequately packaged, and labeled as the agreement requires.
   C. Be of average quality, including fungible goods.
   D. Pass without objection in trade under the contract description.

___ 11. An implied warranty of _____ guarantees that goods are fit for the usual purpose for which they are sold.
   A. Fitness for a particular purpose.
   B. Merchantability.
   C. Due course.
   D. Fitness and merchantability.

___ 12. Which of the following is *not* needed for the implied warranty of fitness for a particular purpose?
   A. The buyer purchased the goods for a particular purpose.
   B. The seller knew of the buyer's purpose in purchasing the goods.
   C. The buyer relied on the seller's expertise.
   D. The seller knew of the buyer's reliance.

___ 13. In highly concentrated industries with few competitors, when all of the competitors offer the same, unfair "take it or leave it" contracts, these contracts are known as _____ contracts.
   A. Adhesion.
   B. Adhesive.
   C. "Take it and run."
   D. Packaged.

__ 14. The buyer's remedies under the UCC include canceling the contract and recovering as much of the price that has been paid, and then:

   I. Covering.
   II. Recovering damages for non delivery.

   A. II only
   B. I and II
   C. I or II
   D. I only

__ 15. Which of the following sales is the only one covered by the CISG?
   A. Electricity.
   B. Stocks.
   C. Auctions.
   D. Commercial goods.

Essay Questions

1. Why is a firm offer irrevocable without consideration?

2. Why are contracts for the sale of goods for $500 or more governed by the statute of frauds?

3. Distinguish FOB seller's and buyer's place of business.

4. Under UCITA, how would you as a manager distinguish between a good such as a computer with computer software installed on the hard drives, versus a Palm Pilot PDA? Which rules govern the sale of these different goods?

CHAPTER 9
TORTS

INTRODUCTION

A tort is a civil wrong resulting in injury to a person or property. This chapter first discusses intentional torts, then addresses torts of negligence (including an accountant's liability to third parties), strict and vicarious liability and apportioned responsibility. The chapter also examines the evolving law on toxic torts.

I. **ELEMENTS OF AN INTENTIONAL TORT**.

    A. In order for a party to prevail in a tort action, the plaintiff must prove **four elements**:

        1. The tortfeasor possessed actual or implied intent;

        2. The tortfeasor's act was voluntarily;

        3. But for the tortfeasor's act, there would be no injury (causation); and

        4. The plaintiff suffered a cognizable injury or harm

    B. **Intent**. The torfeasor's intent can be actual or implied.

        1. *Actual* intent can be shown by evidence that the defendant intended a specific consequence.

        2. *Implied* intent occurs when the defendant knew or was substantially certain that the particular consequences causing said injury or harm would occur.

        3. Intent may be transferred. E.g., if the defendant intended to hit one person but instead hit the plaintiff, the court will find the presence of the intent requirement is met.

II. **TYPES OF INTENTIONAL TORTS AND DEFENSES**. There are a number of particular intentional torts recognized in law (*infra*). Even if a plaintiff can show the four elements, the defendant-tortfeasor has legal defenses, including consent. If the plaintiff consented to the act of the defendant, e.g. a surgery, playground soccer game, etc., there is no tort.

III. **INTENTIONAL TORTS TO PROTECT PERSONS**.

    A. **Battery** is defined as an intentional, non-consensual, harmful, or offensive contact with the plaintiff's body or with something in contact with it, even if there is no physical injury.

B. **Assault** is an intentional, non-consensual act that gives rise to the apprehension (though not necessarily fear) that a harmful or offensive contact is imminent. No contact is required.

C. **False Imprisonment** is the intentional, non-consensual confinement by physical barriers or by physical force or threats of force. The plaintiff must have known he or she was confined or suffered harm as a result of the confinement. A merchant's defense can be based on good faith, reasonable manner and cause.

D. **Intentional Infliction of Emotional Distress**. In most jurisdictions, to prove intentional infliction of emotional distress, a plaintiff must show an intentional outrageous act that caused foreseeable emotional suffering and distress. Often courts require some physical manifestation to prevent frivolous claims.

E. **Defamation.**

1. Definition. Communication (publication) to a third party of an untrue statement of fact that injures the plaintiff's reputation by exposing him or her to "hatred, ridicule or contempt." *Libel* is written defamation, and *slander* is spoken defamation.

2. Slander Damages. Plaintiff must prove actual harm, such as the loss of credit, a job, or customers, unless the statement is slander *per se*.

3. Libel Damages are presumed. No actual harm need be shown unless the statement on its face is not damaging.

4. Defenses to Defamation are based on privilege.

   • *Absolute* privilege gives defendant right to publish false statements if made under certain conditions (political broadcast, official government proceedings).

   • *Qualified* privilege can be used to protect business interests, such as employment reviews and credit reports if made in good faith.

5. Public Figures and Media Defendants. When commenting on a "public official or figure," the media has a qualified privilege that is almost absolute. A public figure can only recover damages for defamation, if she can show the statement was made with *actual malice*.

F.   **Invasion of Privacy** covers violations of one's right to keep personal matters private. The tort can be intrusive, appropriation of a name, or a public disclosure of private facts.

> **Case 9.1--*Bodah v. Lakeville Motor Express, Inc.*,** 663 N.W.2d 550 (Minn. 2003). Defendant (LME) wrongly sent a fax with names and Social Security numbers of its employees to 16 trucking terminals in surrounding states. Employees filed a class-action suit alleging the tort of invasion of privacy (arguing that the plaintiffs might have been victims of identity theft). The Minnesota Supreme Court defined the three factors that constitute a *prima facie* claim for the tort of invasion of privacy as: (1) defendant publicizes some aspect of the plaintiff's life; (2)the public has no legitimate concern with such information; and (3) a reasonable person would see the disclosure as offensive. The Court concluded that the faxes were not issued to the public and dismissed the complaint.

IV.   **INTENTIONAL TORTS THAT PROTECT PROPERTY.**

A.   **Trespass to Land** is an entry on real property without consent of the owner. The land need not be injured by the trespass. The trespass may occur either above or below the land. Throwing trash on the land, or shooting bullets over it, may be trespass, though the perpetrator never entered plaintiff's land.

B.   **Nuisance** is **a** non-trespassory interference with the use and enjoyment of property by, e.g., odor or noise.

C.   **Conversion** is the exercise of dominion and control over personal property of another.

View from Cyberspace: Suing to Stamp Out Spam. Earthlink and AOL sued spammers on a theory of trespass to chattels arguing that excess spam limited the efficiency of their service and the ISPs lost customers. In 2004, G. W. Bush signed into law an anti-spam measure, the Controlling the Assault of Non-Solicited Pornography and Marketing Act (CAN-SPAM).

D.   **Trespass to Personal Property** (trespass to chattels)—the intent to interfere with or control another's personal property.

> **Case 9.2--*Intel Corp. v. Hamidi*,** 71 P.3d 296 (Cal 2003). Hamidi, a former Intel employee sent six messages to approximately 35,000 Intel e-mail addresses over 21 months. He took the addresses from a floppy disk he had received anonymously. On a theory that Hamidi had committed a trespass to chattels, Intel won an injunction against Hamidi and he

appealed. The California Supreme Court overturned and dismissed the suit holding that Intel had suffered no injury to its personal property or legal interests in said property.

V. INTENTIONAL TORTS THAT PROTECT CERTAIN ECONOMIC INTERESTS AND BUSINESS RELATIONSHIPS.

A. **Disparagement** is the publication of statements derogatory to the quality of the plaintiff's business, the business in general, or the plaintiff's personal affairs, intended to discourage others from dealing with her.

B. **Injurious Falsehood** occurs through a false statements made knowingly. Only pecuniary losses related to business operations are recoverable. Defendants have defenses of privilege and honesty.

C. **Fraudulent Misrepresentation** (or fraud) requires a plaintiff show that the defendant: (1) intentionally misled the plaintiff by (i) making a material misrepresentation of fact (ii) upon which the plaintiff relied, or (2) omitted to state a material fact when (i) the defendant had a duty to speak and (ii) had a special relationship with plaintiff.

D. **Malicious Prosecution and Defense**. Plaintiff must prove that a prior proceeding was instituted against her maliciously and without probable cause or factual basis. Plaintiff can recover attorneys' fees, injury to reputation, and emotional distress. Courts disfavor this tort.

E. **Interference with Contractual Relations and Participation in a Breach of Fiduciary Duty**. Plaintiff must prove that the defendant, who knew about the existence of the contract, intentionally induced a third party to breach her contract with plaintiff. Truth is a defense to this claim.

F. **Interference with Prospective Business Advantage**. Plaintiff must prove the defendant intentionally interfered with a relationship the plaintiff sought to develop and that the interference caused plaintiff's loss. This tort is not viewed favorably by the courts. Truth is a defense and most jurisdictions recognize a privilege to act for one's own financial gain.

G. **Bad Faith** is a claim separate and independent from a breach of contract claim. Typically bad faith torts are brought by an insured against an insurance company for breaching a duty to act in good faith in re a payment of claims.

VI. NEGLIGENCE. Negligence is conduct that involves an unreasonable risk to cause injury to another or damage to property. To establish liability under a theory of negligence, plaintiff must show: (1) the defendant owed a duty to the plaintiff to act in conformity with a certain standard of conduct; (2) the defendant breached that duty; (3) the defendant's breach caused the resultant injury; and (4) the plaintiff suffered an actual loss or injury.

A.   **Duty**. A person has a *legal* duty, to act reasonably to avoid harming another.

1.   Duty to Rescue. Generally, there is no duty to rescue, but once a rescue effort is undertaken, one has a duty to act reasonably and not abandon the effort unreasonably. Some relationships create a legal duty to rescue: employer-employee; innkeeper-guest; teacher-student; and employee of a common carrier-passenger, etc.

2.   Duty of Landlord or Tenant.

- An owner of land (or possessor, e.g., tenant) has a legal duty to keep the property reasonably safe. Landowner-Tenant can be liable for injury that occurs outside or on the premises. Landowners must exercise care in the demolition or construction of buildings on their property and excavation of their land.

- In all jurisdictions, a landowner has a general duty to inspect her land and keep it in repair, and she may be liable if, e.g., a showroom window, a downspout, a screen, or sign injures someone.

3.   Traditional Approach to Liability for Injuries on Premises depends on the status of the injured party: trespasser, licensee, or invitee.

- Duty to Trespassers. Generally, a landowner owes no duty to an undiscovered trespasser, unless a substantial number of trespassers are in the habit of entering at a particular place. Trespassing *children* are owed a higher level of duty.

- The *attractive nuisance* doctrine imposes liability for physical injury to child trespassers caused by conditions on the land if the landowner knew or should have known that children were likely to trespass.

- Duty to Licensees. A licensee enters the land with express or implied consent for his or her own purposes. Landowners must exercise reasonable care for the protection of the licensee *before* they enter the land.

- Duty to Invitees. An invitee is a customer (or business visitor) who enters the premises for purposes of the possessor's business. The possessor must protect invitees against known dangers and also those dangers that he might discover with reasonable care.

- Contractors who create a dangerous condition while working at a construction site may be held liable for injury caused by the dangerous condition.

- This duty may include an obligation to protect invitees from criminal conduct by third parties.

4.   Reasonable Care Approach. The trespasser, licensee, or invitee distinction is problematic and not universally accepted. Some courts apply a standard of *reasonable care under the circumstances,* which requires all landowners to act in a reasonable manner with respect to entrants on their land, with liability hinging on the foreseeability of harm. See *Basso v. Miller*, 352 N.E.2d 868 (N.Y. 1976).

5.   Duty of Landlord to Tenant. Generally, a landlord has a duty to take steps to provide adequate security to protect tenants from foreseeable criminal acts of a third party. Courts balance the foreseeability of the harm against the burden to be imposed on the landlord in taking precautionary measures. See *Sharon P. v. Arman*, Ltd., 989 P.2d 121 (Cal. 1999).

B.   **Breach of Duty and *Res Ipsa Loquitur*.**

1.   Once it is determined that the defendant owed the plaintiff a duty, the next issue is whether the defendant breached the duty. Generally, the court judges whether the defendant met a standard of conduct of a "reasonable person" unless there is special training or a trade in which the person will be held to the higher standard, e.g., doctor, architect, pilot, attorney, etc.

2.   Negligence *per se*. If the defendant fails to comply with a relevant statute or regulation, she has breached her duty and the burden shifts to the defendant to prove that she was not negligent.

3.   *Res Ipsa Loquitur* allows the plaintiff to prove breach of duty and causation indirectly when an accident occurs, if it would not have happened absent someone's negligence (e.g., a medical clamp left in plaintiff's abdomen). Generally, the burden of proof shifts to the defendant.

C. **Causal Connection**. A plaintiff must prove that the defendant's breach of duty caused their injury. The causation requirement has two parts: actual cause and proximate (or legal) cause.

1. Actual Cause. This is the "but for" test: plaintiff must show that less the defendant's negligent conduct, plaintiff would not have been harmed. When more than one defendant is involved, courts use the "substantial factor" test.

2. Proximate Cause. Once actual cause is proved, plaintiff must prove that the plaintiff's injuries were *foreseeable*, which places limits on the defendant's liability. Courts apply the foreseeability requirement in one of two ways: some limit the defendant's liability to those *consequences* that were foreseeable. Others look to whether the plaintiff was within the *zone of danger* caused by the defendant's careless conduct.

> **Case 9.3--*Gaines-Tabb v. ICI Explosives USA, Inc.*,** 160 F.3d 613 (10th Cir. 1998). On 19 April 1995 a truck filled with explosives blew up the Murrah Federal Building in Oklahoma City, killing 168 people and injuring hundreds of others. Those who suffered injuries sued ICI, the manufacturer of the ammonium nitrate (AN), used to make the explosives. Plaintiffs alleged that ICI mislabeled explosive-grade AN and sold it as fertilizer grade to a retailer. Ultimately either Terry Nichols or Timothy McVeigh purchased the mislabeled AN and made a bomb. The district court dismissed the action as unforeseeable. The appeals court held that it was not foreseeable that criminals like Nichols or McVeigh would purchase AN and make a bomb designed to destroy a federal building. Because ICI's error was not the proximate cause of the victim's injuries, the dismissal was upheld.

D. **Injury**. Plaintiff must prove *legal* injury. Even if a defendant is negligent, the plaintiff cannot recover if he cannot show that the harm suffered was the result of the defendant's conduct.

VII. **DEFENSES TO NEGLIGENCE.** In some jurisdictions, defendant may be absolved of part or all of the liability by proving that the plaintiff was also negligent.

A. **Contributory Negligence**. In states supporting this doctrine, a plaintiff was negligent to any degree cannot recover *any* damages from the defendant. Most courts do not follow the doctrine of contributory.

B.   **Comparative Negligence: Ordinary and Pure**.

    1.   In *ordinary comparative negligence*, the plaintiff may recover only if he or she is 50 percent or less liable than the defendant.

    2.   In *pure comparative negligence*, the plaintiff may recover for any amount of the defendant's negligence, even if the plaintiff was 80 percent liable.

C.   **Assumption of Risk** requires defendant to show that the plaintiff knew the risk was present and understood its nature and voluntarily chose to incur the risk. This defense relieves the defendant of any liability.

VIII.   **LIABILITY OF ACCOUNTANTS AND OTHER PROFESSIONALS TO THIRD PARTIES**.

A.   **International Misrepresentation** (or fraud) by an accountant leaves the accountant liable to the client. A suit can also be brought by any person whom the accountant reasonably should have foreseen would rely upon the intentional misrepresentation.

B.   **Negligent Misrepresentation**. Professional negligence is called malpractice. A professional owes a duty to her client, but not to a third party with whom she does not have a contractual relationship.

    1.   Accountants. Under the New York approach, a third party may sue an accountant under a three-part test. See *e.g.*, *White v. Guarantee*, 372 N.E.2d 315 (N.Y. 1977). A more liberal view extents accountant' liability to anyone whom could have been reasonably foreseen to rely on the account. This position is noted in the Restatement (Second) of Torts § 552.

    2.   Attorneys. Lawyers may be liable to corporate investors and directors. And may be liable to non-professionals who rely on their opinions. See *Petrillo v. Bachenberg*, 65 A.2d 1354 (N.J. 1995).

        Case 9.4--*Chem-Age Industries, Inc. v. Glover*, 652 N.W.2d 756 (S.D. 2002). Alan Grover represented Byron Dahl. Acting as Dahl's agent, Grover negotiated with Pederson and Shepard to invest in Chem-Age (CAI). After they invested, Pederson and Shepard noticed that CAI accumulated credit card debt for Dahl's personal purchases. Glover reassured the investors about the company's solvency and that all debts would be paid. CAI failed to pay its taxes and then dissolved. Shepard and Pederson sued Dahl and Glover for negligent misrepresentation and sued Glover for malpractice. Though Shepard and Pederson could not recover for negligent misrepresentation or malpractice, as Dahl owed a fiduciary duty to them, and Glover aided and abetted Dahl's breach of that duty, Glover was liable to Shepard and Pederson.

3.   Investment Bankers have a duty of care when authoring fairness opinions over leveraged buyouts. Questions center on the reach of said liability *in re* shareholders and the degree to which they reasonably rely on the banker.

IX.   **NEGLIGENT HIRING AND LIABILITY FOR LETTERS OF RECOMMENDATION.** Employers face liability for hiring incompetent employees and for harm caused by former employees for whom the prior employer wrote a wrongfully favorable letter of recommendation.

A.   **Negligent Hiring**. An employer may be held liable for the negligent or tortious conduct of its employee if the employer breached its duty to use due care in hiring competent employees.

B.   **Duty of Employers to Third Parties Based on Letters of Recommendation**. Employers face a dilemma when dealing with recommendations for former employees. Providing "too much" information might be deemed negative and thus gives rise to a defamation suit by the former employee. On the other hand, disclosure of "too little" negative information leaves the former employer liable to injured third parties for negligent misrepresentation. See e.g., *Randi W. v. Muroc Joint Unified School District*, 929 P.2d 582 (Cal. 1997).

X.   **STRICT LIABILITY**. Liability without fault, that is, without either intent or negligence that is imposed in two circumstances: (1) in product liability cases (*see* Chapter 10), and (2) in cases involving abnormally dangerous (or ultrahazardous) activities.

A.   **Ultrahazardous Activities**. Defendant is strictly liable for injuries resulting from abnormally dangerous activity that is not commonly performed and involves risk of serious injury which cannot be avoided through utmost care.

B.   **Standard of Care Irrelevant**. Once a court determines an activity is abnormally dangerous, it is irrelevant that the defendant observed a high standard of care.

XI.   **VICARIOUS LIABILITY AND *RESPONDEAT SUPERIOR***. It is possible for one person to be held vicariously liable for the negligent, or in some cases the intentional, conduct of another.

A.   ***Respondeat superior*** holds an employer vicariously liable for the torts of the "servant" or employee if the employee was acting within the scope of his or her employment.

1. Liability for Torts Committed Within the Scope of Employment

- The employer is directly liable for her own negligence in supervising or hiring an employee.

- The employer is also liable for her employee's wrongful acts, even if the employer had no knowledge of them and in no way directed them, so long as the acts were committed while the employee was acting within the scope of employment. E.g., *Chastain v. Litton Sys., Inc.*, 694 F.2d 957 (4th Cir. 1982).

- The employer is generally liable for his or her employee's intentional torts if the wrongful act in any way furthered the employer's purpose, however misguided the manner of furthering that purpose.

2. Employer Liability Based on the Aided-in-the-Agency Doctrine. When employees commit intentional torts that do not further the employer's business, liability may be attributed on the grounds that the employer empowered the employee via provision of authority, opportunity, access or assets. See e.g., *White v. County of Orange*, 212 Cal. Rptr. 493 (Cal Ct. App. 1985).

> **Case 9.5 *Fearing v. Bucher***, 977 P.2d 1163 (Or. 1998). From 1970 through 1972, Bucher, a priest employed by the Archdiocese of Portland, acted as youth pastor, confessor, and priest to Fearing and his family. Bucher began to spend substantial periods of time with Fearing, then a minor, and committed a series of sexual assaults upon him. Years later, Fearing filed claims against the Archdiocese for vicarious liability (under the doctrine of *respondeat superior*) and negligent retention, supervision and training of Bucher. The trial court dismissed, and the court of appeals affirmed. The Supreme Court of Oregon reversed finding the allegations sufficient to state a claim of vicarious liability against the Archdiocese based on the doctrine of *respondeat superior*. Plaintiff was permitted to proceed with the lawsuit.

B. **Vicarious Liability.** At times an employer maybe indirectly (vicariously) liable for the acts of employees. Courts find employers liable due to their acts or omissions that created a foreseeable harm or injury. *Robertson v. LeMaster*, 301 S.E.2d 563 (W. Va. 1983). But see also *Otis Eng'g Corp. v. Clark*, 668 S.W. 307

(Tex. 1983).

XII. **SUCCESSOR LIABILITY**. Individuals or entities that purchase a business may be held liable for the tortious acts of the previous owner, e.g., Dow Chemical which bought Union Carbide, might be responsible for the chemical disaster in Bhopal.

XIII. **DAMAGES**. Tort damages generally attempt to restore the plaintiff to the same position he or she was in before the tort occurred. Tort damages may include punitive as well as compensatory damages.

  A. **Actual Damages** also known as *compensatory damages*, measure the cost to repair or replace an item, or the decrease in market value caused by the tortious conduct. Actual damages may also include compensation for medical expenses, lost wages, and pain and suffering.

  B. **Punitive Damages** also known as *exemplary damages*, may be awarded to punish the defendant and deter others from engaging in similar conduct. Punitive damages are awarded only in cases of outrageous misconduct.

POLITICAL PERSPECTIVE: THE CHANGING TIDE OF TORT REFORM. There has been much political debate about the American tort system. Complaints center on the range of jury awards, different state laws, and resultant higher costs for insurance and goods. Still punitive damage awards are rare. Congress has sought to impose federal rules to limit and liability for drug companies and other tortfeasors.

XIV. **EQUITABLE RELIEF**. If a monetary award cannot adequately compensate for the plaintiff's loss, courts may apply *equitable relief* such as an *injunction*.

XV. **LIABILITY OF MULTIPLE DEFENDANTS**. The plaintiff may name numerous defendants. In some cases, the defendants may ask the court to join the action, or add other defendants. If a court determines what liability exists, it must allocate the damages among multiple defendants.

  A. **Joint and Several Liability**. This doctrine holds multiple defendants jointly (collectively) liable and also individually liable. If the court determines multiple defendants are at fault, the plaintiff may collect the entire judgment from any one of them, regardless of the degree of the particular defendant's fault.

  B. **Contribution and Indemnification** mitigate joint and several liability. *Contribution* distributes the loss among several defendants by requiring each to pay its proportionate share to one defendant. *Indemnification* allows a defendant to shift its individual loss to other more blameworthy defendants.

XVI. TOXIC TORTS. Since the 1970s tort law has evolved in response to the effects of toxic substances.

    A.   **Definition**. A toxic tort is a wrongful act that causes injury via exposure to a harmful, hazardous, or poisonous substance. Liability can attach to manufacturers, distributors, or even government agencies.

    B.   **Expensive to Defend**. Toxic tort claims are among the most difficult and expensive to defend or prosecute. Cause-and-effect relationships are difficult to establish. When illness or injury does occur, it is often years after exposure occurred.

    C.   **Strict Liability**.

        1.   Some courts hold that hazardous-waste disposal is an ultra-hazardous activity. These courts have imposed strict liability for injuries resulting from such waste disposal. See *Sterling v. Velsicol Chem. Corp.*, 855 F.2d 1188 (6th Cir. 1988); *Farm Bureau Mutual Ins. Co. v. Porter & Heckman, Inc.*, 560 N.W.2d 367 (Mich. Ct. App. 1996).

        2.   Federal law, CERCLA imposes strict liability for cleanup costs on: (a) the current owner or operator of the property; (b) the owner or operator at the time the hazardous substance was discharged; *and* (c) the parties responsible for transporting and disposing of the waste.

    D.   **Theories of Damages**.

        1.   Plaintiffs who prove exposure to a toxic substance and defendant's liability still might not receive a damage award for the law requires proof of an *actual* injury, and some plaintiffs may not develop injuries for years.

        2.   Frequently courts are asked to allow awards for emotional distress in the absence of either physical symptoms.

        3.   Another novel remedy is an award to cover future costs of medical monitoring and treatment to limit physical injury of disease.

XVII. RESPONSIBLE MANAGER: REDUCING TORT RISKS. Managers should implement programs of education and monitoring to reduce the risks of tort liability. Because torts can be committed in numerous ways, the programs should cover all possible sources of liability. Managers should:

- respond quickly to allegations of sexual harassment;
- be aware that statements can constitute defamation;
- define "scope of employment" clearly to insulate liability from employees who commit intentional, reckless, or negligent acts;
- avoid actual interference with contractual relations of rival firms; and
- draft and implement policies regarding the handling, distribution, and use of toxic substances, including a contingency plan for responding to toxic accidents.

XVIII. **INSIDE STORY: TAKING AIM AT THE GUN INDUSTRY.** In 2001 an Illinois court held that gun dealers and gun makers could be held liable under a theory of public nuisance. Courts in Ohio and Florida allowed gun makers to be held liable for injuries from their guns. Still some judgments are overturned, and since 1998 at least 30 states have passed laws to grant manufacturers immunity – save California.

STUDY QUESTIONS

True-False Questions

___ 1. The definition of an intentional tort requires that the defendant have intended the result of their action.

___ 2. Courts allow plaintiffs to show transferred intent in a tort claim.

___ 3. The most frequently raised defense to a tort is consent.

___ 4. Putting poison in someone's food is a battery.

___ 5. If Bud said to Lou, "If I were not such a nice guy, I would break your legs" Bud would be committing an assault.

___ 6. State legislation for the shopkeeper's privilege as a legal defense came about because too many lawsuits were brought against shopkeepers for false arrest.

___ 7. Abusive, threatening, or profane language is, per se, a tort.

___ 8. Libel is written defamation and slander is spoken defamation.

___ 9. A qualified privilege, by definition, cannot be lost.

___ 10. The law in most states assumes that the plaintiff has a good reputation unless the defendant proves otherwise in a defamation suit.

___ 11. In a slander *per se* tort, damages are presumed.

___ 12. Fraud requires the intent to mislead the plaintiff, reliance by the plaintiff, and an injury as a result of the reliance.

___ 13. For a plaintiff to recover for the tort of interference with contractual relations, the defendant's creation of the opportunity to breach the contract is all one needs to show.

___ 14. Standard of care is a material factor in a lawsuit based on strict liability.

___ 15. A homeowner who has an in-ground pool, but does not have a fence around it, may be liable for an attractive nuisance if a child walks to the pool, falls in, and dies.

Multiple-Choice Questions

___ 1. Intentional torts require all but which of the following?
     A. Actual intent.
     B. Voluntary act by the defendant.
     C. Causation.
     D. Injury to the plaintiff.

___ 2. If a pitcher hit a batter in the head with a thrown ball during batting practice, the batter who sues will probably:
     A. Win.
     B. Lose; he consented to the contact.
     C. Lose; defense of others.
     D. Win; *res ipsa loquitur*.

___ 3. Which of the following is *not* a defense to an intentional tort?
     A. Truth.
     B. Self-defense.
     C. Consent.
     D. Defense of others.

___ 4. Tony slaps the hat off of Mike's head. This is
     A. An assault.
     B. An intentional infliction of emotional distress.
     C. A battery.
     D. Defamation.

___ 5. At the I Tappa Keg fraternity party, Melissa tries to leave by the door through which she

entered. The fraternity members will not let her exit. There are other doors nearby that she can use. Melissa complains for five minutes refusing to exit except through the front door. Melissa sues for false imprisonment. Melissa will most likely:
A. Lose.
B. Lose; she was not held long enough.
C. Win; she was intentionally held against her will.
D. Win; she was detained for a sufficiently long period.

___ 6. In a television broadcast, Hall calls Goldberg a thief, which is not true. Goldberg could win a lawsuit for:
A. Assault.
B. Intentional infliction of emotional distress.
C. Slander.
D. Libel.

___ 7. In regard to the trespass to land tort, which statement is *false*?
A. It is an interference with a property right.
B. Land need not be injured by the trespass.
C. The intent required is the intent to enter the property, not the intent to trespass.
D. A mistake as to ownership is relevant to the suit.

___ 8. A public nuisance is usually brought by the
A. injured plaintiff.
B. government.
C. plaintiff who was injured by the trespass.
D. Any of the above.

___ 9. Which of the following is *not* a private nuisance?
A. Destruction of crops by flooding caused by another.
B. Pollution of a stream.
C. Gas leaking from an underground tank that seeps into adjoining property.
D. Air pollution that causes the city's population to have burning eyes.

___ 10. Injurious falsehood allows recovery for:
A. Emotional damages.
B. Pecuniary losses related to personal reputation.
C. Pecuniary losses related to business.
D. Loss of reputation.

___ 11. A victorious plaintiff in a malicious prosecution suit can recover for:

I. Attorney's fees for the prior suit.
II. Injury to reputation.

III. Psychological distress.

A. I, II, and III.
B. I and II.
C. II only.
D. III only.

__ 12. To establish negligence, the plaintiff must show all of the following *except:*
A. A duty owed to the plaintiff.
B. An intentional breach.
C. Causation.
D. Damages.

__ 13. A(n) _____ is anyone who is on the land of another with the possessor's express or implied consent.
A. Invitee.
B. Trespasser.
C. Licensee.
D. Business invitee.

__ 14. Who would be held to provide the highest standard of care?
A. Engineer.
B. Architect.
C. Pharmacist.
D. Surgeon.

__ 15. Sarah bungee jumps after reading an explicit release form. She is injured in the jump and sues. The defendant will probably use which defense?
A. *Respondeat superior.*
B. Pure negligence.
C. Assumption of the risk.
D. Successor liability.

Essay Questions

1. Compare and contrast assault and battery.

2. Compare and contrast private and public nuisances.

3. What are the requirements for *res ipsa loquitur*?

4. In what ways may a consumer have a cause of action for trespass to chattels for spam (unwanted email) that is being delivered into his or her inbox?

CHAPTER 10
PRODUCT LIABILITY

INTRODUCTION

Product liability is the legal liability manufacturers and suppliers have for defective products that injure a purchaser, user, bystander, or property. Liability extends to anyone in the chain of distribution: manufacturers, distributors, wholesalers, and retailers. The general trend is towards strict product liability, hence an injured person may recover without showing the manufacturer was negligent. The chapter discusses the evolution of the strict liability doctrine. It then focuses on the bases for strict liability. The chapter examines who may be held liable for defective products and the allocation of liability among multiple defendants. Defenses to a product liability claim are discussed, along with legislative reforms. Finally, the chapter describes the law of product liability in the European Union.

I. **THEORIES OF RECOVERY**. The primary theories on which a product liability claim can be brought are breach of warranty, negligence, and strict liability.

    A. **Breach of Warranty**. In a warranty action, the question is whether the quality, characteristics, and safety of the product were consistent with the implied or express representations made by the seller.

        1. UCC Warranties may be either express or implied, for merchantability or a particular purchase, as set forth in Chapter 8.

        2. Privity of Contract is a breach-of-warranty is based on contract law. Generally, an injured person can only recover for a breach of warranty if he is in a contractual relationship (*privity*) with the seller (of the product).

    B. **Negligence**. To prove negligence for product liability, plaintiff must show that the defendant did not use reasonable care in designing or manufacturing its product or failed to provide adequate warnings or to comply with statutory requirements. Generally, plaintiffs cannot prove negligence by introducing evidence of "upgrades" designed to improve a product. *MacPherson* is the landmark case in which the manufacturer was found liable for negligence though there was no contractual relationship between manufacturer and plaintiff.

        Case 10.1--*MacPherson v. Buick Motor Co.*, 111 N.E.2d 1050 (N.Y. 1916). MacPherson purchased a new car from a Buick dealer, who had purchased the car directly from the manufacturer. MacPherson was injured when the car ran into a ditch after a wheel collapsed due to faulty spokes of that wheel. The wheel was not made by Buick. MacPherson sued Buick and won. The court held that Buick owed a duty to any person who might suffer a foreseeable injury as a result of a defect in Buick's cars.

C.   **Strict Liability in Tort**. A person injured by an unreasonably dangerous product can recover damages from the manufacturer or seller of the product. The basis of liability is the product defect, even if the manufacturer exercised all possible care in its manufacture and sale of the product.

　　1.　　Rationale. Strict liability is grounded in public policy holding that law should protect consumers from unsafe products. The goal of strict product liability is to force companies to internalize the costs of product-caused injuries.

　　2.　　Elements of Strict Liability Claim. Plaintiff must prove that the plaintiff (or their property) was harmed by a defective product, which caused the plaintiff's injury, and that the defect existed at the time the product was in defendant's control.

　　3.　　Strategy and Punitive Damages. Negligence and warranty actions are generally secondary to strict liability. Strict liability is easier to prove for the plaintiff need not prove negligence or privity of contract.

II.   **DEFINITION OF PRODUCT**. Strict liability in tort applies only to products, not services, ideas or improvements to land. What a court qualifies as a *product* is unclear at times. See holding of the Alabama Supreme Court.

III.   **WHAT MAKES A PRODUCT DEFECTIVE?** Plaintiffs must prove that the product was defective when it left the manufacturer or seller, and the defect made the product unreasonably dangerous.

A.   **Manufacturing Defect** is a flaw in the product that occurs during production, such as a failure to meet the design specifications.

View from Cyberspace: Jurisdictional Disputes. Various jurisdictions seek to protect manufacturers or suppliers. The inherently international character of e-commerce poses fodder for legal disputes over which jurisdiction will hear a case. In 2000 the European parliament granted jurisdiction to the country receiving goods in contract sales. Congress has not adopted a uniform standard or signed onto any international conventions on product liability and jurisdiction for e-commerce.

B.   **Design Defect** occurs when inadequate design or poor choice of materials makes a product dangerous, even though it is manufactured correctly.

C.   **Inadequate Warnings, Labeling, or Instructions**. A product may be defective if it does not carry adequate warnings of the risks involved in the normal use of the product.

1.   Causation Requirement. Plaintiff must show that defendant breached a duty to warn *and* that the defendant's failure to warn was the proximate cause of plaintiff's injuries.

2.   Bilingual Warnings. In states with a substantial non-English-speaking population, a manufacturer is not yet, but may be liable for not printing the warnings in more than one language.

> **Case 10.2--*Ramirez v. Plough, Inc.*,** 863 P.2d 167 (Cal. 1993). Jorge Ramirez, four months old, was given St. Joseph's Aspirin for Children, for a cold or upper respiratory infection, by his mother. Jorge developed Reye's Syndrome, resulting in severe neurological damage and retardation. Plough, the manufacturer, knew Hispanics purchased its product, but the warning on the label was only in English. Ramirez's family sued but their claim was dismissed on the grounds that but the U.S. federal government and the State of California only require warning labels in English.

D.   **Unavoidably Unsafe Product**. Nearly every state follows the Restatement (Second) of Torts which immunized manufacturers for making products that are inherently dangerous, if the benefit of proper use outweighs the risk of harm. .

IV.   **WHO MAY BE LIABLE**. In theory, each party in the chain of distribution may be liable: manufacturers, distributors, wholesalers, and retailers. Manufacturers of component parts are frequently sued as well.

A.   **Manufacturers of Products and Component Parts**. So long as the manufacturer sells the product (even just a component part), it is strictly liable for defects regardless of how remote the manufacturer is from the final user. Liability may attach even if there is distributor (dealer) final inspections, corrections, and adjustments of the product.

> **Case 10.3 *Jimenez v. Superior Court of San Diego County*,** 58 P.3d 450 (Cal. 2002). The Jimenez family purchased a home, built with others in a housing development. Like others in the development, the Jimenez family noticed problems which stemmed from faulty windows. The court held that the window manufacturer was strictly liable.

B. **Wholesalers** are generally strictly liable for defects in the products they sell. Some courts find no liability for latent or hidden defects if the wholesaler sells the products in exactly the same condition it received them.

C. **Retailers** are often held strictly liable for they have a duty to inspect and care for products they acquire and sell.

D. **Sellers of Used Goods and Occasional Sellers**. Occasional sellers of used goods are usually not held strictly liable as they are not within the original chain of distribution and their products are sold "as is." A seller of used goods is, however, strictly liable for any defective repairs or replacements she makes.

E. **Successor Liability**. A successor corporation that purchases or acquires the assets of another (through merger) is liable for its debts (and defective products) if the successor corporation is merely continuing the practices of the original corporation. See e.g., *Allenberg v. Bentley Hedges Travel Serv., Inc.*, 22 P.3d 223 (Okla. 2001); *Conway ex rel. Roadway Express, Inc. v. White Trucks*, 639 F. Supp 160 (M.D. Pa. 1986).

F. **Market-Share Liability**. If multiple manufacturers produce identical products, the injured party might not be able to prove which manufacturer caused the injury. In certain cases, *e.g.,* prescription drugs, the court may allocate liability on the basis of each defendant's share of the market.

G. **Premises Liability**. Recently, courts have recognized liability for asbestos-related diseases against a building owner may be found liable for violating its general duty to manage the premises and warn of asbestos dangers.

H. **Defenses**. Defenses to product liability include the following:

    1. Traditional tort defenses: assumption of risk; comparative negligence (fault)

    2. Other defenses: obvious risk; unforeseeable use; statute of limitations; government-contractor; and state-of-the-art

    3. Federal pre-emption.

I. **Assumption of Risk**. When a person voluntarily and unreasonably assumes the risk of a known danger, the manufacturer is not liable for any resulting injury.

J. **Comparative Fault**. Contributory negligence by the plaintiff is not a defense in a strict liability action. However, damages may be reduced by the degree to which plaintiff's negligence contributed to the injury.

K.   **Obvious Risk**. Generally manufacturers are not liable for injuries if a product carries an obvious risk.

L.   **Unforeseeable Misuse of the Product**. Generally, manufacturers are not liable for injuries resulting from *abnormal* use of a product. However, an unusual use that is reasonably foreseeable may give rise to liability. E.g., operating a lawn mower with the grass bag removed was foreseeable, so the manufacturer was liable to a bystander injured by an object shot out of an unguarded mower.

> **Case 10.4--*James v. Meow Media Inc*.**, 300 F.3d 683 (6th Cir. 2002). In 2002, a teenager shot and killed eight people in his school in Paducah, Kentucky. The families of the victims sued the video game maker. The court dismissed the suit on the grounds that the child's criminal acts were not a reasonably foreseeable outcome of his playing the game and that the video game was not a product, hence there could be no product liability.

M.   **Government-Contractor Defense**. A manufacturer of products under contract to the government can avoid product liability if the product was manufactured according to government specifications. The manufacturer acquires immunity when acting as an agent of the government.

N.   **State-of-the-Art Defense**. A manufacturer might be shielded from liability if courts recognize there is no possible safer product design. However, a manufacturer might still be liable for manufacturing a defective product. See *Potter v. Chicago Pneumatic Tool Co*., 694 A.2d 1319 (Conn. 1997)

O.   **Preemption Defense** can be used to preclude *State* product liability law when manufacturer complies with federal laws. The defense depends largely on the language and context of the federal statute at issue. See e.g., PL 107-296.

> **Case 10.5--*Geier v. American Honda Motor Company, Inc*.**, 529 U.S. 861 (2000). While driving a 1987 Honda Accord, Alexis Geier crashed into a tree and was seriously injured. Though the car had manual shoulder and lap belts that Geier was using, it had no airbags or other passive restraints. Geier and her parents sued American Honda under *state law* for failing to include a driver's side airbag. The Federal Motor Vehicle Safety Standard (FMVSS) 208, promulgated pursuant to the National Traffic and Motor Vehicle Safety Act required auto makers to equip 10 percent of their national fleet with passive restraints, but did not require airbags. The district court dismissed the plaintiff's claim on the grounds that the state law was preempted by federal law. The ruling was upheld by both the U.S. Court of Appeals and the U.S. Supreme Court.

BASES FOR PRODUCT LIABILITY AND DEFENSES	
Theory of Liability	**Defenses**
Breach of Warranty	No privity of contract
Negligence	Defendant used reasonable care Contributory or comparative negligence
Strict Liability in Tort	Unavoidably unsafe product Comparative fault (only reduces damages) Assumption of risk Obvious risk Abnormal misuse Government contractor Preemption State of the art

V.   **OTHER LEGISLATIVE LIMITS ON LIABILITY.** Since the 1980s a number of state legislatures have enacted a number of laws to reduce or limit product liability.

   A.   **Limitations on Non-Manufacturers' Liability**. Some states absolve mere non-manufacturers sellers in the chain of distribution of a product from strict liability claims.

   B.   **Limitations on Joint Liability**. Rejecting the common-law rule, at least 37 states have restricted or eliminated joint and several liability. See e.g., ORS § 18.485 (2003).

   C.   **Caps on Punitive Damages**. More than 30 states have enacted legislation limiting punitive damages awards: placing limits on when punitive damages are available; requiring a higher standard of evidence; outright caps on punitive damages. The Supreme Court suggested that punitive awards should not be more than 10 times the compensatory damages. *State Farm Mutual Automobile Ins. Co. v. Campbell*, 538 U.S. 1028 (2003).

   D.   **Penalties for Frivolous Suits**. Under statute, or by the rules of equity and common law, all states allow courts to impose penalties against those who bring wrongful or frivolous suits (and their attorneys).

VI.   **STATUTE OF LIMITATIONS, REVIVAL STATUTES, AND STATUTES OF REPOSE.** Generally a lawsuit must be brought within a certain time period. The "clock" begins when the person is injured.

   A.   **Statute of Limitations**. When the date of injury is uncertain (e.g. from asbestos) the statute of limitations does not begin to run until the person discovers their injury.

B.   **Revival statutes** permit plaintiffs to file lawsuits that had been barred previously by a statute of limitations (*e.g.*, silicone breast implants).

C.   **Statutes of Repose**. A statute of repose cuts off the right to assert a cause of action after a specified period of time from the delivery of the product or the completion of the work.

VII.   **TOBACCO AND GUNS**. Dramatic applications of product liability law have been applied against tobacco and gun companies. Litigation by private individuals against gun companies has had mixed results.

A.   **Tobacco**. Forty-six states and the federal government brought lawsuits and reached settlements with the tobacco industry. Litigation has occurred outside the United States as well.

B.   **Guns**. In 2000 officials from the Clinton administration presented the gun industry with a list of demands to improve gun safety. Smith & Wesson largely agreed. The approach of legislation via negotiation appears more effective than lawsuits against gun makers.

VIII.   **PRODUCT LIABILITY CLASS ACTIONS**. Class action suits are procedural devices that allow a large number of plaintiffs to recover against a defendant in a single case. Litigation involving the tobacco industry, asbestos, silicone breast implants, and harmful diet drugs were all resolved through class actions. In some class actions, the class may base its suit on a *future* illness or physical injury resulting from drug ingestion or exposure to a toxic product. Still there have been some legal problems note *Amchem Products, Inc. v. Windsor*, 521 U.S. 591 (1997); *Ortiz v. Fibreboard Corp.*, 527 U.S. 815 (1999); *Wilson v. Brush Wellman Inc.*, No. 2003-0048 (Ohio Nov. 17, 2004)

IX.   **PROBLEMS WITH THE PRODUCT LIABILITY SYSTEM AND THE RESTATEMENT (THIRD) APPROACH TO DESIGN DEFECTS**. The current product liability scheme has been criticized for it assumes that manufacturers are in the best position to insure against loss or to spread the risk of loss among their customers which leads to higher manufacturing costs, ultimately taking its toll on industry efficiency and competitiveness.

A.   **Restatement (Third) of Torts: Product Liability**. The new Restatement avoids the term "strict liability" proposing instead that any claim of design defect be supported by a showing of a *reasonable alternative* design. The intent is to force plaintiffs to prove that defendants acted wrongly or negligently in choosing an improper design.

   Case 10.6--*Wright v. Brooke Group Ltd.*, 652 N.W.2d 159 (Iowa 2002). Robert and DeAnn Wright sued tobacco companies on the ground that the cigarettes had a design defect. The Iowa Supreme Court rejected previous case law on the Restatement (Second) of Torts and instead adopted Sections 1 and 2 of the Restatement (Third) and compelled plaintiffs to show an alternative to the design defect.

B. **GLOBAL VIEW: PRODUCT LIABILITY IN THE EUROPEAN UNION.** The EU directive's basic purpose is to hold manufacturers strictly liable for injuries caused by defects in their products. This is a fundamental change for manufacturers of products marketed in Europe. The EU product liability directive and legal defenses are similar to the strict liability doctrine of the United States. Unlike in the United States, a supplier or wholesaler is not strictly liable unless the injured party is unable to identify the manufacturer. Further, a producer can escape liability by proving that the state of scientific knowledge when the product went into circulation was insufficient to allow it to discover the defect.

X. **THE RESPONSIBLE MANAGER:** *Reducing Product Liability Risk.* Managers have the responsibility to minimize their company's exposure to liability in the design, manufacture, assembly, and sale of its products. They should:

- Implement a product-safety program in order to ensure that products are sold in a legally safe condition,
- Implement internal loss-control procedures, obtain insurance protection, and seek the advice of product liability counsel from the earliest stages of product development,
- Check the safety of their products both in their intended use and in reasonably foreseeable misuse and develop adequate instructions and comprehensive warnings,
- Consider the reasonably foreseeable risks of using the product, ways to avoid those risks, and the consequences of ignoring the risks,
- Have a thorough understanding of all statutes, regulations, and administrative rulings to which a product must conform,
- Keep internal records of their product engineering and manufacturing decisions,
- Continuously monitor field reports of injuries caused by both use and misuse of their company's products,
- Send post-sale information to purchasers about upgrades and recalls, and
- Establish a product-safety committee and to conduct regular safety audits in order to identify and correct problems.

XI. **INSIDE STORY: BIG FOOD FACING BIG LAWSUITS.** Over the decades various products have been the target of tort suits: asbestos, tobacco, breast implants, and guns. Now fast food is a target. Companies like McDonald's have been sued for promoting obesity and its foods generating serious health problems in customers. Consider that McDonald's targets children through happy meals and toys. Further McDonald's has agreed that it mislabels food and with suits pending, the fast food industry is lobbying for statutory relief.

STUDY QUESTIONS

True-False Questions

__ 1. The UCC provides for only express warranties.

__ 2. Contractual recovery requires privity of contract; hence, bystanders cannot recover.

__ 3. An injured person may recover in strict liability even if the manufacturer has exercised all possible care in the manufacture and sale of the product.

__ 4. The Restatement (Third) proposes to eliminate strict liability.

__ 5. Strict liability is easier to prove than either negligence or breach of warranty.

__ 6. Sellers of used goods are usually held strictly liable because they are within the foreseeable original chain of distribution of the product.

__ 7. Market-share liability was developed by Congress.

__ 8. The defendant in a product liability suit can raise the assumption of the risk defense.

__ 9. Contributory negligence by the plaintiff is a defense in strict liability cases.

__ 10. Ordinarily, the statute of limitations starts to run when the plaintiff becomes aware of the injury.

__ 11. A seller of used goods is usually strictly liable for any defective repairs or replacements made.

__ 12. The majority of states deem "state-of-the-art" to refer to what is technologically feasible at the time of design.

__ 13. A statute of limitation cuts off the right to assert a cause of action after a period of time from the delivery of the product or the completion of the work.

__ 14. In a strict liability action today, defendants are always held jointly and severally liable.

__ 15. Traditionally, most EU member states imposed strict liability on defective products.

Multiple-Choice Questions

__ 1. For a defendant to be held strictly liable, the plaintiff must prove the:

   I.   Plaintiff or property was harmed by the product.
   II. Injury was caused by a defect in the product.
   III Defect existed at the time the product left the defendant and did not substantially change afterwards.

   A. I and II.
   B. II and III.
   C. I, II, and III.
   D. I and III.

__ 2. The principle of strict liability is based on which rationale?
   A. The law should protect consumers against unsafe products.
   B. Manufacturers should not escape liability simply because there is no contract with the end user of the product.
   C. Manufacturers and sellers of products are in the best position to bear the costs of the injuries caused by their products.
   D. All of the above.

__ 3. In a strict liability case, what must the plaintiff show to establish a defective product?

   I.   The product was defective when it left the defendant or seller.
   II. The defect made the product unreasonably dangerous.

   A. I or II.
   B. I and II.
   C. Neither I nor II.
   D. II only.

__ 4. A product may be dangerous because of a:
   A. Manufacturing defect.
   B. Design defect.
   C. Labeling inadequacy.
   D. All of the above

__ 5. The Ford Pinto was an example of a _____ defect.
   A. Design.
   B. Manufacturing.
   C. Warning.
   D. Labeling.

__ 6. Which of the following is *not* normally in the chain of distribution?
    A. Distributor.
    B. Retailer.
    C. Seller of used products.
    D. Wholesaler.

__ 7. A brake manufacturer builds brakes to an auto manufacturer's specifications. The brakes
    fail to work properly because of a flaw in the automobile braking system. Who would be
    liable for the braking problem?
    A. Brake manufacturer.
    B. Automobile manufacturer.
    C. Neither.
    D. Both.

__ 8. In service industries, there is liability for:

        I.   Negligence.
        II. Strict liability.
        III. Design defects.

    A. I only.
    B. II only.
    C. I and II.
    D. I, II, and III.

__ 9. A corporation purchasing or acquiring the assets of another is liable for its debts if there
    is a(n):
    A. Merger.
    B. Express or implied agreement to assume such obligations.
    C. New corporation, not a continuation of the selling corporation (via successor
       liability).
    D. Both A and B.

__ 10. Lucky uses his lawn mower as a hedge trimmer, resulting in a seriously injured hand.
    The owner's manual says to not use the mower for this purpose or in this manner. The
    mower manufacturer's best defense in a suit by Lucky is:
    A. Contributory negligence.
    B. Comparative fault.
    C. Assumption of the risk.
    D. Market-share liability.
__ 11. Which statement is *false* concerning what a manufacturer has to show to avoid product
    liability under the government-contractor defense?
    A. The product was produced according to government specifications.
    B. The manufacturer possessed less knowledge about the specifications than the

government.
   C. The manufacturer exercised proper care in production.
   D. The manufacturer deviated from the specifications.

___ 12. Which of the following is a defense to a breach of warranty claim?
   A. No privity of contract.
   B. Reasonable care used.
   C. Contributory negligence.
   D. Comparative negligence.

___ 13. Which of the following is *not* a defense to a negligence claim for product liability?
   A. Use of reasonable care.
   B. No privity of contract.
   C. Contributory negligence.
   D. Comparative negligence.

___ 14. Which of the following could *not* be successfully utilized as a defense to a strict liability tort action?
   A. Reasonable care used.
   B. Assumption of the risk.
   C. Preemption.
   D. State of the art.

___ 15. A statute of _____ measures the time to litigate from the time the injury occurred.
   A. Repose.
   B. Limitation.
   C. Warranty.
   D. Jurisprudence.

Essay Questions

1. A hair dryer has a label on it, which states it should not be used in the shower. The same statement appears on the box the dryer came in, and in the manual for the dryer. Should this be sufficient to protect the manufacturer of the hair dryer if a purchaser uses the dryer in the shower and is injured? Explain.

2. Why has market-share liability been rejected in many jurisdictions?

3. What is the preemption defense?

CHAPTER 11
INTELLECTUAL PROPERTY

INTRODUCTION

Intellectual property is an essential part of business. In legal terms *intellectual property* (IP) is any product or result of a mental process that is given legal protection against unauthorized use. Intellectual property represents about 87% of a firm's value. There are four types of IP: patents; copyrights; trademarks; and trade secrets.

A patent is a government grant to exclude others from making, using or selling an invention without the patent owner's permission. A copyright grants right to prevent others from copying an original expression embodied in a tangible medium. A trademark, in the form of words or symbols, is an exclusive mark of a given business. A trade secret is private information that provides a company an advantage over its competitors, e.g. the formula for Coca-Cola.

This chapter describes the law of patents, copyrights, mask work rights, trademarks, trade secrets. It also covers efforts to enact new legislation to protect databases, technology licensing, and concludes with a discussion of international intellectual property laws.

I. **PATENTS** form the basis for many industries, e.g., instant cameras, industrial plastics, and biotechnology. Article I of the U.S. Constitution specifically grants Congress the authority to grant patents. Subsequently the Congress created the Patent and Trademark Office of the Dept. of Commerce to issues patents.

  A. **Types of Patents**

  1. Utility Patents protect any novel, useful, and non-obvious process, machine, manufacture, or composition of matter, or any novel, useful, and non-obvious improvement. For issuance of a utility patent, the application must show that the "invention" has both utility and is novel.

  - Biotechnology. In *Diamond v. Chakrabarty*, 447 U.S. 303 (1980), the Court held that patent statutes should include "anything under the sun that is *made* by man" thus allowing a patent for living organisms, e.g., bacteria. This has opened the door for DNA-based patents.

  - Computer Software. Since *Diamond v. Diehr*, 450 U.S. 175 (1981) patents may contain mathematical formulae or applications in a structure or process," hence programmers may obtain patents on computer programs.

- Business Method Patents, allowed since 1998, are granted for methods dealing with Internet applications, electronic commerce, and computer-based systems for managing mutual fund investments.

2. Design Patents protect any novel, original (rather than non-obvious), and ornamental design for an article of manufacture. Design patents protect against copying the appearance or shape of an article, e.g., the shape of a "Coca-Cola" bottle, a typeface, and screen displays of computer programs. Design patents are easier to obtain than utility patents.

3. Plant Patents are granted for man-made inventions of any distinct and new variety of plant that is asexually reproduced.

B. **FILING FOR PATENT PROTECTION**. In order to obtain patent protection in the United States, the inventor must file a patent application with the U.S. Patent and Trademark Office (PTO). Each patent application contains four parts:

1. Specifications must describe the invention in its best mode, manner and process of making and using the invention so that a person skilled in the relevant field could make and use it.

2. Claims must describe those elements of the invention that will be protected by the patent. Any element not specifically set forth in the claims is unprotected by the patent.

3. Drawings must show the claimed invention.

4. Declaration by the inventor must state that the inventor has reviewed the application and believes that she is the first inventor of the invention with full disclosure to avoid relevant prior art.

5. Continuation application (or appeal). The PTO rejects 99 percent of all initial applications. One may file an appeal to the PTO and after exhausting administrative remedies, to the U.S. District Court for the District of Columbia or the U.S. Court of Appeals for the Federal Circuit.

6. Provisional applications. Since 1995, inventors can file a provisional application without formal patent claims. This tool allows an inventor to file earlier than they would otherwise.

II. **PATENT INFRINGEMENT.**

A. **Types of Infringement**. There are three ways to infringe upon a patent.

1. Direct Infringement is the innocent or intentional making, use, or sale of any patented invention within the United States during the term of the patent. The doctrine of equivalents allows a patent holder to claim infringement when the replication works in substantially the same way as the patented device.

2. Indirect infringement is defined as the active inducement of another party to infringe a patent.

3. Contributory infringement occurs when one party knowingly sells an item that has one specific use that will result in the infringement of another's patent.

B. **Defenses**. One accused of patent infringement has a variety of legal defenses.

    1. Noninfringement asserts that the allegedly infringing matter does not fall within the claims of the issued patent.

    2. Invalidity. A court may rule a patent invalid if the invention was not novel, or failure to meet statutory requirements.

    3. Patent Misuse is an affirmative defense that the patent holder has abused her patent rights and therefore should lose her right to enforce them.

    4. Innocent Infringement asserts that the defendant lacked adequate notice of the patent.

C. **Remedies**. Patent holders may seek remedies for alleged infringement of their patent rights.

    1. Injunctive Relief prevents infringement of the patent pending the court's ultimate decision. Permanent injunctive relief is available if infringement is found.

    2. Damages may also be awarded, based on a reasonable royalty for the infringer's use of the invention, as well as court costs and attorney's fees. See the example of *Polaroid Corp. v. Eastman Kodak Co.*, 789 F.2d 1556 (Fed. Cir. 1986).

III. **COPYRIGHTS**. Books, novels, films, software and CDs are all copyrightable. Under the U.S. Copyright Act, works must be fixed in a tangible medium and original. Names, commonly known phrases, government documents, and facts are not protected by copyright. If an author can establish fixity and originality, copyright protection is automatic.

A. **Ownership and Scope of Protection**. The author is either the creator of the work or, in the case of a work made for hire, the party for whom the work was prepared. The author of a work for hire is a third party, usually an employer, for a work created by an employee within the scope of employment.

　　1. Expression Versus Idea. The copyright law prohibits unauthorized copying, but the ideas embodied in the work can be used freely. However if an expression is merged with an idea, it is not copyrightable.

　　2. Useful Article Doctrine. Copyright protection does not extend to the useful application of an idea. E.g., blank forms used to record, rather than convey, information are non-copyrightable, useful articles.

B. **Preemption of State Law**. The Copyright Act, as a federal statute, preempts any state law that conflicts with it, though it allows application of other state laws designed to prevent unfair competition. E.g. the federal copyright law did not preempt state tort claims, *Brown v. Ames*, 201 F.3d 654 (5th Cir. 2000).

C. **Term of Protection**. Copyright now extends for: (1) the life of the author plus 70 years (if the author is known); or (2) the lesser of 95 years after the first publication or 120 after the creation of works of unknown authors. The Supreme Court upheld the extension. *Eldred v. Ashcroft*, 537 U.S. 186 (2003).

D. **Copyright Formalities**. Using proper copyright notices and registering copyright works afford the copyright owner substantial benefits.

　　1. Copyright Notice is not required, but advisable for it prevents a claim of innocent infringement. A proper notice for works distributed within the U.S. includes these elements: "Copyright" or "Copr." or "©"; the year of first publication; and the name of the copyright owner.

　　2. Copyright Registration with the U.S. Copyright Office is required prior to filing an infringement suit for a work of U.S. origin. Damages of up to $100,000 per violation and attorney's fees are available.

E. **Exclusive Rights**. Copyright owners are given certain exclusive rights in the work to: (1) reproduce the copyrighted work; (2) prepare derivative works; (3) distribute copies of the copyrighted work; (4) perform the work publicly; and (5) display the copyrighted work publicly.

IV. **COPYRIGHT INFRINGEMENT** includes copying, modification, display, performance, or distribution of a work without the permission of the copyright owner.

A.   **Types of Infringement.**

1.   Direct infringement occurs when one party violates at least one of the five exclusive rights of the copyright holder by its own actions.

2.   Contributory infringement occurs when the defendant induces or causes or participates in the infringing conduct of another.

3.   Vicarious infringement occurs when the defendant has the right and ability to control the infringer's act and receives a direct financial benefit from the infringement. See *A & M Records, Inc. v. Napster*, 239 F.3d 1004 (9th Cir. 2001).

> **Case 11.1--*Metro-Goldwyn-Mayer Studios v. Grokster*, 380 F.3d 1154 (9th Cir. 2004).** In the matter of file sharing, copyright holders sued Grokster and StreamCast Networks (software distributors) for contributory and vicarious copyright infringement. The two defendants provided free software enabling users to connect to a decentralized file-sharing network of computers. Neither defendant maintained any control over the network. The district court granted summary judgment for the defendants. The appeals court agreed holding that defendants neither provided material aid nor had control over those who shared files and thus were not liable for copyright infringement.

B.   **Defenses to Copyright Infringement** include fair use, first sale and copyright misuse.

1.   Exclusive Right Exception: "Fair Use" Doctrine. A person may infringe on a copyrighted work if the activity involves literary criticism, social comment, news reporting, education, scholarship, or research. Parody enjoys broad protection. See *Campbell v. Acuff-Rose Music, Inc.*, 510 U.S. 569 (1994). The following case shows how courts considered whether copying software is fair use.

> **Case 11.2--*NXIVM Corp. v. The Ross Institute*, 364 F.3d 471 (2nd Cir. 2004).** Rick Ross acquired materials from NXIVM and posted them on his website where he criticized cults and mind-control organizations. NXIVM sought an injunction to have their information removed from Ross' website but were denied on the grounds that Ross transformed data and did not seek economic gain from the NXIVM materials.

2. First Sale Doctrine. Once the copyright owner sells the copyrighted item and thereby puts it in the stream of commerce, the owner has waived his exclusive statutory right to control distribution of the item.

3. Copyright Misuse. Similar to patent misuse, a defendant may allege that the copyright holder seeks to exercise authority outside the scope of the copyright.

C. REMEDIES.

1. Piracy and Current Responses. Software companies lose billions of dollars through piracy. In the music area, the Recording Industry Association of America is using technology and lawsuits to prevent file sharing.

2. Civil Copyright Remedies. A plaintiff is entitled to recover actual damages and the defendant's profits attributable to the infringement, as well as attorneys' fees.

3. Digital Millennium Copyright Act may apply to copyright. The DMCA outlaws devices used to copy software illegally and criminalizes circumvention of anti-piracy measures in commercial software. The court may also order injunctions and the destruction of equipment used to violate the copyright.

4. Criminal Liability. Infringers may face criminal penalties including fines and imprisonment under the No Electronic Theft Act of 1997. The law requires no proof that the defendant made profits from the violation. Defendants may also suffer liability under the DMCA.

ECONOMIC PERSPECTIVE. INTELLECTUAL PROPERTY RIGHTS AND INCENTIVES TO INNOVATE. Neo-classical economic theory advocated free markets as to maximize productive efficiency and allocative efficiency. Intellectual property laws are seemingly in opposition to free-market principles. But the rationale of granting monopoly power to inventors and holders of patents is to encourage innovation and invention. Yet the IP system also extends state-of-the-art technology to reduce "waste."

V. **REGISTERED MASK WORK**. The Semiconductor Chip Protection Act of 1984 protects registered masks as intellectual property for ten (10) years, but allows reverse engineering. The remedies for infringement are an injunction, damages, and the impoundment of the infringing mask and chips.

VI. **TRADEMARKS**. Trademark law concerns itself with how trademarks are created, how its rights arise, are preserved, and why certain trademarks gain more protection than others.

A.   Ownership and Scope of Protection

1.   Definition. The Lanham Act and the 1988 Trademark Law Revision Act[1] define a trademark as "any word, name, symbol, or device or any combination thereof adopted and used by a manufacturer or merchant to identify and distinguish his or her goods, including a unique product, from those manufactured or sold by others, and to indicate the source of the goods, even if that source is unknown."

2.   Purpose: There are four different purposes of a trademark:

   • to provide an identification symbol for a particular merchant's goods,
   • to indicate that the goods to which the trademark has been applied are from a single source,
   • to guarantee that all goods to which the trademark has been applied are of a constant quality, and
   • to advertise the goods.

3.   Distinctive Characteristics. Trademark law also protects distinctive shapes, odors, packaging, and sounds. For instance, there is trademark protection for the unique shape of the Coca-Cola bottle and NBC's three chimes. Color may also qualify as a trademark. See *Qualitex Co. v. Jacobson Products Co.*, 514 U.S. 159 (1995).

B.   Other Marks. Trademarks should not be confused with other forms of legally protected identifying marks, such as service marks, trade names, and certification marks.

1.   Service Marks are used in connection with services.

2.   Trade Names identify a company, partnership, or business.

3.   Certification Marks placed on a product indicate that the product has met the certifier's standards of safety or quality ("Good Housekeeping" seal).

VII.   CHOOSING A TRADEMARK. Under trademark law, the degree of protection is based on its distinctiveness. Marks that are the most distinctive generally have the greatest protection.

A.   Fanciful and Arbitrary Marks, often called strong marks, need no proof of distinctiveness.

---

[1] 15 U.S.C. §§ 1051-1072 (1994).

1. Fanciful Marks have no meaning until used as a trademark in connection with a particular product (Exxon).

2. Arbitrary Marks are real words whose ordinary meaning has nothing to do with the trademarked product (Apple, Camel).

B. **Suggestive Marks** suggest something about the product without directly describing it (Chicken of the Sea tuna).

C. **Descriptive Marks** specify certain characteristics of the goods, such as size, quality or color (Gold Medal flour).

1. Geographic Terms are generally non-distinctive.

2. Personal Names are not inherently distinctive. However the PTO granted a trademark to AOL for its "buddy list." *America Online, Inc. v. AT&T Corp.*, 243 F.3d 812 (4th Cir. 2001).

3. Secondary Meaning. Marks can become protected if they acquire *secondary meaning*, that is, a mental association by the buyer that links the mark with a single source of the product (Microsoft "Windows").

D. **Generic Terms**. Trademark law grants no protection to generic terms, such as "spoon" or "software," not even via a secondary meaning. Many terms that were once enforceable trademarks have become generic (escalator, aspirin, Xerox, etc.). Note the case of *Microsoft Corp. v. Lindows.com, Inc.*, 2004 WL 329250 (W.D. Wash. Feb. 10, 2004).

VIII. **CREATING RIGHTS IN A TRADEMARK**. Trademark rights are obtained through use of the mark in commerce or the filing of an intent-to-use application with the PTO. Via use in interstate commerce, additional rights may be obtained by federal registration. State registration requires only intrastate use.

A. **Trademark Searches**. Companies should discover if an intended mark is freely available. Trademark searchers can be conducted online at the U.S. Patent and Trademark Office (http://www.uspto.gov). Though some trademarks are not registered, searching is evidence of a good faith effort to determine whether any other entity has pre-existing rights in a mark.

B. **Common Law Rights of Use**. A trademark is used in commerce if it is physically attached to goods that are then sold or distributed. Generally, ownership of inherently distinctive marks in the United States is governed by priority of use—unless a subsequent user creates a strong mark in a particular geographic area.

C. **Federal Registration**. Though not required, registration on the federal Principal Register provides legal advantages such as constructive notice of ownership within the U.S., the "incontestable" right to use the mark, and the right to prevent importation articles bearing an infringing mark.

D. **State Registration** does not provide as much protection as federal registration, but is quicker and less costly. Note that State protections are pre-empted by federal law.

IX. **LOSS OF TRADEMARK RIGHTS**. Failure to use one's mark may result in the loss of rights.

A. **Actual Abandonment** occurs when an owner discontinues use of the mark with the intent not to resume use.

B. **Constructive Abandonment** results when the owner does something, or fails to do something, that causes the mark to lose its distinctiveness (allowing "thermos" to be used as a noun rather than a brand name).

X. **TRADEMARK INFRINGEMENT**. To establish infringement, a trademark owner must prove a valid mark, priority of usage of the mark, and a likelihood of confusion in the minds of the purchasers.

A. **The Federal Trademark Dilution Act of 1995** allows owners of famous trademarks to sue for damages and injunctive relief from defendants who willfully trade on the reputation of the famous mark owner or cause dilution of the famous mark.

B. **Defenses** against trademark infringement include first sale and fair use doctrines, nominative use, genericity, and the First Amendment.

1. First Sale Doctrine provides a trademark seller cannot act against resellers. Resale by the first purchaser of the original product is neither trademark infringement nor unfair competition.

2. Fair Use Doctrine allows a competitor to use a rival's trademark to identify the other's product.

3. Nominative Use. A defendant is not in violation of trademark infringement if the defendant only talks about the mark itself. Courts use a

three-part test to determine nominative use. See *New Kids on the Block v. News Am. Publ'g, Inc.*, 971 F.2d 302 (9th Cir. 1992).

> **Case 11.3--*Playboy Enterprises v. Welles*, 279 F.3d 796 (9th Cir. 2001).** Terry Welles was Playboy Playmate of the Year 1981. Welles used the PEI trademarks on her website. Though she noted that her website was not associated with PEI. The suit was largely dismissed as mere nominative use.

4. Genericity. The defense holds that the trademarked term is a generic term. E.g., *Microsoft v. Lindows.com*

5. First Amendment. Parties may use trademarked names in their political expressions.

C. **Remedies**. Owners can petition for injunctive relief, an accounting for lost profits due to customer confusion, and damages on a case-by-case basis.

XI. **TRADE DRESS**. The Lanham Act also protects *trade dress*, that is, the packaging or dressing of a product. Elements of trade dress infringement parallel those of trademark infringement – the likelihood of consumer confusion being the core issue. See *Best Cellars, Inc. v. Grape Finds at Dupont, Inc.*, 90 F. Supp. 2d 431 (S.D.N.Y. 2000).

XII. **TRADE SECRETS** law is designed to prevent the unauthorized disclosure of sensitive information.

A. **Scope of Protection**. Generally trade secret law is covered by state laws on contracts and tort. Some awards range in the millions.

VIEW FROM CYBERSPACE: DOMAIN NAMES AND CYBERSQUATTING. Internet addresses, *domain names,* are regulated by the Internet Corporation for Assigned Names and Numbers (ICANN). Domain names are registered on a first-come, first-served basis and are the intellectual property (or trademark) of its brand owner. Registering a domain name that violates a person/firm's trademark and selling it to the real owner for a "ransom" is called "cyber-squatting" and is illegal. ICANN defines cybersquatting as the registration of a domain name that is confusingly similar or identical to a protected trademark, where the domain name has no legitimate interest in the particular domain name and the domain name is registered and used in bad faith. The Lanham Act was amended to include the Anti-cybersquatting Consumer Protection Act (ACPA) to create a federal remedy for cybersquatting if the defendant breaches the standard of "bad faith intent to profit." Critics of ACPA see it as bad policy in that it is unilateral and may infringe on free speech.

B. **Common Law**. Section 757(b) of the Restatement (Second) of Torts addressed trade secrets. Courts examine five factors to determine liability.

C. **The Uniform Trade Secrets Act** defines trade secrets and covers (1) information that has potential value from being secret; (2) information regarding one-time events; and (3) negative information, such as test results showing what will not work for a particular process or product. The UTSA is more flexible than the common law test.

D. **Criminal Liability Under the Economic Espionage Act** falls upon any person who intentionally or knowingly steals a trade secret or knowingly receives or purchases a wrongfully obtained trade secret. The Act applies to any violation outside of the United States by a U.S. citizen or resident alien or by an organization organized in the United States.

XIII. **CREATING AND PROTECTING A TRADE SECRET.** There is no formal process to establish a trade secret. The information merely must remain private. Protection of the trade secret is best maintained through the implement of a protection program covering notification, identification, security, and exit interviews.

A. **Notification** must be written and made explained to all employees at orientation. Use of "confidential" stamps and signs should also be used. There should be confidentiality (or non-disclosure) agreements between the company and contractors.

B. **Identification** of trade secrets is not clear. One extreme is the view that everything within the workplace is a trade secret; the other holds that there must specific identification of each trade secret seeking protection.

C. **Security** measures must be taken. The disclosure of any trade secret for any reason, even by carelessness, destroys the legal protection. Digital information should be encrypted.

D. **Exit Interviews** should be conducted for employees leaving the company to reinforce disclosure of trade secrets and legal remedies against the employee if warranted.

XIV. **MISAPPROPRIATION OF TRADE SECRETS.** Individuals misappropriate trade secrets when they use or disclose another's secret or learn of a trade secret by an improper means.

A. **Inevitable Disclosure Doctrine** recognizes that former employees who work for a competitor may rely on or disclose the trade secrets gained through former employment. Some companies are attempting to ameliorate this problem privately. For example, in November 2000, Intel and Broadcom settled on undisclosed terms litigation sparked by Broadcom's hiring of three former Intel workers.

B. **Remedies**. The typical trade secret case may involve more than one form of relief:

　1. Injunction if there is irreparable harm, and/or

　2. Damages when trade secret owner has suffered financial harm, based on a contract or tort theory. The contract theory measures damages based on the loss of value of the trade secret. The tort theory measures damages harm or unjust enrichment.

　3. Punitive Damages are available for willful violations.

C. **Criminal Liability**. The Federal Economic Espionage Act and state statutes impose criminal sanctions on theft or wrongful use of trade secrets.

XV. **DATABASE PROTECTION**. In the United States, databases have no copyright protection, but the do in the EU. However one court may grant relief on the theory of trespass to chattels. E.g., *eBay v. Bidder's Edge*, 100 F. Supp. 2d 1058 (N.D. Cal. 2000).

INTELLECTUAL PROPERTY PROTECTION: COMPARATIVE ADVANTAGES				
	Trade Secret	**Copyright**	**Patent**	**Trademark**
Benefits	Very broad protection for sensitive, competitive information; very inexpensive	Prevents copying of a wide array of artistic and literary expressions, including software; very inexpensive.	Very strong protection; provides exclusive right to exclude others from making, using, and selling an invention; protects the idea itself.	Protects marks that customers use to identify a business; prevents others from using confusingly similar identifying marks.
Duration	So long as the information remains valuable and is kept confidential	Life of author plus 50 years; for corporations, 75 years from date of first publication or 100 years from date of creation, whichever is shorter.	20 years from date of filing utility or plant patent application; 14 years from date of filing design patent application.	As long as the mark is not abandoned and steps are taken to police its use.
Weaknesses	No protection from accidental disclosure, independent creation by a competitor, or disclosure by someone without a duty	Protects only particular way an idea is expressed, not the idea itself; hard to detect copying in digital age.	Must meet high standards of novelty, utility, and non-obviousness; often expensive and time consuming to pursue (especially when overseas patents are needed); must disclose invention to public.	Limited scope; protects corporate image and identity but little else; can be costly if multiple overseas registrations are needed.

	to maintain confidentiality.			
Required Steps	Take reasonable steps to protect— generally a trade secret protection program.	None required; however, notice and filing can strengthen rights and filing is required before an action for infringement can be filed.	Detailed filing with U.S. Patent and Trademark Office that requires search for prior art and hefty fees.	Only need to use mark in commerce; however, filing with U.S. Patent and Trademark Office is usually desirable to gain stronger protections.
International Validity of U.S. Rights?	No. Trade secret laws vary significantly by country, and some countries have no trade secret laws.	Generally, yes	No. Separate patent examinations and filings are required in each country unless they file international patent application under Patent Cooperation Treaty or file in the European Patent Office for the EU countries.	No. Separate filings are required in foreign jurisdictions, and a mark available in the U.S. may not be available overseas.

TECHNOLOGY LICENSING. Technology owners can benefit from technology by using it themselves or by licensing others to use it.

GLOBAL VIEW: THE MOVE TOWARD HARMONIZATION OF INTELLECTUAL PROPERTY REGIMES. Several multinational treaties coordinate the registration and patent process among the signatory countries. Among others are the Paris Convention and the Patent Cooperation Treaty. The Paris Convention (The International Convention for the Protection of Industrial Property Rights) encourages reciprocal recognition of patents, trademarks, service marks, and similar forms of intellectual property rights among signatory nations. The Patent Cooperation Treaty (the PCT) allows an inventor to file one international patent application with, for example, the World Intellectual Property Organization (WIPO), to receive patent protection in each signatory country. The *Madrid* Agreement Concerning the International Registration of Trademarks allows for centralized international registration of trademarks. The owner of a trademark in its home country can file at WIPO in Geneva for registration of its trademark in those signatory countries that it specifies. In addition, the Pan American Convention and the EU Community Trade mark (CTM) offer relief for those who claim violations of their intellectual property rights.

XVI. **THE RESPONSIBLE MANAGER:** Protecting Intellectual Property Rights. Some of a company's most important assets may be intangible forms of intellectual property. Managers seeking to protect their intellectual property should:

- Provide written notice to all employees that it has a policy for IP and trade secrets and violating the policies will result in civil and criminal liability.
- Reminded exiting employees of their obligations
- Inspect materials and computers from exiting employees.

- Develop a global patent strategy that accommodates the different international legal requirements for protection and enforcement.
- File all copyrightable matters with the U.S. Copyright Office as a prerequisite for filing an infringement suit for a work of U.S. origin.
- Work to preserve trademarks from dilution and infringement.
- Examine the benefits and liabilities of technology licensing.
- Examine insurance policies for intellectual property, data, e-commerce and licensing provisions.

XVII. **INSIDE STORY: DIGITAL MILLENNIUM COPYRIGHT ACT.** Clinton signed the DMCA in October 1998. The DMCA implemented the WIPO Copyright Treaty and the WIPO Performances and Phonograms Treaty. The DMCA applied to creative works transmitted in digital form over the Internet. Scientists, professors, librarians and others opposed the DMCA because it did not allow immunity for educational use. Congress later added such exemptions. In its applications the DCMA academics and programmers who sought to publish academic papers and share software faced civil and criminal penalties for violating the DMCA. Critics of the DMCA claim that copyright holders were already protected under pre-existing laws. There have been proposals to amend the DMCA.

STUDY QUESTIONS

True-False Questions

___ 1. Trademarks are the oldest recognized forms of intellectual property.

___ 2. Under the Constitution, the Executive Branch has exclusive right to determine who may receive a patent and how long the patents run.

___ 3. Utility patents are the most frequently used type of patent.

___ 4. A design patent lasts for 14 years from the date on which the patent application was filed.

___ 5. Plant patents protect any distinct and new variety of non-naturally existing plant that is asexually reproduced.

___ 6. Anti-file estoppel prevents a patent owner from asserting a claim interpretation that is at odds with the application on file in the Patent Office.

___ 7. Plaintiffs rarely waive their right to a jury trial in patent infringement cases.

___ 8. Facts are copyrightable.

__ 9. When an idea and its expression are inseparable, the unit doctrine dictates that the expression is not copyrightable.

__ 10. Copyright infringers may face civil and criminal penalties.

__ 11. The Supreme Court held that a parody that uses no more than is necessary of the original work as to make it recognizable is a fair use of the work and therefore not actionable.

__ 12. Courts have been strongly against copyright protection for computer code.

__ 13. Trade names cannot be registered under federal law unless they have been used as trademarks or service marks.

__ 14. Trademarks benefit only producers.

__ 15. Secondary meaning is necessary to establish trademark protection for descriptive marks, geographic terms, and personal names.

Multiple-Choice Questions

___1. U.S. patent law provides for all of the following kinds of patents *except:*
A. Utility.
B. Engineering.
C. Design.
D. Plant.

__ 2. The patent owner has the exclusive right to use the work for a nonrenewable period of ___ years from the date the patent application was filed.
A. 20.
B. 10.
C. 17.
D. life plus 50.

__ 3. Which would get a patent?
A. A statement of scientific principles.
B. A film about the laws of nature.
C. A technique to discover naturally occurring, yet previously unknown, substances.
D. None of the above.

__ 4. A _____ patent protects any novel, original, and ornamental design for an article of manufacture.
A. Utility.

    B. Plant.
    C. Design.
    D. Software.

__ 5. Each patent application contains all of the following *except* the:
    A. Claims.
    B. Specifications.
    C. Drawings.
    D. Deposition of the inventor.

__ 6. All of the following are types of patent infringement except?
    A. Direct.
    B. Negligent.
    C. Indirect.
    D. Contributory.

__ 7. Which of the following is a defense to a patent infringement action?

    I. Noninfringement.
    II. Invalidity.
    III. Misuse.
    IV. Recklessness.

    A. I, II, and III.
    B. I, II, and IV.
    C. I, II, III, and IV.
    D. II, III, and IV.

__ 8. A patent is presumed to be valid. A court may find a patent invalid for all of the following reasons *except:*
    A. The invention was not novel.
    B. The patent was for a mental process.
    C. A requirement of patent law was not met.
    D. None of the above.

__ 9. Which of the following is a remedy for patent infringement?

    I. Damages.
    II. Injunction.
    III. Court costs.

    A. I, II, and III.
    B. I and II.
    C. II and III.

D. I and III.

__ 10. Under the first sale doctrine, once the copyright owner sells it, the owner has:
   A. Not lost absolute control over the item.
   B. Retained control over the copyright for twelve months.
   C. Waived her exclusive statutory right to control distribution.
   D. Retained her right to control subsequent distribution.

__ 11. Jessica writes and copyrights a book. How long will the copyright last?
   A. Her lifetime.
   B. Her lifetime plus 70 years.
   C. 95 years after it is first published.
   D. 120 years after she writes the book.

__ 12. Software companies estimate they lose $_____ a year to pirated software.
   A. 15 billion.
   B. 100 billion.
   C. 100 million.
   D. 500 million.

__ 13. One can obtain a trademark of which of the following?

   I.   Distinctive sounds.
   II. Distinctive shapes.
   III. Distinctive odors.
   IV. Distinctive colors.

   A. I, II, and IV.
   B. I, II, III, and IV.
   C. I, III, and IV.
   D. II and IV.

__ 14. _____ marks are real words whose ordinary meaning has nothing to do with the trademarked product.
   A. Suggestive.
   B. Inherent.
   C. Fanciful.
   D. Arbitrary.

__ 15. Which if the following is *not* a factor used to determine whether or not something is a trade secret?
   A. The extent the information is known outside the business.
   B. The ease of duplicating the information.
   C. The cost of the information.

D. The extent to which measures are taken to protect the information.

Essay Questions

1. Why do many experts believe that the PTO is issuing business software patents too readily?

2. Why should fair use be allowed?

3. What is the purpose of a trademark?

CHAPTER 12
THE EMPLOYMENT AGREEMENT

INTRODUCTION

Managers must know employment law to minimize the legal risks for their companies. This chapter examines traditional at-will employment, and various exceptions to the rule, e.g. wrongful termination, and public policy. The chapter also explores various common law principles on labor and employment. Further the chapter examines employment procedures such as drug and polygraph testing. Then topics tied to federal law and immigration law are reviewed.

CHAPTER OUTLINE

I.   **AT-WILL EMPLOYMENT**. Most Americans are hired "at will." They have no written employment contract, no express agreement as to how long the job will last, and either the employer or employee may terminate the arrangement without cause. The modern trend, however, is toward some level of protection against discharge in certain circumstances. Exceptions include:

    A.   **Employees Not Subject to the At-Will Rule.**

        1.   Public Employees. Most employees of federal, state, and local government agencies have long worked under civil service or merit systems that provide for tenure, require just cause for discharge, and guarantee administrative procedures to determine whether there is "just cause" for discharge.

        2.   Employees with Individual Contracts. Private-sector employees can avoid at-will status by negotiating a contract that provides for a specific term of employment and defines how the contract can be terminated.

        3.   Union Contracts usually require just cause for termination with arbitration procedures whereby an employee can challenge his or her discharge.

    B.   **WRONGFUL DISCHARGE** is the termination of employment without good cause, against public policy and, at common law, breached an implied contract and implied covenant of good faith.

        1.   The Public Policy Exception. The employer is prohibited from discharging the employee for reasons that violate public policy. Greatest protection is given for an employee's refusal to commit an unlawful act at employer's request.

- Remedies. Some courts hold that an employee may seek both tort and contract actions, damages for pain and suffering, and possibly punitive damages.

- State Sources of Public Policy. Across the states, there are different rules for causes of action as well as available remedy. E.g. *Ness v. Hocks* 526 P.2d 512 (Or. 1975) (allowing the excuse of jury duty to bar termination of an at-will contract).

- Federal Sources of Public Policy. Some federal statutes forbid termination in retaliation for an employee report of a violation of rights or statute. See OSHA and the FLSA.

- Nongovernmental Sources include professional codes of conduct and ethics, e.g. the Professional and Ethical Standard for Attorneys.

- Whistleblower Statues. Whistle blowers reports illegal or unethical activity of their companies or supervisors to legal authorities. In particular one federal law is the Sabanes-Oxley Act of 2002 (SOX, named after its legislative co-sponsors). Save an applicable state or federal statute an employee can be terminated for such reports.

  > **Case 12.1--*Collins v. Beazer Homes USA, Inc.*,** 334 F. Supp. 2d 1365 (N.D. Ga. 2004). Judy Collins accepted a job as director of marketing for the Florida division of Beazer Homes, subject to a 90-day, at-will period. Collins reported what she perceived as criminal and unethical behavior of her supervisor, Marty Schaffer, to Beazer's vice president of Sales. Schaffer terminated Collins. Collins sued for a violation of SOX. Collins was allowed to sue as SOX trumped the at-will provision of her contract.

2. **Implied Contracts**. Some employees work so long, and have established a given relationship with the employer that courts will see the relationship was as if there were a contract. E.g., *Toussaint v. Blue Cross & Blue Shield of Michigan*, 292 N.W.2d 880 (Mich. 1980). Finding of an implied contract only bars dismissal without cause.

3. **Implied Covenant of Good Faith and Fair Dealing**. Employers cannot terminate at-will employees solely to deprive them of earned bonuses or pay.

II.   **Right to Fair Procedure**. Some courts acknowledge a common-law right to fair procedure, protecting individuals from arbitrary exclusion. Individuals having this right must be given notice of the charges against them and an opportunity to respond to those charges.

III. **Fraudulent Inducement**. During difficult economic times, a business may engage in puffery and exaggeration to keep and attract highly qualified personnel (*infra*). Further employers cannot induce employees to quit or retire for fraudulent reasons. *Rodowicz v. Massachusetts Mutual Life Insurance Co.*, 192 F.3d 162 (1st Cir. 1999).

> **Case 12.2—*Lazar v. Rykoff-Sexton, Inc.*,** 90 P.2d 981 (Cal. 1996). Lazar was President of a family-owned restaurant equipment company in New York. In September 1989, a vice-president of Rykoff-Sexton, Inc. (Rykoff) contacted Lazar and asked him to move to Los Angeles. The company intensively recruited Lazar through February 1990 promising him significant pay increases, advancement, security and a long-term relationship with the company. Rykoff represented that the company was strong financially and anticipated profits and growth. Based on these representations, Lazar and his family moved to L.A. Lazar performed in an exemplary manner. Lazar was terminated three months later and discovered the representations were materially false. Lazar was unable to find comparable employment and sued Rykoff. Lazar was due recovery on a cause of action for fraudulent inducement.

IV.   **NON-COMPETE AGREEMENT (COVENANT NOT TO COMPETE)** is a contractual provision or clause which is part of another agreement (e.g., employment contract) that is designed to protect a company's interests by limiting a former employee's ability to use trade secrets when working for a competitor, or in a competing business. Courts will enforce only reasonable restrictions on competition that do not place a great hardship. Generally employees cannot leave and take the employer's clients.

> **Case 12.3--*BDO Seidman v. Hirshberg*,** 712 N.E.2d 1220 (N.Y. 1999). Hirshberg was employed in the Buffalo, New York office of BDO, an accounting firm. As a condition of promotion, Hirshberg signed a "Manager's Agreement." Paragraph SIX of the agreement provided that if, within eighteen months following the termination of his employment, Hirshberg served any former client of BDO Buffalo office, then he would be required to compensate BDO Seidman "for the loss and damages suffered" in an amount equal to one-and-a-half times the fees BDO Seidman charged that client over the last fiscal year of patronage. Hirshberg resigned from BDO and BDO claimed it lost 100 clients who were billed $138,000 in the year Hirshberg left the firm. BDO sued and the trial court invalidated the reimbursement clause on the grounds that it

constituted an overbroad and unenforceable anticompetitive agreement. BDO appealed. The Court of Appeals reversed and found the agreement was reasonable and largely enforceable.

V. **AT-WILL EMPLOYMENT AND EMPLOYMENT PRACTICES.** Courts consider statements made during pre-employment interviews and on application forms when determining employment parameters. If an employer wants to preserve the traditional legal right to discharge employees at-will, it should see that limitations on this right are not inadvertently created. Employers should do the following: (a) make overt expressions about the at-will relationship in the employment application or the personnel manual; (b) draft personnel policies to ensure the language expressly reserves those rights that the employer wishes to maintain, especially with respect to discharge; (c) treat employees fairly and consistently; (d) train managers to use internal discipline that may lead to termination; (e) compel binding on employee; and (f) establish an internal grievance procedure.

VI. **RECOMMENDATIONS FOR FORMER EMPLOYEES.** References from former employers are problematic; they should be fair and not impugn the reputation of former employees. As well, when an employer gives an untrue assessment of a former employee, the former employer may be liable not only to the new employer who relies on the recommendation, but also to third persons physically harmed as a foreseeable result of the recommendation.

    A. **Conditional Privilege.** Employers have a conditional privilege to communicate information concerning a former employee to a prospective employer. Under the *doctrine of self-publication* an otherwise defamatory communication by an employer to an employee may constitute publication when the employer could foresee that the employee would be required to repeat the communication to a prospective employer. Most jurisdictions require a showing of abuse on the part of the former employer.

    B. **Waiver.** If an employee signed a waiver and release, the employer may be protected against liability for defamation claims by that former employee.

VII. **EMPLOYER TESTING AND SURVEILLANCE.** Employers are increasingly adopting drug-screening programs in an effort to avoid decreased productivity, quality control problems, absenteeism on the job, accidents, and employee theft that can result from drug and alcohol abuse.

    A. **DRUG TESTING.** Employees may challenge the testing on the following grounds: (a) breach of employment contract; (b) no justification for the test; (c) violation of public policy in re privacy; (d) defamation based on an erroneous test; (e) emotional distress; (f) discrimination.

Generally drug testing is permissible depending on four factors: (a) the scope of the testing program (random testing is hard to defend); (b) whether the employer is a public or private employer, (c) whether the state constitutional guarantees of right to privacy; and (d) whether there are state statutes regulating drug testing.

1. Public Employees are afforded greater protection than private employees against unreasonable searches and seizures under the Fourth Amendment and the right to privacy. With only a few exceptions, there is no federal constitutional limitation on urine and drug testing in the private sector.

2. Constitutional Protection. Under the U.S. Constitution one has protection against state actors, but some state constitutions extend Fourth Amendment-type privacy rights to prevent private searches. Contrast *Luddtke v. Nabors Alaska Drilling, Inc.*, 768 P.2d 1123 (Alaska 1989) with *Semore v. Pool*, 217 Cal. App. 3d 1087 (Cal. Ct. App. 1990).

3. Statutory Regulation. Some states have legislation regulating when, how, and where employers can compel drug tests from employees.

B. **HEALTH SCREENING AND GENETIC TESTING** involves many of the same issues that arise in the context of drug testing. As of January 2005, Congress had failed to enact any legislation banning genetic testing. At least 31 states have outlawed genetic discrimination in the workplace. Employees may have a right of action to sue for genetic discrimination under the Fourth Amendment, Title VII, and the ADA.

C. **POLYGRAPH TESTING OF EMPLOYEES**. The Employee Polygraph Protection Act of 1988[1] (EPPA) does not ban polygraph testing, but makes it unlawful for employers to require employees to take a polygraph, to rely on the results, or to threaten adverse action if the test is not taken. Employees cannot be compelled to waive their EPPA rights in advance. Still Employers may test employees who are reasonably suspected of conduct injurious to the business, as well as applicants or employees in certain businesses involving security services or the handling of drugs. But many states ban the use of polygraph results to punish employees.

D. **EMPLOYEE SURVEILLANCE**. Over 80 percent of surveyed companies engage in monitoring their employees. Employers have a legitimate interest in observing their employees to ensure quality control and productivity, but some surveillance may transgress the employee's privacy rights. Employee's rights must be balanced by the "operational realities" of the workplace. See *O'Connor v. Ortega*, 480 U.S. 709 (1987).

---

[1] 29 U.S.C. §§ 2001-2009 (1988).

Case 12.4--*TBG Insurance Services Corp. v. Superior Court of Los Angeles County*, 96 Cal. App. 4th 443 (Cal. Ct. App. 2002). Robert Ziemski was an executive for TBG. Ziemski agreed that he would use TBG computers for business purposes only and consented to be monitored. Ziemski visited pornographic sites and was terminated. Ziemski claimed there were pornographic pop-ups and that others used the TBG computer at his home. Given the agreements Ziemski had no reasonable expectation of privacy and a trial court would have to determine if Ziemski was fired for cause.

VIII. **RESPONSIBILITY FOR WORKER SAFETY**. Both federal and state laws require employers to provide a reasonably safe workplace.

A. **OCCUPATIONAL SAFETY AND HEALTH ADMINISTRATION** requires that employers establish safe and healthy working environments, and regulates such things as exposure to hazardous chemicals, protective gear, fire protection, and workplace temperatures and ventilation. Employers have a duty to provide a place of employment that is free from *recognized hazards* that are causing or are likely to cause death or serious physical harm to employees. OSHA inspectors are allowed to conduct surprise inspections at worksites. There is a trend toward increasing the number of criminal prosecutions of employers for OSHA violations. A manager can be held criminally responsible for serious workplace-safety violations.

VIEW FROM CYBERSPACE: BIG BROTHER IS READING YOUR E-MAIL. Employees are frequently using e-mail and instant messages. Nearly 75% of employers are monitoring their employee communications. Most court uphold the employer's right to review such electronic messages. To avoid problems employers should develop and post clear guidelines about private and work-related communications.

1. Criminal Prosecutions. OSHA makes it a misdemeanor to cause the death of a worker through willful violation of safety laws. Such violations may be prosecuted under state law as well. Since 1982, more than 170,000 Americans have been killed on the job. Federal and state officials only investigated one-quarter of those. Nearly 2,200 were determined to have been caused by willful safety violations.

2. State Analogues to OSHA. Many states have OSHA-type laws. California has the strictest laws.

B.   **State Criminal Prosecutions**. State prosecutions beyond OSHA bring charges for battery, reckless homicide, and more. Prosecutions against corporate managers have been mixed.

C.   **Liability for Terrorist Attacks**. Since September 11, 2001, OSHA has encouraged employers to have emergency action plans and many businesses have created such.

D.   **Tort Liability for Violence in the Workplace**. Employers also face potential liability for violence in the workplace perpetrated by employees or their former lovers or spouses. Once an employer is informed about the risk of violence or takes an interest in the case, it exposes itself to liability for negligence if it fails to take reasonable steps to prevent injury.

IX.   **WORKERS' COMPENSATION**. State workers' compensation statutes provide for coverage of income and medical expenses for employees who suffer work-related accidents or illnesses.[2] The statutes are based on a "no-fault" principle that holds that the risks of injury in the workplace should be borne by industry. Workers' compensation can be provided through insurance policies. Generally the benefit paid through workers' compensation is the only payment the injured worker will receive and bars lawsuits.

X.   **MINIMUM WAGE, OVERTIME, AND CHILD LABOR.** Under the Fair Labor Standards Act (FSLA) of 1938 the federal government has set a baseline for wages and work hours. Some states impose stricter standards and higher minimum wage laws.

A.   **Who Is Covered**. FLSA applies nearly all employees and employers. FLSA does not apply to independent contractors, or other occupations like waiters or farm workers. If the law is violated both individuals and corporations can be held liable.

B.   **Hours Worked**. As long as there is compensation for overtime, FLSA does not limit the number of hours that an employee may work. Employees may take *Comp time*, extra paid vacation time, in lieu of extra pay for overtime work.

Case 12.5--*Christensen v. Harris County*, 529 U.S. 576 (2000). Sheriff Thomas of Harris County, Texas, and 127 deputy sheriffs agreed to accept compensatory time, instead of cash, for overtime. As they accumulated comp time, Harris County became concerned that it lacked the financial resources to pay employees who (1) worked overtime after reaching the statutory cap on comp time accrual or (2) left their jobs with large amounts of accrued time. So Harris County implemented a policy to cap comp

---

[2] *See* Constance E. Bagley & Craig E. Dauchy, *The Entrepreneur's Guide To Business Law*, p. 378-89 (1998).

time. The sheriffs sued, claiming that the policy violated FLSA. The Supreme Court upheld Harris County's policy requiring employees to use comp time rather than accrue it.

C. **Compensation**. FLSA requires that employees be compensated for all hours worked. In the case of professional or off-site employees, the number of hours worked is often contested. Travel time to and from work is not generally considered as work time. *Kavanagh v. Grand Union Co.*, 192 F.3d 269 (2d. Cir. 1999).

D. **Minimum Wage**. FLSA requires that, with some exceptions, every non-exempt employee be paid one and one-half times the regular rate of pay for hours worked in excess of forty in a work-week. Some cities are imposing so-called living wage ordinances. See *RUI One Corp. v. City of Berkeley*, 371 F.3d 117 (9th Cir. 2004).

E. **Overtime**. The Department of Labor establishes guidelines as to declare which jobs fall under FLSA protection. Exempt employees are not covered by the hours and wage guidelines. Generally, an *exempt employee* is paid a minimum salary per week or month (*e.g.* executive, administrative, and professional employees), while *non-exempt employees* are often paid an hourly wage. Those in management with subordinates, or who can work with minimal oversight are usually exempt.

     1. Minimum Salary. Employees who earn less than $455 per week or $23,660 per year are non-exempt. For those earning between $23,600 and $100,000 the Department of Labor examines the particulars of the job to determine if one is exempt from the FLSA.

     2. Salary Basis Test. If employers make salary deductions for taxes and other benefits, the employee may be deemed non-exempt.

     3. Duties Test. Department of Labor will review the duties of different types of workers to determine their status. Executives, Administrators, Professional employees, Computer programmers, and Outside Sales Employees will be exempt of they meet DOL criteria.

F. **Child Labor under FLSA**. The FLSA was designed to prevent child labor and abuse. In general those under 18 cannot work. Children under 14 cannot work except in specified agricultural occupations. Those from 14-15 may work in some occupations, but only if the employment occurs outside of school hours and does not exceed daily and weekly hour limits. Teens aged 16-18 may work but not in hazardous manufacturing occupations.

G. **Modern-Day Slavery**. Many workers are trafficked to the U.S. from Latin America, China, other parts of Asia, Africa and Europe. They are brought to work in factories, on farms, as domestic servants, or in sweatshops. Under federal law, the Department of Justice has prosecuted some of these cases.

XI. **Immigration Law**. In October 2003 federal officials arrested nearly 300 immigrant workers at 61 different Wal-Mart locations. Workers were arrested and deported, Wal-Mart was threatened with fines. Since 1986 it is illegal to hire undocumented workers.

A. **Obtaining Authorization**. Foreign workers must obtain work visas, e.g., an H-1B, available only for professional and highly skilled employees.

B. **Verifying Authorization**. The federal government requires that employers use an I-9 form to verify one's employment eligibility.

C. **Amnesty Proposal**. Given the high number of undocumented workers from Mexico and Latin America, George Bush advocated an amnesty program for aliens. Congress never took action on the proposal.

ECONOMIC PERSPECTIVE: OUTSOURCING. American companies are increasingly importing manufactured components. As former blue-collar manufacturing jobs are lost to cheap labor overseas, the trend has extended to white-collar work in computer programming, communications, tele-marketing. Economists see that the short-term dislocations should not have a long-term detrimental effect on the economy.

XII. LABOR-MANAGEMENT RELATIONS. Since the 1930s, federal law has been implemented to smooth labor-management relations.

A. **National Labor Relations Act**. Grants rights to employees, not independent contractors, or supervisors.

B. **Union Representation**. Under the NRLA, workers may hold elections and choose to form a union, or not. If certified, the employer must negotiate with the union instead of individual employees.

C. **Unfair Labor Practices by Employers**. Under the NRLA, employers cannot interfere with union organizing, spy on employees, or induce employees to reject the union. Employers cannot retaliate against employees who support union activities.

D. **Lawful and Unlawful Strikes and Economic Action**. Laborers may conduct strikes for better pay, compensation and working conditions. Such is legal unless there exists a court order or consent decree whereby the union is barred from withholding its labor. The NRLA forbids other types of economic protest including recognitional picketing and secondary boycotts.

E. **Non-Strike-Related Unfair Labor Practices by Unions**. Union members cannot coerce workers to join or discriminate against others based on race, gender, creed, or religion. Unions cannot encourage employers to discriminate against non-union members.

GLOBAL VIEW: THE RIGHT TO CONTINUED EMPLOYMENT. Various nations have different rules about labor-relations and "at-will" employment. The EU has not harmonized laws across the different nations. Though distinct, each nation generally allows employees to challenge dismissal. In the United Kingdom, the law largely parallels that of the United States. Under current British law employees may be terminated for cause and misconduct, otherwise the employee may challenge their dismissal. France extends greater protections. Generally the employee must receive written notice. In Japan employers must give employees 30 days notice of termination or be paid one month's salary at termination. Under Indian law, courts have wide latitude to intervene over employment decisions and employers with businesses with more than 100 workers must gain permission before terminating workers.

THE RESPONSIBLE MANAGER: Avoiding Wrongful Discharge Suits. Courts appear to be moving toward providing all employees the protection against discharge without good cause, what was traditionally offered only by union contracts. More often employers are being sued for wrongful discharge. In order to reduce liability management should articulate the kind of contractual relationship it wishes to have with its employees, commit to a code of conduct, established processes, and fairness. Lastly managers need to be familiar and comply with all FLSA issues. Further though American managers typically mistrust unions, studies show that a unionized workplace has higher productivity and fewer days lost from illness.

INSIDE STORY: WORKING "OFF THE CLOCK." Though the FLSA requires overtime pay for work in excess of 40 hours per week, many employers are finding way around the rule. They demand employees clock-out, yet remain on the job, threaten termination, cheat employees from earned pay, and make promotions contingent upon unpaid overtime. The practice is common in the service industry, poultry plants and places were immigrants work. Companies like Wal-Mart, T-Mobile, Kinko's, Nordstrom's and others commonly force employees to work "off the clock."

STUDY QUESTIONS

True-False Questions

___ 1. A contract that allows an employee to quit any time, and an employer to fire the employee at any time, even without notice, is called a free-will contract.

__ 2. Termination for refusing to commit an illegal act is known as a retaliatory discharge.

__ 3. A whistle-blower statute is an example of a statutory protection for at-will employees.

__ 4. When there is an implied employment contract, an employer may not legally terminate an employee suspected of misconduct without good cause.

__ 5. Most states have recognized the implied covenant of good faith and fair dealing .

__ 6. A covenant not to compete restricting a real estate agent from competing with the former real estate broker for three years within a 200 miles radius of the broker would probably be valid.

__ 7. A statement on an employment application form stating that all employment is at-will, will probably not be upheld if an employee handbook states that employees will not be terminated without just cause.

__ 8. Random drug testing is the most difficult for employers to defend.

__ 9. The EPPA completely bans the use of polygraph exams for employment reasons.

__ 10. OSHA requires employers to provide a place of employment that is free from *all hazards* that are causing or are likely to cause death or serious physical harm to employees.

__ 11. Under OSHA, managers and officers of corporations have been prosecuted for serious violations that have led to the death of employees.

__ 12. Employers have a conditional privilege to communicate information concerning a former employee to a prospective employer.

__ 13. The Fair Labor Standards Act absolutely limits the number of hours an employee may work in a workday or week.

__ 14. Drug testing in the private sector has no federal constitutional limitations.

__ 15. Managers should re-evaluate disciplinary policies and employee handbooks for exempt personnel to avoid reclassification of their employees.

Multiple-Choice Questions

__ 1. Wrongful discharge is *NOT* supported by which of the following theories?

A. Tortious interference with contracts.
B. Public policy.
C. Implied contract.
D. Implied covenant of good faith.

__ 2. Which of the following can be a wrongful termination because of public policy?

I. Criminal statute.
II. Civil statute.
III. Professional code of ethics.

A. I, II, and III.
B. I and III.
C. II and III.
D. I and II.

__ 3. The employer's right to terminate an employee without cause may be subject to and restricted by:
A. Civil service systems.
B. Union contracts.
C. Whistle-blower contracts.
D. All of the above.

__ 4. Unreasonableness in a covenant not to compete can be found on which grounds?

I. Geography.
II. Duration.
III. Employer protection.
IV. Over-specificity.

A. I, II, III, IV
B. I, II, IV
C. I, II, III
D. II, III, IV

__ 5. Which statement is *false* concerning pre-employment practices?
A. The employer should decide whether or not to establish an internal grievance procedure.
B. An employer cannot enter into an agreement with an employee to resolve disputes by arbitration.
C. If there is a progressive discipline policy, appropriate supervisors need to be trained on the policy.
D. The handbook and manuals need to be consistent.

__ 6. Why are drug tests for employees of limited use?

I. Duration of the drugs in the body.
II. Erroneous results.
III. Time of ingestion.

A. I and III.
B. II and III.
C. I, II and III.
D. I and II.

__ 7. The EPPA generally makes it unlawful for employers to do all but which of the following?
A. Request an applicant to take a polygraph test.
B. Rely on the results of a polygraph test given an employee.
C. Take adverse action against an employee for refusing to take a polygraph.
D. All of the above.

__ 8. _____ is authorized by Congress to govern work issues concerning fire protection and workplace temperatures and ventilation.
A. EPPA.
B. OSHA.
C. EPA.
D. HMO.

__ 9. OSHA inspectors are allowed to conduct surprise inspections at worksites in all of the following situations *except* which?
A. When OSHA believes there is imminent danger.
B. If an employee has filed a compliant.
C. When a fatality may occur.
D. None of the above

__ 10. Types of OSHA violations include all but which of the following?
A. *De minimis* violations.
B. Nonserious violations.
C. Serious violations.
D. Capital violations.

__ 11. Workers' compensation can be provided through:
A. Self-insurance.
B. Insurance purchased from the state.
C. Insurance purchased from a private insurer.

D. All of the above.

___ 12. The FLSA was established to regulate all of the following *except:*
   A. Minimum wage.
   B. Overtime pay.
   C. Child labor.
   D. Maximum number of hours worked per week.

___ 13. Generally a child cannot work if she is below____ years of age.
   A. 14.
   B. 15.
   C. 16.
   D. 18.

___ 14. Under the NRLA, employers may not:
   A. Fire all unionized workers.
   B. Refuse to negotiate with a recognized union.
   C. Pay non-union workers more than unionized employees for the same job at the same place of business.
   D. Engage in any of the above activities.

___ 15. Striking workers cannot be arrested and put in jail for which of the following?
   A. Establishing a secondary boycott.
   B. Protesting unsafe working conditions.
   C. Marching in front of a plant against police orders to disperse.
   D. Electing to reject a 30-year-old consent decree that they did not negotiate

Essay Questions

1. What are some of the factors that can give rise to an implied obligation to an employee only for good cause?

2. What do employers accomplish with covenants not to compete?

3. Why should a former employer not give an overly positive letter of recommendation about a former employee?

CHAPTER 13
CIVIL RIGHTS AND
EMPLOYMENT DISCRIMINATION

INTRODUCTION

Civil rights laws help ensure that every member of society has the opportunity to reach his or her full potential. Managers who fail to enact and enforce polices to ensure compliance with federal legislation prohibiting employment discrimination put their companies at risk of being penalized by large fines and judgments. This chapter provides an overview of federal legislation barring employment discrimination, with special attention to Title VII, the Age Discrimination in Employment Act, the Americans with Disabilities Act, and the Family and Medical Leave Act. It also illustrates the various legal theories pursued under each piece of legislation, and how those theories relate to legal and appropriate behavior by managers in a business environment. The chapter concludes with an application of discrimination laws to pre-employment practices, and a brief discussion of how these laws apply to persons hiring contingent or temporary workers.

I. **OVERVIEW OF CIVIL RIGHTS LEGISLATION.**

   A. **Scope**. The federal statutes discussed herein generally apply only to employees, not independent contractors. Though the laws in place since 1963 have tried to level the playing field, women still earn less than men on average.

   B. **Definition of Adverse Employment Action**. An employee must establish that the employer subjected him or her to an "adverse employment" action. There are differing views:

      1. Some courts hold an *expansive view* of adverse action, which includes such actions as demotions, refusals to hire or promote, unwarranted negative job evaluations, disadvantageous transfers or assignments, requiring an employee to work without lunch break, and changing an employee's schedule without notification.

      2. Other courts hold adverse action to mean only an act that materially affects the terms and conditions of employment, such as employee compensation or privileges.

      3. Other courts have adopted the most *restrictive* view, holding that only hiring, firing, promoting and demoting are adverse employment actions.

II. **ENFORCEMENT**. The Equal Employment Opportunity Commission (EEOC) is the primary enforcer of U.S. civil rights legislation, and often uses equally qualified "testers" to apply for entry-level positions in an effort to determine whether employment-discrimination by race, gender, national origin, or disability influences employment decisions.

III. **TITLE VII.**

A. **Scope**. Title VII bans discrimination based on an individual's race, color, religion, national origin, or gender.

B. **Traditional Discrimination Claims.**

1. **Disparate Treatment**. Plaintiff must prove that the employer intentionally discriminated against him or her by denying a benefit or privilege of employment because of his or her race, religion, gender, or national origin based on the following procedures:

   - The employee must first prove a *prima facie* case: (i) he or she is a member of a class of persons protected by Title VII and (ii) he or she was denied an available position or benefit he or she sought and for which he or she was qualified.

   - Next, the employer must present evidence that it had legitimate, nondiscriminatory grounds for its decision.

   - The employee must then prove that the grounds offered by the employer were only a pretext for intentional discrimination.

2. **Disparate Impact**. Plaintiff does not have to prove intentional discrimination; rather plaintiff must show that an employment practice, though neutral on its face, had a disparate *impact* on a protected group. To prove the case, plaintiff must show:

   - The specific employment practice caused, for example, a statistically significant disproportion between the racial composition of the persons holding the jobs at issue and the racial composition of the *qualified* persons in the relevant labor market. The employer then has the burden to demonstrate that the challenged practice is job-related and consistent with business necessity.

   - If the job requires no special skills, then all members of the labor pool are considered when doing the statistical analysis necessary to determine whether a facially neutral policy has a disparate impact.

- The business justification offered by the employer to justify the disparate impact must relate to job performance.

C.   **Harassment** claims typically address sex or gender bias or mistreatment, but may include harassment on the grounds of race, ethnicity, religion, etc.

  1.   Sexual Harassment.

    - *Quid Pro Quo* **Harassment** occurs when a specific, job-related adverse action, such as denial of a promotion, is in retaliation for a person's refusal to respond to his or her supervisor's sexual advances. The employer is always liable in cases of *quid pro quo* harassment.

    - **Hostile Environment Harassment**. The *threat* of adverse job action in retaliation for rebuffing sexual advances is not *quid pro quo* if the threat is not carried out. Instead, it is a form of hostile environment.

    - **Defining a Hostile Work Environment**. Courts consider the frequency of the conduct, whether it is physically threatening or humiliating or a mere offensive utterance, and whether it unreasonably interferes with an employee's work performance.

    - **Same Sex Sexual Harassment**. In *Oncale v. Sundowner Offshore Services*, 505 U.S. 75 (1988) the U.S. Supreme Court held that same-sex harassment involving heterosexuals or homosexuals may be actionable under Title VII.

    - **Sexual Orientation Harassment**. The federal circuits are split on whether on has a cause of action under Title VII for harassment on the basis of sexual orientation. Contrast *Simonton v. Runyan*, 232 F.3d 33 (2d Cir. 2000) with *Rene v. MGM Grand Hotel*, 305 F.3d 1061 (9th Cir. 2002).

  2.   Racial, National Origin, and Religious Harassment claims must follow the rule in *Harris v. Forklift Systems, Inc.*, 510 U.S. 17 (1993). Though plaintiff usually must show a pattern, harassment from a superior may be sufficient. See *Taylor v. Metzger*, 706 A.2d 685 (N.J. 1998).

  3.   Liability for Hostile Environment. Employers are responsible for all torts committed by employees acting within the scope of employment. If a supervisor fails to promote a woman due to her gender, the employer is

liable for sex discrimination. However, if a supervisor harasses an employee, that falls outside the scope of employment.

- Negligence. The employer is negligent with respect to sexual harassment if he knew or should have known of the harassment, but failed to stop it by taking appropriate corrective measures. E.g., *Ferris v. Delta Airlines*, 277 F.3d 128 (2d. Cir. 2001).

VIEW FROM CYBERSPACE: HARASSMENT IN THE VIRTUAL OFFICE. In 1989, Tammy Blakely, a pilot at Continental began to suffer sexual harassment. Shortly thereafter, male pilots posted derogatory remarks about her on bulletin board. The on-line bulletin board was provided by CompuServe but Continental required its pilots to use it to see flight schedules. Given the overt nature of the postings, the court held that Continental management knew of the hostile work environment and had a duty to stop it. *Blakely v. Cont'l Airlines, Inc.*, 751 A.2d 538 (N.J. 2000).

- Aided-in-the-Agency Relation and Supervisor Harassment. Employers are vicariously liable for harassment. See *Faragher v. City of Boca Raton*, 524 U.S. 775 (1998). But there are affirmative defenses. Management must show it took steps to address or prevent harassment.

    Case 13.1 *Hill v. American General Finance, Inc.* 218 F.3d 639 (7th Cir. 2000). Louise Hill was subject to racial and sexual harassment from her immediate supervisor, Darin Brandt. Ms. Hill complained to upper management, Gary English. English told Brandt to stop, later fined Brandt but also transferred Hill – limiting her capacity to earn commissions. Hill resigned and sued for harassment. The district court dismissed and the ruling was upheld on the grounds that AGF took adequate and appropriate steps to prevent and stop harassment.

- Personal Liability. Generally supervisors cannot be held personally liable for the harassment of their immediate subordinates. However see *Patterson v. County of Oneida, New York*, 375 F.3d 206 (2d Cir. 2004).

D.   **Duty to Accommodate Religious Beliefs**. Employer should accommodate religious beliefs but need not suffer hardship. See *Endres*, *infra*.

    Case 13.2 *Endres v. Indiana State Police*, 349 F.3d 922 (7th Cir. 2003). Endres, a police officer, was assigned, randomly, to work as a Gaming

Commission agent at a casino. Endres requested a transfer on religious grounds, but was denied. He then refused to report for work and was fired. Endres sued, and the defendant moved for dismissal. On appeal the Seventh Circuit held that it would be impractical for police officers to refuse assignment without creating a hardship on the employer. Endres suit was dismissed.

E.   **Retaliation**. Employers can be held liable for retaliation against employees who have complained about sexual harassment or other types of discrimination. Actions allegedly taken to prevent further harassment may be deemed retaliatory if they harm the employee's employment situation. E.g., *White v. Burlington Northern & Santa Fe Railway Co.*, 364 F.3d 789 (6th Cir. 2004).

F.   **Special Applications of Title VII**. The civil rights legislation was designed to prevent discrimination on race, religion, and sex. The law has expanded to reach more subtle forms of discrimination.

1.   Pregnancy Discrimination is, on its face, a form of sex discrimination under Title VII. Employers must provide the same compensation for disabilities related to pregnancy and childbirth as they provide for any other disability. But see *Stout v. Baxter Healthcare Corp.*, 282 F.3d 856 (5th Cir. 2002).

2.   Fetal-Protection Policies. Certain chemicals are harmful to an unborn child and can create an action for an unsafe work environment. Some companies used "fetal-protection policies" and bar women from certain jobs, but such can be found discriminatory. Compare *Automobile Workers v. Johnson Controls, Inc.*, 499 U.S. 187 (1991) with *Asad v. Continental Airlines*, 328 F. Supp. 2d 772 (N.D. Ohio 2004).

3.   English-Only Laws. The EEOC takes the position that "English-only" workplace rules are akin to discrimination against race or national origin. *EEOC v. Premier Operator Servs., Inc.*, 113 F. Supp. 2d 1066, (N.D. Tex 2000).

4.   Dress Codes at the workplace are generally allowed, but must not impose gender or religious discrimination.

G.   **Defenses under Title VII**. There are a number of statutory defenses.

1.   Bona Fide Occupational Qualification (BFOQ) allows an employer to hire an individual on the basis of religion, gender, or national origin, *if* such a quality is a BFOQ for that particular business.

2. Seniority and Merit Systems for distinguishing pay are expressly excluded from Title VII.

3. After-Acquired Evidence. If, during discovery, an employer learns that the plaintiff violated company rules, the plaintiff's claim may be dismissed on the grounds the employer could have discharged the employee for misconduct. But see *McKennon v. Nashville Banner Publishing Co.*, 513 U.S. 352 (1995).

H. **Remedies Under Title VII** include: (1) lost salary and benefits, (2) reinstatement or "front pay" equal to what the employee would have received had the individual not been discharged, (3) injunctive relief to stop prohibited discriminatory actions, (4) future losses, (5) emotional pain and suffering, (6) inconvenience, and (7) punitive damages.

1. Punitive Damages. Plaintiff must demonstrate that the employer engaged in a discriminatory practice with *malice* or *reckless indifference* to the federally protected rights. The employer may not suffer vicariously liability if the company has engaged in "good-faith efforts" to comply with Title VII. See *EEOC v. Wal-Mart Stores, Inc.*, 187 F.3d 1241 (10th Cir. 1999).

2. Caps on Liability are set in the legislation noting maximum damage awards. But such caps do not apply to intentional racial discrimination.

IV. **AGE DISCRIMINATION.**

A. **ADEA.** The federal Age Discrimination in Employment Act prohibits age discrimination to individuals aged forty years or older. But see *O'Connor v. Consolidated Coin Caterers Corp.*, 517 U.S. 308(1996). It generally prohibits age-based retaliation, employee hiring, firing, compensation, etc. There are four parts to a prima facie case of age discrimination. See *Reeves v. Sanderson Plumbing Products, Inc.*, 530 U.S. 133 (2000). The federal circuits are split on claims alleging a disparate impact.

B. **OWBPA.** The Older Workers' Benefit Protection Act prohibits age discrimination in providing employee benefits.

C. **DEFENSES** are construed very narrowly. A defendant-employer may show: (1) that age was a reasonably necessary BFOQ (this is extremely difficult to prove); (2) differential treatment is based on something other than age; (3) there is a bona fide seniority system or employee benefit plan; or (4) the discharge/discipline was for good cause.

D. **REMEDIES UNDER THE ADEA.** Plaintiffs are entitled to equitable relief and monetary damages including back pay.

V. **DISABILITY DISCRIMINATION.** The Americans with Disabilities Act (ADA) prohibits employers from discriminating because of a disability in regard to job applications, hiring, training, work, compensation or benefits. Employers may use criteria that are job-related. However an employer may not exclude a disabled individual if that individual, with some "reasonable accommodation." Employers may ask "pre-employment" questions about reasonable accommodations. The ADA also covers employee benefit packages.

A. **IMPERMISSIBLE DISCRIMINATION.** Employers cannot intentionally discriminate against disabled persons or engage in employment practices that have the effect of discriminating against disabled persons. Under the ADA "discriminate" is construed to include an extensive set of behaviors.

B. **DEFINITION OF "DISABILITY."** The ADA defines a person with a disability as one with physical or mental impairment to include the idea of a *substantial limit* on one or more of that person's *major life* activities.

1. Physical or Mental Impairment as defined in the ADA and relevant CFRs examines one's capacity to function due to physical ailments, not social or environmental factors.

2. Substantially Limits a Major Life Activity. An impairment is only a disability if such prevents one from the capacity to perform. Major life activities include sexual reproduction (*Bragdon v. Abbot*), eating (*Lawson v. CSX Transp., Inc.*) but not carpal tunnel syndrome (*Toyota v. Williams*) or post-traumatic stress disorder related to being raped (*McKenzie v. Dovala*).

> **Case 13.3--*Sutton v. United Air Lines, Inc.*,** 527 U.S. 471 (1999). Sutton and Hinton were twins with severe myopia. Though their myopia prevented them from conducting some activity, they could, with glasses or contact lenses, function as individuals with normal vision. They applied to United Air Lines to be pilots, but were told that they did not meet UAL's minimum vision requirements (uncorrected vision of 20/100 or better). Plaintiffs filed suit, alleging violation of the ADA. The case was dismissed because the Plaintiffs did not have a disability. The Supreme Court affirmed ruling that a "disability" exists only where an impairment "substantially limits" a major life activity, not where it "might."

3.   Regarded as Disabled. Under the ADA no employer may engage in a practice grounded in societal stereotypes and prejudice about individuals with disabilities.

4.   Exclusions. The ADA specifically excludes drug addiction, homosexuality, bisexuality, sexual-behavior disorders, compulsive gambling, kleptomania, and pyromania from the definition of a disability. Importantly an employee or applicant involved in or having completed a supervised drug or alcohol rehabilitation program may be regarded as disabled.

C.   **Reasonable Accommodation**. ADA requires employers to make reasonable accommodations to an employee's disability. Such includes making facilities accessible, modifying work tasks or schedules, acquiring devices, providing interpreters, etc. At a minimum the employer must discuss potential accommodations with the employee. Reassignment may be a form of reasonable accommodation.

D.   **Defenses Under the ADA**. The ADA notes three defenses for failure to comply: undue hardship; business necessity; and permissible exclusion.

1.   Undue Hardship. Activity requiring significant difficulty or expense in light of the circumstances, including the employer's financial status, the number of employees, and cost of the accommodation, may pose an undue hardship. E.g., *Gaul v. Lucent Techs, Inc.*, 134 F.3d 576 (3d. Cir. 1998).

2.   Business Necessity may excuse the employer from ADA compliance. Depending upon the alleged disability or necessity the employee might have the burden to prove the ADA violation.

3.   Permissible Exclusion. A worker may be refused employment if she cannot perform the essential functions of the job or if her employment poses a significant risk to the health or safety of others.

- **Inability to Perform Essential Functions**. The applicant or employee does not have to prove his or her ability to perform all the functions of the job, only the essential functions.

- **Direct Threat**. The threat to the employee or public safety must be direct, not a future injury or speculative.

Case 13.4 *Echazabal v. Chevron USA, Inc.*, 536 U.S. 73 (2002). Echazabal worked for maintenance contractors at a

Chevron oil refinery in California. Echazabal then applied for a position at Chevron. Chevron rescinded its offer after learning about Echazabal's liver disease. Chevron also demanded that the contractor remove Echazabal from the refinery or place him in a position that eliminated his exposure to toxic chemicals. Echazabal filed a complaint against Chevron, alleging a violation of the ADA. The district court dismissed. The appellate court reversed holding that the ADA's direct threat defense does not permit employers to shut disabled people out of jobs on the ground that the worker puts their health at risk.

E.   **HIV Discrimination**. The ADA does not specifically list HIV as a disability, but in *Bragdon v. Abbott*, 524 U.S. 624 (1998) the Court held that asymptomatic HIV-positive individuals are disabled due to their limited reproductive capacity. Within the workplace, medical records must remain confidential lest employers are sued for violations of privacy and or slander.

F.   **Genetic Discrimination**. Approximately 18 states ban genetic discrimination. The EEOC has determined that the ADA prohibits discrimination based on genetic testing that shows the possibility of a future sickness.

G.   **Enforcement and Remedies** are the same as Title VII of the Civil Rights Act.

VI.   **Family and Medical Leave Act (FMLA) of 1993** grants up to twelve weeks of unpaid leave per calendar year. To be eligible employees must have worked at the place of employment for at least 12 months and have completed at least 1,250 hours of service during that 12-month period. Employees may use FMLA leave to: (a) give birth to a child; (b) accept placement of an adopted or foster-care child; (c) take care of a child, a parent, or a spouse; or (d) recuperate from serious health condition that renders the employee unable to do his job. After one's leave the employer is supposed to restore the employee at the equivalent benefits and pay.

VII.   **AFFIRMATIVE ACTION**. Affirmative-action programs are generally viewed as a means to remedy past acts of discrimination. Under standing executive orders, federal contractors must refrain from wrongful discrimination and take affirmative steps to prevent discrimination. However, In *Adarand Construction v. Pena*, 515 U.S. 200 (1995), the U.S. Supreme Court held that government-mandated affirmative action plans are subject to *strict scrutiny* and hence the government must justify minority preference programs on the basis of correcting historical discrimination.

VIII.   **APPLICABILITY OF CIVIL RIGHTS LAWS TO TEMPORARY WORKERS**. The EEOC has extended discrimination liability to temporary workers. If both the staffing firm and its client have the right to control the worker, then the two are treated as joint employers, subject to liability for back and front pay, as well as compensatory and punitive damages.

IX. **THE EXTRATERRITORIAL REACH OF AMERICAN LAW**. In 1991 Congress amended title VII of the Civil Rights Act to cover U.S. citizens employed overseas by a U.S. or U.S.-controlled employer. Such companies must follow the ADEA and the ADA as well.

ECONOMIC PERSPECTIVE: GLOBALIZATION, CULTURAL NORMS, AND WORKPLACE DISCRIMINATION. In 2004 an Indian software firm settled a sexual harassment suit. In the current era of globalization companies must learn to implement anti-discrimination practices that incorporate local culture and law. More often American companies and those of other nations realize the multicultural interaction demands policies of tolerance and respect yet with clear guidelines for what is unacceptable behavior.

X. **GLOBAL VIEW: DISCRIMINATION AND DIVERSITY**. Managers must familiarize themselves with the discrimination laws of the region and nation. In the EU, Japan, and India there are differences of which one must be aware. In Europe, the law puts the burden on the employer to show that there is no discrimination, and has lifted caps on awards. Conversely, in Japan the anti-discrimination law is not very developed – despite strong language in her constitution. Gender bias against women in the Japanese workplace is still present. India has seen a long political struggle for equality among its Dalit and "indigenous" communities. Recently the Indian government has placed guarantees for gender equality and recognized the rights of people with disabilities.

XI. **THE RESPONSIBLE MANAGER: Honoring Employees' Civil Rights**. Managers must be diligent in preventing and correcting any unlawful discrimination either in the pre-employment process or during employment. Management should develop a written policy that: (a) outlines discriminatory acts prohibited by federal, state, and local statutes; (b) prohibits retaliation against employees who complain about discrimination; and (c) clearly states violations of the policy will result in poor performance reviews or termination.

Managers should also create a working environment in which they model ethical, courteous behavior and where employees feel comfortable in bringing complaints against fellow workers and supervisors. This means managers must not tolerate retaliation against employees who have filed discrimination claims. In conjunction managers need to create nondiscriminatory hiring policies and non-discrimination training procedures for new employees.

Lastly, managers should look to reduce liability by purchasing employment practice liability insurance (EPLI) to protect against discrimination claims; remain proactive and engage in an interactive "paper trail" process with employees who may have disabilities that are requesting accommodation; and draft policies that encompass dating and romantic relationships, which can sour into harassment claims.

STUDY QUESTIONS

True-False Questions

__ 1.   Section 1981, as amended, applies to hiring and firing, but not working conditions.

__ 2.   The Equal Pay Act covers all public and private employers.

__ 3.   The ADEA protects persons 50 years and older from discrimination based on age.

__ 4.   The ADA applies to all employers with twenty or more employees.

__ 5.   The Family and Medical Leave Act applies to women and men.

__ 6.   The EEOC documented a significant increase in religious discrimination claims in the first half of the 1990s.

__ 7.   Lost future earnings compensate an employee for a lifetime of diminished earnings resulting from the harm to one's reputation suffered as a result of discrimination.

__ 8.   In discrimination suits, punitive damages are available to the plaintiff if compensatory damages were awarded in the case.

__ 9.   In a mixed-motive case, the employer has done nothing illegal, so no damages can be awarded.

__ 10. Generally, a one-time incident is insufficient to create a hostile work environment.

__ 11. Generally, the BFOQ defense is not available for race or color discrimination.

__ 12. Seniority systems are not covered by Title VII.

__ 13. Employers must provide the same compensation for pregnancy and childbirth that they provide for other disabilities, but these protections are not absolute.

__ 14. Sexual harassment can be heterosexual, but not homosexual, in nature.

__ 15. Sexual stereotyping is equivalent to puffing in sales: not favored, but not legally actionable.

Multiple-Choice Questions

___ 1. The first legislation in employment and civil rights was passed in:
   A. 1964.
   B. 1866.
   C. 1981.
   D. 1881.

___ 2. Which of the following is a *false* statement concerning the Equal Pay Act?
   A. The act covers all employers.
   B. The act is enforced by the EEOC.
   C. The act applies to the federal government.
   D. The act covers private employers with 20 or more employees.

___ 3. Title VII, as amended, applies to all of the following types of discrimination *except:*
   A. Race.
   B. Religion.
   C. Pregnancy.
   D. Sexual preference.

___ 4. The ADA's definition of a disability includes:

   I.   Alcoholism.
   II. Mental disease.
   III. HIV infection.
   IV. Cancer.

   A. I, II, III, IV.
   B. I, II, III.
   C. II, III, IV.
   D. I and III.

___ 5. Which act provided a commission to study the affects of "glass ceilings"?
   A. Civil Rights Act of 1991.
   B. Equal Pay Act.
   C. Americans with Disabilities Act.
   D. Family and Medical Leave Act.

___ 6. Which of the following is *not* a remedy under Title VII?

   I.   Lost wages.
   II. Front pay.
   III. Injunctive relief.
   IV. Mental anguish compensation.

A. II and IV.
B. II only.
C. IV only.
D. None of these.

___ 7. A plaintiff claiming disparate _____ must prove the employer intentionally discriminated against him or her by denying a job benefit because of a protected factor.
A. Impact.
B. Treatment.
C. Feelings..
D. Harassment.

___ 8. The City of Nirvana's policy for hiring firefighters is that the applicants must be at least six feet tall and weigh at least two hundred pounds. Several women sue; they should challenge the policy on the theory of: _____.
A. Disparate treatment.
B. Disparate impact.
C. Negligence.
D. Tortious interference with contract.

___ 9. Which of the following would *not* be a valid BFOQ?
A. Hiring only females to be bikini models.
B. Considering only black males to play the part of Malcolm X.
C. Hiring only blacks for a movie about Africa.
D. Interviewing exclusively Baptist ministers to be a pastor in a Baptist church.

___ 10. Threats of adverse job action that are not carried out constitute _____.
A. *Quid pro quo* harassment.
B. No harassment.
C. Hostile work environment.
D. Disparate impact treatment.

___ 11. An employer is liable for the torts of employees not acting within the scope of employment in all but which situation?
A. The employer intended the conduct.
B. The employee was negligent.
C. The employee's high rank made him or her the alter ego of the employer.
D. The employee was aided in the tort by the agency relationship.

___ 12. Which of the following is *false*?
A. The ADEA prohibits discrimination against those age 40 and older.
B. Individuals under age 40 have no protection from age discrimination.
C. The substantive provisions of the ADEA is similar to Title VII.

D. The ADEA applies to all employers that affect interstate commerce and employ at least fifteen employees.

___ 13. Which of the following is the most difficult to prove?
A. Age as a BFOQ.
B. Age is not a factor in employee treatment.
C. A bona fide seniority system.
D. Discharge of a 50-year-old employee was for good cause.

___ 14. Which is *not* a prohibited practice under the ADA?
A. Classifying an applicant by disability for employment status.
B. Using job-related tests for employment.
C. Utilizing employment agencies that discriminate against disabled people.
D. Refusal to make accommodations for any job.

___ 15. Which is *not* a situation for leave under the Family and Medical Leave Act?
A. The birth of a child.
B. The adoption of a child.
C. The care of a parent, child, or sibling.
D. None of the above.

Essay Questions

1. Why do some consider the ADA as the most sweeping civil rights measure since 1964?

2. How does the plaintiff prove a disparate impact claim?

3. In same-sex sexual harassment, must the plaintiff show the defendant was homosexual? Why or why not?

CHAPTER 14
CRIMINAL LAW

INTRODUCTION

Criminal law is a powerful tool for controlling corporate behavior and ensuring ethical conduct. This chapter examines what a crime is, what the basics of criminal procedure are, and the major constitutional issues involving criminal procedure. The chapter also introduces other federal statutes involving such areas as white-collar crime, computer crime, and environmental law.

I. **DEFINITION OF A CRIME**. A *crime* is an offense against the public at large that consists of two elements.

    A. **The Criminal Act (*Actus Reus*)** is the guilty act or wrongful act in question.

    B. **The State of Mind (*Mens Rea*)**. Generally a criminal actor can only be guilty if they possess the required mental intent at the time of the act.

        1. Strict Liability is generally disfavored for criminal laws and only allowed for crimes dealing with issues of public health and safety.

        2. *Mens Rea.* There are three mental states associated with crime, negligence (failure to foresee a negative outcome), recklessness (conscious disregard or indifference to a substantial risk) and intent (overt desire to commit a given act or obtain a criminal outcome).

    C. **Sources of Criminal Law**. The federal government and State governments have criminal statutes. Such divide offenses into *felonies* is a crime punishable by death or by imprisonment for more than one year, and *misdemeanors* is a less serious crime, punishable by a fine or a jail sentence of one year or less. In order to harmonize criminal law, many states have adopted the Model Penal Code.

    D. **Criminal versus Civil Liability**. *Civil* law (*e.g.,* negligence) compensates the victim for legal wrongs committed against the person or her property. *Criminal* law protects society by punishing the criminal. The burden of proof in a *civil* trial is the *preponderance of the evidence* (more likely than not). For *criminal* trials the defendant is presumed innocent until proven *guilty beyond a reasonable doubt,* and is entitled to numerous constitutional protections.

II.   **CRIMINAL PROCEDURE.** A criminal action begins with the arrest of the person suspected of a crime and proceeds through a preliminary hearing to plea bargaining and trial.

       A.   **Arrest**. If one is taken into custody an arresting officer then files a report with the prosecutor. Prosecutor (District Attorney) decides whether to press charges against the arrested person. If charges are brought, many states require that the accused be taken before a judge to be informed of the charges against him. Bail, if appropriate or necessary, is often determined during this initial appearance.

       B.   **Plea**. For felonies, after the initial appearance there may be a preliminary (probable cause) hearing where the D.A. must introduce evidence that the defendant committed the felony. Following the hearing, formal charges are filed either through an information, or by a grand jury indictment.

       C.   **Arraignment**. The accused is informed of the charges against him or her and asked to enter a plea of guilty or not guilty. If the defendant enters a plea of not guilty, the case is set for trial. The accused may plead *nolo contendere*, meaning she shall not contest the charges.

       D.   **Plea Bargaining**. A prosecutor may agree to reduce the charges in exchange for a guilty plea. Sometimes defendants provide the D.A. with testimony incriminating an accomplice, in exchange for a reduced sentence or immunity from prosecution. Some corporate defendants accept *consent decrees* to court orders that the defendant will take measures to remedy the problem that led to criminal charges.

       E.   **Trial**. The process is similar to civil trials. There are opening statements, direct examination and cross examination of witnesses, and closing arguments. If requested, a jury then deliberates to reach a verdict. Guilty verdicts must be unanimous.

III.   **CONSTITUTIONAL PROTECTIONS.** The U.S. Constitution guarantees certain protections for criminal defendants.

       A.   **Ex Post Facto Clause**. A person can be convicted of a crime only if the person's actions constituted a crime at the time they occurred.

       B.   **Fourth Amendment Protections**. The Fourth Amendment applies only to actions by government officials, unless a private person is acting on behalf of the government.

            1.   The Arrest Warrant Requirement. No arrest is valid without probable cause, a reasonable belief that the suspect has committed a crime or is about to commit a crime. However no warrant is necessary for an arrest in a public place when the officer has "reasonable suspicion" that a crime has been committed or was committed in the officer's presence.

2. Searches and Seizures and Reasonable Expectations of Privacy. Law enforcement agent must obtain a warrant when the suspect has a reasonable expectation of privacy under the circumstances. In the home there is a strong expectation of privacy, but less so in a business during business hours. No warrant is necessary for government search of bank records.

- Searches Employing New Technology. *Thermal Imaging* devices can only be used if police have a warrant. *Kyllo v. United States*, 533 U.S. 27 (2001). *Cordless and Cellular Phones and E-mail*—a search warrant is required for land-based telephones (wiretapping), but *not* for cordless or cellular telephones because communications on the units could be overheard by other users.

- Suspicionless and Administrative Searches and Seizures. Generally, a search or seizure is "unreasonable" without some suspicion of wrongdoing, unless there are "special needs," for example: random drug-testing of students; administrative searches of a "closely regulated" business; brief detainment of motorists at Border Patrol checkpoints; and sobriety checkpoints.

- Obtaining a Search Warrant. A warrant is signed by a "neutral and detached" magistrate, based on probable cause and supported by affidavit that sets forth in specific detail (with particularity) what is to be searched or seized. The government may obtain a broad warrant to conduct a sweeping raid of a company only when the government has made a showing that a company is pervaded by fraud.

C. **The Exclusionary Rule** prohibits the introduction of illegal evidence in a criminal trial obtained by an unconstitutional search or seizure in violation of the Fourth Amendment. There are exceptions: **Good Faith**, evidence gathered in good faith will not be excluded from trial, even if it was obtained in violation of the Fourth Amendment; and **Inevitable Discovery**, evidence is admissible if it would have been found by other legal means.

D. **Fifth Amendment Protections** are tied to self-incrimination, double jeopardy and due process.

1. Self-Incrimination. The Fifth Amendment provides that no person "shall be compelled in any criminal case to be a witness against himself."

> **Case 14.1--*Missouri v. Seibert*,** 124 S. Ct. 2601 (2004). Seibert was convicted of second-degree murder after she admitted of a plot to burn her mobile home in which a persons inside was killed inadvertently. Seibert confessed after her arrest, but prior to receiving her *Miranda* warning. Though Seibert signed a confession – it was based on a pre-*Miranda* confession. As this confession was the primary evidence against her, the Supreme Court overturned her conviction.

- <u>Business Records and Papers and the Collective Entity Doctrine.</u> Corporations (and other business entities) enjoy no protection. The custodian of records for a corporation may not resist a subpoena for such records on Fifth Amendment grounds.

- <u>Foreign Prosecutions.</u> A witness may not refuse to convey testimony or evidence on the grounds that she would face prosecution in another country.

2. **Double Jeopardy** prohibitions apply to the authority of one sovereign to prosecute a defendant for the same offense more than once. However a single act may result in both criminal and civil prosecutions (*e.g.*, O.J. Simpson trials). Enduring a Civil ***and*** Criminal Prosecution does ***not*** create a violation of the double jeopardy clause.

3. **Due Process and Voluntary Confessions**. The Due Process clauses of the Constitution bar the government from using the involuntary confessions.

E.   **Sixth Amendment Protections.**

1. Assistance of Counsel. A defendant has the right to effective legal representation, and must be informed of this right. If the defendant cannot afford an attorney, he will be entitled to a court-appointed attorney, but may have to reimburse the costs to the state if he is convicted.

2. Jury Trial. Most defendants in criminal cases have the right to a jury trial. Jury trials are not required if the punishment for the charged offense is six months or less. A jury is not required in juvenile proceedings. State court

juries consist of six to twelve individuals, with a minimum of six jurors. Federal courts have twelve.

3. Other Procedural Rights. The Sixth Amendment also guarantees the rights to a speedy trial, to confront and cross-examine witnesses.

IV. **NONCONSTITUTIONAL PROTECTIONS**. Both sides may be compelled to turn over evidence, prosecutors must reveal any exculpatory evidence. Further, defendant communications with their attorneys are generally private and protected by **Attorney-Client Privilege**.

V. **SENTENCING**. Generally statutes specify penalties for criminal transgressions, though judges have some discretion in sentencing.

A. **Federal Sentencing Guidelines**. Under the federal guidelines, federal judges were to consider a number of factors when imposing sentence.

1. Individuals. The federal system has no parole. Individuals must serve at least 85% of their sentence.

2. Organizations. Under the federal sentencing guidelines, organizations could receive stiff fines and heavy penalties for fraud, anti-trust violations and corporate crime.

- Determining the Sentence. Under the old federal guidelines, judges determined levels of punishment and then made upward or downward departures based on levels of culpability and cooperation with prosecution.

- Letting Employees Take the Rap. Under the federal system, corporations have an incentive to set up one employee as a fall guy.

B. **Constitutional Challenge to the Federal Sentencing Guidelines**. Recently there have been challenges to the federal sentencing guidelines on the grounds that they violate the Sixth Amendment.

Case 14.2--*United States v. Booker*, 125 S. Ct. 738 (2005). Two separate defendants were convicted of drug crimes. In both instances, the judges sentenced the convicts on a finding of an amount of drugs greater than the jury found (if the jury made a definitive finding at all). The Supreme Court held that as defendants were subject to a judicial, rather than a jury, finding (with a mere preponderance standard), defendants were denied their Sixth Amendment guarantee to have all elements of the crime presented before and found by a jury beyond a reasonable doubt. The convictions were upheld, but the sentences were vacated.

VI.   LIABILITY FOR CRIMINAL ACTIONS

A.   **INDIVIDUAL LIABILITY.** An officer, director, or employee who commits a crime against the corporation (theft, embezzlement, or forgery) will be prosecuted as an individual, even if they were trying to benefit the corporation.

1.   Direct Liability. If an employee commits a crime against the corporate employer, individuals will be prosecuted even if acting at the behest or for the benefit of the company.

2.   Vicarious Liability. Officers, directors, and managers are criminally liable for acts committed by employees under their supervision, if supervisors fail to provide adequate supervision or fail to satisfy a duty imposed by a criminal statute.

- Responsible Corporate Officer Doctrine holds that a corporate officer may be found responsible for the actions of their subordinate if the officer bore a reasonable relation to the violation. *United States v. Park*, 421 U.S. 658 (1975).

- Impossibility Defense. A corporate officer might not be held strictly (and vicariously) liable she did everything possible to ensure legal compliance, yet the company was unable to comply with the law. According to the U.S. Court of Appeals for the Second Circuit: "To establish the *impossibility defense*, the corporate officer must introduce evidence that he exercised extraordinary care and still could not prevent violations of the Act."[1]

B.   **Corporate Liability.** A corporation is liable for criminal offenses committed by employees if the acts were committed within the scope of their employment. See *Commonwealth v. McIlwain Sch. Bus Lines*, 423 A.2d 413 (Pa. Super 1980). A corporation is liable if it adopts a policy or issues instructions that cause an employee to violate the law. *Commonwealth v. Penn Valley Resorts, Inc.*, 494 A.2d 1139 (Pa. Super 1985).

---

[1] *United States v. Gel Spice Co.* 773 F.2d 427 (2d Cir. 1985) (quoting *United States v. New England Grocers Co.,* 488 F. Supp. 230 (D. Mass. 1980)). (Emphasis added.)

Deciding Whether to Prosecute: The Thompson Memorandum. One federal prosecutor outlined nine factors to consider before seeking to indict a corporation. Given the Thompson memo, many corporations are electing to cooperate with prosecutors and waive attorney-client privilege.

VII.   IN BRIEF: LIABILITY FOR CRIMINAL ACTIONS.

Type of Defendant	Standard for Liability
Individual	The individual must have performed *actus reus* (criminal act) with *mens rea* (guilty mind). An individual can perpetrate a crime against the corporate employer (e.g., the embezzlement) or for the benefit of the corporation (e.g., price-fixing).
Corporate Officers	Officers can be directly liable for failing to supervise subordinates. In addition to individual liability for their own acts, officers may be vicariously liable for crimes committed by other employees. Under the responsible corporate officer doctrine, officers can be liable for criminal actions of their subordinates if the officer bore a "responsible relation" to the violation of law. Typically, the doctrine is used to impose criminal liability only for violations of strict-liability statutes involving public health where the officer is charged with a misdemeanor or the prosecution proves—through direct or circumstantial evidence—that the officer knew of the violation.
Corporations	*Respondeat superior* liability. A corporation is criminally liable for (1) all misdemeanor offenses and regulatory crimes committed by any of its agents or employees; (2) all crimes committed pursuant to top management's corporate policy or express instructions; (3) all crimes committed by employees if the acts were committed (a) within the scope of their employment (whether actual or apparent and in some states, also in furtherance of the corporation's business interests), or (b) tolerated by top management.

VIII.   WHITE-COLLAR CRIME.
A white-collar crime is a violation of the law by a corporation (or other business entity) or one of its managers. Many white-collar criminal statutes do not require criminal intent to break the law.

   A.   **Crimes against the Employer**. Examples of crimes committed by an employee against his or her employer include:

   1.   Theft (larceny) ranges from taking home pens and paper from the office to stealing money through the company's computer system.

2. Embezzlement the taking of money or property that is lawfully in the employee's possession by reason of his or her employment.

3. Fraud, any deception intended to induce someone to part with property or money.

4. Acceptance of a bribe may also be a crime against the employer.

B. **CRIMES BY THE CORPORATION AND ITS AGENTS.** Crimes include consumer fraud, securities fraud, tax evasion, and environmental pollution. Corporations can also commit crimes against other corporations (*e.g.,* price fixing or violation of trademark laws).

1. Racketeering under the Racketeer Influenced and Corrupt Organizations Act (RICO). RICO is designed to combat organized "white collar" crime and provides an enforcement mechanism against syndicate bosses. More often it is used against insider-trading.

   • RICO Requirements: "Enterprise" and Racketeering Activity. An enterprise is a partnership, corporation, association, union or group of associated individuals, or legal entity. Racketeering Activity includes mail and wire fraud and fraud in the sale of securities. Almost any business fraud can serve as the basis for a RICO violation. Government must show at least two related acts during the previous ten-year period.

   • Limits on the Use of RICO. RICO is most effective against groups of traders, brokers, and others who have developed a continuous relationship of passing and trading on inside information. But cannot be applied against accountants. *Reeves v. Ernst & Young,* 507 U.S. 170 (1993).

   • Private Civil Actions. The RICO statute allows civil actions for statutory violations whereby plaintiffs can receive treble damages and attorneys' fees.

2. Mail and Wire Fraud. Under the Mail and Wire Fraud Act individuals and corporations can be convicted if the Government demonstrates: (a) a scheme intended to defraud or to obtain money or property by fraudulent means, and (b) the use of the mails or of interstate telephone lines in furtherance of the fraudulent scheme.

3.   False Claims to the U.S. Government. The federal False Statements Act is similar to the Mail and Wire Fraud Act and is commonly used against companies who deal with federal agencies. E.g., *United States v. Yermian*, 581 F.2d 595 (7th Cir. 1978).

HISTORICAL PERSPECTIVE: WHITE COLLAR CRIME. White Collar crime is associated with high status professions. Socialist Edwin Sutherland argued that crime is not merely a product of lower classes and base violence, but is rife among the elite. Though White Collar crime was noted in the acts of robber-barons, and within securities, it was not until the 1960s when such acts were punished with prison time. It was not until the 1970s when White Collar prosecutor become relatively common. By the 1980s and 1990 high-profile cases involving securities and savings and loans came to public light. Still the comparative prosecution and penalty of corporate crime is slight. S & L crooks stole millions yet only faced an average of three years in prison – comparably, petty thieves receive around 56 months. In 1992 the total value of all bank robberies was $35 million, less than 1% of the amount looted by executives at the Lincoln Savings & Loan.

4.   False Claims to the U.S. Government and Health-Care Fraud. Since the 1980s, the government has used the False Claims Act to attack contract fraud. Further private parties can sue on the government's behalf as *qui tam* plaintiffs. As well due to fraud in the health care industry there have been more criminal prosecutions. Since 1996, they have come under HIPAA.

5.   Computer Crime takes many forms. People use computers to steal company or government funds through fraud. Most computer crime can be prosecuted under state law.

- The Computer Fraud and Abuse Act **(CFAA)** prohibits: (a) accessing a computer without authorization, (b) knowingly transmitting a computer code or program that causes "damage" to a protected computer, or (c) knowingly transmitting computer viruses resulting in damage or "denial of service" attacks.

    Case 14.3--*Shurgard Storage Centers, Inc. v.Safeguard Self Storage, Inc.*, 119 F. Supp. 2d 1121 (W.D. Wash 2000). Shurgard sued a competitor, Safeguard, for embarking on a "systematic" scheme to hire away key employees to obtain trade secrets. Shurgard claimed a Safeguard employee used Shurgard computers to access various trade secrets and proprietary information belonging, and sent e-mails containing the information to Safeguard. Shurgard alleged misappropriation of trade secrets, conversion, unfair competition, tortious interference with a business expectancy, and violations of the Computer Fraud and Abuse Act. Safeguard moved to dismiss the CFAA claims. The motion to dismiss was denied for [T]he CFAA was intended to control interstate computer crime, and since the advent of the Internet, almost all computer use has become interstate in nature.

- Computer Piracy is theft or misuse of computer software. Congress amended the Copyright Act to address computer software as a means to stop or remedy computer piracy.

6. The Foreign Corrupt Practices Act makes it a crime for any U.S. firm to make payments to an official of a foreign government in an attempt to influence the actions of that official or a foreign government.

7. Crimes Involving Intellectual Property. Companies lose over $200 billion annually to IP fraud, crime, and theft.

8. Antitrust Laws. Under the Sherman Anti-trust law, most companies are prosecuted for restraints on trade, price-fixing and monopoly.

VIEW FROM CYBERSPACE: FIGHTING CYBERCRIME. Cybercrime, as financial and consumer fraud, is more common. Government efforts to prevent cybercrime are finally paying off as the government is catching spammers and software pirates.

9. SECURITIES LAW VIOLATIONS

Federal Securities Laws—Securities Act of 1933 and the Securities Exchange Act of 1934, administered by the Securities and Exchange Commission (SEC) establish penalties for illegal securities trading.

State Blue Sky Laws can be more restrictive than their federal counterparts.

Case 14.4--*Mueller v. Sullivan*, 141 F.3d 1232 (7th Cir. 1998). Mueller controlled Farm Loan Services, an auction house for the sale of securities. Mueller and Stopple were charged with violating Wisconsin's version of the Uniform Securities Act, for willful omission of material facts in connection with the purchase of sale of securities. The trial judge instructed the jury that Mueller could be convicted under the act if the prosecution proved that defendants knew that the investors were not being told relevant, material information. Mueller and Stopple were subsequently convicted. Mueller challenged claiming that Due Process protections required a more stringent showing of mental state, required in cases under Section 10(b) of the Securities Exchange Act of 1934 (1934 Act). The federal appeals court upheld the conviction holding that Due Process permits conviction for violation of state securities laws even if defendants did not know their action was illegal.

10.   Obstruction of Justice, Perjury, and Related Offenses. Sarbanes-Oxley increases penalties for and expands definitions of obstruction of justice. When convictions are not made for obstruction, perjury charges are brought. Such was the fate of Martha Stewart and Frank Quattrone.

IX.   **OTHER FEDERAL REGULATORY AND TAX OFFENSES.**

A.   **The Environmental Laws**. Individuals may be prosecuted under the Clean Water Act (CWA) which requires all industrial and municipal entities to obtain a permit from the EPA prior to discharging specified pollutants into water. The Resource Conservation and Recovery Act (RCRA) provides for monitoring, transportation and record-keeping of hazardous-waste material.

B.   **Worker Safety Laws.**

1.   The Occupational Safety and Health Act (OSHA) usually imposes civil penalties unless there are continuing willful violations.

2.   State Law Prosecutions of Workplace Safety Hazards. State prosecutors are taking an aggressive approach to enforcing state laws, as OSHA does not pre-empt such prosecutions.

C.   **Tax Laws**. Federal tax violations, including fraud and willful evasion can lead to fines and prison sentences.

X.   **AMNESTY AND LENIENCY PROGRAMS.** In an effort to promote self-policing and regulation, several federal agencies and offices have offered amnesty programs.

A.   **Amnesty for Cartels**. As a public policy matter offering amnesty may be necessary due to the difficulty in obtaining insider information.

B.   **EPA Incentives for Self-Policing.** The audit policy of the EPA on self-policing is designed to enhance protection of human health. If a party meets all the EPA conditions, the agency will forbear on criminal prosecutions.

C.   **OSHA and Voluntary Self-Audits.** In 2000 OSHA issued its policy on self-reporting audits. The purpose of the policy was to allow employers to identify and correct hazardous conditions.

XI.   **THE RESPONSIBLE MANAGER: Ensuring Criminal Law Compliance.** Senior management can take various actions to encourage criminal law compliance.

- Managers should develop a code of ethics with an enforcement mechanism that clearly states that violations will result in sanctions and, in extreme cases, termination of employment.
- Managers should develop corporate compliance and education programs to ensure compliance with laws and regulations.
- The company should expect ethical behavior at all levels.
- Criminal misconduct within a corporation is often a function of goals and performance measures that induce people to cut corners.
- In-house counsel should be independent and report directly to the board of directors, and not succumb to pressure from division managers.
- Managers should use outside firms to audit the corporation's methods of ensuring criminal law compliance.
- If faced with criminal investigation, acting quickly is important, managers should turn over information about internal investigations to prosecutors but guard against waiving attorney-client privilege.

INSIDE STORY: THE CEO AS FELON. In response the Enron and other corporate scandals, President Bush created a Corporate Fraud Task Force. Between 2000 and 2004, a number of high-profile cases resulted in prosecution and convictions of corporate CEOs. With convictions and pleas from Dennis Kozlowski at Tyco, Andrew Fastow at Enron and Bernie Ebbers at WorldCom, it looks at though the government has put Wall Street on notice that corporate malfeasance will not be tolerated.

STUDY QUESTIONS

True-False Questions

___ 1.   A crime is defined as an offense against the victim.

___ 2.   Thoughts and dreams about a crime are not a crime.

___ 3.   Normally, to be guilty of a crime, you need to have the intent to commit the crime when you commit the crime.

___ 4.   Criminal prosecutions can be brought by either the city, state, or federal government.

___ 5.   A federal judge has less discretion in sentencing than a state judge.

___ 6.   Congress placed new restrictions on federal parole in 1992.

___ 7.   One shortcoming of the Federal Sentencing Guidelines for Organizations is that it encourages companies to adopt all the compliance form without actually having much compliance substance.

___ 8.   In a civil suit subsequent to a criminal conviction, the judge in the civil case will accept the criminal conviction as sufficient proof of negligence for the civil case.

___ 9.   *Nolo contendre* is the equivalent to a guilty plea for civil and criminal proceedings.

___ 10. In general, arrest warrants are required for arrests made in a suspect's home or in another person's home.

___ 11. A warrant is required to search airline passengers before boarding a plane.

___ 12. No search warrant is required for a search of the phone numbers a person has called.

___ 13. The exclusionary rule prohibits any introduction of evidence that was obtained by an illegal search or seizure in violation of the Fourth Amendment.

___ 14. A prosecution and a civil suit for the same event would violate the double jeopardy clause.

___ 15. The responsible corporate officer doctrine holds that a corporate officer may be found responsible for the actions of their subordinate if the officer bore a reasonable relation to the violation.

Multiple-Choice Questions

___ 1.   The elements necessary for a crime are:

   I.   Guilty act (*actus reus*).
   II.   Guilty mind (*mens rea*).

III. Motive (*actus lex*).

A. I and II.
B. I and III.
C. II and III.
D. I, II and III.

__ 2. Which of the following is *not* a form of *mens rea?*
A. Negligence.
B. Carelessness.
C. Recklessness.
D. Intention.

__ 3. Monica could receive a sentence of five years, but is sentenced to nine months in prison. Monica was convicted of a: _____.
A. Violation.
B. Misdemeanor.
C. Felony.
D. Tort.

__ 4. The criminal burden of proof is guilty beyond: _____.
A. A shadow of a doubt.
B. A doubt.
C. All doubt
D. A reasonable doubt.

__ 5. A formal charge filed by a grand jury is called an: _____.
A. Information.
B. Indictment.
C. Introduction.
D. Initial plea offer.

__ 6. _____ prohibits any criminal prosecution of the witness that relates to any matter discussed in his or her testimony.
A. Transactional immunity.
B. Use immunity.
C. *Nolo contendere.*
D. Testimonial immunity.

__ 7. The prohibition against unreasonable searches and seizures is found in the ____ Amendment.
A. 4th.
B. 5th.

C. 1st.
D. 8th.

__ 8. A police officer stops a driver suspected of driving under the influence of alcohol. After observing her swerving across lanes of traffic and accelerating and decelerating in an erratic manner, and administering a field sobriety test, the police officer may:
   A. Arrest her.
   B. Not arrest her.
   C. Arrest her if he has a warrant.
   D. Not arrest her, due to a lack of probable cause.

__ 9. In which situation would a search warrant be required?
   A. A border search.
   B. A search of dumpster in an alley.
   C. A search of a home.
   D. A search of a business during business hours limited to what is visible to a customer.

__ 10. A valid search warrant must do all but which of the following?
   A. Be based on probable cause.
   B. Be supported by an oath or affirmation.
   C. Contain a general description of what is to be searched or seized.
   D. All of these are required.

__ 11. Which of the following is *not* in the Fifth Amendment?
   A. Self-incrimination.
   B. Right to counsel.
   C. Double jeopardy.
   D. Due process.

__ 12. Which of the following rights is *not* in the Sixth Amendment?
   A. Speedy trial.
   B. Confrontation of witnesses.
   C. Cross-examination of witnesses.
   D. Self-incrimination.

__ 13. A bank teller who takes $100 out of his or her drawer and pockets the money for his or her own use has committed:_____.
   A. Embezzlement.
   B. Larceny.
   C. Fraud.
   D. Bank fraud.

__ 14. The RICO statute prohibits all but which of the following?

A. Investment in any enterprise of income derived from racketeering.
B. Acquisition of an interest in an enterprise through a pattern of racketeering activity.
C. Participation in an enterprise through a pattern of racketeering activity involving at least two related predicate acts in a twenty-year period.
D. Conspiracy to commit racketeering.

___ 15. The Computer Fraud and Abuse Act prohibits gaining access to a computer without authorization, if by such access the user obtains:

I. Financial records from a financial institution.
II. Any information from a United States agency or department.
III. Information from any protected computer involved in interstate commerce.

A. I or II.
B. I, II, or III.
C. II or III.
D. I or III.

Essay Questions

1. To reduce culpability under the Federal Sentencing Guidelines, what strategies must a company have in place?

2. Why are there different burdens of proof in civil and criminal cases?

CHAPTER 15
ENVIRONMENTAL LAW

INTRODUCTION

Environmental law consists of federal, state, and local laws designed to protect human health. Some industries have long been regulated, but more often real estate developers, insurance and financial institutions face environmental regulations. This chapter reviews environmental laws that cover a wide array of business activities: the Clean Air Act, the Clean Water Act, and the Resource Conservation and Recovery Act. The chapter also addresses the potential liability under the environmental laws of shareholders, directors, officers, and managers, as well as affiliated companies and lenders. It outlines elements of effective compliance programs and audits, and it concludes with a discussion of international considerations.

I. ENVIRONMENTAL LAWS

   A. **Common-Law Nuisance**. Historically, lawsuits based on common-law nuisance were used to control industrial and agricultural activities that interfered with the health or comfort of the community. Today, state and federal regulatory programs have largely replaced common-law nuisance as a means of pollution control.

   B. **Statutes and Regulations**. Federal and state statutes now authorize the executive branch or an administrative agency, *e.g.*, the Environmental Protection Agency, to adopt and enforce environmental policies. Three general areas of regulation.

      1. Discharge of Pollutants into the air, water, or ground. Examples include the Clean Air Act, the Clean Water Act, the Solid Waste Disposal Act, as amended by the Resource Conservation and Recovery Act (RCRA); and the Comprehensive Environmental Response, Compensation, and Liability Act (CERCLA or Superfund).

      2. Manufacture and Sale of Pollutants the regulation of pesticides under the Federal Insecticide, Fungicide and Rodenticide Act, and the Toxic Substances Control Act, which applies to all chemical substances both manufactured in and imported into the United States, excluding certain substances that are regulated under other federal laws.

      3. National Environmental Policy Act (NEPA) requires decision makers to consider the effect of their decisions on the quality of the environment, permitting and licensing.

C. **Natural Resources Laws** contribute to the protection of natural resources, but do not include wilderness preservation, energy conservation, or land-use regulation/zoning.

D. **Industry Participation.** Due to complexity of issues and science, lawmakers often welcome industry participation in setting up regulatory schemes.

II. **ADMINISTRATION OF ENVIRONMENTAL LAWS**

A. **The Environmental Protection Agency (EPA)** created in 1970 by an executive order and operates under the supervision of the president. The EPA administrator and assistant administrators are appointed by the president with the advice and consent of the Senate.

B. **State Programs** many states have laws that are more stringent and more comprehensive than the federal laws. The EPA may authorize or approve a state program in lieu of the federal program in that state.

III. **THE CLEAN AIR ACT (CAA)** requires the EPA to (1) establish *national* ambient air quality standards, (2) require that air quality not deteriorate from these standards, (3) preserve natural visibility within the major national parks and wilderness areas, and (4) establish emission standards that protect public health.

IV. **THE CLEAN WATER ACT (CWA)** seeks to eliminate the discharge of pollutants into the navigable waters of the United States, waters used in interstate commerce, and freshwater wetlands that are adjacent to all other covered waterways.

A. **National Pollutant Discharge Elimination System (NPDES)** administered largely by approved state programs, with supervision by the EPA, and requires permits for the discharge of pollutants from any point source to navigable waters.

B. **Individual Liability of Corporate Officers.** A corporate officer can be civilly responsible under the CWA if she had authority to exercise control over the corporation's activity that caused the unlawful discharge. The officer can be criminally liable if she knowingly violated the act.

V. **THE RESOURCE CONSERVATION AND RECOVERY ACT (RCRA)** governs the management of hazardous wastes by identifying and listing hazardous wastes, and setting standards for the construction and operation of hazardous-waste treatment, storage, and disposal facilities.

A. **Cradle-to-Grave Responsibility.** RCRA imposes "cradle-to-grave" responsibility on generators of hazardous waste, by requiring detailed federal permitting and record-keeping processes for transportation, storage and disposal of hazardous waste.

ECONOMIC PERSPECTIVE: STRATEGIC ENVIRONMENTAL MANAGEMENT. Many companies have moved beyond mere compliance with law. Companies like Monsanto, AT&T, Lockheed and others are searching for eco-efficient strategies. Through integrated economic and ecological approaches companies are looking to reduce energy costs, and ecological externalities. As well social and political concerns about pollution have given economic opportunities for hybrid cars, alternative energy, and more.

B.   **Criminal Liability**. The RCRA imposes strict civil liability on corporations or individuals who fail to comply with codes for storage, treatment, or disposal of wastes. Criminal liability requires some sort of knowledge that hazardous waste was transported to a facility that does not have a permit.

VI.   **THE FEDERAL SUPERFUND LAW (CERCLA)** authorizes the federal government to investigate and take remedial action in response to a release or threatened release of hazardous substances to the environment. CERCLA established the *Hazardous Substance Superfund* to finance federal response activity.

A.   STRICT LIABILITY. CERCLA imposes strict liability for "responsible persons," even if the waste was disposed of on the land by a previous owner or tenant though the "innocent landowner defense" can be established.

B.   POTENTIALLY RESPONSIBLE PARTIES are liable under CERCLA and may be compelled to do remedial clean-up.

1.   Owner or Operator at the Time of Disposal.

> **Case 15.1--*Carson Harbor Village, Ltd. v. Unocal Corp.*, 270 F.3d 863 (9th Cir. 2001). Carson Harbor Village (CHV) sued Unocal for the costs of an environmental clean-up. Unocal had owned the law, but did not contribute to contamination. Contamination had migrated through the soil. Unocal was found liable because it was the owner at the time of the disposal of the contamination.

2.   Lessee as Owner. At least one court has held that a lessee, is a de facto owner for the purpose of CERCLA. *Commander Oil Corp. v. Barlo Equip. Corp.*, 215 F.3d 321 (2d Cir. 2000).

C.   **Joint and Several Liability**. Though multiple parties might be responsible for environmental damage, one party might have to bear all the costs or liability. In some cases parties might only have to bear a portion of the liability, *Browning-Ferris Industries of Illinois v. Ter Maat*, 195 F.3d 953 (7th Cir. 1999) or no liability, *United States v. Alcan Aluminum Corp.*, 990 F.2d 711 (2d. Cir. 1993).

D.   **Liability of Affiliated Companies and Piercing the Corporate Veil**. Both the parent company and its subsidiaries can be held liable under CERCLA.

E.   **Successor Liability**. Ordinarily, a purchaser of corporate assets, as opposed to a purchaser of all the stock of corporation, does not assume any liabilities from the seller. Federal courts have created such liability as corporations sought to avoid liability by selling off assets.

F.   **Liability of Lenders and Fiduciaries**. Lenders can be liable if they foreclose on a contaminated property, as it gives the lender title and ownership to the land. However, a lender is not an owner or operator of a facility if it did not participate in the management of a facility prior to foreclosure. Liability of a fiduciary is limited to the assets held in trust.

G.   **Retroactive Application**. Owners can be held liable for hazardous waste disposed of before CERCLA became law. But see *Gen. Elec. Co. v. EPA*, 360 F.3d 188 (D.C. Cir. 2004).

H.   **Defenses**. There are four CERCLA Defenses to Liability: (a) release of hazardous substances was caused by an *act of God* (e.g., natural disaster); (b) an *act of war*; (c) the act or omission of a *third party*; (d) purchaser of *brownfields*.

1.   Third-Party or Innocent Landowner Defense: defendant must show that the true responsible third party was not an employee and had no contractual relationship with defendant/purchaser, who had no reason to know that hazardous substances were disposed at the facility

Case 15.2--*Western Properties Service Corp. v. Shell Oil Co.*, 358 F.3d 678 (9th Cir. 2004). In 1920 a family sold the rights to dump noxious waste into pits on a ranch. Neighbors began to complain, but sludge pits developed and animals ended up falling into these acidic pits. By 1986 the property was owned by Western Properties. The State of California ordered a clean up which cost $5 million, and Western sued Shell which had dumped toxins on the site. The court held that Western was not an innocent owner, and so it did not have a complete shield from liability. Shell and other oil companies were also liable in part.

2.   Recyclers are exempted from CERCLA liability for private actions, but liable for suits by the government.

3.   Brownfields and Ready for Reuse Certificates. The Brownfields Revitalization Act makes it possible for those who acquire contaminated sites to avoid liability.

I.   **Extraterritorial Application**. One court applied CERCLA against a Canadian smelter.

> **Case 15.3--*Pakootas v. Teck Cominco Metals, Ltd.*,** 2004 U.S. Dist. LEXIS 23041 (E.D. Wash. Nov. 8, 2004). Native American plaintiffs sued to enforce EPA regulations against TCM, a Canadian company. TCM moved to dismiss on the grounds of lack of jurisdiction. The District court found that TCM activities touched U.S. territory and that Congress did not prohibit application of CERCLA to parties outside the U.S. TCM appealed.

VII.   **ENVIRONMENTAL JUSTICE** considers how incinerators, dumps, factories, and other sources of pollution affect poor and minority communities. Often toxic sites are located away from wealthier populations who have more political influence over zoning and environmental regulations.

VIII.   **ENFORCEMENT OF ENVIRONMENTAL LAWS** includes monitoring, compliance and remediation.

A.   **Agency Inspections**. Agencies have broad powers to conduct on-site inspections of plant facilities, collect samples, and execute search warrants if criminal activity is suspected. Violations may be the subject of civil or criminal enforcement actions.

B.   **Self-Reporting Requirements** concerning concentrations and/or the amounts of pollutants discharged from a facility are required. There are penalties for filing false reports, but the EPA may reduce or eliminate fines for civil or administrative violations by companies that discover such violations through their own systematic compliance reviews and notify the EPA.

C.   **Administration and Civil Enforcement Actions**. Government offices are given latitude to enforce environmental laws. The first violation may result in a warning and a schedule for compliance with more aggressive action for repeated violations. In egregious cases the EPA may initiate a civil lawsuit and/or a criminal prosecution and/or shut down the violator's operations.

D. **Criminal Prosecutions**. Federal Prosecutions are the highest level of enforcement. Courts may impose heavy fines and prison sentences.

> **Case 15.4--*United States v. Hansen*,** 262 F.3d 1217 (11th Cir. 2001). Christian Hansen founded the Hanlin Group. Through a subsidiary LCP, Hanlin purchased a chemical plant in Brunswick, Georgia where hazardous materials had been dumped. LCP constructed a wastewater treatment facility, but OSHA cited LCP for safety hazard violations. Hanlin declared bankruptcy, LCP lost its license to dump waste water and ultimately the plant was closed and the EPA clean up cost $50 million. U.S. attorneys then indicted Hansen and others. Hansen was convicted of violating the CWA, RCRA, and CERCLA. Defendants appealed on the grounds that as owners, they were not responsible as plant operators. Their convictions were upheld.

IX. **MANAGEMENT OF ENVIRONMENTAL COMPLIANCE**. Knowledgeable corporate officials recognize the need to develop policies to ensure legal compliance and practices to promote a safe environment.

A. **Corporate Policy** compliance with environmental laws may not be enough. Corporate policy should encompass stringent measures and require every employee to comply with environmental laws.

VIEW FROM CYBERSPACE: THE EPA LAUNCHES ECHO. The Enforcement of Compliance History online program is designed to provide the public access and information about a company's environmental record. The system combines various databases, but critics believe that as the system is limited, and may be misleading.

B. **Well-Defined Organization and Crisis-Management Plan**. Companies should have a crisis-management plan in place which designates someone other than the CEO to coordinate the response and control the crisis. Because corporate officers can be held liable for the acts of employees, education and training of staff and management is necessary.

C. **Record Keeping, Accounting, and Disclosure**. Companies must comply with federal (EPA and SEC) disclosure and reporting requirements, including record-retention policies and cost-accounting procedures. Management must also make sure that whistle-blowers are not subject to retaliation.

D. **Periodic Environmental Audits** measure compliance with occupational health and safety requirements; federal, state, and local environmental laws and regulations. Various states have granted immunity to corporations which produce self-audits. The EPA has also developed programs to certification that companies are compliant with environmental laws.

E.   **Procedures for Agency Inspections**. Federal inspectors may conduct surprise visits. Management should designate a liaison to accompany the inspector and prepare are report to supervisors.

F.   **Public and Community Relations**. The public favors corporate responsibility and environmental sensitivity. A company can gain credibility and respect by handling an environmental accident in a proactive and fair manner. Eastman Kodak took proactive measures to help homeowners in Rochester, New York, who faced economic losses due to toxic groundwater caused by Kodak's chemical processes.

G.   **Long-Term Strategies**. The best companies develop plans to minimize pollutants produced, ways to recycle and dispose of waste, and new technologies to render wastes non-hazardous.

GLOBAL VIEW: SUSTAINABLE DEVELOPMENT, GLOBAL WARMING, AND THE KYOTO CLIMATE PROTOCOL. Sustainable development holds that environmental resources are limited and that economic development must plan for and account for the idea that certain resources, from petroleum to landfill space, will run out. At the same time, economic planning can seize on the opportunities created by this recognition. One prevalent concern is global warming and the thought that human production of greenhouse gases are having a deleterious effect on human climates and weather. Under the Kyoto protocols, nations agreed to reduce their greenhouse gas emissions, but some industries complained that it would provide economic advantages to nations like China and India over the U.S. Some nations are seeking to provide incentives for industries and companies that reduce emissions.

X.   **THE RESPONSIBLE MANAGER: MANAGING RISKS OF ENVIRONMENTAL LIABILITY.** In evaluating a company for purposes of acquisition, investment, or financing, a manager must consider that the company's earnings may be affected by the costs of compliance with environmental laws.

- Equipment values may be affected by regulatory limitations that make the equipment obsolete.
- Corporate expansion may be impaired by air emission standards or waste treatment or disposal facilities.
- Failure to comply with regulations may lead to the imposition of substantial penalties.
- A small company may not be able to survive CERCLA liability and remediation costs.
- Companies must engage in due diligence, a systematic and ongoing process for determining whether property contains or emits hazardous substances and whether the company is in compliance with environmental laws.

- Considering the demands of CERCLA, the company may have to negotiate contracts that shift liability to third parties.
- Lenders too need to be aware of potential environmental hazards and legal liabilities on lands and properties.

INSIDE STORY: DREDGING UP THE HUDSON. The Hudson River, along New York City is one of the dirtiest rivers known. General Electric has used the river as a dump for its waste for years. In 2001, the EPA ordered GE to dredge the river due to past years of dumping PCBs. GE repeated protests centered on the fact that at the time it dumped PCBs into the Hudson, such activity was legal. Further there is a chance that by dredging up the toxins, local communities will be re-exposed. In 2004 a federal appeals court ruled that application of CERCLA against GE for its activity pre-1977, would be unconstitutional. *Gen. Elec. Co. v. EPA*, 360 F.3d 188 (D.C. Cir. 2004).

STUDY QUESTIONS

True-False Questions

___ 1. Historically, public officials relied on the common-law theory of nusiance to control environmental problems.

___ 2. The largest category of environmental laws consists of laws that regulate the release of pollutants in to the air, water, or ground.

___ 3. Congressional and administrative agency staffs may be unaware of how a proposed law or regulation may affect a particular industry.

___ 4. Environmental laws generally do not cover zoning.

___ 5. The EPA operates under the supervision of Congress.

___ 6. Many states have environmental laws that are more stringent and comprehensive than federal laws.

___ 7. The EPA may authorize a state program in lieu of a federal program in a state.

___ 8. Navigable waters include freshwater wetlands adjacent to covered waterways.

___ 9. Under the RCRA, unlike most other environmental laws, "person" includes both corporations and individuals.

__ 10. The RCRA can impose both civil and criminal sanctions.

__ 11. Environmental regulatory programs can both increase costs and create opportunities for cost savings.

__ 12. CERCLA affects businesses and individuals that do not produce pollutants.

__ 13. The average cost of response by the EPA at a Superfund site is about $25 million.

__ 14. CERCLA has no retroactive applications.

__ 15. CERCLA does not allow for punitive damages.

Multiple-Choice Questions

__ 1. Environmental statutes:

I.   Establish policy.
II. Set goals.
III. Authorize agencies to adopt regulations.

A. III only.
B. I and II.
C. I and III.
D. I, II, and III.

__ 2. Which act is *not* covered in the same category of environmental law?
A. Clean Air Act.
B. Clean Water Act.
C. Safe Drinking Water Act.
D. Solid Waste Disposal Act.

__ 3. Which of the following is *not* a category of environmental law?

I.   Governing the sale and manufacture of chemicals as commercial products.
II. Regulation of the release of pollutants into the air, water, and ground.
III. Toxic chemicals and wastes.
IV. Requiring government agencies to use a cost-benefit analysis on new environmental decisions.

A. II and IV.

    B. III.
    C. IV.
    D. II.

__ 4. The EPA administrator is:

    I.   Appointed by the President.
    II.   Confirmed by Congress.
    III.   Confirmed by the Senate.
    IV.   Confirmed by the House.

    A. I and III.
    B. I and II.
    C. I and IV.
    D. I only.

__ 5. Which is *not* a goal of the Clean Air Act?
    A. The EPA will establish regional ambient air quality standards.
    B. Air quality in compliant areas cannot be allowed to deteriorate.
    C. Preservation of natural visibility in national parks and wilderness areas.
    D. The EPA will establish emission standards that protect public health.

__ 6. SIP's are _____ Plans
    A. State Improvement.
    B. State Implementation.
    C. Statutory Implementation.
    D. Statutory Improvement.

__ 7. Before construction of major sources of emissions in noncontainment areas, case-by-case determinations of the _____ for the sources are required.
    A. Best available control technology.
    B. Best achievable emission rate.
    C. Lowest achievable emission rate.
    D. Highest achievable emission rate.

__ 8. The Solid Waste Disposal Act, as amended, authorizes the EPA to all but which of the following?
    A. Identify and list hazardous wastes.
    B. Develop standards for managing hazardous wastes.
    C. Develop standards for destroying hazardous wastes.
    D. Set standards for operation of hazardous waste storage facilities.

__ 9. CERCLA stands for the _____ and Liability Act.
    A. Comprehensive Environmental Response, Compensation,

B. Comprehensive Environmental Required Clean-up
C. Comprehensive Environmental Reaction, Costs,
D. Critical Environmental Response, Compensation,

___ 10. Under CERCLA, "responsible persons" includes all but which if the following?
A. The present owner or operator of the facility.
B. Any former owner or operator of the facility.
C. Anyone who arranged for disposal of hazardous waste at the facility.
D. Any person who transported hazardous substances to and selected the facility.

___ 11. To protect plaintiffs against corporate schemes to merely evade responsibility, courts may _____ for affiliated companies.
A. Do nothing.
B. Order a stock split.
C. Pierce the corporate veil.
D. Pierce the corporate subsidiary.

___ 12. Which is *not* a defense to liability under CERCLA?
A. An act of God.
B. An act of war.
C. The innocent landowner defense.
D. The innocent third party defense.

___ 13. In most instances, courts are authorized to impose penalties of

I. $25,000 to $100,000 per day of violation.
II.   Jail terms of one year or more to individuals.
III. Closure of the business.

A. I and II.
B. II and III.
C. I and III.
D. I, II and III.

___ 14. The most essential component of good environmental management is:
A. Good public relations.
B. Comprehensive education and training.
C. Solid reporting policies and procedures.
D. Periodic assessment.

___ 15. An environmental audit does *not* measure which of the following items?
A. Compliance with OSHA requirements.
B. Compliance with federal and state emissions limits.

C. Current hazardous waste disposal practices.
D. Current sustainable development.

Essay Questions

1. Why may congressional or administrative agency staffs be unaware of how proposed regulations may affect a particular industry?

2. The EPA establishes performance standards based on the best control technology available for a category of similar sources. Why?

3. In general, what is successor liability?

CHAPTER 16
ANTITRUST

INTRODUCTION

In recent years corporate giants ADM and BASF,AG have paid record fines for price-fixing. Both the United States and EU authorities brought criminal actions against these firms under antitrust laws. In general companies may not restrict competition, which raises prices for consumers. This chapter offers a general overview of the federal antitrust laws, pointing out which aspects are settled and which are not. It begins with a discussion of Sections 1 and 2 of the Sherman Act, and then addresses the Clayton Act provisions relating to mergers and combinations. The chapter outlines the Robinson–Patman Act's prohibitions on price discrimination, references the Federal Trade Commissions Act. It concludes with a discussion of extra-territorial application of the U.S. antitrust laws, EU competition laws, and their extra-territorial application.

CHAPTER OUTLINE

I. **AGREEMENTS IN RESTRAINT OF TRADE: SECTION 1 OF THE SHERMAN ACT** provides that "Every contract, combination in the form of trust or otherwise, or conspiracy, in restraint of trade or commerce among the several States, or with foreign nations, is declared to be illegal." Courts have interpreted § 1 to refer only to those restraints of trade that *unreasonably* restrict competition.

    A. **Trade and Commerce**. The Sherman Act applies to trade and commerce, thus extends to practically all economic activity. See *Summit Health, Ltd. v. Pinhas*, 500 U.S. 322, 329 n.10 (1991) and *Hamilton Chapter of Alpha Delta Phi, Inc. v. Hamilton Coll.*, 128 F.3d 59 (2d Cir. 1997).

    B. **Proving a Violation of Section 1**. To make a *prima facie* case the plaintiff must prove: (1) there is a contract, combination, or conspiracy among separate entities; (2) that it unreasonably restrains trade; (3) that it affects interstate commerce; and (4) that it causes an antitrust injury.

    C. **What Constitutes a Contract, Combination, or Conspiracy?** Section 1 does not prohibit unilateral activity in restraint of trade. Because such conspiracies are secretive courts develop mechanisms to determine the merits of § 1 claims, namely *horizontal vs. vertical Agreements*.

HISTORICAL PERSPECTIVE: POLITICS AND ECONOMICS. The Sherman Act grew out of a period of American history where oil and Steel industries had organized to restrict competition.

More than a century later, with U.S. firms competing in a global economy, many wonder if federal law is needed to regulate markets against trusts and monopolistic practices.

1.   Proving a Horizontal Conspiracy. Plaintiffs need not show an overt agreement. Conspiracy can be shown via parallel behavior between otherwise competing firms. E.g., *Theatre Enters, Inc. v. Paramount Film Distrib. Corp.*, 346 U.S. 537 (1994).

> **Case 16.1--*Williams Oil Co. v. Phillip Morris USA*,** 346 F.3d 1287 (11th Cir. 2003). Between 1993 and 2000, Phillip Morris (PM) and three other companies produced 97% of all cigarettes sold in the U.S. In 1993 PM reduced its retail price for Marlboro cigarettes by 40 cents per pack. Others followed suit. Subsequently, RJR raised its prices and PM and others also raised prices. Wholesalers sued for a violation of the Sherman Act. Because wholesalers could not show any actions taken against economic interest or other "plus factors" the suit was dismissed.

2.   Proving a Vertical Conspiracy. Vertical agreements between, e.g., an automaker and a car dealership, reduce intrabrand competition – competition between local car dealers. Such arrangements might increase interbrand competition with different dealers selling different makes of cars. Courts will allow reductions in intrabrand competition when interbrand competition increases.

D.   What Constitutes an Unreasonable Restraint of Trade?

1.   *Per se* Violations are practices completely void of competitive rationales. The number of truly *per se* violations of the antitrust laws has declined.

2.   The Rule of Reason posits whether, on balance, the activity promotes or restrains competition, whether it helps or harms consumers.

E.   Types of Horizontal Restraints.

1.   Horizontal Price-Fixing (*per se* violation of § 1)—agreement between retailers to set a common price for a product such as: (a) setting prices (including maximum prices); (b) setting the terms of sale, such as customer credit terms; (c) setting the quantity or quality of goods to be manufactured or made available for sale; or (d) rigging bids (agreements between or among competitors to rig contract bids). The Justice Department views price-fixing as "hard crime" punished by jail sentences whenever possible.

2.   Horizontal Market Division and Nonprice Horizontal Restraints (*per se* violation of § 1). Competitors divide up a market according to class of customer or geographic territory or restrict product output. Agreements among competitors not to compete on non-price matters may violate § 1.

3.   Group Boycotts and Trade Associations (may be *per se* violation of § 1). Boycotts are agreements between or among competitors that deprives another competitor of something it needs to compete effectively. However, not all boycotts are *per se* violations. Courts do not look favorably upon attempts at self-regulation by trade and professional associations, particularly when such attempts result in group boycotts.

F.   **Types of Vertical Restraints** are restraints between firms at different levels in the chain of distribution, including price-fixing, market division, tying arrangements, and some franchise agreements.

1.   Vertical Price-Fixing (may be *per se* violation of § 1) occurs through agreements on price between firms at different levels of production or distribution. Also known as resale price maintenance (RPM) when the agreement fixes minimum prices.

2.   Nonprice Vertical Restraints and Vertical Market Division come about through arrangements imposed by a manufacturer on its distributors or dealers that limits the freedom of the dealer to market the manufacturer's product. They are judged under the rule of reason. The central question is whether a reduction in intrabrand competition is justified by interbrand competition.

> **Case 16.2--*Concord Boat Corp. v. Brunswick Corp.*,** 207 F.3d 1039 (8th Cir. 2000). In 1983, Brunswick had 75% share of the stern-drive engine market for motor boats. Brunswick offered discounts to boat manufacturers. In December 1986 Brunswick purchased two of the largest boat builders. Given its control of the market, other boat manufacturers were "taxed" as Brunswick would not granted them the bulk "discount." Though plaintiffs won at the trial court, the ruling was overturned. Brunswick engaged in competitive, not monopolistic and unfair practices, i.e., volume discounts and lower prices.

> • Exclusive Distributorships. A manufacturer limits itself to a single distributor in a given territory or, perhaps, line of business. Such are legal under the rule of reason.

- <u>Territorial and Customer Restrictions</u> prevent a dealer or distributor from selling outside a certain territory or to a certain class of customers.

- <u>Dual Distributors</u> manufacturers that sell their goods at both wholesale and retail.

3. Product Bundling and Other Tying Arrangements (may be *per se* violations of § 1)—seller agrees to sell product A (the *tying,* or desired, product) to the customer only if the customer agrees to purchase product B (the *tied* product) from the seller. Violation if:

   - The tying and tied products are separate products,
   - The availability of the tied product is conditioned upon the purchase of the tying product,
   - The party imposing the tie has market power ("the power to force a purchaser to do something that he would not do in a competitive market") to force the purchase of the tied product, and
   - A "not insubstantial" amount of commerce in the tied product is affected.
   - Unlike other *per se* violations, a tying arrangement may be upheld if there is a business justification for it (quality of parts for business image).

4. Franchise Agreements in which one party (the franchisor) grants to another party (the franchisee) the right to use the franchisor's name, logo and distribute the franchisor's products. Section 1 issues arise when franchisor wants to promote uniformity and name recognition, imposes certain types of limitations on the franchisee.

II. **MONOPOLIES: SECTION 2 OF THE SHERMAN ACT**. Section 2 of the Sherman Act defines monopoly activity and declares that such is a felony. No agreement is required and unilateral action may violate Section 2. A defendant's monopoly power is considered with a relevant market and unilateral action will be deemed wrongful if a defendant willfully acquired or maintained that power through anticompetitive acts.

A. **Market Power (Monopoly Power)** is marked by prices that are higher than they would be in a competitive market over an extended period of time and the unavailability of substitute goods or services.

   1. Defining Relevant Market. Markets have two components: a product and location or geography.

- <u>Multiple-Brand Product Market</u> has product or service offerings by different manufacturers or sellers that are economically interchangeable.

- <u>Single-Brand Product Market</u> is dominated by one brand, and parts are controlled by one manufacturer. *Eastman Kodak Co. v. Image Technical Services, Inc.* 504 U.S. 451 (1992).

- <u>Geographic Market Competition</u> denotes restraints on product movement. Contours of geographic markets can also be affected by government regulations.

- <u>Market Share.</u> Once a relevant market is determined, plaintiff must show that, within that market, the defendant has monopoly power, inferred from market share, allowing defendant to control prices. Plaintiff must also show that there are significant barriers to entry.

- <u>Barriers to Entry.</u> Common barriers to entry include patents, licenses, buyer preferences, up-front capital requirements, etc.

2. Monopolistic Intent. Once a *prima facie* case is proved, the defendant's intent may be relevant. If relevant, monopolistic intent can be proved by evidence of conduct (not merely statements), it is inherently anticompetitive.

ECONOMIC PERSPECTIVE: THE REGULATION OF NATURAL MONOPOLIES. In a world of perfect competition, productive efficiency would go hand in hand with allocative efficiency. In some areas, like telephone service, duplication of infrastructure is not cost effective. Hence natural monopolies are allowed. By 1974, AT&T grew so large that the federal government brought suit for violation of the Sherman Act. In 1984, under a consent decree AT&T was broken up into the Baby Bells, and other long-distance carriers were allowed to use AT&T lines.

3. Predatory Pricing is the attempt to eliminate rivals by undercutting their retail prices to the point where the rivals will lose money and go out of business after which the monopolist can raise prices because it is no longer restrained by competition.

> **Case 16.3--*LePage's, Inc. v. 3M*,** 324 F.3d 141 (3d Cir. 2001). LePage's challenged 3M which had a 90 percent share in the transparent tape market. Part of 3M's marketing strategy involved bundling rebates which the court of appeals likened to predatory

pricing – making the cost of entering the market too high. LePage's was awarded nearly $69 million.

4. Refusal to Deal. Generally, antitrust laws do not prevent a firm from deciding with whom it will or will not deal, unless the firm owns or manages an *essential facility*, i.e., some resource necessary to its rivals' survival that they cannot feasibly duplicate.

5. Derivative Markets. If a firm with monopoly power in one market can use that power to gain an advantage in a separate market, it violates § 2.

6. Other Anticompetitive Acts include allocation of markets and territories, price-fixing, fraudulently obtaining a patent, or engaging in sham litigation against a competitor.

III. **PRICE DISCRIMINATION: THE ROBINSON–PATMAN ACT (SECTION 2 OF THE CLAYTON ACT).** Price discrimination—selling the same product to different purchasers at the same level of distribution at different prices—is illegal under the Clayton Act. Generally, private individuals are involved in litigation.

A. **Elements of a Robinson-Patman Act**: (1) Discrimination in price; (2) Some part of the discrimination must involve interstate commerce; (3) The discrimination must involve sales for use, consumption, or resale within the United States; (4) There must be discrimination between different purchasers; (5) The discrimination must involve sales of tangible commodities of like grade and quality; and (6) There must be a probable injury to competition.

B. **Defenses**. Even if the elements are shown, there are defenses.

1. Availability. Robinson-Patman permits discrimination when discounts are offered to all competing customers.

2. Meeting Competition. Discriminatory prices are not prohibited if the seller acted in "good faith to meet an equally low price of a competitor."

3. Cost Justification. Price differentials are allowed if due to cost of manufacture, sale or delivery resulting from the differing methods or quantities in which the goods are sold and delivered.

4. Changing Conditions. Section 2(a) does not prohibit price changes due to fluctuating market conditions.

IV. **MERGERS: SECTION 7 OF THE CLAYTON ACT.** If a merger or acquisition unreasonably restrains trade, it violates § 1. If it results in monopolization, it violates § 2.

A. **Hart–Scott–Rodino Antitrust Improvements Act**. An amendment to § 7, provides that if a merger is large enough, in economic terms, there is a pre-merger notification procedure whereby the FTC and Justice Department can review the anticompetitive effects of proposed merger.

B. **Merger Guidelines**. The FTC and Justice Department will: analyze whether the merger will reduce competition based on Sherman Act § 2 criteria; determine the relevant geographic and product markets; calculate the market shares of the companies proposing to merge; and determine the effect the merger will have on the relevant market; all with the use of the *Herfindahl-Hirshman Index*.

C. **Litigation under Section 7.**

1. Horizontal Mergers combine two or more competing companies at the same level in the chain of production and distribution. Lawfulness is determined by: (a) identification of the relevant product and geographic markets, based on § 2 Sherman Act criteria; (b) market shares of the firms involved in the transaction; (c) level of concentration in the market; and (d) whether the market is structurally conducive to anticompetitive behavior.

> *Case 16.4--United States v. Oracle Corp.*, 331 F. Supp. 2d 1098 (N.D. Cal. 2004). Oracle tendered to purchase PeopleSoft, Inc. The Department of Justice sought to enjoin the merger on the grounds it would create an effective duopoly. The court held that the government as plaintiff could not meet its burden to show that the merger would reduce competition.

2. Vertical Mergers occur as one company acquires another along a higher or lower level in the chain of production and distribution. Courts tend to focus on whether the merger has excluded competitors from a significant sector of the market.

3. Conglomerate Mergers are the acquisition of a company by another company in a different line of business. Federal efforts to prohibit conglomerate mergers have largely been abandoned. It can be argued a merger violates § 7 if: (a) the market is highly concentrated; (b) one of the merging firms is an actual, substantial competitor; (c) entry of that firm would be likely to have pro-competitive effects; and (d) but for the merger, the smaller firm would enter the market.

V.   **UNFAIR METHODS OF COMPETITION: SECTION 5 OF THE FEDERAL TRADE COMMISSION ACT**. The FTC Act is broader than the Sherman Act. Congress granted the FTC authority to regulate unfair methods of competition and deceptive practices.

VI.   **ANTITRUST ENFORCEMENT**. Both government-led and private suits are available.

    A.   **Criminal Violations**. The Federal Trade Commission (FTC) refers cases to the Department of Justice. Corporations and individuals can be found in violation.

    B.   **Civil Suits**. The Justice Department enforces Sherman and Clayton acts in civil suits. Robinson-Patman violations are prosecuted by the FTC. Private plaintiffs are able to recover three times their damages sustained by the wrongful acts of defendant.

    C.   **Enforcement of the Hart-Scott-Rodino Antitrust Improvements Act**. If a defendant is found in violation, courts may order payments of fines, restitution and a number of equitable remedies including: divestiture, sell-offs, sharing of technology, etc.

VII.   **ANTITRUST INJURY**. To recover damages, a plaintiff must establish that it sustained an *antitrust injury*: a loss due to a competition-reducing aspect or effect of the defendant's behavior.

VIII.   **LIMITATIONS ON ANTITRUST ENFORCEMENT**. The courts have limited the private enforcement rights of individual citizens and states by invoking the doctrine of standing. They have also limited the liability of state governments by applying state-action exemptions.

    A.   **Standing**. Plaintiffs must show that they have suffered an injury from the defendant in order to bring a suit in antitrust.

    B.   **State-Action Exemption**. The Sherman Antitrust Act only applies to anticompetitive actions by private parties, not to anticompetitive actions by state legislatures or administrative bodies. State action is exempt so long as: (1) there is a clear state purpose to displace competition; and (2) the state provides adequate public supervision.

IX.   **THE EXTRATERRITORIAL REACH OF U.S. ANTITRUST LAW**. The Sherman Act included trade or commerce with foreign nations. But the Clayton Act on price discrimination has no application outside the U.S. Practices by foreign firms inside the U.S. are examined to the extent that they are extensions of policies of foreign governments (exempt) and the purpose and effects test. See *Hartford Fire Insurance, Co. v. California*, 509 U.S. 764 (1993).

Case 16.5--*United States v. Nippon Paper Industries Co.*, 109 F.3d 1 (1st Cir. 1997). NPI, a Japanese manufacturer of fax paper, met in Japan with unnamed co-conspirators to fix prices of paper in the United States. The court of appeals held that NPI could be prosecuted for violations of the Sherman Act in the United States for NPI acts committed in Japan.

X. **U.S. CONTROL OVER OFFSHORE MERGERS AND OTHERS CONSOLIDATIONS.** Both the Justice Department and the FTC require HSR reports regarding U.S. and non-U.S. based mergers and acquisitions. Companies are often fined for failure to give timely reports. Subsequent amendments have placed simple economic guidelines on reporting requirements.

XI. **GLOBAL VIEW: ANTITRUST LAWS IN THE EUROPEAN UNION.** The EU sets rules on mergers and acquisitions in Articles 81 and 82 of the Treaty of Amsterdam. Article 81 is similar to § 1 of the Sherman Act, but the EU is stricter on vertical arrangements. Article 82, parallel to § 2, does not have an expansive definition of market share. Still the EU will punish importers who abuse their dominant market position, e.g. Microsoft.

XII. **THE RESPONSIBLE MANAGER: Avoiding Antitrust Violations.** To minimize antitrust violations, a manager should:

- *not* discuss products or pricing among competitors, trade and professional associations,
- *not* disseminate information that may result in market division or output restriction,
- be wary of highly-concentrated markets,
- encourage employees to inform the manager whenever any of the above "red flags" appear,
- seek assistance from competent counsel in analyzing any activity that might violate the antitrust laws, and
- if ever she hears competitors discussing price or other terms of sale, make a memorable and noticeable exit.

STUDY QUESTIONS

True-False Questions

__ 1. Read literally, Section 1 of the Sherman Act would outlaw almost every type of business transaction.

__ 2. Interpreting Section 1, courts have found only prohibitions against unreasonable restrictions on competition.

__ 3. The top criminal price-fixing fine is almost $75 million dollars.

__ 4. No matter what an individual does, an individual cannot violate Section 1.

__ 5. A parent corporation and its wholly owned subsidiary can violate Section 1.

__ 6. A vertical agreement can be proved by direct evidence that there was an agreement, or by circumstantial evidence that tends to exclude the possibility of independent action.

__ 7. Parallel pricing of similar products or services is illegal price-fixing.

__ 8. Price competition between local dealers selling the same manufacturer's products is known as inter-brand competition.

__ 9. Once an act is identified as illegal *per se*, all that remains for liability to attach is proof of an impact on the market.

__ 10. Under the Federal Sentencing Guidelines, a person convicted of horizontal price-fixing would usually receive a six to twelve month jail sentence as a first time offender.

__ 11. The Supreme Court has emphasized that horizontal market division by potential as well as actual competitors is *per se* illegal.

__ 12. Manufacturers and distributors may advertise suggested retail prices.

__ 13. Exclusive distributorships are illegal.

__ 14. Tying arrangements are illegal under both the Sherman Act and the Clayton Act.

__ 15. Antitrust laws apply to anti-competitive actions by private parties, state legislatures, and administrative agencies.

Multiple-Choice Questions

__ 1. The Sherman Act can be enforced by:
   A. Prosecutions as felonies.
   B. Civil actions by the Justice Department.
   C. Private lawsuits.
   D. All of the above.

__ 2.   Sherman Act violations can punish violators in which of the following ways?

I.   Corporate fines of up to $1 million.
II.   Individual fines of up to $300,000.
III.   Imprisonment of individuals up to 5 years in prison.

A.   None of the above.
B.   II and III.
C.   I only.
D.   I and II.

__ 3.   To prove Section 1 liability, a plaintiff must prove all but which of the following?
A.   There is a contract or conspiracy among one or more entities.
B.   The conspiracy unreasonably restrains trade.
C.   It affects interstate or foreign commerce.
D.   There is an antitrust injury.

__ 4.   _____ agreements are those between firms at different levels of distribution.
A.   Horizontal.
B.   Vertical.
C.   Parallel.
D.   Circular.

__ 5.   The objective to determine for the rule of reason includes all but which of the following?
A.   Whether the activity promotes or restrains trade.
B.   The structure of the market.
C.   The defendant's actions.
D.   Whether the activity has a substantial net effect to reduce competition.

__ 6.   Which is *not* an example of a horizontal price-fixing agreement?
A.   Setting minimum prices.
B.   Setting the terms of the sale.
C.   Setting the quantity or quality of the goods.
D.   Competitive bidding process.

__ 7.   Which is an example of a horizontal market division?
A.   Classification of customers.
B.   Geographic territories.
C.   Product output restrictions.
D.   All of the above.

__ 8.   A _____ among competitors is when they refuse to deal with another competitor
A.   Horizontal agreement.

B.   Vertical agreement.
C.   Group boycott.
D.   *Per se* agreement.

__ 9. Which of the following is an unlawful horizontal restraint?
A.   Price-fixing.
B.   Market division.
C.   Tying arrangements.
D.   None of the above.

__ 10. Vertical price-fixing is also known as _____ maintenance.
A.   Retail price.
B.   Resale price.
C.   Repressive price.
D.   Resale parity.

__ 11. Vertical market divisions may establish: _____.
A.   Exclusive distributorships.
B.   Territorial restrictions.
C.   Customer restrictions.
D.   All of these.

__ 12. Tying arrangements have traditionally been held to be: _____.
A.   No violation.
B.   A *per se* violation.
C.   A recommended business practice.
D.   An unsubstantial effect on interstate commerce.

__ 13. Which is a *false* statement about Section 2 of the Sherman Act?
A.   As a practical matter, violators of Section 2 are not prosecuted criminally.
B.   Like Section 1, Section 2 requires proof of an agreement or any other collective action.
C.   Section 2 does not prohibit the mere possession of monopoly power.
D.   A company that has monopoly power thrust upon it does not violate Section 2.

__ 14. The Justice Department cannot seek _____ for a Clayton Act violation.
A.   a divestiture action
B.   a sale of particular subsidiaries
C.   criminal sanctions
D.   temporary restrictions on the defendant's output

__ 15. The Herfindahl-Hirshman Index evaluates the effect of mergers by examining all of the following except: _____.
A.   A company's market share.

B.   The market share of competitors.
C.   Market concentration.
D.   Estimated increased consumer costs.

Essay Questions

1. Why does § 1 of the Sherman Act *not* penalize a manufacturer advertising suggested retail prices?

2. Why can a franchise agreement specify that another franchise will not be awarded in the same geographic area?

3. Briefly discuss the justifications for the defenses to an allegation of a Robinson-Patman Act violation.

CHAPTER 17
CONSUMER PROTECTION

INTRODUCTION

This chapter explores the major acts that focus on consumer protection and fairness. Issues of consumer health and safety are also covered. Additionally, which agencies handle which consumer issues is addressed.

CHAPTER OUTLINE

I. **COMMISSIONS AND AGENCIES**. Federal offices involved in consumer protection are either independent commissions or agencies. Commissions are: the Federal Trade Commission, the Federal Communications Commission, the Securities and Exchange Commission, the Federal Reserve System, and the Consumer Product Safety Commission. The executive branch agencies are: the Food and Drug Administration, Environmental Protection Agency, and the National Highway Traffic Safety Administration.

II. **CONSUMER HEALTH AND SAFETY.** Federal, state, and local regulatory agencies protect consumers' health and safety (*e.g.*, the FDA and the Consumer Product Safety Commission). The FTC regulates labeling and packaging. States regulate the availability of alcohol, tobacco, and gambling; no-smoking areas; and licensing of professional workers through the granting of various occupational licenses.

III. **FOOD SAFETY AND LABELING.**

   A. **Product Definition under FDCA: Food or Drug?** The distinction is important because of different provisions of the Food, Drug and Cosmetic Act (FDCA). Drugs include: (i) articles intended for use in the diagnosis, cure, mitigation, treatment, or prevention of disease; and (ii) articles (other than food) intended to affect the structure or any function of the body. Food is defined as: (i) articles used for food or drink, (ii) chewing gum, and (iii) articles used for components of either.

   B. **FDA Standards for Food Condemnation**. The FDA protects consumer health through confiscation of contaminated or adulterated food. Standards depend on whether the FDA examines an additive or considers food adulterated. Additives are anything not inherent in the food product. If the additive is injurious, the product is deemed "adulterated." Natural Foods are adulterated if they consist of, in whole or part, any filthy, putrid or decomposed substance.

C. **Role of the U.S. Department of Agriculture (USDA)**. The USDA inspects slaughterhouses and meat processing, poultry and egg plants; prevents the sale of mislabeled food; and offers producers a voluntary grading program for various agricultural products.

D. **Pesticides and Human-Made Bugs**. Under the Food, Drug, and Cosmetic Act, the FDA and EPA share responsibility or regulating pesticide residues on food.

E. **Genetically Modified Food**. In April 2000 the National Academy of Sciences advised the federal government to increase regulation of GMO foods. Europeans largely reject GMO foods and more Americans are skeptical as well.

F. **Irradiated Foods** an FDA authorized irradiation of fresh and frozen meat to kill bacteria.

G. **Organic Foods**. USDA standards ban the use of pesticides, genetic engineering, growth hormones, and irradiation. Foods grown and processed according to these standards can bear the seal "USDA Organic."

H. **Food Labeling**. The FDA has primary responsibility for regulating the packaging and labeling of most food (save that covered by USDA), drugs, medical devices, and cosmetics. Under the Fair Packaging and Labeling Act labels must contain the name and address of the manufacturer, packer, or distributor; the net quantity of food; the quantity in servings, number of serving per unit; and other information.

     1. Nutrition Facts. The Nutrition Labeling and Education Act requires labeling of "Nutrition Facts" by ingredients, but restricts nutrient health claims. An Illinois court found that the NLEA preempts suits for inadequate labeling of McDonald's foods. *Cohen v. McDonald's Corp.*, 86 Antitrust & Trade Reg. Rep. (BNA) 220 (Ill App. Ct. Feb. 13, 2004).

     2. Health Claims. Since 1990 manufacturers can make certain health claims previously certified by the FDA.

IV. **DRUGS AND MEDICAL DEVICES.**

A. **FDA Standards for Drug Approval**. The FDA certifies drugs (and their particular uses) and has authority to require that certain drugs be available only by prescription. DEA classifies drugs into one of five different schedules.

B. **Labeling of Medical Devices**. The FDA has jurisdiction over medical devices. Though a manufacturer provides the FDA-mandated warnings, it still could be found liable under state product liability law. *Ogilvie v. Int'l Playtex, Inc.*, 821 F.2d 1438 (10th Cir. 1987).

C.   **Drug Advertising**. Since 1997 the FDA recently relaxed rules for the advertising of prescription drugs on television and radio. Companies need not state all the side effects of the drug.

V.   **HEALTH CLAIMS AND LABELING OF DIETARY SUPPLEMENTS**. Under the Dietary Supplement Health and Education Act, dietary supplements are regulated only if the supplement contains a new dietary ingredient or poses a safety risk. The Nutrition Labeling and Education Act allows manufacturers to make health claims on dietary supplements.

HISTORICAL PERSPECTIVE: FOOD AND DRUG REGULATION. Thalidomide tragedy spurs new laws, 1962. Thalidomide was developed as a sleeping drug. In conjunction with thalidomide a number of women gave birth to babies born without fully developed arms and legs. Shortly thereafter, Congress adopted stricter standards for drug approval.

VI.   **LABELING OF OTHER PRODUCTS.**

A.   **Clothing**. The FTC has primary responsibility for regulating the packaging and labeling of commodities including clothing for the purpose of protecting consumers against misbranding and false advertising.

B.   **Alcohol**. The Bureau of Alcohol Tobacco Tax and Trade regulates labels on alcohol and requires warning labels.

C.   **"Made in USA"** labels can be issued in accordance with rules promulgated by the FTC.

D.   **State Labeling Laws**. Many states have taken steps to protect consumers from dangerous products. Historically, these laws have sought to protect consumers from dangers of imminent bodily harm.

VII.   **BROADCASTING AND THE INTERNET.**

A.   **Broadcasting**. The FCC seeks to ensure that broadcast media are competitive and operate for the public's benefit and use. FCC enforcement power comes through license renewal primarily. Licenses cannot be transferred or assigned unless the FCC determines it is in the public interest.

B. **Internet**. Though generally open as a free speech medium, primary regulation has come about to prevent fraud, auction fraud, pyramid schemes, and securities fraud.

VIII. **THE CONSUMER PRODUCT SAFETY COMMISSION (CPSC)**. The CPSC protects the public against unreasonable risks of injury associated with consumer products (including infant products and toys) and provides assistance to consumers in evaluating the comparative safety of such products. Any interested person may petition the CPSC to adopt a standard or begins a proceeding to develop a standard by publishing a notice in the *Federal Register* inviting any person to submit an offer to do the development. Under the Consumer Product Safety Act it is unlawful to manufacture for sale, offer for sale, distribute in commerce, or import a consumer product that does not conform to CPSC standards. Violators are subject to civil penalties, criminal penalties, injunctive enforcement and seizure, private suits for damages, and private suits for injunctive relief. The CPSC may require manufacturers to repair, modify, or replace the product, or refund the purchase price.

IX. **AUTOMOBILES**. The National Highway Traffic Safety Administration (NHTSA) has the power to establish motor vehicle safety standards, prohibit manufacture or importation of substandard vehicles, and develop tire safety. States refusing to comply with established federal standards are denied federal highway funds.

X. **PRIVACY PROTECTIONS** - Technological developments, especially the Internet, have made it possible to amass large amounts of detailed personal information.

A. **State legislation**. State departments of consumer affairs protect the public by examining and licensing firms and individuals who possess the necessary education and demonstrated skills to perform their services competently. Among the occupations generally regulated are accountants, architects, barbers, contractors, cosmetologists, dentists, dry cleaners, marriage counselors, nurses, pharmacists, physical therapists, physicians, and social workers. Attorneys are regulated by state bar associations and the courts. State departments of consumer affairs also investigate and resolve consumer complaints and hold public hearings involving consumer matters.

B. **Federal Trade Commission Actions**. For years the FTC has taken the position that companies must honor their own privacy agreements. In 2004 the FTC proposed a rule to require consumer reporting agencies and others to take reasonable measures to protect against unauthorized access to use of such information.

VIEW FROM CYBERSPACE: PRIVACY IN THE ELECTRONIC AGE: ELI LILLY'S PROZAC WEBSITE IS A DOWNER. In June 2001 Eli Lilly inadvertently disclosed e-mail addresses of its customers. The FTC sued Eli Lilly for failure to maintain the confidentiality of subscribers. In

January 2002 Eli Lilly agreed to a settlement whereupon Eli Lilly would impose new security training, conduct annual reviews, check for security risks and adjust the program as necessary.

C.   **Financial Information: Grimm-Leach- Bliley Act** requires financial institutions and others e.g. travel agencies, to ensure privacy protections to consumers and restricting the right to give out personal information. The act also requires institutions to disclose their privacy policy, and to give customers the right to opt-out of information disclosures to third parties.

D.   **Medical Information: The HIPAA.** Under the Health Insurance Portability and Accountability Act both health care professionals and insurance providers must maintain strict privacy of patient information.

E.   **Children's Online Privacy Protection Act (COPPA)** prevents companies from collecting, disclosing or selling information about children through websites.

XI.   **JUNK FAXES, SPAM, AND THE DO-NOT-CALL LIST.**

A.   **Fax Blasts.** The Telephone Consumer Protection Act (TCPA) bans unsolicited facsimile transmission. In 2000 the FCC imposed a $5 million forfeiture against Fax.com.

B.   **Telemarketing and the Do-Not-Call List.** Under the TCPA the FCC adopted rules to protect people against telemarketers and unsolicited pre-recorded messages.

POLITICAL PERSPECTIVE: STOPPING SPYWARE. Spyware is a type of computer software that imbeds in a computer operating system or hard drive. Certain types of spyware are illegal under the Electronic Communications Privacy Act and other federal laws. In 2004 the FTC appealed to the software industry to prevent spyware, but ultimately Congress took action. State governments have also taken steps to criminalize spyware.

C.   **Spam.** About 10 million unsolicited e-mails are sent every minute in the United States. The federal CAN-SPAM Act preempts state laws and prohibits certain types of information farming and imposes prison sentences and fines for convictions. Since 2003, AOL, Microsoft and Yahoo have taken steps to reduce spam. Various ISPs also brought lawsuits against spammers and "spimmers."

XII.   **UNFAIRNESS, DECEPTION, AND FRAUD.** Agencies, such as the FTC, the FDA, the FCC and the SEC, regulate unfair and deceptive trade practices and consumer fraud. The federal agencies regulate advertising, packaging and labeling, pricing, warranties, and numerous sales practices.

A. **Deceptive Advertising and Warranties**. Companies sometimes make claims that are deceptive or false. Legal solutions involve three separate approaches: the common law, statutory law, and regulatory law.

1. Common Law provides two remedies for a consumer who has been misled by false advertising. The consumer can sue for breach of contract and fraud (deceit) under tort.

2. Statutory Law. The UCC and the Lanham Act may protect consumers from false advertising. Under the UCC, the consumer can sue for breach of express warranty. The Lanham Act forbids the use of any false "description or representation" in connection with any goods or services. See *Coca-Cola v. Tropicana Prods., Inc.*, 690 F.2d 312 (2d Cir. 1982).

3. FTC Regulatory Law. The Federal Trade Commission is charged with preventing unfair and deceptive trade practices, including false advertising. FTC may negotiate consent orders or issue cease and desist orders to enforce civil laws.

   - Deceptive Price. FTC rules forbid sale of advertised items at higher prices to unaware customers as well as *bait and switch advertising*.

   - Quality Claims made without any substantiation are deceptive. Conversely obvious exaggerations and vague generalities are considered to be "puffing" and not deceptive.

     Case 17.1--*Lavie v. Procter & Gamble Co.*, 129 Cal. Rptr.2d 486 (Cal. App. 1st Dist. 2003). Lavie developed an ulcer after using Aleve, a product of P&G. P&G advertised Aleve as being gentler on the stomach than aspirin. Lavie sued for false advertising. The courts held that as P&G did not target naïve consumers, thus ads were not fraudulently misleading.

   - Testimonials and Mock-ups. Ads showing people who endorse a product but have not, in fact, used it, are considered to be deceptive.

4. Infomercials are ads presented in the format of half-hour television shows. The National Infomercial Merchandising Association has elected self-regulation to the FTC to prevent abuse or deception.

5. UCC Warranties. Advertisements may create implied warranties, enforceable in court.

6. Magnuson–Moss Warranty Act. When a seller offers a written warranty on goods costing more than $15, it must "fully and conspicuously disclose in simple and understandable language the terms and conditions of the warranty." On goods of at least $10 the seller must note the warrant as full or limited. A written warranty may not disclaim *implied warranties*, such as the implied warranty of merchantability.

7. State Lemon Laws deal with warranties on new cars and new mobile homes. In general a new car must conform to the warranty given by the manufacturer. If, after a reasonable number of attempts (usually four), the manufacturer or dealer is unable to remedy a defect, the car must be replaced or the purchase price refunded.

8. Sales Practices. States and federal agencies have laws to protect consumers from unfair and deceptive sales practices, e.g., making false promises, and fraud.

9. State Deceptive Practices Statutes seek to prohibit sellers from providing false and misleading information to consumers.

10. UCC Unconscionability Principle. Section 2-302 prohibits the enforcement of patently unfair contracts.

11. Door-to-Door Sales require notice of a three-day "cooling off" period during which the consumer can rescind the contract.

12. Referral Sales and Pyramid Sales. Pyramid schemes (multi-level marketing) are illegal and involve the recruitment of additional sellers, commissions on sales to recruits.

13. Telemarketing. The use of auto-dialers and "900" numbers is covered by the Telephone Consumer Protection Act (TCPA) and regulated by the FCC.

14. Mail-Order Sales. Unsolicited merchandise may be kept without cost. The U.S. Postal Service has authority to enforce statutes against mail fraud.

15. Industry-Specific Sales Practices. Since the 1980s the FTC has developed guidelines to regulate specific industries, e.g., car sales.

16. Real Estate Sales require certain disclosures under a host of federal laws. Common-law and state statutes also regulate such sales.

XIII. **STATE OCCUPATIONAL LICENSING.** State governments have departments of consumer affairs which ensure credentials and licenses for jobs that require certain skills or training.

XIV. **CONSUMER CREDIT AND THE CONSUMER CREDIT PROTECTION ACT (CCPA).**

    A. **Truth-in-Lending Act (TILA)** requires clear disclosure of credit terms for sales, loans, and leases between creditors and consumers. Corporations and other entities are not protected. Regulation Z requires that credit card companies display interest rates and terms of the contract. The TILA has different disclosure requirements for *open-end* vs. *closed-end* credit. Consumers may be required to arbitrate their claims if they agreed to do so when applying for credit, but the TILA limits the liability of credit-card holders to $50 per card for unauthorized charges made before a card issuer is notified that the card has been lost or stolen.

        1. Home Equity Lending Plans. Consumers have a right of rescission, available for three days if all procedures are properly followed by the lender, or for three years if they are not.

        2. Credit Advertising. Any advertised specific credit terms must actually be available, and any credit terms must be explained fully.

            Case 17.2--*Rossman v. Fleet Bank (R.I.) National Association*, 280 F.3d 384 (3d Cir. 2002). Rossman took out a credit card in which Fleet promised no annual fee. Within a few months, Fleet imposed a fee. Rossman sued and the trial court dismissed. The appeals court reversed on the grounds that Fleet engaged in a deceptive practice.

        3. Credit Billing requires creditors to respond to consumer complaints, followed by a reasonable investigation to determine whether the complaint is justified. Companies cannot evade this requirement by canceling a cardholder's account.

    B. **Extortionate Credit Transactions** are prohibited under the CCPA.

    C. **Restrictions on Garnishment**. The CCPA sets a maximum on the amount that the creditor may retrieve via garnishment.

    D. **Fair Credit Reporting Act (FCRA)** allows consumers to request all information (except medical information) on themselves, the source of the information, and any recent recipients of a report. The FCRA gives consumers a right to accurate copies of their credit report sent to creditors. Credit bureaus must investigate disputes and resolve consumer complaints within 30 days.

E.   **Equal Credit Opportunity Act** prohibits discrimination in the granting of credit on the basis of race, color, religion, national origin, sex or marital status, age, receipt of public assistance.

F.   **Fair Debt Collection Practices Act** regulates debt collectors and debt-collection practices of third-party collectors and provides a civil remedy for anyone injured by a violation of the statute.

> **Case 17.3--*Chuway v. National Actions Financial Services Inc.*,** 362 F.3d 944 (7th Cir. 2004). Chuway received a letter from a collection agency which both told her that she owed an exact amount and that called into question if she owed another amount. The appeals court held that the letter violated the FDCPA and Chuway was able to collect damages awarded under law.

G.   **Electronic Fund Transfer Act: Debit Cards and Preauthorized Fund Transfers**.   Under the ETA, customer liability is usually limited to no more than $50; receipts must accompany every ATM transaction. For Preauthorized Fund Transfers banks must provide notice within two days or notify customers where to call for confirmation. ATMs require PIN to protected cards issued by banks. *Off-Line Debit Cards* can be used without a personal identification number.

H.   **State Laws Regulating Consumer Credit**. The Uniform Consumer Credit Code (UCCC) has not worked as credit card companies simply work around the laws. Usury statutes and credit card fee limits in effect only the state in which the credit card company is located. *Marquette Nat'l Bank of Minneapolis v. First of Omaha Serv. Corp.*, 439 U.S. 299 (1978).

GLOBAL VIEW: INTERNATIONAL PRIVACY PROTECTION. Other nations have more comprehensive laws and view individual information as personal property rather than that of the companies with the databases. The EU law prohibits transfer of personal information outside the EU unless the receiving nation has adequate protection for personal privacy. American companies may take steps to comply with EU regulations. Japanese privacy law applies to companies outside Japan – and companies may note the specific purpose for obtaining and using personal information. India does not have a comprehensive law and there is little recourse for breaches of privacy. Canadian law prohibits information transfers without individual consent. Australian law also demands consent, when available, but allows transfers if firms belief such comports with Australian law.

THE RESPONSIBLE MANAGER: COMPLYING WITH CONSUMER PROTECTION LAWS. Managers should:

- ensure that employers are aware of, and in compliance with, various federal and state consumer protection regulations;
- put procedures in place to educate employees about important consumer law topics, especially civil and criminal liabilities;
- recall products if necessary to correct a defective product;
- consider implementing an internal product safety committee to conduct regular product safety inspections;
- refrain from making claims that may be deceptive or false;
- be aware that many discriminatory practices in the extension of credit are illegal; and
- endeavor to self-regulate or work with a regulatory agency to establish industry standards that meet the concerns of both the agency and the company.

INSIDE STORY: WHAT'S IN A NAME? FIGHTING IDENTITY THEFT. Identity theft is increasingly common. Via the internet and the proliferation of electronic databases, personal information is easier to obtain. Both state governments and the Congress have passes laws to fight identify theft. A recent *Time* magazine article outlines eight steps to prevent identity theft through computer technology. Through the use of firewalls, internet blocks, and caution one is less likely to download virus or spyware that can upload personal information.

STUDY QUESTIONS

True-False Questions

___ 1. Federal regulatory agencies that are not independent commissions are part of the legislative branch.

___ 2. The TILA sets maximum interest rates for credit cards.

___ 3. Visa and MasterCard companies typically offer closed-end credit.

___ 4. Congress directed the FTC to interpret and enforce the TILA.

___ 5. Regulation Z applies to any transaction that involves an installment contract that has payments made in two installments or more, and when the credit is for personal, family, or household purposes.

__ 6. The TILA limits a credit-card holder's liability to $50 for unauthorized use if prompt notification is made.

__ 7. Unlike the other section of the TILA, there is no private cause of action for a consumer to sue credit advertisers directly.

__ 8. The Fair Debt Collection Practices Act is enforced by the FCC.

__ 9. Unlike credit cards, banks are prohibited from sending out debit cards except in response to a consumer's request.

__ 10. A bank with credit cars operations in South Dakota can charge a New York resident higher rates of interest and fees than would be allowed in New York.

__ 11. Bait and Switch sales are unethical, but legal.

__ 12. A product with any connection to the United States can have the label "Made in the USA."

__ 13. Puffing is actionable under the Lanham Act.

__ 14. Unsolicited, properly addressed merchandise sent by U.S. mail is a gift.

__ 15. For purposes of regulations, the definitions of "food" and "drugs" are essentially the same thing.

Multiple-Choice Questions

__ 1. _____ is *not* an independent commission.
   A.   FTC.
   B.   SEC.
   C.   FDA.
   D.   FCC.

__ 2. Which of the following is *not* part of the Consumer Credit Protection Act?
   A.   Fair Credit Card Billing Act.
   B.   Truth-in-Lending Act.
   C.   Fair Credit Reporting Act.
   D.   Equal Credit Opportunity Act.

__ 3. The TILA applies to _____ between two consumers.
   A.   Sales.

B.   Leases.
C.   Loans.
D.   Secured contracts.

___ 4.   Which commercial practice has the least amount of federal regulation?
A.   Organic food production.
B.   Car sales.
C.   Infomercials .
D.   Spam.

___ 5.   Amendments to the FCRA impose new restrictions on the use of credit reports by employers. These are designed to ensure that individuals
A.   Are aware their credit reports may be used for employment purposes.
B.   Agree to the use for employment purposes.
C.   Are notified promptly if the report results in a negative employment decision.
D.   All of the above

___ 6.   Which of the following is *not* a prohibited category of discrimination in credit?
A.   Marital status.
B.   Sexual orientation.
C.   Age.
D.   Religion.

___ 7.   Under the EFTA, a customer is liable for no more than _____.
A. $25.
B. $50.
C. $100.
D. $75.

___ 8.   The _____ Act requires a warranty on goods costing more than $15 that is "fully and conspicuously disclose in simple and understandable language the terms and conditions of the warranty."

A.   Warren-Patman Warranty.
B.   Sarbanes-Oxley Warranty.
C.   Magnuson-Moss Warranty.
D.   The Federal Warranty.

___ 9.   The _____ Act requires financial institutions and others e.g. travel agencies, to ensure privacy protections to consumers and restricting the right to give out personal information. The act also requires institutions to disclose their privacy policy, and to give customers the right to opt-out of information disclosures to third parties.

A.   HIPAA.
B.   Gram-Rudman Credit Protection Act.
C.   Consumer Credit Counselling Act.
D.   Grimm-Leach- Bliley.

__ 10.   Which is not regulated by the USDA?
A.   Organic vegetables.
B.   Edible drugs.
C.   Eggs.
D.   All of these.

__ 11.   Traditional common-law approaches to false advertising are: _____.

I.   Breach of contract.
II.   Breach of express warranty.
III.   Deceit.

A.   I and III.
B.   II and III.
C.   I, II, and III.
D.   III only.

__ 12.   FTC remedies for deceptive advertising include all but which of the following?
A.   Affirmative advertising.
B.   Damages.
C.   Corrective advertising.
D.   Criminal prosecution.

__ 13.   Which of the following can regulate packaging and labeling?

I.   The FDA.
II.   The FTC.
III.   The states.
IV.   The FCC.

A.   I, II, and IV.
B.   II, III, and IV.
C.   I, II, and III.
D.   I, II, III, and IV.

__ 14.   In door-to-door sales, consumers get _____ to rescind a sale.
A.   Forty-eight hours.
B.   Three days.
C.   Seven days.
D.   One day.

__ 15. Which of the following is *not* normally regulated by state agencies?
   A.   Dentists.
   B.   Clergy.
   C.   Social workers.
   D.   Dry cleaners.

Essay Questions

1. Why does the TILA provide for a right of rescission for home equity loans?

2. What can you, as a consumer, request under the Fair Credit Reporting Act?

3. What is "bait and switch" advertising?

CHAPTER 18
REAL PROPERTY AND LAND USE

INTRODUCTION

This chapter discusses the forms of real estate ownership and the transfer of ownership, the role of brokers, and the effect of express and implied warranties concerning the condition of the property. The chapter outlines the alternatives to acquiring real property for cash, including tax-deferred exchanges, sale and leasebacks, and real estate investment trusts. Finally, the chapter outlines governmental regulation of the use of real property through the exercise of police and condemnation powers, and the circumstances in which government restrictions on land use are deemed "takings" and require compensation of the owner under the U.S. Constitution.

CHAPTER OUTLINE

I.   FORMS OF OWNERSHIP. Real property can be held in a variety of ways.

    A.   **Individual Ownership** is common, but imposes personal liability. There are four common types of ownership.

        1.   Tenancy in Common. At least two persons (tenants) own an undivided interest in a parcel of real property. Each tenant in common has an equal right to possession of the property and can exclude a third party but not a co-tenant. Co-tenants share the income and burdens of ownership. A tenant's interest is assignable and is passed to his or her heirs upon death.

        2.   Joint Tenancy. The property is owned in *equal* shares by two or more individuals. When a joint tenant dies, his or her interest passes automatically to the remaining joint tenant(s).

        3.   Tenancy by the Entirety is special type of co-ownership between husband and wife. Husband and wife have equal rights to the possession, use, and revenues of the property.

        4.   Community Property exists among spouses. Each spouse owns an undivided one-half interest in the property. Property acquired *prior* to the marriage or by gift or inheritance during the marriage is separate property. Separate property can become community property.

            •   Conveyance: (a) Both spouses must execute the instrument by which the conveyance is affected; (b) A spouse can leave his or her interest to a third party in his or her will. Without a will, community property automatically passes to the other spouse.

- Divorce affects property ownership differently in each state.

5. Trust. Property may be held in trust. The trustee controls the property for the benefit of another or others (*beneficiaries*).

B. **General Partnership**. Partners have rights similar to those of co-tenants. Each partner is liable for all the debts of the partnership. A partner may not assign his interest in specific partnership property. A partner may convey the entire partnership property to a bona fide purchaser.

C. **Limited Partnership**. Partners manage real property. Each partners' liability is restricted to their capital contribution. The powers of general partners are set forth in the partnership agreement and state law.

D. **Corporate Ownership**. Corporations can own real property. The power to convey is governed by the corporation's articles of incorporation and by-laws, and state laws. The board of directors must authorize most transfers of real property.

E. **Limited Liability Company** is the preferred business entity for realty. The authority to convey property is governed by the operating agreement and state law for LLCs. The board of managers must authorize most transfers of real property.

II. **TRANSFER OF OWNERSHIP**. Transfers of land from seller (grantor) to buyer (grantee) require a deed which is recorded at a public office, typically a county recorder. Most real estate is transferred as a "fee simple" interest (absolute ownership).

A. **Title**. The seller is required to sell land with "marketable title," *i.e.*, a fee simple interest free from defects, including liens. The type of interest and quality of title are set forth in a deed. The type of deed determines the scope of warranties granted.

B. **Types of Deeds**. An interest in real property can be conveyed only by a signed deed that specifically describes that interest and is delivered to and accepted by the named grantee.

1. Grant Deed contains implies warranties that the grantor has not previously conveyed the same property or any interest in it to another person, and the title is marketable.

2.   Quitclaim Deed contains no warranties; the grantor only conveys whatever right, title, and interest it holds, if any.

3.   Warranty Deed contains implied warranties of a grant deed as well as quiet possession of the property

C.   **Adverse Possession**. At common-law one may acquire land by adverse possession through specific practices and legal notices.

D.   **Representatives and Implied Warranties**. Current law rejects the old rule of *caveat emptor*.

1.   Implied Warranty of Habitability. Builders guarantee to the first buyer that the house is livable.

2.   Seller's Duty to Disclose. In most states sellers have a duty to disclose any defects that affect the property's value that the buyer could not reasonably discover.

> **Case 18.1--*Strawn v. Canuso***, 657 A.2d 420 (N.J. 1995).
> Developers of new houses and real estate brokers marketing the new houses did not disclose to 150 new home buyers that the houses had been constructed near an abandoned hazardous waste site. The court held that the developers and brokers violated their duty to disclose, among other duties.

3.   Contractual Protections and Due Diligence. Buyers should safeguard their purchases with contractual protections.

III.   **RECORDING STATUTES**. Deeds and other instruments of conveyance must be recorded with a government official in a public office, where copies will be available for public notice. The record in the public office is the principal basis for determining the authenticity of one's real estate title. There are three general types of recording systems.

A.   **Race statutes**. The first to record a deed has superior rights, regardless if the first recorder knows that someone else had already bought the property.

B.   **Pure Notice Statutes**. A person who has notice that someone else has already bought the property cannot validate her deed by recording it first. Notice may be actual or constructive (where reasonable inquiry would have disclosed the prior interest).

C.   **Race–Notice Statutes** protect those good faith subsequent purchasers who record their deed before the prior purchaser records its deed.

IV.   **TITLE INSURANCE**. Title insurance companies offer some safeguard about the title or priority of one's property interest.

     A.   **Extent of Coverage**. Title insurance usually covers for losses incurred as a result of undisclosed liens or defects in title to the property; or errors in the abstraction of the title, that is, in the summary of the relevant recorded deeds and liens.

     B.   **Escrow**. Title companies act as fiduciaries to the buyer and seller for closing. Title companies hold the purchase money in escrow until the conditions for the sale have all been met. If the sale does not go through, the money is returned to the would-be purchaser. Banks also perform this service, and in some jurisdictions there are separate escrow companies, which act as neutral parties.

> **Case 18.2--*Schoepe v. Zions First National Bank*.**, 750 F. Supp. 1084 (D. Utah 1990). Lion Hill, a Nevada partnership, contracted to sell mining property to Pacific Silver. Both parties signed an escrow agreement with Zions whereby Pacific Silver would make installment payments to Zions as the escrow agent. During the installment period, Zions made loans to Pacific Silver; Lion Hill was unaware of these loans. Subsequently, Pacific Silver defaulted on the payments to Lion Hill. Lion Hill sued claiming that Zions should have disclosed its loans to Pacific Silver given Zions was an escrow agent. Given its role as a neutral party, Zions had no legal duty to Lion Hill to disclose.

V.   **BROKERS** serve to maintain the market by putting together buyers and sellers.

     A.   **Compensation**. Generally brokers are retained by the seller and compensated by a payment based on a percentage of the gross selling price.

     B.   **Listing Agreements**. Typically Brokers will agree to one of three payment arrangements.

         1.   Open Listing. The listing broker receives a commission only if she is the first to procure a ready, willing, and able buyer.

         2.   Exclusive Listing grants the broker the right to sell the property; any sale of the property during the term of the listing will entitle the broker to a commission.

         3.   Net Listing schemes give the broker any sales proceeds in excess of the net listing amount specified by the seller. Net listings are uncommon.

C. **Regulation of Brokers**.

    1. Licensing. Brokers are generally required to have a license to perform. Brokers may also be required to meet continuing education requirements and rules regarding the particulars of real estate loans.

    2. Agency Relationship. Brokers are fiduciaries of the seller and may not work for more than one person in a transaction without the knowledge and consent of all parties.

VI. **ACQUISITIONS AND DISPOSITIONS**. In real Estate sales, parties rely on detailed contracts, with heavy concerns on the warranties.

A. **Tax-Deferred Exchanges**. A seller may exchange property for another parcel with favorable tax consequences, including deferral of the capital gains tax.

B. **Sale and Leaseback** agreements involve a simultaneous two-step transaction with favorable tax consequences: (1) the institutional lender purchases real property from a corporation; (2) the property is leased back to the corporation for its use; and (3) lessee has the option to purchase.

C. **Synthetic Lease** is a lease where the lessee treats the transaction as though she purchased the property. Payments are treated as debt service on the loan, and the lessee may take favorable interest payment deductions as well as depreciation write-offs.

D. **Real Estate Investment Trusts (REITs)**. As long as at least 95 percent of a REITs net income is distributed to shareholder-beneficiaries, the REIT itself pays no income tax; taxes are paid at the shareholder-beneficiary level only. REITs may not have five persons with more than 50 percent of the REIT's beneficial interests.

E. **Transactions with Foreigners**. Sales of real property interests to nonresident aliens are regulated by the federal government. Under the Foreign Investment in Real Property Tax Act (FIRPTA), the purchaser of a U.S. real property interest from a foreign person is required to withhold 10 percent of the purchase price to ensure that U.S. capital gains tax is paid on the sale.

F. **Environmental Due Diligence**. The buyer must conduct due diligence, he may be liable under federal and state environmental laws and regulations for toxic or hazardous substances on or under the property. Under CERCLA (the "Superfund") the current owner or operator is jointly and severally liable for the costs associated with clean up. Liability attaches *unless* the owner can prove it made an extensive due diligence investigation.

VII. **PRELIMINARY AGREEMENTS**. When the parties are unable to reach a general agreement on terms and conditions, they may negotiate specific representations and warranties or to investigate the sale further.

    A. **Option Contract**: A potential buyer pays the seller for the right to purchase the property during a given time period. To be enforceable, the option must be in writing and consideration must be paid to the seller.

    B. **Right of First Refusal** is conferred by a written contract, to purchase the property on the same terms offered by or to a third party.

    C. **Letter of Intent**: creates a right to acquire an interest in a specific property on general terms and conditions until a formal acquisition agreement can be signed. Courts increasingly view letters of intent as enforceable contracts.

VIII. **FINANCING**. Financing the purchase of real estate often involves borrowing funds, with such being secured through a mortgage.

    A. **Permanent Loans** are usually repaid over five or ten years, and sometimes up to twenty years.

        1. Fixed-Interest Loans: an interest rate does not change over the term of the loan. Some lenders may insert a pre-payment penalty if the loan is paid off early.

        2. Variable-Interest Loans. The rate of interest is set at a fixed number of percentage points over a base rate (e.g., the *prime rate*). Over the term of the loan, the interest rate fluctuates.

        3. Points. Real estate lenders often charge a loan fee. The fee is fixed percentage of the loan. Each point is one percent of loan value.

    B. **Construction Loans** are provided for construction projects. Upon completion of the job, a construction lender may be repaid from either permanent (take-out) financing or interim (gap) financing.

    C. **Development Loans** are made in relation to the acquisition, subdivision, improvement, and sale of residential properties.

D.   **Equity Participation by Lender**. Many lenders attempt to increase their yield from real estate projects by participating in the *equity,* or ownership, of the property.

E.   **Wraparound Financing** occurs as a second lender lends the owner additional funds and takes over the servicing of the first loan. In exchange, the owner executes a mortgage and an all-inclusive note, covering the combined amount of the first and second loans.

VIEW FROM CYBERSPACE: ELECTRONIC CLOSINGS. More frequently, real estate deals are closed with the aid of computer technology, instead of through face to face signings. Documents are being scanned, which saves on space and paper. The Uniform Real Property Electronic Recording Act can standardize this process.

F.   **Foreclosure and rights of redemption**. Legal process by which a mortgagee (lender) may put up a piece of property for sale in the public arena to raise cash in order to pay off a debt owed by the mortgager (buyer) to the mortgagee.

IX.   APPRAISAL METHODS. Income-producing property is generally appraised by the income approach, which establishes the present value of the estimated annual cash flow over the anticipated holding period.

X.   PROTECTIVE LAWS FOR BORROWERS. Though States generally do not have usury laws, some still penalize unconscionably high interest rates. Federal law prohibits racial discrimination in lending.

XI.   COMMERCIAL LEASING. A commercial lease is a conveyance and a contract that governs the respective rights and obligations of the parties during the lease term.

A.   **Types of Leases.**

1.   Offices Leases usually are at a standard rate, unless the tenant occupies a substantial part of the building.

2.   Retail Leases frequently contain a percentage rent clause that requires the tenant to pay, in addition to a base monthly rent, a percentage of its gross sales to the landlord.

3.   Industrial Leases tend to have a five-year term with renewal options and are almost always *triple net,* which means the tenants pay all taxes, insurance, and operating maintenance expenses.

4. Ground Leases are very long-term leases. Ground leases are used when a landowner desires to obtain a steady return of income from undeveloped commercial property without the expense of improving or managing the property.

B. **Assignments and Subleases**. An assignment is a complete transfer of tenant rights to a third party who assumes the lease. A sublease allows the original tenant to re-enter. Generally landlords may restrict subleases.

C. **Hidden Issues**. Some property leases have early termination clauses while others use standard out clauses. Renters should take care to negotiate and note all terms and conditions.

XII. **GOVERNMENT REGULATION OF LAND USE**. States and local governments have varied rules about land use and environmental regulations. Responsible managers need to review competing federal, state and local rules.

A. **National Environmental Policy Act**. NEPA requires all federal agencies to preserve and enhance the environment and requires all agencies of the federal government to include an environmental impact statement (EIS).

1. EIS Requirement. Though some federal laws exempt the need for an EIS, the EPA may exempt an EIS after completion of an environmental assessment.

2. State Law Counterparts. Most states have adopted environmental quality laws similar to NEPA, requiring state and local agencies to consider the environmental impacts of development projects.

3. Planning for NEPA compliance includes permits and an EIS to minimize adverse effects on the environment.

B. **The Police Power** is the inherent authority of government to regulate activity tied to public health, safety, and welfare.

C. **Rent Control** is a legitimate exercise of police power; and does not violate the Fifth Amendment "taking" clause as it prevents owners from exploiting housing shortages by charging unreasonably high rents. See *SMB, Ltd. v. Superior Court of Los Angeles County*, 968 P.2d 993 (Cal. 1993).

D. **Regulatory Takings** ("inverse condemnation") are unconstitutional violations of the Fifth Amendment when the regulation (i) does not substantially advance legitimate state interests, or (ii) denies the owner all economically viable use of its land.

Case 18.3--*Tahoe-Sierra Preservation Council Inc. v. Tahoe Regional Planning Agency*, 535 U.S. 302 (2002). Plaintiffs owned property in the Lake Tahoe Basin. Due to rapid development a significant increase in nutrients washed into Lake Tahoe causing algae to grow, turning the lake green and opaque. To halt the increasing environmental damage, TRPA withheld development permits for several years. Plaintiffs sued TRPA claiming that the moratorium constituted an unconstitutional taking for which compensation was due. The district court ruled that certain property owners were due compensation. TRPA appealed. The Court of Appeals reversed.

XIII. REGULATORY SCHEMES. The fundamental components of most land-use regulatory schemes are a general plan, a zoning ordinance, and a subdivision ordinance.

A. **The General Plan**—many cities have a general development plan as a long-range, comprehensive planning document addressing the physical development and redevelopment of a city. The plan includes goals, objectives, policies, and programs related to these concerns.

B. **Other Planning Documents** are more specific than the general plan.

C. **Zoning** is the division of a city or county into districts with specific land-use regulations in each district. The two classes of zoning are: (1) regulations of structural and architectural design; and (2) regulations regarding building uses, e.g., commercial, residential, industrial, etc.

    1. Traditional Zoning separates land uses as residential, commercial, industrial.

    2. Planned Unit Development Zoning. Land-use regulations for a given piece of property reflecting a mixture of uses, residential, office, and retail.

    3. Zoning Relief. *Variances* allow a landowner to construct a structure or to carry on an activity not otherwise permitted. *Conditional use* permits allow uses not permitted as a matter of right under the zoning ordinance.

    4. Nonconforming Use—existing use that was originally lawful, but that does not comply with a later-enacted zoning ordinance.

D. **Subdivision** a separate parcel that allows the city to regulate new development and limit harm, promote water quality, and reduce soil erosion.

E. **Conditions**. Restrictive building permits or compelled easements can amount to a "taking" of land under the Fifth Amendment. See *Nollan v. California Coastal Commission* 483 U.S. 825 (1987); and *Dolan v. City of Tigard*, 512 U.S. 374 (1994).

F. **Environmental Assessment**. Many States and local governments require assessments prior to allowing development.

G. **Vested Development Rights**. Until rights are vested, developers may lose the capacity to build via re-zoning. As a means to reduce uncertainty, some States have adopted early vesting policies.

XIV. **PHYSICAL ACCESSIBILITY TO COMMERCIAL FACILITIES**. The ADA requires full and equal enjoyment of accommodation in any place of public accommodation.

A. **New Construction**. Any new renovations or alterations to commercial facilities must be accessible to disabled persons, including those in wheelchairs. Violators may be required to pay damages as well as civil penalties of up to $50,000 for a first violation and $100,000 for subsequent violations.

B. **Minor Changes** that are "readily achievable" need to be made to existing workplaces to accommodate disabled workers. ADA protections are available to disabled individuals *unless* the individuals pose a significant risk to the health or safety of others that cannot be mitigated by reasonable modifications.

C. **Discrimination**. The ADA prohibits discrimination on the basis of disability when applied to zoning.

> **Case 18.4--*Oregon Paralyzed Veterans of America v. Regal Cinemas Inc.*, 339 F.3d 1126 (9th Cir. 2003). Plaintiffs sued the movie theater for failing to provide patrons in wheelchairs with a clear line of sight. The trial court granted a dismissal. The appeals court reversed and entered a judgment for the plaintiffs.

XV. **THE RESPONSIBLE MANAGER: BUYING AND USING REAL ESTATE**. Acquisition and management of real estate is fraught with regulatory and administrative schemes that affect a company's liability. Before acquiring real estate, the manager should:

- Determine whether the property is properly located for the company's operations;
- Determine whether the improvements, if already built, comply with applicable building codes and are suitable;
- Determine whether the facility complies the Americans with Disabilities Act;

- Determine whether previous owners have complied with federal, state, and local environmental and hazardous-waste laws and evaluate company's liability;
- Decide whether the company should lease or buy the property;
- Decide for how long and under what terms the property should be leased;
- Decide, if the property is for sale, how best to negotiate the purchase contract and finance the purchase; and
- Keep senior executives and/or the board of directors informed about the manager's actions and decisions throughout the process.

INSIDE STORY: RECLAIMING BROWNFIELDS. Brownfields, dumps and waste sites have gone unused for years. The last two decades of law restricting urban and suburban sprawl has limited the land available for development and increased the value of brownfields. Through federal legislation which limits liability for bona fide purchasers, these areas are being developed.

STUDY QUESTIONS

True-False Questions

___ 1.   In a tenancy in common, a co-tenant has the right to exclusive possession against any third party.

___ 2.   The interest of a tenant in common is assignable, but not inheritable, without the consent of the other co-tenants.

___ 3.   With regard to tax issues, community property is generally a more favorable form of ownership than joint tenancy.

___ 4.   Ownership of land is transferred by a bill of sale.

___ 5.   A grant deed coveys after-acquired title.

___ 6.   A pure notice statute protects a good faith subsequent purchaser.

___ 7.   All parties involved in real estate sales needs a broker's license.

___ 8.   A contract for the sale of a real property interest must be in writing.

___ 9.   Under CERCLA, if a prior owner is insolvent or nonexistent, the current owner can be responsible for the entire cleanup.

___ 10. Sales of real property interests to foreign persons are regulated by the federal government.

___ 11. Letters of intent are often viewed as enforceable by the parties, but courts have increasingly treated them as unenforceable.

___ 12. Permanent loans traditionally have level interest rates throughout the term of the loan.

___ 13. Gap financing is financing that a developer obtains to pay off the construction loan when it becomes due before the permanent financing is available.

___ 14. The sale of property to raise cash to pay off a debt on the property is called a lien.

___ 15. A work letter agreement states the percentage of the renovation costs the owner will pay.

Multiple-Choice Questions

___ 1. _____ each own an undivided fractional interest in real property.
   A. Tenants in common.
   B. Joint tenants.
   C. Tenants by the entirety.
   D. Communal property holders.

___ 2. Scott Hall and Kevin Nash own property together with a right of survivorship. This is a: _____.
   A. Tenancy in common.
   B. Joint tenancy.
   C. Tenancy by the entirety.
   D. Sole proprietorship.

___ 3. Which statement is false?
   A. Tenancy by the entirety includes a right of survivorship, like joint tenancy.
   B. The parties in a tenancy by the entirety cannot destroy the right of survivorship.
   C. Historically, in a tenancy by the entirety, only the husband has a right to possess and use the property.
   D. Slightly over half of the states recognize some form of tenancy by the entirety.

___ 4. The "manager" of a trust is called the: _____.
   A. Trustor.
   B. Trustee.
   C. Grantor.
   D. Beneficiary.

__ 5. A _____ deed contains no warranties.
   A.   Grant.
   B.   Warrant.
   C.   Quitclaim.
   D.   Warrantless.

__ 6. Which of the following is a type of recording statute?

        I.   Race.
        II.   Race notice.
        III.   Pure notice.
        IV.   Pure race.

   A.   I, II and III.
   B.   I, II, and IV.
   C.   II, III, and IV.
   D.   I, II, III, and IV.

__ 7. A(n) _____ listing is one in which a listing broker will receive a commission only if a buyer is secured for the property.
   A.   Open.
   B.   Exclusive.
   C.   Net.
   D.   Seller.

__ 8. When a broker acts for both the buyer and the seller, the relationship is called a(n) _____ agency.
   A.   Illegal.
   B.   Simultaneous.
   C.   Concurrent.
   D.   Dual.

__ 9. The implied warranty of habitability is like _____ under the UCC.
   A.   An implied warranty of merchantability.
   B.   An implied warranty of fitness for a particular purpose.
   C.   An implied warranty of fitness.
   D.   A dual agency.

__ 10. As long as ___ percent of a REIT's net income is distributed to shareholder-beneficiaries, the REIT itself pays no income tax.
   A.   95.
   B.   75.
   C.   85.

D.   51.

__ 11. A(n) _____ is when the buyer pays consideration to keep the offer open for a definite stated time period.
   A.   Right of first refusal
   B.   Letter of intent
   C.   Option contract
   D.   Form offer

__ 12. On a $100,000 loan, two points would equal
   A. $200.
   B. $2,000.
   C. $20,000.
   D.   Prime plus 2%.

__ 13. Which is *not* an appraisal method?
   A.   Fair market price.
   B.   Market approach.
   C.   Improvement costs.
   D.   Estimated property revenue.

__ 14. A(n) _____ is a temporary transfer of the lease to a third party.
   A.   Assignment.
   B.   Sublease.
   C.   Lease.
   D.   Retail lease.

__ 15. A(n) _____ is an existing use that was originally lawful, but now does not comply with current zoning ordinances.
   A.   Nonconforming use.
   B.   Conditional use.
   C.   Variance.
   D.   Easement.

Essay Questions

1. The modern view of tenancy by the entirety is that it converts to a tenancy in common upon divorce. Why?

2. Briefly discuss the types of recording statutes.

3. How does a sale and leaseback operate?

CHAPTER 19
FORMS OF BUSINESS ORGANIZATIONS

INTRODUCTION

One of the first questions facing any entrepreneur wishing to start a business is which form of business organization will best suit the enterprise. Entrepreneurs selecting a form of business entity enjoy a broad range of options. This decision comes in the earliest stages in the life of a business, but it is nonetheless a crucial one. This chapter discusses the most frequently used forms of business organization, and their basic tax treatments.

CHAPTER OUTLINE

I. **SOLE PROPRIETORSHIP** is the simplest and most prevalent form of business enterprise. One person owns all of the assets of the business and is solely liable for all of its debts and loses. Advantages of a sole proprietorship include the flexibility afforded by having one person in complete control of the business. A sole proprietorship ends upon either the discontinuation of the business or the death of the proprietor.

II. **GENERAL PARTNERSHIP** is created when two or more persons agree to place their money, efforts, labor, or skills in a business and to share the profits and losses. The partnership agreement can be express or implied. Absent an express agreement to the contrary, each partner has some control over the business, and each may have the authority to bind the other partner with respect to third parties.

    A.   **Advantages and Disadvantages**. A partnership does not pay income taxes as a separate entity. Instead, the profit earned "passes through" to the individual partners, who report it as income on their individual returns. Individual partners are subject to personal liability for the obligations of the partnership. If the partnership is unable to pay its debts, creditors of the partnership have claims against the assets of individual partners.

    B.   **Joint Venture** is a one-time partnership of two or more persons for a specific purpose; it terminates when the project is completed. Like a general partnership, a joint venture requires that the parties: (1) share a community of interest; (2) have the mutual right to direct and govern; (3) share the partnership's profits and losses; and (4) combine their property, money, efforts, skill, or knowledge in the undertaking.

III. **LIMITED LIABILITY PARTNERSHIPS** (LLPs) are a recently developed form of business organization, usually for lawyers and accountants. The main function of an LLP is to insulate its partners from vicarious liability for certain partnership obligations, such as liability arising from the malpractice of another partner. Like other forms of partnerships, LLPs retain pass-through taxation treatment. LLPs are created by filing appropriate forms with a central state agency.

IV. **LIMITED PARTNERSHIP.** A limited partnership is a special type of partnership consisting of at least one (1) general partner and one (1) limited partner. General partner(s) of a limited partnership remain jointly and severally liable for partnership obligations. Limited partners assume no liability for partnership debts beyond the amount of capital they have contributed, and they have no right to participate in the management of the partnership. Limited partnerships are often used to raise capital and their limited liability makes them attractive to investors. Courts are generally strict about enforcing the formal requirements of limited partnership status.

V. **CORPORATIONS.** A corporation is an organization authorized by state law to act as a legal entity distinct from its owners. The corporation operates under state charter with limited powers to achieve specific purposes and has various legal advantages.

    A. **C Corporations and "S" Corporations**. C Corporations face taxes on corporate revenues and shareholder dividends. S corporations avoid double taxation and are taxed as a pass-through entity, like a partnership. To qualify for S corporation status, a corporation must meet certain criteria including: (1) it cannot have no more than seventy-five shareholders, all of whom must be citizens or U.S. resident aliens, or certain types of tax-exempt organizations, trusts, or estates; and (2) the corporation generally may not own 80 percent or more of any other corporation.

    B. **Close Corporations** have a limited number of shareholders who explicitly designate the close corporation in the charter. Some states allow shareholders to agree not to observe corporate formalities relating to meetings of directors or shareholders in connection with the management of its affairs, thus bypassing of these formalities may not be considered a factor in deciding whether to pierce the corporate veil.

    C. **Closely Held Corporations** have a limited number of shareholders, but the stock is not available to the public.

VI. **LIMITED LIABILITY COMPANIES.** A limited liability company (LLC) combines the tax advantages of a pass-through entity with the limited liability advantages of a corporation. The LLC is a creature of state law. To form an LLC, a charter document must be filed with the appropriate state agency (usually the office of the secretary of state). The members elect the managers who are responsible for managing the business, property, and affairs of the company. LLCs will be taxed as a "pass through" entity like a partnership. Even the controlling persons in LLCs can limit their liability to the amount invested. The main advantage of the LLC form over the S corporation is the lack of restrictions on shareholders and the ability to have more than one class of securities; its investors can be corporations, partnerships, and foreigners.

VII. INCOME TAX CONSIDERATIONS: COMPARING SEPARATE TAXABLE ENTITIES WITH PASS-THROUGH ENTITIES. The tax treatment of a C corporation is different from that of pass-through entities. Each may have favorable or unfavorable tax consequences, depending upon the circumstances.

  A. Property Transfers. C corporations are separate taxable entities, the transfer of cash or any other property between the corporation and the owners is a taxable unless it comes within one of the statutory exceptions. A corporation will be taxed on the appreciation in value just as if it had sold the property for cash. In LLC/Partnership it is easier to transfer property to and from a partnership or LLC on a tax-free basis than it is with either a C corporation or an S corporation. Neither the partnership nor the LLC is subject to tax on the appreciated property, and the partner receiving the property is not taxed until he or she subsequently sells the property.

  B. Cash Distribution. The income of a C corporation is taxed at the corporate level, and again at the individual level when distributed. Cash distributions from Partnerships and S corporations are tax-free to the recipients, up to the amount of their previous capital contributions less any income previously passed through to them.

  C. Operating Losses. In C Corporations, operating losses will be recognized at the corporate level. The corporation receives no benefit until it has operating income against which its prior losses can be deducted. For LLC/S Corporations Operating losses each year will be passed through to the individual partners or shareholders, which may be deductible on personal income tax returns. Passive investors may not deduct such losses from ordinary income, but can use passive losses to offset passive gains (such as capital gains on the sale of stock).

  D. Capitalization. There are no tax-law restrictions on corporate capitalization. The corporation may issue common stock, preferred stock, bonds, notes, warrants, options, and other instruments.

  E. Allocation of Losses. For an LLC or Partnership income or loss generally can be allocated to specific partners (or members) at specific times as long as these allocations have a substantial economic effect apart from tax considerations. No comparable allocation can be made by a C corporation, except to a limited extent by capitalizing the corporation with different classes of stock and debt.

VIII. CHOICE OF BUSINESS ENTITY: PROS AND CONS. The following chart lists the principal considerations in selecting the form of business entity and applies them to the C corporation, S corporation, general partnership, limited partnership, limited liability company, and limited liability partnership.

	C Corp.	S Corp.	General Partnership	Limited Partnership	Limited Liability Company	Limited Liability Partnership
Limited Liability	Yes	Yes	No	Yes (A)	Yes	Yes (B)
Flow-through Taxation	No	Yes	Yes	Yes	Yes	Yes
Simplicity/ Low Cost	Yes	Yes	No	No	No	No
Limitations on Eligibility	No	Yes	No	No	No	No
Limitations on Capital "Structure"	No	Yes	No	No	No	No
Ability to Raise Venture Capital	Yes	No	No	No	No	No
Ability to Take Public	Yes	Yes (C)	No (D)	No (D)	No (D)	No (D)
Flexible Charter Documents	No	No	Yes	Yes	Yes	Yes
Ability to Change Structure without Tax	No	No	Yes	Yes	Yes	Yes
Favorable Employee Incentives (including incentive stock options)	Yes	Yes/No (E)	No (F)	No (F)	No (F)	No (F)
Qualified Small Business Stock Exclusion for Gains	Yes (G)	No	No	No	No	No
Special Allocations	No	No	Yes	Yes	Yes	Yes
Tax-Free In-Kind Distributions	No	No	Yes	Yes	Yes	Yes

(A) Limited liability for limited partners only; a limited partnership must have at least one general partner with unlimited liability.

(B) Partners in LLPs generally are protected from liability for malpractice and other wrongful conduct of fellow partners; states are split on whether LLP partners can be held individually liable for other partnership liabilities, such as commercial debt.

(C) S corporation would convert to C corporation upon a public offering because of the number of shareholders.

(D) Although the public markets are generally not available for partnership offerings, partnerships (including LLPs) and LLCs can be incorporated without tax and then taken public.

(E) Although an S corporation can issue incentive stock options (ISOs), the inability to have two classes of stock limits favorable pricing of the common stock offered to employees.

(F) Although partnership and LLC interests can be provided to employees, they are poorly understood by most employees. Moreover, ISOs are not available.

(G) Special low capital gains rate for stock of U.S. C corporations with not more than $50 million in gross assets at the time stock is issued if the corporation is engaged in an active business and the taxpayer holds the stock for at least five years.

IX.   **ABILITY TO RAISE VENTURE CAPITAL.** C Corporations are preferred: (A) venture capital firms raise money from large institutional investors, who can receive income and capital gains tax-free only if the issuer of the securities is not a pass-through entity (B) most start-ups will issue two classes of stock.

X.   **AGENCY LAW AND LIMITED LIABILITY.** Individuals must make clear when they represent themselves or are acting as agents of a legal entity. As well, when owners and partners take an active role in the operation of a business entity, they may be held liable in tort.

>   **Case 19.1--*Estate of Countryman v. Farmers Cooperative Association of Keota***, 679 N.W.2d 598 (Iowa 2004). In 1999, a propane tank explosion killed seven and injured others. Numerous plaintiffs sued Double Circle and FCA. Double Circle had delivered the tank and FCA owned 95% of Double Circle. The legal question was whether a manager of the LLC, FCA, could be held responsible for the acts of a member of the LLC, Double Circle. The court found that FCA was directly responsible for the acts of Double Circle in re the propane tank and therefore could be held liable.

XI.   **GENERAL PARTNERSHIP MECHANICS.** The following section describes in more detail how general partnerships are formed, operated, and terminated.

>   A.   **Formation of a General Partnership**. A general partnership can be created with nothing more than a handshake and a general understanding between the partners. A partnership does not require a minimum of capital in order to be formed. Partners usually contribute cash or property, but in some instances, a partnership interest may be received as a gift.

>   >   1.   Without a Written Agreement. If there is *no written* partnership agreement, the laws in the state where the parties are doing business will determine the rights and duties of the partnership.

Case 19.2--*Holmes v. Lerner*, 88 Cal. Rptr. 2d 130 (Cal. Ct. App. 1999). Sandra Lerner was wealthy entrepreneur. She met Holmes and the two talked about setting up a cosmetics business, Urban Decay. Holmes received assurances from Lerner about finances and setting up the business. Later Lerner negotiated a separate deal without including Holmes. Later Lerner had articles of incorporation drafted which noted Holmes had only a one percent interest in Urban Decay. Holmes sued insisting that she should have been a full and equal partner. The courts found in favor of Holmes, no written expression nor discussion of profits is a prerequisite to form a partnership.

2. With a Written Agreement. Partners can avoid misunderstandings and craft mechanisms for dispute resolution. A written partnership agreement usually includes: the name and addresses of the partners, the term of the partnership's existence, the capital characteristics of the partnership, the division of profits and losses, partnership salaries or withdrawals, the duties of the partners, and the consequences to the partnership if a partner decides to sell his or her interest in the partnership or becomes incapacitated or dies.

3. Operation of a General Partnership may be informal. A lack of formality does not mean a lack of legal responsibility. Partners have direct owner management and control of the business. The partners may elect a "managing" partner to control the business. If the partners in an informal partnership cannot agree on a decision, they may disband the partnership, distribute its assets, and terminate it.

4. Fiduciary Duty. Under the Revised Uniform Partnership Act, and at common-law, partners owe one another certain fiduciary duties such as loyalty and trust.

5. Dissolution and Winding Up of a General Partnership. Dissolution occurs when the partners no longer carry on the business together. Upon dissolution, all of the partners' authority ceases except their authority to complete transactions begun but not yet finished, and to wind up the partnership. *Winding up* involves settling the accounts and liquidating the assets of the partnership for the purpose of making distributions and terminating the concern. The liabilities and obligations of the partners do not end at dissolution; the partnership continues throughout the winding-up period. During the winding-up process, the partners' fiduciary duties to one another continue.

B. **Termination of the General Partnership** occurs when all the partnership affairs are wound up and the partners' authority to act for the partnership is completely extinguished. A dissolved partnership may terminate or may be continued by a new partnership formed by the remaining partners (including perhaps the estate or heirs of a deceased partner).

XII. **LIMITED PARTNERSHIP REQUIREMENTS.** The basic rules that govern formation, operation, and termination of general partnerships apply to limited partnerships. Some additional requirements placed on limited partnerships are discussed below.

A. **Formal Requirements.** A certificate of limited partnership must be filed with the appropriate state authority. The partnership agreement must designate the limited partners as such, or they may suffer liability and apparent authority attaching to each partner.

B. **Limited Participation.** A limited partner's liability is limited *unless* she takes part in the control of the business. A limited partner may contribute money or property to the partnership, but generally not services. The limited partner's name cannot appear in the name of the partnership without incurring unlimited liability.

XIII. **INCORPORATION** is the process by which a corporation is formed, set forth in laws of the state, where the corporation is domiciled, usually based on the Model Business Corporation Act. A corporation can do business as a foreign corporation in another state by filing documents with the appropriate secretary of state and tax authorities.

A. **Where to Incorporate.** Corporations may incorporate in any state; it need not be the state in which most of their business is located. If the corporation will be large from the outset or plans to engage in substantial interstate business, incorporation in a jurisdiction with the most advantageous corporate statutes and case law should be considered, often Delaware.

B. **How to Incorporate.** The minimum steps required to form a corporation are: (1) select a corporate name and agent for service of process; (2) file a certificate of incorporation; (3) adopt bylaws; (4) designate directors.

C. **Defective Incorporation.** Any defect in the incorporation process can have the effect of denying corporate status with the result that the entity may be a legal partnership opening the shareholders to personal liability.

1. *De Jure* Corporation the entity is a corporation by right and cannot be challenged.

2. *De Facto* Corporation. If the incorporators cannot show substantial compliance, a court may treat the entity as a *de facto* corporation, even though it is not a corporation by law.

3. Corporation by Estoppel. An entity that is neither a *de jure* nor a *de facto* corporation may be a *corporation by estoppel*. If a third party, in all of its transactions with the enterprise, acts as if it were doing business with a corporation, the third party is prevented from claiming that the enterprise is not a corporation.

XIV. **PIERCING THE CORPORATE VEIL**. Generally, shareholders enjoy a "veil" of limited liability from third-party claims. However, a court will pierce this veil if necessary to prevent evasion of statutes, perpetration of fraud, or other activities against public policy, based on various legal theories.

A. **Alter Ego Theory** applies when the owners of a corporation have so mingled their own affairs with those of the corporation that the corporation does not exist as a distinct entity; instead, it is an alter ego of its owners.

1. Domination of the Controlling Shareholder. If an individual owns too much of the stock as to exercise near absolute control, courts may find the corporation is not independent.

2. Commingling of Assets may give the appearance that the directors used the corporation for personal affairs.

3. Bypassing Formalities. If executives act without board approval, where it is typically necessary, a court may pierce the veil.

B. **Undercapitalization Theory** applies when the corporation is a separate entity, but its deliberate lack of adequate capital allows it to skirt potential liabilities. Such undercapitalization constitutes a fraud upon the public.

> **Case 19.3--*Walkovszky v. Carlton***, 223 N.E.2d 6 (N.Y. 1966), Defendant was a shareholder in the cab company, Seon, responsible for hitting Walkovszky. Plaintiff sued Calton due to the undercapitalization of Seon, which only had a $10,000 insurance policy. The court rejected plaintiff's suit, holding that the level of capitalization was a matter for the legislature to decide.

C. **TORT VERSUS CONTRACT**. Depending the particular claim of the plaintiff, a court may be more or less amenable to a legal claim that will pierce the corporate veil.

XV.   CORPORATE MANAGEMENT. Corporate control is apportioned among the directors, officers, and shareholders. The directors are the overall managers and guardians. The officers are day-to-day managers. Shareholders owner the corporation, but do not participate directly in management.

   A.   Directors. Typically corporations have a board of directors, which selects a chief executive officer (who may also be a member of the board).

   B.   Officers usually serve at the pleasure of the Board, but with a contract that incorporates the corporation's bylaws.

   C.   Shareholders.

      1.   Voting Rights. Shareholders elect the members of the board of directors (their vote may be via proxy). No action can be taken at a shareholder meeting unless there is a quorum. Depending upon the reason for a vote, e.g. to select board members or direct policy, the voting scheme may be based upon cumulative or class voting procedures.

      2.   Including Shareholders Proposals in the Company's Proxy Statement. Though not normally allowed to be involved in day-to-day decisions, SEC rules allow shareholder proposals to be voted on including: (a) compensation packages; (b) pension benefits; (c) advertising plans; and (d) dividend payouts.

      3.   Shareholder Nomination of Directors. New SEC proposals advocate the shareholders have the right to nominate directors to the board without having costly proxy votes.

      4.   Shareholder Inspection Rights and Access to the Shareholder List. Shareholders have a common-law right to inspect the corporate books and records, including the stock register and/or shareholder list, the minutes of board meetings and shareholder meetings, the bylaws, and books of account. The corporation must grant shareholders access to other shareholders

      5.   Shareholder Suits come in two forms (a) against the CEO, usually for corporate mismanagement; or (b) a derivative suit, on behalf of the corporation.

XVI.   STRUCTURAL CHANGES IN A CORPORATION. State laws establish mechanisms by which the fundamental structure of the corporation can be changed. Changes range from a reorganization to the end of the corporation. State corporation law prohibits certain changes, such as a merger or sale of all of the corporation's assets, unless first approved by both the board of directors and shareholders

A. **Merger** is the combination of two or more corporations into one. The "target" corporation becomes part of the surviving corporation. The surviving corporation becomes responsible for all of the liabilities and debts of the target. In a non-cash merger shares of the target corporation are automatically converted into shares in the surviving corporation. With a cash ("freeze out") merger some shareholders are required to sell their shares.

B. **Sale of Assets**. A company may want to acquire the assets of another, but not its liabilities. It can thus purchase all or most of the other company's assets without merging. The proceeds of the sale can be distributed to shareholders.

> **Case 19.4--*Cargo Partners AG v. Albatrans Inc*.**, 352 F.3d 41 (2d Cir. 2003). Albatrans agreed to buy Chase-Leavitt. Chase-Leavitt's chief shareholder was to be retained by Albatrans. Chase-Leavitt acquired a debt to Cargo Partners prior to Albatrans' buy out. Cargo Partners sued Albatrans on the theory that there existed a de facto merger between Albatrans and Chase-Leavitt. The court held that a *de facto* merger had not been completed, hence Albatran's was not liable.

C. **Appraisal Rights**. Shareholders who disapproved of a merger are entitled to sell their stock and receive fair market value for them.

XVII. TENDER OFFERS AND STOCK REPURCHASES

A. **Tender Offers** are public offers to all the shareholders of a target corporation to buy their shares at a stated price, usually higher than the market price. The offeror is called the *bidder*, or raider, for a hostile bid. The target shareholders are free to reject or accept the tender offer without the approval of the board of the target.

B. **Leveraged Buyouts**—any tender offer can be structured as a *leveraged buyout* (*LBO*), where a stock purchase is financed by debt.

C. **Self-Tender Offers and Going-Private Transactions**. A corporation may repurchase its own stock. If fewer than 300 people own all the stock, the corporation is no longer bound by SEC reporting rules and outside the requirements of the Sarbanes-Oxley Act.

THE RESPONSIBLE MANAGER: CHOOSING THE APPROPRIATE BUSINESS ORGANIZATION. In order to maximize profits the manager must lay out goals and a business plan in conjunction with the proper type of business organization. Written documents are a good way to reduce future liability and problems of the forgotten founder. Once the corporation has been established, managers must address questions of capitalization and finance.

INSIDE STORY: FOCUS ON FRANCHISES. Franchises are unique types of corporations that have benefits and risks. There are a number of considerations when deciding how, when and where to run a franchise.

A. **Advantages and Disadvantages**. Franchises offer customers familiarity but limit the independence of owners.

B. **Definition and Formation**. Franchising is commonly understood to refer to an arrangement whereby the *franchisor* receives cash up front, followed by monthly payments based on a reseller's gross receipts, in exchange for granting the *franchisee* the right to use the franchisor's trademarks and marketing plan.

C. **The Marketing Plan Definition** of a franchisee is pursuant to that plan or system is substantially associated with the franchisor's trademark, service mark, trade name, logotype, advertising, or other commercial symbol designating the franchisor or its affiliate; and the franchisee is required to pay, directly or indirectly, a franchise fee.

D. **The Community Interest Definition** of a franchisee, according to the state of New Jersey, means: (1) a written arrangement for a definite or indefinite period; (2) in which a person grants another person a license to use a trade name, trade mark, service mark, or related characteristics; and (3) in which there is a community of interest in the marketing of goods or services at wholesale, retail, by lease, agreement, or otherwise.

E. **Venue and Resolving Disagreements**. Typically the venue of the franchise resides where the particular offense occurs.

F. **State Registration and Disclosure Requirements**. Thirteen states require franchisors to register in order to sell franchises.

G. **State Franchise Laws: No termination without good cause**. Most state statutes prevent non-renewal without just cause.

H. **FTC's Franchise Rule**. The FTC requires franchisors to provide prospective franchisees detailed written disclosures of its Franchise Rule.

I. **Franchise Relationship Issues**. FTC rules do not address what franchisees see as the most pressing problem, overbearing and abusive power of the franchisor.

Franchisor's often allow competing franchisees to encroach upon one another and thus prevent franchisees from meeting their contractual obligations.

STUDY QUESTIONS

True-False Questions

__ 1. The sole proprietorship is the most common form of business in the United States.

__ 2. It is more difficult for sole proprietorships to raise capital.

__ 3. A general partnership agreement must be an express agreement.

__ 4. A partnership is, in effect, a mutual agency.

__ 5. A partnership is a tax reporting entity.

__ 6. In a joint venture, there is not mutual agency unless the partners specifically provide for it.

__ 7. The Revised Uniform Limited Partnership Act was been adopted by every state except Louisiana.

__ 8. Limited partners can participate in management of the partnership.

__ 9. A corporation is a separate legal entity authorized by a state, and owned by shareholders.

__ 10. An S corporation is a partnership—corporation hybrid.

__ 11. The LLC charter document is typically called the articles of initiation.

__ 12. A partnership need not be given a name.

__ 13. A general partnership is characterized by direct owner management and control of the business.

__ 14. Delaware is known as a pro-shareholder state, thus explaining its popularity for incorporation.

__ 15. A court will pierce the corporate veil only to prevent fraud.

Multiple-Choice Questions

__ 1.   Which is *not* an advantage of a sole proprietorship?
        A.   Flexibility of one owner.
        B.   Easiest to establish.
        C.   Least costly.
        D.   Raising capital.

__ 2.   Partners may agree to terms for a partnership as long as they are not

              I.   Illegal.
              II.   Contrary to public policy.
              III. Unethical.

        A.   I and II.
        B.   II and III.
        C.   I and III.
        D.   I, II and III.

__ 3.   Which is a *false* statement?
        A. Partners may make contributions in the form of money or services.
        B. Partnerships pay taxes as a separate entity.
        C. Partnerships are pass-through entities.
        D. Partnerships need two or more people to form them.

__ 4.   A joint venture requires all but which of the following?
        A. Common interest
        B. Mutual right to govern and direct
        C. Share of the profits, but not the losses
        D. Combination of the partners money and skills for the venture

__ 5.   Which is *not* a corporate characteristic?
        A.   Perpetual life.
        B.   Democratic management.
        C.   Limited liability.
        D.   Free transferability of interest.

__ 6.   Which of the following would violate the requirements for an S corporation?
        A. It must have no more than 25 shareholders.
        B. It can only issue one class of stock.
        C. It may not generally own 80 percent or more of another corporation.
        D. It must elect to be treated as an S corporation.

__ 7. An exchange of property for a share of the entity is tax-free for a: _____.

     I.   Corporation.
     II.   Partnership.

A.   I only.
B.   II only.
C.   both I and II.
D.   neither I nor II.

__ 8. A partnership agreement usually includes: _____.

     I.   Term of existence.
     II.   Division of profits and losses.
     III.   Duties of the partners.
     IV.   Consequences of incapacity of a partner.

A.   I, II, and IV.
B.   II, III, and IV.
C.   I, II, and III.
D.   I, II, III, and IV.

__ 9. Dissolution of a general partnership occurs when: _____.
A.   The stated term expires.
B.   There is agreement by the partners.
C.   There is a death of a partner.
D.   All of the above.

__ 10. Which would probably cause liability for a limited partner?

     I.   Having one's name in the partnership name.
     II.   Voting to remove a general partner.
     III.   Participating in business decisions.

A.   I and III.
B.   I, II, and III.
C.   II and III.
D.   I and II.

__ 11. A corporation that is technically not a corporation by law is called a(n) _____ corporation.
A.   *De jure.*
B.   *De minimis.*
C.   *De facto.*
D.   *Estoppel.*

___ 12. When the owners of a corporation disregard the corporate entity, this is known as the
_____ theory.
   A.   Fraud.
   B.   Alter ego.
   C.   Commingling.
   D.   Undercapitalization.

___ 13. A director who is not also an officer of the corporation is called a(n) _____ director.
   A.   Outside.
   B.   Inside.
   C.   Simultaneous.
   D.   Objective.

___ 14. Who are agents of the corporation?
   A.   Officers.
   B.   Directors.
   C.   Shareholders.
   D.   All of these.

___ 15. A _____ is a public offer to all shareholders to buy their shares at a stated price.
   A.   Leveraged buyout.
   B.   Merger.
   C.   Tender offer.
   D.   Sale offer.

Essay Questions

1. Shareholders elect the directors. Directors hire the officers. The officers run the corporation
    day to day. Therefore, the shareholders run the corporation day to day. Explain.

2. Explain corporate double taxation.

3. Why are staggered boards favorable to incumbent management?

CHAPTER 20
DIRECTORS, OFFICERS, AND CONTROLLING SHAREHOLDERS

INTRODUCTION

Directors and officers are agents of the corporation and, along with controlling shareholders, owe a fiduciary duty of care and loyalty to the corporation and its shareholders. This chapter examines the duty of care, the business judgment rule, duties of good faith and loyalty and concludes with the duties of directors and controlling shareholders.

CHAPTER OUTLINE

I. **THE BUSINESS JUDGMENT RULE AND THE DUTY OF CARE.** In cases involving suits for a breach of the duty of care, as long as certain standards are met, a court will presume that the directors have acted in good faith. The business judgment (BJR) rule is an available defense as long as the director can show no conflict of interest and an informed decision.

  A. **Informed decision.** A board's decision is reasonably informed with reports of officers and outside experts, and if necessary, an outside appraiser should prepare a valuation study on the financial fairness of the transaction. Passive reliance on such reports may result in an insufficiently informed decision.

    Case 20.1--*Smith v. Van Gorkom*, 488 A.2d 858 (Del. 1985). Van Gorkom, chairman Trans Union, asked the CFO to work out a price per share for Trans Union stock. The CFO did not try to fix the intrinsic value of the company, but came up with a cash-flow and debt-financing price. Van Gorkom used that price to negotiate a merger plan with Pritzker. A board meeting was called with one day's notice. The board approved the plan after a two-hour meeting. Plaintiff, shareholder, sued challenging the stock price as too low. The Delaware Supreme Court found the Trans Union directors grossly negligent in making an uninformed decision. The case was settled for $25.5 million.

    1. Reliability of Officers' Reports. Not every statement of an officer can be relied upon, and no statement is due blind reliance.

    2. Reliability of Experts' Reports. The expert advice must be from a reputable banking firm and the directors must exercise reasonable oversight.

B.   **Reasonable Supervision**. Directors must exercise supervision over corporate operations.

Case 20.2 *In Re Caremark International Derivative Litigation*, 698 A. 2d 959 (Del. Ch. 1996). Caremark was charged with many felonies and entered agreements to pay nearly $250 million. A shareholder derivative suit was filed seeking to make the directors personally liable for this amount. The proposed settlement included no personal payments by directors, only a series of procedures the company would implement. The court found the settlement acceptable and said that shareholders could elect new directors.

C.   **Disinterested Decision**. The Business Judgment Rule (BJR) only applies to "disinterested" decisions in which the directors have no financial or other personal interest in the transaction at issue.

D.   **The Duty of Candor**. Directors have a duty of disclosure. See *Malone v. Brincat*, 722 A.2d 5 (Del. 1998).

II.   **Statutory Limitations on Directors' Liability for Breach of Duty of Care**. Delaware limits the liability of directors for breaches of the duty of care in shareholder or corporation suits. The limit does not apply to suits brought by third parties.

A.   **Delaware's Statute** does not limit or eliminate director liability of directors for breaches of fiduciary duties, bad faith, unlawful and interested action.

B.   **California's Statute** also makes directors liable for recklessness, inattentiveness, and allows suits against quasi-foreign corporations.

III.   **Duty of Good Faith**. The duty of good faith is distinct from the duty of loyalty. Good faith includes proactive stewardship and active oversight, especially in relation to corporate compliance with law.

Case 20.3--*In re Abbott Laboratories Derivative Shareholders Litigation*, 325 F.3d 795 (7th Cir. 2003). Abbott Labs had entered a consent decree to pay $100 million to the FDA and withdraw commercial products. Shareholders sued Abbott's directors for failing to take corrective steps in response to FDA communications and warnings. Though the trial court dismissed the complaint, the appellate court reversed citing repeated omissions of the board constituted a breach of a duty of good faith.

IV.   **DUTY OF LOYALTY**. Directors and managers must subordinate their own interests to those of the corporation and its shareholders. If a court concludes a transaction was unfair or unreasonable to the corporation and in favor of the directors, the transaction may be voided.   <u>Corporate Opportunities</u>: Neither directors nor managers may take advantage of an opportunity that rightfully belongs to the corporation. Courts have a test to determine whether individual directors are taking such opportunities. See *Guth v. Loth, Inc.*, 5 A.2d 503 (Del. 1939).

V.   **DUTIES IN THE CONTEXT OF TAKEOVERS, MERGERS, AND ACQUISITIONS.** In deciding whether to sell a company, directors should act in good faith by considering the following key factors.

A.   **The Company's Intrinsic Value** is more than the market price of a share of company's stock. Directors must assess the intrinsic or fair value of the company (or division) and look to internal and external sources for guidance.

B.   **Delegation of Negotiating Authority**. If members of management are financial participants in the proposed transaction, delegation of negotiation to management or inside directors will expose the board to greater liability. See *Hanson Trust PLC v. ML SCM Acquisition, Inc.*, 781 F.2d 264 (2d Cir. 1986).

C.   **Nonprice Considerations** are factors other than share price, and interests of constituencies, and future corporate employee opportunities.

D.   **Takeover Defenses**. The BJR creates a powerful presumption in favor of actions taken by the directors to prevent a merger or hostile takeover.

   1.   Unocal Proportionality Test. Board rejection of a merger or takeover must be based on a reasonable belief of a threat.

   2.   Duty to Maximize Shareholder Value under *Revlon*. Directors must ensure the best price for shareholders, but need not consider every conceivable alternative. *Barkan v. Amsted Industries*, 567 A.2d 1279 (Del. 1989).

   3.   When is a Company in *Revlon* Mode? It occurs when the board faces two competing buy-out offers, and one bidder is hostile. See *Paramount Communications, Inc. v. QVC Network, Inc.*, 637 A.2d 34 (Del. 1994).

E.   **Deal Protection Devices** are part of friendly mergers and can be defensive moves to prevent merger.

   1.   No-Talk Provisions which limit the board's right to make decisions are not favored by courts. Courts prefer more flexible negotiation contracts. *Ace Ltd. v. Capital Re Corp.*, 747 A.2d 95 (Del Ch. 1999).

2. Breakup Fees are contractual guarantees to pay the bidder if the merger is not completed

3. Options. Put options might demand an excessive penalty and will not be honored. *Paramount Communications, Inc. v. QVC Network, Inc.*, 637 A.2d 34 (Del. 1994).

4. Other Devices. Must directors always submit a buy-out offer to the shareholders?

> **Case 20.4--*Omnicare, Inc. v. NCS Healthcare, Inc.***, 818 A.2d 914 (Del. 2003). NCS became insolvent due to limited government reimbursements and various third party providers. Omnicare offered to buyout NCS and later, another company, Genesis made a more appealing offer. The NCS board elected to accept what it saw as a firm offer from Genesis that included a contractual provision that effectively prevented shareholders from choosing to accept the Omnicare offer. The contract was invalid as it prevented the NCS board from accepting a better offer.

VI. **ALLOCATION OF POWER BETWEEN THE DIRECTORS AND THE SHAREHOLDERS**. In theory the board of directors is the guardian of the shareholders' interests, but the interests and obligations of the two groups sometimes conflict.

  A. **"Poison Pills" (Shareholder Rights Plans)**. The board may pass a resolution that makes any takeover unapproved by the directors prohibitively expensive for the new corporation. But see *Blasius Indus. v. Atlas Corp.*, 564 A.2d 651 (Del. Ch. 1988).

  B. **Protecting the Shareholder Franchise and the Blasius Standard of Review**. Courts distinguish between power over corporate assets and the power relationship between the board and shareholders. A board's unilateral action, without compelling reason, will not be upheld (*Blasius*) in the name of protecting shareholders.

VII. **DUTY OF DIRECTORS TO DISCLOSE PRELIMINARY MERGER NEGOTIATIONS-** Directors may be required to disclose negotiations even if parties have not reached an agreement in principle. A management buy-out (MBO) poses a conflict of interest problem.

VIII. **DUTIES OF CONTROLLING SHAREHOLDERS**. A controlling shareholder might owe a fiduciary duty to the other shareholders, and always owe minority shareholders the duty to control the corporation in a fair, just, and equitable manner. *Sugarman v. Sugarman*, 797 F.2d 3 (1st Cir. 1986).

A.   **Sale of Control**. A controlling interest usually commands a higher price per share than the minority interest. Controlling shareholders normally have a right to derive a premium from the sale of a controlling block of stock, however, controlling shareholders must allow minority shareholders to participate in the financial benefits.

> **Case 20.5--*Jones v. H. F. Ahmanson & Co.*,** 460 P.2d 464 (Cal.1969). The majority shareholders of United Savings and Loan traded their shares to United Financial Corporation and became the majority shareholders UFC. Minority shareholders were not allowed to do make a similar transaction. The court held that the new majority shareholders, who did not allow minority to exchange their shares, breached a fiduciary duty to the minority shareholders. The court ordered defendants to pay damages to minority shareholders.

B.   **Freeze-outs**. A majority shareholder *may* freeze out the minority, so long as the transaction is fair and is designed to maximize shareholder value. *Weinberger v. UOP, Inc.*, 457 A.2d 701 (Del. 1983).

IX.   **GREENMAIL** is the purchase of a dissident's shares above market price. Shareholders may challenge greenmail through a derivative suit. However, the board can argue the BJR.

THE RESPONSIBLE MANAGER: CARRYING OUT FIDUCIARY DUTIES. Officers, directors, and controlling shareholders (managers) must act as fiduciaries and protect other stockholders in the following way:

- Show an undivided loyalty.
- Exercise good faith with no conflict of interest.
- Act with the care a reasonable person would use to manage their own property.
- Make only informed decisions.
- Not rely blindly on the advice of other people, even experts.
- Use due diligence after reviewing all information and the effects of both the monetary and the non-monetary aspects of the transaction.
- Not vote on a transaction that might bring personal benefit to fiduciaries
- Leave conflicted decisions to disinterested directors.
- Ensure fair transactions by using independent committees, financial consultants and counsel.
- Maximize shareholder value.
- In the event of change of control, not adopt a scorched-earth policy that leaves the successful bidder with a depleted target.

INSIDE STORY: THE LONG TWILIGHT OF IMPERIAL CEOS. In 2004, New York State Attorney General, Eliot Spitzer brought a civil suit against Marsh & McLennan. The insurance company undertook a number of illegal and unethical business practices. The stock price crashed and directors at Marsh & McLennan cooperated rather than face criminal indictment. Simultaneously directors at Disney came under fire for agreeing to a $140 million severance for Michael Ovitz. Stockholders brought a derivative suit. As well the financial meltdown of WorldCom showed that CEO's were acting with near impunity and without true board oversight.

STUDY QUESTIONS

True-False Questions

___ 1. The business judgment rule precludes a court from examining the economic decisions of a board of directors.

___ 2. Not every statement of a corporate officer can be relied on in good faith, and no statement is entitled to blind reliance.

___ 3. Directors need not attempt to ensure that an investment banker's compensation does not impair the banker's independent opinion.

___ 4. The question of what constitutes reasonable supervision by directors is necessarily judged by a uniform legal standard.

___ 5. Stockholders can either sue the board of directors directly or in a derivate suit whenever stockholders believe the board made a bad economic decision.

___ 6. Outside directors are usually viewed as more objective and disinterested than inside directors.

___ 7. When managers and directors are engaged in self-dealing, courts will void the transaction, unless it can be shown that the deal was fair to the corporation.

___ 8. Most states use the expectancy of interest test to determine whether or not an opportunity belongs to the corporation.

___ 9. Directors have no fiduciary duty to familiarize themselves with non-price provisions of a proposed agreement.

___ 10. The business judgment rule is always a defense in lawsuits regarding take-over bids.

___ 11. Once the decision has been made to sell the corporation, the directors have a fiduciary duty to get the best available price for the shareholders.

___ 12. If directors' and shareholders' interests are in conflict, the directors' interests may prevail, as in accord with business judgment rule.

___ 13. More than half of the Fortune 500 companies have poison-pill plans in effect.

___ 14. If the controlling shareholder knows the purchaser of the shares intends to use controlling power to the detriment of the corporation, the controlling shareholder is forbidden from transferring the power.

___ 15. A majority shareholder may never freeze-out minority shareholders.

Multiple-Choice Questions

___ 1. Which statement is *false* concerning the business judgment rule?
   A.   It is applicable only if it is an informed decision.
   B.   Passive reliance on officers' reports may result in an insufficiently informed decision.
   C.   Directors should not have a conflict of interest.
   D.   If the business judgment rule does not apply in a case, the plaintiffs have the burden of proof to show the director's acts were grossly negligent.

___ 2. A leading business judgment rule case that was discussed in the text was: _____.
   A.   *Smith v. Romans.*
   B.   *Smith v. Van Gorkom.*
   C.   *Van Gorkom v. Romans.*
   D.   *Pritzker v. Van Gorkom.*

___ 3. Concerning the reliability of expert's reports, _____.

   A.   Directors have a duty to make a reasonable inquiry and exercise reasonable oversight.
   B.   A conclusory fairness opinion is not a sufficient basis for a board decision.
   C.   An expert's opinion must be in writing and be reasoned.
   D.   All of these statements are true.

___ 4. In Delaware, the certificate of incorporation cannot eliminate or limit the liability of a director for all but which of the following?
   A.   Any breach of the director's duty of loyalty.
   B.   Acts of omissions not in good faith.
   C.   Unlawful payments of dividends or stock purchases.

D.   An unexcused pattern of inattention that amounts to abdication of the director's duties.

___ 5.   The corporate _____ doctrine states that officers and directors may not take personal advantage of a business opportunity that rightfully belongs to the corporation.
A.   Opportunity.
B.   Fiduciary.
C.   Loyalty.
D.   Business.

___ 6.   Under the _____ test, if an officer, director, or controlling shareholder learns of an opportunity that is proper for the business in the course of his or her business for the corporation, he or she cannot keep the opportunity for him- or herself.
A.   Fiduciary.
B.   Opportunity-in-business.
C.   Line-of-business.
D.   Loyalty-in-business.

___ 7.   Which is *not* a factor that courts have said directors should consider when deciding to sell the company?
A.   Nonprice considerations.
B.   The company's book value.
C.   The reliability of expert's reports.
D.   Investment banker's fee structure.

___ 8.   Directors must not only assess the adequacy of the premium and how the premium compares with that paid in other takeovers in the same or similar industries, but they must also assess the intrinsic value of the company

I.   As a going concern.
II.   On a liquidation basis.
III.   In a distressed sale.

A.   I and II.
B.   I and III.
C.   II and III.
D.   I, II, and III.

___ 9.   Analyzing a take-over bid and its effect on the corporate enterprise, the board may consider all but which of the following?
A.   The nature and timing of the offer.
B.   The risk of non-consummation.
C.   The impact on constituencies other than the employees.
D.   The quality of the securities being offered in exchange.

__ 10. When a company has an obligation to maximize shareholder wealth, the company is said to be in _____ mode.
   A.   *Paramount.*
   B.   *Barkan.*
   C.   *Revlon.*
   D.   *Time-Warner.*

__ 11. A corporate executive's generous severance agreement is known as a _____ parachute.
   A.   Silver.
   B.   Golden.
   C.   Platinum.
   D.   Tin.

__ 12. A shareholder who owns sufficient shares to out-vote the other shareholders is known as the _____ shareholder.
   A.   Material.
   B.   Commanding.
   C.   Conquering.
   D.   Controlling.

__ 13. Normally, to whom does the control premium belong?
   A.   The corporation.
   B.   The majority shareholder.
   C.   All shareholders.
   D.   It is divided between the majority shareholder and the corporation.

__ 14. The payment of a much higher than market price for stock of a corporation dissident is known as
   A.   Greenmail.
   B.   Blackmail.
   C.   Hushmail.
   D.   Extortion.

__ 15. Contrasting greenmail and hushmail, which is true?
   A.   Hushmail is at least twice as expensive.
   B.   Greenmail is paid to try to insure silence.
   C.   Hushmail is paid to try to insure silence.
   D.   Greenmail is legal and hushmail is illegal.

Essay Questions

1. When can an officer or director rely on the company's procedures for determining what disclosure is required?

2. What is wrong with re-pricing executive stock options if the stock price falls?

3. What factors will favor keeping a poison pill in place?

CHAPTER 21
EXECUTIVE COMPENSATION AND EMPLOYEE BENEFITS

INTRODUCTION

In 2002, Tyco disclosed a patter of illegal activity of then CEO Dennis Kozlowski. Kozlowski loaned himself millions of dollars of corporate funds, and subsequently forgave much of the debt. He misused corporate funds for parties and committed other abuses. Kozlowski, like other corporate heads, engaged in insider trading and induced employees to lose millions in worthless company retirement schemes. Generally executive compensation is regulated by state law while employee retirement is governed by ERISA. With recent law, the federal government has entered into regulating corporate practices tied to CEO compensation in re securities. This chapter reviews corporate compensation, laws and regulations tied to them and looks at international trends with CEO compensation.

I. **REGULATION OF EXECUTIVE COMPENSATION.**

    A. **State Regulation.** Though the Boards of Directors approve CEO and executive compensation packages, they must adhere to statutes and case law on fiduciary responsibility.

        Case 21.1--*In re The Walt Disney Company Derivative Litigation*, 825 A.2d 275 (Del.Ch.2003). CEO Michael Eisner chose personal friend Michael Ovitz to be president of Disney. By 1996, Ovitz was looking to resign and Eisner drafted a no fault termination package whereby Ovitz would not lose any of his benefits all without board approval. Stockholders brought a derivative suit against the directors for a breach of fiduciary duty. As alleged the directors' actions fell outside the business judgment rule and a suit could go forward against the directors for personal liability.

    B. **Federal Regulation.** Chiefly under the SEC Acts of 1933 and 1934 the SEC requires CEOs and executives to disclose the stockholdings.

        1. **Disclosures and Shareholders Proposals.** Since 1992, SEC requires corporations to disclose: (a) compensation of the top five executives; (b) comparisons of its stock performance versus others in the industry; (c) the rationale for the compensation.

2. **Compensation Committees** are supposedly independent and report to the Board of Directors with recommendation for executive salaries. In fact members of these committees are not completely independent.

II. **STOCK OPTIONS** offer employees the right to purchase a number of shares at a particular price.

HISTORICAL PERSPECTIVE: EFFECTS OF TAX LAWS ON STOCK OPTIONS. The use of stock options grew as a way to encourage non-owner directors to have an interest in the company. By the 1970s, federal tax law had discouraged the use of stock options in executive compensation. By the 1980s federal law had changed and options were common. After 1993, Congress compelled stock options to be performance-based. Now around 25% of public companies use stock options and such ranges from 10 to 20% of executive compensation.

A. **Exemption from Federal Registration of Stock Option Plans**. Non-public companies are limited as to the amount of stock it can issue in one year. Under Section 701, they can exceed the $1 million value limit.

B. **Tax and Accounting Treatment of Stock Options**. Companies can deduct the difference in the strike price from the fair market value of the stock when employees exercise their options. Individuals are taxed whether they sell the stock or not.

C. **Impact of Underwater Stock Options**. If the Strike price is higher than the current market price, optionees suffer a relative loss. Companies have used a variety of approaches to address such losses, extending the option period, buying back the options, and lowering the strike price.

D. **Stock Option Litigation**. Some wrongful termination suits have had at their source, stock options. *Fleming v. Parametric Technology Corp.*, 187 F.3d 647 (9th Cir. 1999); *Greene v. Safeway Stores, Inc.*, 210 F.3d 1237 (10th Cir. 2000).

Case 21.2--*International Business Machines Corporation v. Bajorek*, 191 F.3d 1033 (9th Cir.1999). Bajorek was a 25-year employee. He exercised $900,000 worth of options. In his last week Bajorek worked for Komag, an IBM competitor – then worked for them full-time after leaving IBM. IBM cancelled his stock options. The appellate court held that IBM had the right to cancel, under New York law, as Bajorek violated his non-compete clause.

III. **OTHER TYPES OF STOCK OWNERSHIP PLANS**. Critics argue that options provide perverse motives to inflate stock prices through short-term planning, *pump and dump* schemes. As companies look to move away from stock option programs, there are at least three alternatives.

A.   **Restricted Stock Plans** provide employees the right to purchase a limited amount of shares, yet take possession later. Employees must file their purchases with the IRS.

B.   **Employee Stock Purchase Plans** must (1) include most groups of employees; (2) receive shareholder approval; (3) not allow a transferable right to purchase.

C.   **Phantom Stock and Stock Appreciation Rights**. The former is a promise to pay a bonus in the equivalent of value of stocks or the increase in value over a period of time. Stock Appreciation Rights, allow the employees to obtain the future appreciation in the company's stock without risking capital.

IV.   **SEC REGULATION OF EQUITY COMPENSATION PLANS** Since 1996 the SEC eliminated the shareholder approval for stock plans. However some private exchanges do require approval.

V.   **ERISA**. The Employee Retirement Income Security Act is designed to protect private retirement plans.

A.   **Coverage** ERISA establishes a range of standards and parameters regarding: (1) minimum funding requirements and vesting standards; (2) fiduciary obligations; (3) disclosures; (4) types of investments; and (5) annual reports.

> **Case 21.3--*In re Worldcom, Inc. ERISA Litigation***, 263 F. Supp.2d 745 (S.D.N.Y. 2003). WorldCom had an employee retirement pension program. In 2002 it announced a series of accounting problems and miscalculations with earnings reports in the billions of dollars. Subsequently WorldCom filed for bankruptcy. Employees sued CEO Bernard Ebbers and president Dona Miller for breach of their fiduciary duty. Defendants brought a motion to dismiss. The court dismissed claims based on ERISA violations, but allowed recovery for the false statements made by defendants.

B.   **Employee Stock Ownership Plans**, including 401(k) plans, have certain tax advantages, restrictions on sales, and allow companies to borrow against them.

C.   **Pension Plans**. Officers and trustees of pension plans are fiduciaries. Such fiduciaries have wide latitude to act in the best interest of plan participants and beneficiaries. *Hughes Aircraft Co. v. Jacobson*, 525 U.S. 432 (1999).

D.   **HMO's** raise questions about fiduciary duties as well.

> **Case 21.4--*Pegram v. Herdrich*** 530 U.S. 211 (2000). Herdrich was covered by an HMO health plan. Herdrich was seen by a doctor, Pegram, who found a lump in her abdomen. Pegram advised Herdrich to wait a few days to get an ultrasound appointment at a facility within the HMO. Herdrich suffered a ruptured appendix prior to the second appointment, and sued Pegram and the HMO in state court for malpractice and fraud. Defendants claimed that the suit was authorized under ERISA. The Supreme Court held that ERISA does not craft HMOs or their doctors as fiduciaries.

> **Federal Preemption**. Federal law bars state law suits against HMOs. In 2004 the Supreme Court further restricted plaintiff recovery options for malpractice due to HMO service. States still may regulate some insurance practices, including timely notice of claims. *UNUM Life Insurance Co. of America v. Ward*, 526 U.S. 358 (1999).

E.   **Penalties** for failure to comply with ERISA include: suits to recover lost benefits; and civil penalties for fiduciary duties.

VI.   **OTHER LAWS AFFECTING THE EMPLOYMENT RELATIONSHIP**. Most federal laws in this are address union employees.

A.   **Consolidating Omnibus Budget Reconciliation Act** (COBRA) allowed employees to continue their health benefits, formerly supplied by a previous employer for up to 18 months so long as the former employee paid for the insurance. Employers must notify employees who do not work enough hours to be covered by the company's insurance program. Employers can discontinue insurance for a number of reasons such as age.

B.   **Health Insurance Portability and Accounting Act** (HIPPA) provides special protection for those with lifelong illnesses who change jobs. HIPPA prevents employers from discriminating against new employees with existing health conditions. HIPPA tries to fill some gaps of COBRA but does not address small business concerns or set caps on insurance benefits.

C.   **Worker Adjustment and Retraining Notification Act** (WARN) addresses plant closings and workforce reductions by companies with at least 100 employees. Companies must provide 60 days notice, unless certain unforeseen conditions arise. Aggrieved employees may recover back pay, and legal fees.

GLOBAL VIEW: INTERNATIONAL TRENDS IN STOCK COMPENSATION. A survey of MNCs showed that nearly 70 have stock compensation plans. There has been an increase in legislation across the world relating to stock and employee compensation. Most companies use stock options but others use performance-based programs. Stock-purchase programs are commonly used for broader employee groups. Few have ESOPs. U.S. multinationals frequently use plans modeled after the 401(k) plan.

RESPONSIBLE MANAGER: SIX KEY PRINCIPLES RELATED TO COMPENSATION. When looking at compensation, managers should:
- Have an independent compensation committee;
- Incorporate performance-based components;
- Avoid benchmarks that compare the company with others within the industry;
- Use fair and proper accounting, not gimmicks;
- Make executives hold shares to avoid pump and dump scenarios; and
- Make executive compensation transparent.

INSIDE STORY: WHO IS WATCHING THE WATCHDOG? Richard Grasso was CEO and Chairman of the Board of the New York Stock Exchange. His annual salary was at least $2.4 million and he regularly received bonuses in the millions. As Grasso came to retire, he had nearly $140 million in benefits and was entitled to $48 million in deferred compensation. Both members of the private sector and New York's Attorney General complained, the latter brought suit as Grasso's pay was excessive considering Grasso failed to prevent the stock scandals of Enron, WorldCom and others.

STUDY QUESTIONS

True-False Questions

___ 1. A company's board of directors has complete authority to authorize executive salaries and compensation.

___ 2. The Securities and Exchange Commission is the primary executive agency authorized to enforce executive compensation as related to loans and cash payments.

___ 3. Publicly traded corporations must disclose the stock they sell or give to executives and directors.

___ 4. Corporations must have independent compensation committees in order to pay exorbitant salaries, e.g., $100,000 per hour, to members of the board of directors.

___ 5. Stock options are rights to buy stock for a set price at which others on the free market cannot.

___ 6. During the 20th century, Congress passed a series of laws that both increased the value and practicality of stock options.

___ 7. Sometimes an employee's stock option is basically worthless.

___ 8. A corporation always has the right to fire an employee rather than allow the employee to take advantage of a stock option agreement.

___ 9. Pump and Dump stock schemes are usually favored by stockholders and employees with employee retirement plans pegged to a company's stock price.

___ 10. Directors of public companies cannot be held personally liable for mismanagement of employee retirement accounts under ERISA.

___ 11. Even if terminated without cause, an employer can terminate the former employee's health insurance.

___ 12. Employers cannot discriminate in the amount of insurance benefits extended to new employees who require high-cost health care, e.g. cancer treatments.

___ 13. The WARN Act demands that large employers give workers at least 60 days notice before a plant closing or layoff.

___ 14. Wise corporate managers avoid accounting gimmicks and encourage transparency in relation to executive compensation.

___ 15. Given the increase in wealth of the NYSE during his tenure as CEO and chairman, there were no viable legal claims against Richard Grasso or the board at NYSE for a breach of fiduciary duties relate to his compensation.

Multiple-Choice Questions

___ 1. Which of the following is *not* required in corporate disclosures to the SEC about executive compensation?
   A. Corporate gifts to spouses and other family members.
   B. Corporate loans to executives that are forgiven.
   C. Compensation packages for top directors and executives.
   D. Explanation for executive compensation.

__ 2. Shareholders were allowed to bring suit against CEO Michael Eisner and the directors at Disney for giving Michael Ovitz excessive compensation because:
A.   Only the SEC can sue for such a breach of fiduciary duty.
B.   Stockholders are not allowed to bring this type of derivative suit.
C.   Stockholders had a better remedy, i.e., voting out the board and Eisner.
D.   The director's actions were not protected by the business judgment rule.

__ 3. Which of the following stock option plans are exempt from SEC disclosure?
A.   Nonpublic companies issuing over $1 million worth of shares per year
B.   Publicly traded companies issuing over $1 million worth of shares per year.
C.   Publicly traded companies issuing less than $1 million worth of shares per year.
D.   None of these are exempt.

__ 4. Which alternative compensation method is a response to stock option abuses?
A.   Employee stock options.
B.   Performance-based salary
C.   Corporate loans.
D.   Loans plus incentive-based salary.

__ 5. Which of the following are rationales for compensation committees?

I.   To remove the decision on how much to pay the board of directors from the board itself.
II.   To prevent the president from rewarding friends on the board.
III. To protect stockholders at the expense of employees.

A.   I, II, and III.
B.   I and II.
C.   I am III.
D.   None of these are rationales.

__ 6. In response to *pump and dump* stock scandals by heads at WorldCom, Enron and the like, some companies have adopted which of the alternative stock / retirement programs?

I.   Employee Stock Ownership Programs.
II.   Stock Appreciation Rights (SAPs).
III. Restricted Stock Plans.

A.   I and II
B.   I and III
C.   II and III
D.   I, II, and III

__ 7. What is characteristic of 401(k) retirement plans?
   A.   Companies can default on them, leaving employees/retirees with nothing.
   B.   They provide tax shelters for the corporation and individuals.
   C.   Companies borrow against them.
   D.   All the above

__ 8. Which is a cash-based retirement benefit?
   A. HMO.
   B. ESOP.
   C. SSI.
   D. WARN.

__ 9. What is not true about HMOs?
   A.   They can be considered part of employee benefits under ERISA.
   B.   As they are regulated by federal law, state lawsuits are preempted.
   C.   HMO directors are defined as fiduciaries under ERISA.
   D.   None of the above.

__ 10. Under COBRA what are the reasons that an employer may decline to extend health care.

   I.   The employee is fired.
   II.   The employer elects to deny coverage to certain employees.
   III. The employee is old enough to qualify for Medicare.

   A.   I and II.
   B.   I and III.
   C.   II and III.
   D.   I, II, and III.

__ 11. HIPPA applies to which of the following circumstances?
   A.   Wrongful termination.
   B.   High-risk employees.
   C.   Groups of small businesses like hairdressers.
   D.   None of the above.

__ 12. The WARN Act allows:

   I.   Employers to fire employees without notice.
   II.   Plant closings due to acts of war.
   III. The government to recover $30,000 from transgressors, even if the employer saved 10 times that amount via a violation of WARN.

   A.   I only

B.   I and II
C.   II and III
D.   I, II, and III

__ 13. A _____ provide employees the right to purchase a limited amount of shares, yet take possession later. Employees must file their purchases with the IRS.

A.   Restricted Stock Plan.
B.   Employee Stock Purchase Plans
C.   Phantom Stock
D.   None of the above.

__ 14. A _____ gives the person to whom its granted the right to buy a certain number of shares at a fixed price for a fixed number of years.

A.   Stock option.
B.   Grant price.
C.   Underwater stock.
D.   Vesting restriction.

__ 15. An ESOP must:

A.   Not discriminate in favor of highly compensated employees.
B.   Have its stock invested in stock of sponsoring company.
C.   Neither A nor B.
D.   Both A and B.

Essay Questions

1.   What options do directors have in lieu of stock option programs?

2.   What impact have tax laws had on stock options?

3.   What can directors do to minimize the threat of litigation regarding executive compensation?

CHAPTER 22
PUBLIC AND PRIVATE OFFERINGS OF SECURITIES

INTRODUCTION

At some point, most business will look to investment in the company from members of the public. These public "offerings" are heavily regulated by both federal and state securities regulations. This chapter provides an overview of the federal statutory scheme that regulates the offer and sale of securities under the Securities Act of 1933. The chapter gives a description of the public offering process, including the registration of securities, the role of an underwriter, and more. It then covers exemptions and restrictions and various requirements under the Act, liability for failure to meet the statutory registration and prospectus-delivery requirements, who may sue and who may be sued, elements of liability, available defenses, and the civil and criminal penalties and remedies.

CHAPTER OUTLINE

I. **FEDERAL STATUTORY SCHEME** holds three primary beliefs: (1) investors should be provided information; (2) insiders should not gain material advantages over the public; and (3) mislead investors should have some relief.

    A. **The 1933 Act:** requires registration of securities offerings with the SEC, unless the offering is exempt; requires companies have a prospectus with material information for investors prior to investment; and creates private causes of action, in addition to SEC and federal prosecutions.

    B. **The 1934 Act:** requires periodic reporting by publicly-traded companies or those with a certain number of shareholders; and contains anti-fraud provisions and filing requirements for insiders dealing in their own company's stock.

HISTORICAL PERSPECTIVE: GENESIS OF THE 1933 ACT. After the stock market crash of 1929 the Congress attempted to pass legislation to protect investors and public confidence in the markets. Speaker Rayburn decried corporate heads as having swindled millions of Americans and acted outside and without government supervision.

    C. **The Private Securities Litigation Reform Act of 1995** designed to: (1) correct abuses in private securities litigation; (2) prevent the filing of frivolous suits; (3) prevent "fishing expedition" lawsuits; (4) require plaintiffs to plead fraudulent intent; (5) eliminate joint and several liability; (6) create a new safe harbor for "forward-looking" statements.

D. **The Securities Litigation Uniform Standards Act of 1998** limits state lawsuits and forces actions into federal court. However there is an exception. See *Lalondriz v. USA Networks, Inc.*, No. 99 Civ. 1711 (RO) (S.D.N.Y. June 30, 1999).

E. **The Sarbanes-Oxley Act of 2002** has 11 titles (sections) but emphasized the inherent conflict between accountants and their corporate clients. SOX also seeks to regulate corporate directors, insider-trading, and encourage better financial disclosures.

F. **SEC Rules and Regulations** are promulgated to clarify Congressional law, federal policy, and exemptions. E.g. the SEC adopted Rule 144 to clarify definition of the term "underwriter;" the SEC adopted Regulation D in re small businesses and private offerings.

II. **STATE BLUE SKY LAWS** are state securities laws, sometimes more restrictive than federal law. The federal Capital Markets Efficiency Act of 1996 provides more uniformity between federal and state securities regulation, yet also pre-empts certain state rules.

III. **DEFINITION OF TERMS:**

A. **Security** is broadly defined; examples include any note, stock, bond, evidence of indebtedness, investment contract, and limited partnership. But see *Robinson v. Glynn*, 349 F.3d 166 (4th Cir. 2003).

B. **Investment Contract** is a transaction involving an investment of money in a common enterprise with profits to come solely from the efforts of others.

> **Case 22.1--*SEC v. Edwards***, 540 U.S. 389 (2004). Edwards was CEO and sole shareholder of ETS Payphones, its subsidiary, controlled by Edwards sold ETS' phones. Edwards sold lease packages that "guaranteed" a 14 percent annual return to customers. The SEC sued on the grounds that Edwards failed to follow the 1933 and 1934 acts. The Supreme Court held that any scheme of investment that proposes to guarantee a return is regulated by the SEC acts of 1933 and 1934.

C. **Family Resemblance Test.** Promissory notes and other evidences of indebtedness may or may not constitute a security, depending on the factual context.

D.   **Offer**: "every attempt or offer to dispose of, or solicitation of an offer to buy, a security or interest in a security, for value," which is much broader than that in contract law.

E.   **Sale**: "every contract of sale or disposition of a security or interest in a security, for value." The crucial term in this definition is *value*, which is very broad and includes, for example, cash, property, or compensation for past services.

IV.   **REGISTERED OFFERINGS**. Once a company prepares to offer a security, they must register the securities and sale.

A.   **Registration of Securities**. Securities must be registered unless an exemption is available. The process is expensive, but guarantees a secondary market.

B.   **The Role of the Underwriter**. Public offerings are usually underwritten by one or more broker-dealers or investment banking firms.

1.   Firm Commitment Underwriting. Underwriters agree to purchase the entire offering. Once effective, the underwriters attempt to sell the securities that they are obligated to purchase.

2.   Best-Efforts Underwriting. Underwriters do not assure purchase, but agree to seek buyers for the initial public offerings. The risk remains entirely with the securities issuer.

C.   **The Registration Statement**. SEC rules dictate how issuers announce and declare registration.

1.   Forms. Issuers must use prescribed forms which different depending on the type of corporation, their revenues on hand and information about the security.

2.   Prospectus is contained within the registration statement. On the one hand it is a marketing instrument, on the other it is a disclosure statement designed to prevent claims for securities fraud. SEC rules now require the prospectus to use "plain English."

D.   **Due Diligence**. Company directors, underwriters, and their respective counsel must investigate and assure that the information in the prospectus is accurate. See exhibit 22.3 for the "checklist."

E.   **Registration Procedure**. The registration statement must be filed with the SEC and becomes effective on the twentieth day after filing, unless the SEC suspends the registration for being materially defective.

1. Review. The SEC reviews the registration and can comment to the company recommending amendments to the registration.

2. Waiting Period: Is the time between the filing of the registration statement and effective date, during which time issuers and underwriters are limited in what they can say about the planned offer.

3. Going Effective: Once the SEC allows, sales of the securities may begin.

F. **Shelf Registration**. Companies may register securities for later issuance.

Managerial Timeline for a Public Securities Offering

Day 1	Decide upon a public offering of securities to raise capital, and choose a securities underwriting firm
Day 30-60	With the aid of the underwriter, prepare the forms and prospectus for the registration statement.
Day 61-90	File the registration statement with the SEC for review, and submit any amendments to the filing.
Day 91-120	During the quiet period, the underwriter can assemble selling groups, distribute copies of the preliminary prospectus, and solicit offers to sell the securities.
Day 121 +	Once the offering is declared effective and the pricing amendment is filed, sales of the company's securities may begin.

G. **Reorganizations and Combinations**. Rule 145 requires a registration statement and approval by shareholders in relation to corporate investment decisions. There are strict limitations on communications by corporate officers, to the shareholders and public about mergers.

H. **SEC's Proposed Changes to the Registration Process**. In October 2004 the SEC proposed new rules on communications between shareholders and directors.

1. Gun – Jumping. Companies may make announcements prior to filing a registration under certain conditions.

2. Free Writing Prospectuses. Well-known seasoned issuers may use a Form S-3 and publish a free writing prospectus, which can make certain claims, yet is not deemed part of the registration statement and leave the issuers free from Section 11 liability.

3. Shelf Registration would allow well-known seasoned issuers to make offerings with automatic shelf registration.

V.   EXEMPTIONS FOR OFFERINGS BY THE ISSUER. Exemptions from registration fall into two categories: exempt securities and exempt transactions. State blue sky laws have similar exemptions.

A.   Private Offerings Under Section 4(2) are transactions only offered to qualified, sophisticated investors. These *private placements* and subsequent transfer of shares are limited.

> **Case 22.2--*SEC v. Ralston Purina Co.*,** 346 U.S. 119 (1953). Ralston Purina offered stock for market prices to its employees, regardless of job classification. Between 1947 and 1951 Ralston Purina sold $2 million worth of stock to 2,000 employees throughout the United States. The Supreme Court held that these sales were not exempt from SEC registration as a private sale. It is not merely numbers of employees, but the sophistication of them due to access to information.

B.   Regulation D: Safe-Harbor Exemptions for Private Offerings. Regulation D contains three separate exemptions from registration under Rules 504, 505, and 506 (as defined via Rules 501-503).

1.   Accredited Investors (banks, wealthy individuals, large corporations, etc.) are financially sophisticated and do not need all the protections afforded by the securities laws.

2.   Integration of Sales—successive sales within a short period of time may be considered a single sale, not needing standard registration.

3.   Rule 504 exempts offerings of up to $1 million within a twelve-month period with an unlimited number of purchasers.

4.   Rule 505 exempts offerings of up to $5 million within a twelve-month period. General advertising is not permitted and no more than thirty-five unaccredited investors are allowed. A Rule 505 offering normally uses a private-placement memorandum to disseminate information.

5.   Rule 506 exempts offerings that the issuer reasonable believes are limited to no more than thirty-five unaccredited investors and an unlimited number of accredited investors. General advertising is not permitted.

C.   Section 4(6) Exemption. The section exempts offers and sales by any issuer to an unlimited number of accredited investors, not to exceed $5 million in aggregate and without public solicitation or advertising.

VIEW FROM CYBERSPACE: OFFERINGS ON THE INTERNET. In 1995 Spring Street Brewing Company made the first internet offering. Other companies have made small offerings under Section 504. Companies are making registered offerings as well. In April 2000 the SEC proposed rules to govern online offerings. All online offerings must be made by registered brokers. The SEC has an electronic system to regulate efficient internet postings of documents filed with securities offerings. Companies are still liable under Section 11 for misleading representations.

D.   **Regulation A** allows issuers to "test the waters" and solicit indications of interest before filing any required disclosure documents.

  1.   Size of Offering and Eligible Companies is limited to $5 million to be sold in a twelve-month period with no "bad boy" principals or shareholders.

  2.   Testing the Waters. Issuers need only file a solicitation of interest document with the SEC. General solicitation via radio or TV is permitted.

E.   **Offerings to Employees**. SEC rules exempt limited offers and sales of securities made pursuant to a written benefit plans or a written compensation contract. Exempt compensatory benefit plans include purchase, savings, option, bonus, stock-appreciation, profit-sharing, thrift-incentive, and pension plans.

F.   **The Private Placement Memorandum**. The private counterpart to the prospectus. SEC rules determine what the issuer must disclose in the document.

VI.   **EXEMPTIONS FOR SECONDARY OFFERINGS**. Securities issued in a private placement cannot be sold in a secondary offering, unless registered or exempt from registration. Securities issued in a private placement are called *restricted securities*.

A.   **Section 4(1) Exemption**. Transactions by "any person other than an issuer, underwriter, or dealer" are exempt from registration.

B.   **Rule 144** provides objective criteria for deciding whether a person is an underwriter. Some transfer agents may require legal opinions before acquiescing to an unregistered sale.

C.   **Rule 144A** creates a safe harbor for the resale of unregistered securities to qualified institutional buyers under certain conditions. Note exhibit 22.7: Exemptions for Resale.

D.   **Regulation S and Increased Liquidity**. Offers and sales outside the United States are not subject to federal registration requirements. In combination with Rule 144A, unregistered offers and sales of securities have grown is size and value.

VII. **REPORTING REQUIREMENTS OF PUBLIC COMPANIES**. A company with registered securities in a public offering must file periodic reports.

A. **Section 12** requires companies with assets exceeding $5 million to file various reports:

1. 10-Q: unaudited quarterly statement of operations and financial condition.

2. 10-K: annual audited report.

3. 8-K: certain strategic events, e.g., changes in control or acquisitions.

Small Business Issuers must file abbreviated reports on Forms 10-KSB and 10-QSB.

B. **Other Sections of the Act.**

1. Proxy Solicitations correspond to powers of shareholders and their proxies to vote on management and shareholder proposals, as well as vote for the board of directors.

2. Insider Trading Reports. The SEC requires reports by officers, directors, and persons holding more than 10 percent of the company's stock.

3. Tender Offers, an offer to buy shares from shareholders, must comply with rules in Section 14 of the 1934 Act.

4. Schedule 13D. Any person acquiring more than five percent of the shares of a reporting company must disclose their intent in a Schedule 13D within ten days of the acquisition.

VIII. **VIOLATION OF THE REGISTRATION AND PROSPECTUS—DELIVERY REQUIREMENTS OF THE 1933 ACT: SECTION 12(A) (1).** Absent an exemption, all securities must be registered and sold only after delivery of a prospectus.

A. **Elements of Liability**. The defendant is strictly liable if he offers or sells securities through interstate commerce without an effective registration statement.

B. **Damages**. If plaintiff owns the securities, she is entitled to a refund of the investment plus interest. If plaintiff has sold the security, she is entitled to damages, the difference between the original investment and subsequent sale.

C.   **Who May Be Sued**? Clearly the issuer is liable, but certain third parties are not unless they are sellers. *Pinter v. Dahl*, 486 U.S. 622 (1988).

D.   **Who May Sue?** Anyone who purchased shares may sue, class-action suits may be brought as well.

IX.   **SECTION 11 OF THE 1933 ACT** provides remedies for suits alleging misleading registration statements.

A.   **Who May Sue.**

   1.   Tracing Requirement. Plaintiff must show that the particular securities they purchased were tied to a misleading registration statement. See *Lee v. Ernst & Young LLP*, 294 F.3d 969 (8th Cir. 2002).

   2.   Class Actions are available if a class can be determined.

B.   **Who May be Sued?** Issuers, Underwriters, Members of the Board of Directors, and others who approved of the registration statement.

C.   **Elements of Liability**. Plaintiff must show: (1) the registration statement contained false or misleading statements or facts; or (2) omitted material facts. See *TSC Indus. v. Northway, Inc.*, 426 U.S. 438 (1976).

   Case 22.3--*Rosenzweig v. Azurix Corp.*, 332 F.3d 854 (5th Cir. 2003). Azurix, a subsidiary of Enron, made an initial public offering in 1998. Enron later purchased all the public shares and made Azurix private. Shareholders alleged that Azurix misrepresented the company in public statements. The suit was dismissed in that Azurix merely cast its business in a positive light.

D.   **Defenses**. There are three statutory defenses under section 11 to suits alleging misrepresentation.

   1.   No Reliance. A defendant can show that the investor knew that the registration statement was misleading at the time of their purchase.

   2.   No Causation. A defendant can show that the misstatement in the registration statement did not actually cause plaintiff's economic loss.

   3.   Due Diligence. Any defendant (except the issuer) is not liable for a misrepresentation or omission if he acted with due diligence by conducting a reasonable investigation and reasonably believed the statements were true and made in good faith.

Case 22.4--*Escott v. BarChris Construction Corp.*, 283 F. Supp. 643 (S.D.N.Y. 1968). BarChris built bowling alleys with capital raised through public offerings. It obtained money in May 1961, but filed for bankruptcy in October of 1962. A class action suit alleged Section 11 violations against the company, its officers and directors, and underwriters. The court found that only the outside directors could rely on the due diligence defense. Defendants were held liable for misleading statements on their SEC registration statements.

4.   Bespeaks Caution Doctrine. Courts may determine that sufficient cautionary statements render immaterial any misrepresentations or omissions.

Case 22.5--*Steinberg v. PRT Group*, 88 F. Supp. 2d 294 (S.D.N.Y. 2000). PRT offered information technology services. PRT had employees but also hired many independent contractors. PRT made an initial offering of $13 per share. PRT claimed revenues of $1.1 million in the fourth quarter of 1997, but a loss of $3 million in the first quarter of 1998. The stock price dropped by over 50% and investors sued for misrepresentation. As the prospectus warned investors, the suits were dismissed.

5.   Litigation Reform Act Safe Harbor for Forward-Looking Statements. Congress extends two grounds for defense from liability, (a) use of precautionary language; and (b) good faith representations.

E.   **Damages**. Plaintiff-stock owners may recover the difference in the price of the stock at the time purchased and its value when the suit is filed. If a stock has been sold, sellers may recover the difference in purchase price versus sale price.

X.   SECTION 12(2)(a) OF THE 1933 ACT provides remedies for any person who purchases a security of a public offering, by means of a misleading prospectus or oral communication. Section 12(2) does not require that the plaintiff show the defendant had intent to deceive.

A.   **Who May be Sued**? Anyone who sells securities via use of a misleading communication, including underwriters, brokers, and dealers.

B.   **Reasonable Care Defense** relieves defendants of liability if they can prove that they did not know and could not have known about any misrepresentations. However the standard is unclear. *Sanders v. John Nuveen & Co.*, 619 F.3d 1222 (7th Cir. 1980).

XI.   **LIABILITY OF CONTROLLING PERSONS.** Section 15 imposes liability on anyone who "controls any person liable under Section 11 or 12." The term "control" is not defined in the 1933 Act. Generally courts hold that a controlling person is an officer, director, or major shareholder of the company, regardless of whether the person exercised power. *Brown v. Enstar Group, Inc*, 84 F.3d 393 (11th Cir. 1996).

XII.   **CRIMINAL PENALTIES.** In addition to the civil damages, defendants also face criminal fines of not more than $100,000 and up to five years in prison.

THE RESPONSIBLE MANAGER: COMPLYING WITH REGISTRATION REQUIREMENTS. Companies offering securities must comply with both federal and state securities laws. Managers:

- Should be familiar with the four-part *Howey* test, noting that certain contracts, not normally thought of as securities-related, may run afoul of the 1933 and 1934 Acts;
- Should only resell their securities under Rule 144 or in a private offering to sophisticated buyers;
- Face considerable liability for misleading information or omissions, whether registered or exempt from registration.;
- Must work closely with counsel to avoid improper disclosures about securities offerings;
- Must ensure that there are no material misstatements or omissions in any public disclosures (for example, Form 10-K or Form 10-Q).

INSIDE STORY: IMPROPER ALLOCATION OF "HOT" IPO SHARES. During the "dot com" boom of the 1990s, initial public offerings (IPOs) were in high demand. Underwriters engaged in morally questionable activity including distributing IPOs to a select group of corporate executives as a *quid pro quo*. Other investment banks let certain clients in on IPOs so long as customers promised to buy more shares later. Certain brokerage houses paid fines for overcharging fees. As of 2004 the SEC was considering rules of ban improper marketing of IPOs.

STUDY QUESTIONS

True-False Questions

___ 1.   Federal securities acts are typically reactive to market events.

___ 2.   The 1933 Act regulates the original distribution of securities.

___ 3.   Investors are not protected from making highly speculative or foolish investments.

__ 4. The 1934 Act covers the original distribution of securities.

__ 5. The Private Securities Litigation Reform Act of 1995 generally eliminates joint and several liability under section 10(b) of the 1934 Act for unintentional violations.

__ 6. An interest in real estate by itself is considered a security under the *Howey* decision.

__ 7. The 1933 Act definition of "offer" is narrower than the typical contract law definition.

__ 8. The SEC does not have the statutory authority to approve or disapprove an offering on its merits.

__ 9. A public offering must be underwritten by one or more investment banking firms.

__ 10. Some regular SEC registrants do not receive a review of the registration statement at all.

__ 11. A private offering can be consummated more quickly, but with more expense than a public offering.

__ 12. Accredited investors are financially sophisticated investors.

__ 13. Regulation S clarifies the general rule that securities laws apply to S corporations.

__ 14. A Schedule 13D must be filed when an acquirer possesses 10 percent or more of a company's stock.

__ 15. According to the reasonable care doctrine, a court may determine that the inclusion of sufficient cautionary statements in a prospectus renders immaterial any misrepresentations and omissions contained therein.

Multiple-Choice Questions

__ 1. The federal securities acts stand for the proposition that:
   A. Investors should have essential information prior to investing.
   B. Inside trading should not be allowed.
   C. Injured investors should be compensated.
   D. All of the above.

__ 2. The 1933 Act requires registration statements be filed with the:
   A. FTC.
   B. SEC.
   C. NYSE.

D.   FCC.

__ 3. Prior to issuing securities, a corporation must do which of the following?

I.   File a registration statement with the SEC.
II.   Provide a prospectus to potential investors.
III. Allow the SEC Ratings Department to rate the issue.

A.   I and II.
B.   I and III.
C.   II and III.
D.   I, II, and II.

__ 4. What perceived abuses did the 1995 Reform Act seek to correct?

I.   Class actions that coerce settlements.
II.   Acts that chilled corporate disclosure.
III. Acts that increased costs of raising capital.

A.   I and III.
B.   II and III.
C.   I, II, and III.
D.   I and III.

__ 5. The 1995 Reform Act required all but which of the following?
A. Stricter pleading requirements concerning misleading statements.
B. Reasons why the statements are misleading.
C. Proof that the misstatement may have caused a loss.
D. Proof that the defendant acted with the required state of mind.

__ 6. Intrastate regulation of securities is referred to as _____ laws.
A.   Merit review.
B.   Statutory securities.
C.   Blue.
D.   Blue sky.

__ 7. Which of the following can be considered a security?

I.   A note.
II.   An investment contract.
III. Puts and calls.
IV. Voting trust certificates.

A.   I, II, III, IV.
B.   I, II, IV.

C.   II, III, IV.
D.   I, II, III.

___ 8.   In a _____ underwriting, the underwriters agree to purchase the entire offering.
A.   Syndicate.
B.   Firm commitment.
C.   Registration.
D.   Best efforts.

___ 9.   Securities offered in an initial public offering should be filed on a Form _____.
A.   S-1.
B.   SB-1.
C.   S-2.
D.   10-K.

___ 10.   A tombstone ad may *not* have which of the following?
A.   Name of the issuer.
B.   Solicitation to buy securities.
C.   Title of the securities.
D.   Price of the securities.

___ 11.   Exempt securities under the 1933 Act include all securities except those issued by:
A.   The state or the federal government.
B.   Any insurance company.
C.   A charitable organization.
D.   Intrastate sales.

___ 12.   The SEC may recommend an integration of offerings if the offerings
A.   Are part of a single plan.
B.   Involve the same type of consideration.
C.   Are made at the same time.
D.   Any of these.

___ 13.   Rule _____ exempts offerings of up to one million dollars within a twelve-month period to an unlimited number of purchasers.
A.   504.
B.   505.
C.   506.
D.   502.

___ 14.   An annual audited report filed with the SEC within 90 days of the end of an issuer's fiscal year is called a Form
A.   10-Q.
B.   12-K.

C. 10-K.
D. 8-K.

___ 15. Under Section 24 of the 1933 Act, a defendant can be

I.   Sentenced to up to 10 years in prison.
II. Fined up to $50,000 in fines.

A. I only.
B. II only.
C. Both I and II.
D. Neither I nor II.

Essay Questions

1. What are the tests that a court can use to determine if a general partnership is an interest in a security?

2. What is the basic managerial time line for a public securities offering?

3. What is the Rule 505 exemption?

732 - 977 - 7286

CHAPTER 23
SECURITIES FRAUD AND INSIDER TRADING

INTRODUCTION

Some attribute the success of American securities markets to transparency and laws against fraud. This chapter focuses on Section 10(b) and Rule 10b–5 of the 1934 Act. It sets forth the seven elements necessary in a Rule 10b–5 case and the fraud-on-the-market theory of liability. The safe harbor for certain forward-looking statements is discussed. Section 17(a) of the 1933 Act, under which the U.S. government can bring fraud claims, is briefly discussed along with Sarbanes-Oxley. The chapter defines insider trading and the legal elements of insider-trading. Short-swing trading is then defined, and the rules for calculating the recoverable profits are discussed, as well as the requirements for reporting by insiders.

CHAPTER OUTLINE

I. **SECTION 10(b) AND 20 OF THE 1934 ACT AND RULE 10B-5**. Section 10(b) gives the SEC power to prohibit securities fraud and authorizes the SEC to prescribe rules to protect investors. More suits are brought under 10b-5 than any other security law provision.

   A. **Aiding and Abetting**. A private plaintiff may not bring a claim for aiding and abetting suit; the SEC may.

   B. **Conspiracy**. There is no private cause of action for conspiracy under Section 10(b).

   C. **Primary Liability for Secondary Actors**. Secondary actors, e.g. accountants, can be liable if their conduct satisfies the requirements for primary liability.

   > **Case 23.1--*McGann v. Ernst & Young*** 102 F.3d 390 (9th Cir. 1996). Ernst & Young audited Community Psychiatric Centers (CPC). Plaintiffs alleged that Ernst & Young failed to disclose that CPC had accounts receivable problems, thereby issuing a false and misleading audit. Plaintiffs also alleged Ernst & Young knew that CPC would include the audit in its SEC filings. The district dismissed. The appeals court reversed holding that an accounting firm was subject to liability under Section 10(b) when it prepared a fraudulent audit knowing that the client will include it public representations.

View from Cyberspace: SECURITIES FRAUD MOVES FROM THE BOILER ROOM TO THE INTERNET. In 2001 the SEC brought charges against 23 companies and individuals for making fraudulent claims over the internet. One individual was sentenced to three years in prison and fined $330 million.

D.   **Statute of Limitations**. Suits must be brought within one year of the date that the plaintiff discovered or should have discovered the fraud, or within three years of the violation, whichever is shorter.

E.   **Controlling Persons**. Section 20(a) imposes joint and several liability on every person who is in control, directly or indirectly, unless the controlling person acted in good faith and did not directly or indirectly induce the acts

II.   ELEMENTS FOR RULE 10B-5 CAUSE OF ACTION. To recover damages a plaintiff must show each of the following elements: (a) defendant used an instrumentality of interstate commerce or the mails or a facility of a national securities exchange; (b) defendant made a statement that either misrepresented or omitted a fact; (c) the fact was of material importance; (d) the misrepresentation or omission was made knowingly; (e) the statement or mission was made in connection with the purchase or sale of securities; (f) plaintiff relied on the defendant's misrepresentation or on the assumption that the market price of the stock accurately reflected its value; (g) defendant's misrepresentation or omission caused the plaintiff to suffer losses.

A.   **Interstate Commerce**. Defendant must have used interstate commerce, the mails, or a national securities exchange.

B.   **Misstatement or Omission** is relevant only if the statement or omission becomes misleading.

1.   Misstatements. A prediction about the future is only a misstatement if the person making the prediction does not believe it. Silence or a "no comment" response to rumors will not lead to liability if the company has not previously spoken and insiders are not trading or tipping.

Case 23.2--*SEC v. Texas Gulf Sulphur Co.*, 446 F.2d 1301 (2d Cir. 1971). Texas Gulf Sulphur (TGS) drilled a test hole which resulted in a discovery of a significant copper discovery. In a press release, TGS minimized the importance of the discovery so it could acquire surrounding properties cheaply. The court held that this was a misleading statement and a violation of Section 10(b) and Rule 10b-5.

2. Omissions include statements that are true at the time, but later become misleading only if investors rely on the previous statements, while the company fails to disclose the latter information.

> **Case 23.3--*Weiner v. Quaker Oats Co.*,** 129 F.3d 310 (3d Cir. 1997). Quaker was acquiring Snapple for $1.7 billion in cash. The market dropped Quaker's stock by ten percent. Quaker borrowed the money to acquire Snapple, increasing its total debt-capitalization ratio to approximately 4 to 5. In its 1993 Annual Report, Quaker stated that its guideline for the debt ration was in the "upper 60-percent range." Quaker also said it was committed by seven-percent, real earnings growth over time. Plaintiffs alleged that Quaker had a duty to update these statements that were misleading. The appeals court remanded the case to decide if a reasonable investor would find Quaker's statements misleading based on its Annual Reports.

3. Statements by Third Parties and Entanglement. If entangled, a company has a duty to correct misleading statements about the business by third parties.

C. **Material Fact** is that which a reasonable investor would consider important. Material facts affect the market value of the company's stock. A manager can be liable even she did not know an omitted fact or misrepresented fact was material.

D. **Bespeaks Caution Doctrine**. Cautionary language that adequately discloses the risks about projections, estimates, etc., can render misrepresentations or omissions immaterial. See *In re Prudential Sec., Inc. P'ships Litig.*, 930 F. Supp. 68 (S.D.N.Y. 1996).

E. **Scienter and Recklessness**. Misstatements or omissions must be made with the intent to deceive. A majority of the courts regard **recklessness** as sufficient for *scienter*.

> **Case 23.4--*Kasaks v. Novak*,** 216 F.3d 300 (2d Cir. 2000). Plaintiffs sued AnnTaylor Stores Corporation and several of top officers (including Novak) for violation of Section 10(b) and Rule 10b-5. Plaintiffs alleged that defendants knowingly and intentionally issued financial statements that overstated AnnTaylor's financial condition and deliberately failing to adhere to company publicly stated policy. The district court dismissed the complaint for failure to plead *scienter* and fraud with sufficient particularity. The appellate court reversed holding that fraud is pled with sufficient particularity if plaintiffs rely on unnamed confidential sources.

F. **In Connection with the Purchase or Sale of Any Security**. Only persons who actually purchase or sell securities can sue under Rule 10b–5. Parties who make or are responsible for misstatements and omissions in a manner reasonably calculated to influence the investing public can be liable.

G. **Reliance**. To hold the defendant liable, an investor must show that he relied, directly or indirectly, on the misrepresentation or omission.

    1. Direct Reliance can be shown through demonstration of a public document. In the case of an omission, plaintiff will be presumed to have relied on the omission, if it was material.

> **Case 23.5--*Emergent Capital Investment Management, LLC v. Stonepath Group, Inc*, 343 F.3d 189 (2d Cir. 2003).** ECI invested $2 million in NETV, now Stonepath. Lee Hansen, the president of NETV was friends with and contacted Mark Waldon, managing director of ECI. NETV collaborated with Howard Appel, who had been banned from securities trading. NETV did not disclosure their relationship with Appel and claimed that it had $14 million invested in Brightstreet.com but only have $4 million. ECI and NETV then signed a stock purchase agreement. Between January and March 2000 NETV stock ranged between $10-$30 per share. It then sank to less than $1. ECI sued for misrepresentation about the value of Brightstreet.com and the omission about Appel. The court dismissed the first count but allowed suit against NETV for failure to disclosure its relationship with Appel.

    2. Fraud on the Market. Suits may be brought against defendants who made misrepresentations that would have caused the market to rely on the misstatement or omission. Truth on the Market is a defense against this allegation.

H. **Causation**. The plaintiff must prove that the defendant's act or omission caused her to suffer losses.

I. **Calculation of Damages**. Typically the difference between the price paid or received and the fair market value. Plaintiffs can opt for rescission and take prejudgment interest.

III. **LITIGATION REFORM ACT SAFE HARBOR FOR FORWARD-LOOKING STATEMENTS.** Forward-looking statements encourage companies to disclose projections and other information about the company's future prospects. Forward-looking statements provide a safe harbor regarding statements like those: (a) concerning projection of revenues, income, earnings per share, expenditures, etc.; (b) concerning plans and objectives of future operations; (c) of future economic performance, and (d) of assumptions underlying any such statement. The safe harbor protection does not apply to: (a) an IPO; (b) an offering of securities by a blank check company; (c) a going-private transaction; (d) a tender offer; or (e) an offering by a partnership, LLC, or direct participation investment program.

IV. **SECTIONS 17(a).** Prohibits fraud with the sale of securities; it does not require *scienter*, there is no private right of action.

V. **RESPONSIBILITY OF AUDITORS TO DETECT AND REPORT ILLEGALITIES.** The PSLRA promotes disclosures by independent public accountants of illegal acts of their audit clients. The account must notify the client's management of the illegal act(s) and notify the SEC in the event the company does not correct the errors in a timely manner.

VI. **SARBANES-OXLEY ACT OF 2002** creates a new crime for securities fraud of a public company. It is a felony to defraud in connection with publicly traded securities or to obtain via fraud, money or property in relation to a securities trade.

VII. **DEFINITION OF INSIDER TRADING.** Generally, insider trading is stock-trading based on material, non-public, information. Insider trading focuses on the duty to disclose. The U.S. Supreme Court has held that insider trading is illegal only if there is a breach of duty by the person trading or by the person who gave a tip. Rule 10b5-1 creates a presumption against the insider *unless* the trade is pursuant to a pre-existing plan.

    A. **Classical Theory of Insider-Trading.** Insiders include not only traditional insiders—such as officers and directors—but also temporary insiders, such as outside counsel and financial consultants.

    B. **Traditional Insiders** are only persons closely allied with the corporation itself were considered insiders. Examples: (1) Officers and Directors; (2) Employees; (3) Controlling Shareholders; and (4) The Corporation.

        1. Temporary Insiders include those who acquire confidential information through employment: attorneys, accountants, consultants, and investment bankers.

        2. Tippees of Insiders. Tippees may also be subject to liability under Rule 10b–5. However, usually a tippee has no legal duty to the shareholders, unless they know the tipper breached a fiduciary duty. See *Dirks v. SEC*, 463 U.S. 646 (1983).

            Case 23.6--*Dirks v. SEC*, 463 U.S. 646 (1983). Dirks was an investment analyst of insurance company securities for various institutional investors. Secrist, a former employee of Equity

Funding of America contacted Dirks and told Dirks of overvaluation of assets at Equity Funding. Dirks then advised clients to sell Equity Funding shares. When fraud was revealed at Equity Funding, the stock priced dropped. The U.S. Supreme Court held that as Secrist, the tipper, had no fiduciary duty to Equity Funding, Dirks was not liable as a tippee.

3. Breach of Fiduciary Duty. A tipper is liable for wrongdoing if they both profit from their nonpublic knowledge and have a fiduciary duty to the corporation

4. Remote Tippees (tippees of tippees) are not liable unless they knew or should have known that the first-tier tipper was breaching a fiduciary duty in passing on the non-public information. *SEC v. Musella*, 678 F. Supp. 1060 (S.D.N.Y. 1988).

C. **Misappropriation Theory of Insider Trading**. If a person misappropriates non-public information, she has breached a fiduciary duty and is therefore liable under Rule 10b-5 because she converted the confidential information for her own use.

Case 23.7--*United States v. O'Hagan*, 521 U.S. 642 (1997). O'Hagan was a partner in a law firm that represented Grand Met in its acquisition of Pillsbury. O'Hagan traded on this non-public information and made over $4 million in profits. He was convicted on 57 counts of securities violations. The Supreme Court upheld the convictions under Section 10(b) and Rule 10b-5 because O'Hagan misappropriated information in violation of his duty to his partners and client.

VIII. **RICO (RACKETEER INFLUENCED AND CORRUPT ORGANIZATIONS ACT)**. Securities fraud cannot be the basis for a RICO (see Chapter 17) case unless the defendant has been criminally convicted for fraud. Similarly, a criminal conviction under the Wire and Mail Fraud Acts for misappropriation of an employer's confidential information could be the basis for a civil RICO case.

IX. **ENFORCEMENT OF INSIDER-TRADING PROHIBITIONS**. Those who violate insider trading laws are subject to criminal and civil penalties.

A. **Private Actions**. The plaintiff must be an actual purchaser or seller of securities, *and* plaintiff's loss must have been proximately caused by the acts of the defendant. The plaintiff's costs are limited to his or her actual out-of-pocket damages.

B. **Civil Enforcement**. The defendant may be liable for treble damages and enjoined from future trading.

C.   **Criminal Prosecutions** brought by the Department of Justice/U.S. Attorney's Office, if convicted, a defendant faces up to $1 million fine and/or imprisonment for up to ten years.

D.   **Bounty Payments** by the federal government for those whose help leads to successful prosecutions are up to 10 percent of the revenues recovered.

X.   **SELECTIVE DISCLOSURE AND REGULATION FD.** Securities traders are not allowed to make limited disclosures to analysts or institutional investors. Issuers must provide fair disclosures of non-public inside information as soon as possible.

XI.   **OTHER RESTRICTIONS ON TRADING BY OFFICERS, DIRECTORS, AND GREATER-THAN-10 PERCENT SHAREHOLDERS**

A.   **Short-Swing Trading.** Insiders and those with more than 10% of the shares cannot engage in the purchase-sale, or the sale-purchase within a six-month period. Liability is imposed regardless of intent to commit fraud.

1.   Definition of an Equity Security. Any stock, convertible security, right to purchase a security, or the like.

2.   Persons Covered: (a) Officers, Directors, and (b) Greater-than-10 percent Shareholder.

3.   Beneficial Ownership of Shares officers, directors, and greater-than-10 percent shareholders can be liable for short-swing trades of shares owned by spouses, minor children, or any other relatives living in their households.

4.   Purchase and Sale Within Six Months. The clock starts on the day of the purchase or sale and ends at midnight two days before the corresponding date in the sixth month.

5.   Profit Calculation. Ill-gotten profits are calculated by comparing the highest sale price with the lowest purchase price.

6.   Unorthodox Transactions. A director, officer or 10-percent shareholder will not be liable if he did not receive cash and the sale/purchase was involuntary. If the trader received cash, liability can attach.

B.   **Filing of Beneficial-Ownership Reports.** Covered persons must file frequent and regular ownership reports.

GLOBAL VIEW: INSIDER TRADING IN THE EUROPEAN UNION. Each member of the EU has its own civil sanctions regime. For example, Germany created laws to prevent stock manipulation and insider trading.

C.   **Prohibition on Selling Short.** Officers or directors cannot sell a security they do not own. If the trader does not deliver the security within twenty days of the sale, she will be liable unless she acted in good faith and was unable to make the delivery within the specified time, or if satisfying the time requirements would have caused undue inconvenience or expense.

THE RESPONSIBLE MANAGER: PREVENTING SECURITIES FRAUD AND INSIDER TRADING. Companies and managers have obligations:

- Not to mislead investors through public announcements, periodic reports, or speeches.
- To make disclosure if it knows that insiders are trading in the company's securities.
- To comply with forward-looking rules.
- Not to trade while in possession of material non-public information.
- To guard confidential information and enforce confidentiality.
- To establish comprehensive policies on insider trading policies and punishment.
- To disclose short-swing purchases and pay any such profits to the corporation.
- To report their security holdings and trades in a timely manner.

INSIDE STORY: MICHAEL MILKEN AND THE INSIDER TRADING SCANDALS OF THE 1980'S. Three high-profile prosecutions show the problem with insider trading. Dennis Levine and Ivan Boesky traded using stolen information. Boesky ended up paying $100 million fine, and serving jail time. With the cooperation of Boesky, the federal government then prosecuted others at Drexel Burnham Lambert including Michael Milken. Drexel Burnham was engaged in a fraudulent scheme that drove up stock prices. In 1989 Milken pled guilty, paid over $600 million in fines, served two years in prison, and was banned for life from trading.

STUDY QUESTIONS

True-False Questions

___ 1.   Section 10(b) of the 1933 Act gives the SEC power to prohibit individuals or companies from engaging in securities fraud.

___ 2.   More suits are brought under Rule 10b-5 than any other provision of securities law.

___ 3.   Section 20(a) imposes joint and several liability on every person who, directly or indirectly, controls any person liable under the 1934 Act.

___ 4. A private plaintiff may not maintain an aiding and abetting suit under Section 10(b).

___ 5. A secondary actor can be liable in private suits if their conduct satisfies the requirements for primary liability.

___ 6. Accountants must sign a written consent before their audited report can be included in a registration statement.

___ 7. Under section 10(b), a suit must be brought within one year of discovery of the fraud.

___ 8. Use of the mails includes sending a letter within a state because the mail is part of interstate commerce.

___ 9. The fact that information is material does not, in itself, give rise to a duty to disclose.

___ 10. A company incurs a duty to update its financial projections when a projection changes or the company discovers an error in the projection.

___ 11. Materiality is a known constant, just like intent to defraud.

___ 12. If directors and other corporate authorities reply to rumors with "no comment," they will always protect the company from liability for securities fraud.

___ 13. Only persons who actually purchase or sell securities can sue under Rule 10b-5.

___ 14. The forward-looking statement protects only written statements.

___ 15. Every instance of trading on inside information constitutes a securities violation.

Multiple-Choice Questions

___ 1. Which statement is _false_ concerning Rule 10b-5?
   A.   Use of the mails for fraud is a violation.
   B.   To be a violation it must be a direct use of interstate commerce.
   C.   It is a violation to employ any device to defraud.
   D.   It is a violation to make any untrue statement of a material fact.

___ 2. Under Rule 10b-5, managers could be liable for misleading statements contained in all but which of the following?
   A.   Press release.
   B.   Letter to shareholders.
   C.   Speech to a trade association.
   D.   Internal memo to employees.

___ 3. To prove a person is an aider and abettor, it is necessary to show

     I.   The defendant's knowledge of the primary violation.
     II.   The existence of a primary violation under Rule 10b-5.
     III.   Substantial assistance of the violation by the defendant.

     A.   I, II, III.
     B.   I and II.
     C.   II and III.
     D.   I and III

___ 4. Which is a *false* statement concerning a Rule 10b-5 cause of action?
     A.   The fact was of material importance.
     B.   The defendant made a misrepresentation.
     C.   The misrepresentation or omission was made with scienter.
     D.   There was a purchase or sale of securities.

___ 5. A(n) _____ is a misrepresentation of a fact.
     A.   Omission.
     B.   Scienter.
     C.   Misstatement.
     D.   Fraudulent statement.

___ 6. The general rule is that a company has no duty under Rule 10b-5 to reveal corporate developments unless it or its insiders
     A.   Trade in its securities.
     B.   Recommend trading to someone.
     C.   Disclose the information as a tip.
     D.   All of these.

___ 7. If the company itself did not publish the misleading projection or make the statement, it
     A.   May be liable to reveal relevant facts.
     B.   Is not liable.
     C.   Is liable under the 1933 Act.
     D.   None of these.

___ 8. Scienter means _____ with regard to defrauding an investor.
     A.   Negligence.
     B.   Innocent statements.
     C.   Intent.
     D.   Carelessness.

__ 9. The _____ theory states that the market price for a security is correct.
   A.   Efficient market.
   B.   True market.
   C.   Anti-fraud.
   D.   Weak form.

__ 10. Under the _____ theory, the causal connection between the defendant's fraud and the plaintiff's injury is not established by proving that the fraud affected the market price.
   A.   Fraud-on-the-market.
   B.   Fraudulent market.
   C.   Fraud-created-the-market.
   D.   Market creation.

__ 11. Forward-looking statements include all but which of the following?
   A.   A projection of revenues statement.
   B.   A statement of objectives of management for the future.
   C.   A statement of future economic performance.
   D.   A tender offer.

__ 12. Traditional insiders include all but which of the following?

   I.   Officers.
   II.   Directors.
   III.   Employees.
   IV.   Outside auditors.
   V.   Controlling shareholders.

   A.   IV.
   B.   IV and V.
   C.   III and V.
   D.   II, III, and V.

__ 13. A person who receives information from an insider is known as a
   A.   Tipper.
   B.   Tippee.
   C.   Remote tippee.
   D.   Temporary insider.

__ 14. Which of the following are *not* temporary insiders?
   A.   Outside attorneys.
   B.   Investment bankers.
   C.   Employees.
   D.   Consultants.

__ 15. Short-swing profits apply to all but which one of the following?
   A. Officers.
   B. Directors.
   C. Five percent or more shareholders.
   D. All of the above.

Essay Questions

1. What is an S-1 review, and why should an accountant do one?

2. Why is materiality judged at the time of the misstatement or omission?

3. When do courts consider a market efficient?

CHAPTER 24
DEBTOR-CREDITOR RELATIONS AND BANKRUPTCY

INTRODUCTION

When a business is in trouble it will be short of cash and fall behind in its payments. The condition could spur unemployment and send disruptive waves through related industries. Legal tools designed to stem this potentiality are found in the Bankruptcy Code.[1] Under the U.S. Constitution, Congress has sole power to regulate bankruptcy. Corporate bankruptcy is on the rise as companies like Kmart, WorldCom, Enron, United Airlines and others have had record bankruptcies.

This chapter summarizes loan agreements, and categorizes commercial loans types. The discussion turns to a summary of terms of loan agreements. Methods for securing a loan under Article 9 of the Uniform Commercial Code are discussed, equipment leasing, guaranties, and subordination are addressed. This is followed by a review of business bankruptcies under Chapter 7 and Chapter 11, and consumer bankruptcies. The chapter concludes with "workouts" and lender liability.

CHAPTER OUTLINE

I.   **LOAN AGREEMENTS** are usually standard, but may be specifically tailored.

  A.   **Parties to the Agreement** are the lender and borrower. A borrower can be a person or a business entity. An insurance company lender issues a note to purchase agreement.

    1.   Lenders. If two or more banks make the loan it is called a *syndicated loan*. A *participation loan* is that which the original lender sells shares to other parties, called participants.

    2.   Borrowers. Under law a parent company and its subsidiary make take a loan together, but are liable separately.

    3.   Additional Parties can make the loan complex as the lender will want assurances and collateral from borrowers.

  B.   **Commitment to Make a Loan**. A "term sheet" outlines the terms and conditions of the loan. A commitment to make a loan need not be in writing to be

---

[1] Codified in scattered sections of 11 U.S.C.

enforceable. *Landes Constr. Co. v. Royal Bank of Canada*, 833 F.2d 1365 (9th Cir. 1987).

C. **Description of the Loan**. A loan agreement contains the lender's promise to lend a specified amount of money, outlines how the funds will be disbursed, the rate of interest will be, and repayment terms.

   1. Mechanics of Funding usually by wire transfer or cashier's check.

   2. Interest Rates are fixed, floating or fluctuating in relation to e.g., the bank's prime rate. Floating rates may be pegged to the London Interbank Offered Rate (LIBOR) or the certificate of deposit (CD) rate.

   3. Computation of Interest. Interest is generally computed on a daily basis, usually by the 365/360 *method*. The rate must not exceed state usury laws.

   4. Repayment Terms may be flexible or determined as based on parties' agreement.

   5. Asset-Based Loans. Some loans are determined according to the levels of the borrower's available assets.

D. **Representations and Warranties**. Lenders investigate the borrower's financial condition and creditworthiness. The lender will require other information from the borrower.

   1. Qualifications. Borrowers must affirm their representations about their risk and liability.

   2. Truthfulness of Representations. Lender's obligations are conditioned on the veracity of the borrower's attestations.

E. **Conditions to Closing**.

   1. Authority to Approve the Loan. Lenders require a borrower to demonstrate that she has the authority to approve the loan, and sign all related documents.

   2. Completion of Documents. Among other documents, lenders require a promissory note of repayment and a security agreement if available.

   3. Payment of Fees. Certain fees must be paid prior to closing.

4.   Other Conditions may apply, e.g., consummation of a merger; environmental audits; or indemnity agreements.

F.   **Conditions Precedent**. The loan agreements often specify some conditions must be met *before* the lender's obligations arise. If any condition is not met, the agreement may be rescinded.

G.   **Covenants** are borrower's promises to the lender. If a covenant is breached, the lender is free to terminate the loan.

1.   Affirmative Covenants state what the borrower undertakes to do.

2.   Negative Covenants state what the borrower undertakes not to do.

3.   Scope. Covenants cannot impede the borrower's business, and courts will not impose contracts with undue covenants.

H.   **Events of Default** will trigger the lender's right to terminate the loan, accelerate repayment obligations, etc.

Cross-Default. Both borrower and lender may want assurances that breaches of other agreements will not constitute grounds to default the primary agreement.

I.   **Remedies for Default** set out the lender's remedies. If the lender *waives*, decides not to exercise a remedy, it may exact additional consideration from the borrower.

II.   COMMERCIAL LOAN CATEGORIES.

A.   **Loans Categorized by Lender**. Commercial loans are commonly made by banks, insurance companies, and purchasers of commercial paper.

B.   **Loans Categorized by Purpose**. Generally loans cannot be made to purchase stocks.

1.   Term Loans for a specific purpose usually are borrowed and repaid in a lump sum or in installments on specific dates.

2.   Revolving Loans allow the borrower to borrow and re-borrow ("revolving") required sums, up to a specified maximum amount.

3.   Secured Loans. A lender can demand collateral that will become the lender's if the loan is not repaid. If the borrower fails to repay a secured loan, the lender may *foreclose* and either sell the collateral or keep it.

III. **SECURED TRANSACTIONS UNDER THE UCC.** Article 9 applies "to any transaction (regardless of its form) which is intended to create a security interest in personal property or fixtures including goods, documents, instruments, general intangibles, chattel paper or accounts."

    A. **Terminology**. A "security interest" is any interest in personal property or fixtures used as collateral to secure payment by the "debtor"(borrower) for the performance of an obligation to the "secured party" (lender).

    B. **Formal Requirements**. The UCC requires that value has been given in exchange for the security and that the debtor has rights in the collateral making the security interest *attached*.

    C. **Rights and Remedies**. Article 9 sets forth the rights of the secured party as against other creditors of the debtor; rules for *perfecting* a security interest, and available remedies.

    D. **Security Agreements** identify the parties and the property used as collateral. It can also specify the debtor's obligations and the lender's remedies.

        1. Parties to the Agreement. In a loan, the secured party is the lender, the debtor is the borrower. If the third-party owner acts as a guarantor of the obligation, it may also be referred to as the debtor.

        2. Granting Clause. The security agreement must be signed by debtor and must expressly grant a security interest in specified property.

        3. Description of the Collateral. The description of the collateral need only reasonably identify the property. Frequently, a secured party will take a security interest in all of the assets of the debtor.

        4. After-Acquired Property of the debtor may be subject to a security interest.

        5. Proceeds. Unless otherwise agreed, the secured party has an interest in the proceeds if the collateral is sold or otherwise disposed of and creates a *floating lien*.

        6. Debtor's Obligations are all terms and conditions agreed, including the debt, interest and related fees, charges, and expenses.

        7. Cross-Collateralization. Collateral for one loan may be used to secure obligations under another loan.

        8. Remedies for Default for Security Agreement. In the event of default, the secured party has the right to take possession of the collateral, without judicial process, if such can be done without breach of the peace. The secured party must then dispose of the collateral at a public or private sale. Any surplus from the sale is return to the debtor. If there is a deficiency, the debtor remains liable.

IV. **PERFECTING A SECURITY INTEREST**. A lender protects its security interest by perfecting it, which makes it valid against other creditors of the debtor and a trustee in bankruptcy of the debtor.

A. **Methods of Perfection.**

1. By Possession. A security interest in letters of credit, goods, money or negotiable documents is perfected by the secured party's taking possession.

2. By Control. A security interest in deposit account or letter of credit is only perfected through control.

3. By Filing. For other types of collateral, perfection is accomplished by filing a financing statement (a UCC-1 form).

4. Automatic Perfection. Security interests with purchase-money securities require neither possession nor filing. Automatic perfection is of limited duration.

5. Uncertificated Securities are governed under Article 8 of the U.C.C.

B. **Filing Procedure**. Perfection by filing provides notice that the assets of person A are subject to the security interest of B.

1. What to File. Filing a financing statement perfects a non-possessory security interest.

2. Where to File. Such is filed with the Secretary of State or with the County Recorder's office where the real property is located.

3. When to File. The first secured party to file has priority over other parties generally, except in the case of a purchase-money security interest.

V. **EQUIPMENT LEASING**. When companies lease equipment, there are often three parties: the seller (lessor) of the equipment, the leasing company, and the user (lessee) of the equipment.

Differences from a True Lease. An equipment lease that serves the purpose of financing is a finance lease. In a standard lease, the lessor has control over the use, alteration, and location of the equipment. The lessee is required to keep the equipment in good repair and insure it. The finance lease is treated as a long-term debt of the lessee, the lessee may therefore enjoy tax benefits such as depreciation deductions.

VI. **GUARANTIES**. The *guarantor* becomes liable for the obligation of another person, the *primary debtor*. A guaranty must be in writing, with terms and amount of liability being stated in the guaranty agreement.

    A. **Payment versus Collection**.

        1. *Guaranty of Payment*. Guarantor's obligation to pay is triggered when the primary debtor fails to make due payment.

        2. *Guaranty of Collection*. Guarantor becomes obliged to pay only after the lender has attempted unsuccessfully to collect the amount due from the primary debtor.

    B. **Limited Versus Unlimited**. Guarantor may agree to accept limited or unlimited liability.

    C. **Continuing versus Restricted**. *Restricted Guaranty* is enforceable only with respect to a specified transaction or series of transactions. *Continuing Guaranty* covers all future obligations of the primary debtor to the lender.

        1. Revocation. A Continuing guarantee may be revoked.

        2. Discharging the Guarantor. The guarantor is no longer liable if the lender alters the agreement or takes actions that discharge liability.

        3. Guaranties Versus Letters of Credit. A letter of credit can be used in place of a guaranty.

    D. **Fraudulent Conveyances** is a direct or indirect transfer of assets to a third party with the actual intent or the effect of hindering, delaying, or defrauding creditors by putting the assets out of the creditors' reach. A leveraged buyout can be attacked as a fraudulent conveyance.

        1. Upstream Guaranty. A subsidiary guarantees the debt of the parent.

        2. Leveraged Buyouts are often done through acquisition of debt and can be attacked as a fraudulent conveyance.

E.   **Preferences**. A transfer from a debtor to an outsider creditor that results in a reduction in the guaranty liability of an insolvent insider done within one year of the filing of bankruptcy may be voidable.

VII.   SUBORDINATION. A debt subordination agreement occurs when one or more "junior" creditors, of a common debtor, agree to defer claims until the "senior" creditor is paid fully. As long as the debtor is solvent, both the junior and senior creditors can expect to be paid.

A.   **Indebtedness to Insiders**. Lenders require that debt to insiders be subordinated to the lender's debt.

B.   **Lien Subordination** is an agreement between two secured creditors whose respective security interests attach to the same property.

C.   **Equitable Subordination** happens when a creditor's claim is involuntarily postponed in bankruptcy to prevent one creditor from increasing its recovery at the expense of other creditors.

VIII.   LENDER LIABILITY. Recent court decisions have expanded recovery available to borrowers.

A.   **Breach of Contract**. The lender's failure to act or to refrain from acting as required by the terms of a loan document or other agreement.

B.   **Fraudulent Misrepresentation**. The lender can be liable if it represents that it will make a loan to the borrower when, in fact, it has decided not to extend credit.

C.   **Economic Duress** occurs if the lender threatens to do an unlawful act that might injure the borrower's business or property. Compensatory and punitive damages can be recovered for economic duress.

D.   **Tortious Interference**. Lenders can be liable for tortious interference with the borrower's corporate governance.

E.   **Intentional Infliction of Emotional Distress**. The lender is liable when bank officials publicly ridicule the borrower, use profanities, and/or laugh about the borrower's financial difficulties.

F.   **Negligence and General Tort Liability** might arise if the lender fails to exercise a duty of care.

G.   **Statutory Bases of Liability** arises through laws e.g., RICO and CERCLA. Also, a lender can be subject to penalties in cases brought by the SEC for aiding or abetting violations of federal securities laws. This theory has been used by private litigants in lender liability cases.

H. **Breach of Duty of Good Faith** e.g., the lender's failure to act reasonably and fairly in dealing with the borrower and in exercising its rights and remedies under the loan documents and under applicable law.

IX. **SPECIAL DEFENSES AVAILABLE TO THE FEDERAL INSURERS OF FAILED BANKS AND SAVINGS AND LOANS.** Lenders are protected under the *D'Oench, Duhme* doctrine which bars borrowers from enforcing private financial agreements unless such are in writing and approved contemporaneously by the bank's board or loan committee.

X. **BANKRUPTCY LAWS**

A. **Management Duties Shift When Company Enters Insolvency Zone.** Directors owe fiduciary duties to creditors.

B. **Initiation of Bankruptcy Proceeding**

1. Petition. A bankruptcy case is initiated by filing a petition (either voluntary or involuntary).

2. Order for Relief. Petitioner seeks an order for relief, if granted a trustee is appointed to oversee the debtor's estate.

Case 24.1--*In re Marvel Entertainment Group, Inc.*, 140 F.3d 463 (3d Cir. 1998). After Marvel filed for bankruptcy, one creditor assumed control, assuming the roles of Debtor-in-Possession (DIP) and creditor. The DIP filed adverse litigation against the other creditors. Other creditors petitioned for a trustee as the DIP was not neutral. The district court granted the request. The appeals court affirmed, it was in the best interests of the creditors and the estate to have a trustee, though it should be an exception in this type of case.

3. Administration of Claims. Unsecured creditors must file a proof of claim in order for the creditor to participate in the bankruptcy.

4. Bankruptcy Estate equals "all the legal and equitable interests of the debtor …" However, federal bankruptcy law includes state exemptions from the estate as determined by local statutes.

5. Distribution of Property. Secured creditors have priority in claims and unsecured creditors are entitled to obtain assets in priority as defined by their claim under the bankruptcy law. Each superior claimant must be paid in full prior to lower class claimants.

XI.   **PRINCIPLES APPLICABLE TO ALL BANKRUPTCIES**. There are two major types of business bankruptcies: liquidation under Chapter 7 and reorganization under Chapter 11.

A.   **Good Faith Requirements**. Bankruptcy law specifically authorizes the court to convert a case under Chapter 11 to Chapter 7 or to dismiss the petition for cause.

Case 24.2--*In re Integrated Telecom Express, Inc.*, 384 F.3d 108 (3d Cir. 2004). Eighteen months after its IPO, ITE had substantial losses. ITE sought to liquidate and then distribute approximately $105 million to its creditors. However ITE could not settle its debt to a landlord and threatened bankruptcy. The landlord sought to challenge ITE's petition on the grounds that it was done in bad faith as to avoid debts. The appellate court held that mere complicity with law is not good faith and dismissed ITE's petition – meaning ITE would remain liable to the landlord.

B.   **Automatic Stay**. Bankruptcy filings grant an automatic stay, which suspends most litigation and collection activities against the debtor.

C.   **Executory Contracts and Leases**. The DIP has the option of assuming or rejecting pre-bankruptcy executory contracts or unexpired leases. Assumption preserves the debtor's rights and duties under the existing relationship, whereas rejection terminates them.

Case 24.3--*Unsecured Creditors Committee of Robert L. Helms Construction & Development Co. v. Southmark Corp.*, 139 F.3d 702 (9th Cir. 1998) (en banc). Southmark, a Texas corporation, sold the Double Diamond ranch to Double Diamond Limited Partnership, retaining the right to repurchase part of the ranch. Southmark later filed for bankruptcy. Southmark filed a notice of assumption on some executory contracts. Double Diamond filed for bankruptcy in Nevada. The committee administering the Double Diamond bankruptcy decided to sell the ranch that Southmark once owned. It asked the bankruptcy court to allow a free-and-clear sale since Southmark rejected its option under its reorganization plan. The court held that if Southmark had assumed the debt, the option contract was executory, if the option contract was not executory, the lower court was to determine if the parcel belonged to Southmark, hence could not be sold by Double Diamond.

1.   Copyright Licenses. May or may not be assignable depending on the forum.

2.   Patent Licenses. Non-exclusive patents are assignable without consent of the licensor. *Everey Systems v. Cadtrak*, 89 F.3d 673 (9th Cir. 1996)

3.   Trademark Licenses. Appear assignable without consent.

4.   Know-How Licenses. No cases have resolved the question whether such licenses are assignable without consent.

D.   **Sale of Property**. The DIP can sell both interests and disburse the net proceeds proportionately, or sell property free and clear of liens or other interests (which normally will be shifted to the proceeds).

E.   **Avoiding Powers**. Bankruptcy trustees can invalidate or reverse certain pre-bankruptcy transactions.

1.   Fraudulent Conveyances. The trustee may void fraudulent transfers or obligations that occurred within a year of the filing whose purpose was to hinder, delay, or defraud creditors or provide less than reasonably equivalent value in exchange.

2.   Preferences are wrongful transfers to (or for the benefit of) creditors on account of antecedent debts made from an insolvent debtor's property within 90 days before bankruptcy and that enable the creditors to receive more than they would through a Chapter 7 liquidation.

> **Case 24.4--*Adams v. Anderson (In re Superior Stamp & Coin Co.*)**, 223 F.3d 1004 (9th Cir. 2004). Superior Stamp & Coin operated as a full-service auction house specializing in the auction of coins, sports and Hollywood memorabilia, etc. Adams and Superior entered into an auction consignment agreement, Superior agreed to auction Adams's coin collection and pay Adams the net proceeds within thirty days after receiving the funds. Superior failed to remit net proceeds, and negotiated a repayment schedule with Adams to remit the proceeds in six equal payments. Superior came under severe financial strain, its largest creditor, the Bank of California, agreed to fund repayments owed to Adams. Superior failed and filed an involuntary petition for Chapter 11 bankruptcy. The trustee sought to recover the payments to Adams as *voidable preference* transfers. The court held for Adams. The payments made by Bank of California fell within the earmarking doctrine.

3.   Setoff Rights. The creditor may automatically deduct what the debtor owes the creditor from what the creditor owes the debtor.

4.   Statutory Liens. Certain liens can be avoided, as federal bankruptcy law preempts state created liens.

5.   Collective Bargaining Agreements. Bankruptcy petitioners cannot necessarily abrogate contracts with unions. Three conditions must be met.

XII. CHAPTER 11 REORGANIZATIONS. Designed for troubled businesses, chapter 11 seeks to rehabilitate the debtor and maximize return for creditors.

A.   **Obtaining Credit**. A DIP's priority is to stay in business. Assets acquired after the bankruptcy petition is filed are not subject to pre-petition security agreements.

1.   Customer's Payments. Bankruptcy allows the DIP to retain otherwise encumbered revenues from customer payments.

2.   Extension of Unsecured Credit. Post petition, suppliers and creditors might be willing to extend unsecured credit.

3.   Secured Borrowings. Chapter 11 can free up collateral and enhances opportunities to receive secured loans.

4.   Court Oversight. With the protection of the court proceeding, debtors might gain favorable treatment from new lenders.

5.   Turnover of Debtor's Property. Creditors and lenders can be ordered to return property and funds to the estate.

B.   **The Plan**. The reorganization plan divides claims and equity interests into separate classes. The plan may extend time to repay or reduce amounts owed. The plan must be feasible and in the best interests of the creditors. In many cases, creditors exchange all or part of their claims for preferred or common stock or other ownership interests in the business. Plans often provide for payments from cash on hand, future earnings, asset sales, new capital contributions, or some combination of sources.

C.   **Confirmation**. To be confirmed, the plan must meet statutory requirements.

1.   Feasibility. The plan must be economically feasible.

2.   Best Interest of Creditors. Unless accepted unanimously, the plan must treat creditors no worse than under a chapter 7 filing.

3.   Disclosure Statement. Creditors are entitled to receive a disclosure from the court.

4. Acceptance. If two-thirds of the creditors or credit interests vote in favor, the plan is accepted.

5. Impaired Claims limit creditor's rights, but may be accepted.

6. Cramdown Confirmation. The court may compel creditors to accept the plan on the grounds that it is fair.

Case 24.5--*Bank of America National Trust and Savings Ass'n v. 203 North LaSalle Street Partnership*, 526 U.S. 434 (1999). BANTSA was the major creditor of 203 North LaSalle Street Partnership (Partnership). The value of the Partnership property was less than the balance due, leaving the bank with an unsecured deficiency of $38.5 million. Over BANTSA's objections, the Partnership planned (1) to discharge the bank's $38.5 million unsecured deficiency claim for 16% of its present value; and (2) that certain former partners would contribute $6 million over the course of five years, in exchange for the Partnership's ownership of the reorganized company. The old equity holders were the only ones given the right to contribute new capital in exchange for equity. The Supreme Court held that the plan could not be approved over the objections of the BANTSA. Lower courts have allowed plans that only permit old equity holders to buy back equity.

7. Plan Negotiations. Parties may attempt negotiations rather than accept the edict of the court.

D. **Discharge**. Confirmation under Chapter 11 removes the debtor's liability. For individual debtors, however, nondischargeable debts under Chapter 7 are excluded from the Chapter 11 discharge.

E. **Workouts and Prepackaged and Prenegotiated Chapter 11 Cases**.

1. Workouts. The right to file bankruptcy cannot be waived; regardless of its terms, a workout agreement cannot stop the debtor from taking refuge in Chapter 11 if the restructured obligations prove too great.

2. Prepackaged Chapter 11. Companies may solicit affirming votes from a sufficient number of creditors prior to filing. Best used when the sale of assets will exceed the costs of bankruptcy.

Case 24.6--*In re Combustion Engineering*, 391 F.3d 190 (3d Cir. 2004). Combustion Engineering was an asbestos litigation defendant. Suits and payouts brought it to the brink of insolvency.

In 2002 Combustion sought to settle past and pending lawsuits through a pre-packaged Chapter 11 filing. Certain plaintiffs objected, but the courts supported the fairness of the plan. The court concluded the process was not fair and overruled on technical grounds.

3.   Prenegotiated Chapter 11. Debtors may solicit agreements from creditors and thus file the pre-negotiated plan. Such prevents creditors from dumping the debtor's stock.

XIII.   CHAPTER 7 LIQUIDATIONS. A straight bankruptcy where the trustee sells off all debtor assets and pays creditors by right of priority.

A.   **Individual Debtors** are discharged from all obligations except for: (1) taxes; (2) educational loans (generally); (3) spousal or child support; (4) fines or penalties; (5) drunk-driving liabilities; and intentional torts.

HISTORICAL PERSPECTIVE: FROM MOSAIC LAW TO VULTURE CAPITALIST. The idea that debtors should have their debts discharged is noted in the bible. Since the English law of 1542, which treated debtors as criminals, there have been evolutions to protect debtors. However in the late 19th century, through the acquisition of bankrupt enterprises, J. P. Morgan and other extremely wealthy individuals and trusts grew through takeover and consolidation. Congress reacted by amending the 1898 law in 1938, adding Chapter 13. Since the amendment of 1978, and massive defaults in the 1980s, some worry that debtors have too much protection. Some favor the Australian style compelled sell-off. There has also been the birth of a new breed of financier, the vulture capitalist.

B.   **Bankruptcy Abuse Prevention and Consumer Protection Act of 2005.** Under the new law, judges have less discretion to discharge debts and those with modest incomes will have to file under Chapter 13.

C.   **Non-Individual Debtors.** Chapter 7 does not provide a discharge for corporations, partnerships, or similar business entities.

XIV.   CONSUMER BANKRUPTCY UNDER CHAPTER 13. Chapter 13 deals with adjustments to the debt of an individual or married couple with regular income.

A.   **Chapter 13 Requirements** include: (1) Individuals with upwards of $307,000 of unsecured debt and secured debt reaching $922,000; (2) repayment plan for creditors; (3) the debtor's future disposable income must be paid to a trustee for the next three to five years; (4) discharge after completing all plan payments;

Chapter 13 provides for either a composition or extended plan. Debtors may also receive a Chapter 13 "super discharge" of claims for fraud, theft, willful and malicious injury, or drunk driving, but not spousal or child support.

B.   **Advantages of Chapter 13**: (1) filing of a bankruptcy petition stops all creditor collection activity; (2) a Chapter 13 debtor does not surrender any assets; (3) Chapter 13 filer can be forced into Chapter 7 liquidation if debtor is unable to make payments.

GLOBAL VIEW: HARMONIZATION OF INSOLVENCY LAWS. High profile insolvency cases have motivated concern to harmonize international law on bankruptcy. Two prevalent domestic models are universality and territoriality. U.S. law is moving toward universality, treating international cases a single event, not being concerned with the fact that a business may be located in several jurisdictions. The UNCITRAL Model Law on Cross-Border Insolvencies attempts to solve international problems by creating uniform rules for debtors and creditors. The UNCITRAL promotes reorganization and disfavors liquidation. EU rules set binding agreements upon member nations and seeks to prevent forum shopping. The American Law Institute seeks to encourage cooperation of bankruptcy cases involving nations of North America and has set out a number of readily agreed to principles of insolvency in the NAFTA nations. The Cross-Border Insolvency Concordat is a collection of principles designed to assist courts to harmonize insolvency proceedings with two or more nations. Concordat seeks a single administrative forum, with open and public proceedings.

XV.   **THE RESPONSIBLE MANAGER: Managing Debtor–Creditor Relations.** A responsible manager must understand lender liability risks. The following steps will help lenders minimize those risks:

- The lender should indicate clearly that any commitment must be in writing and approved by the loan committee or other appropriate officials of the lender.
- The lender should avoid clauses that attempt to control the borrower's management decisions or day-to-day business activities.
- Loan documents should provide that any amendment, modification, or waiver be signed by both parties.
- The lender can ask the borrower to agree to waive its right to a jury trial and substitute a binding arbitration clause.
- The lender's documents should be accurate and complete; virtually all the documents in the lender's files may be subject to legal discovery
- The lender should refrain from giving any legal, financial, or investment advice to the borrower.
- Consider Chapter 11 as a strategic option for creative business planning.

INSIDE STORY: RJR NABISCO LEVERAGED BUYOUT. In the 1980s, owners of RJR bonds sued RJR after it commenced a leveraged buyout (LBO) because RJR acquired so much debt that its bond value plummeted. The trial court dismissed. Subsequently most underwriters of bonds exact express covenants and terms with the bond issuer to protect against lost value through a

LBO.

STUDY QUESTIONS

True-False Questions

___ 1. Lenders and borrowers may not normally enter into transactions whereby secured credit will be used to acquire stock.

___ 2. If the lender is an insurance company, the loan agreement is called a draft purchase agreement.

___ 3. In a leveraged buyout, the acquisition of a company is financed largely by debt secured by its assets.

___ 4. Under the 365/360 method, the actual rate of interest will be greater than the nominal annual rate.

___ 5. Except for certain types of asset-based financing, the structure of a loan agreement is not affected by whether the loan is secured or unsecured.

___ 6. The risk of representation proving to be untrue is usually placed on the borrower rather than the lender.

___ 7. The main priority for a debtor-in-possession is to stay in business.

___ 8. If the lender waives a default, it may receive additional consideration from the borrower, such as a higher interest rate.

___ 9. Article 9 applies to liens on real property.

___ 10. If the lender forecloses on equipment, any proceeds in excess of the loan amount under the equipment loan are available to pay down a line of credit.

___ 11. The UCC defines perfection of a security interest to aid business people.

___ 12. To facilitate electronic filing, the revised Article 9 will need to eliminate the requirement that the debtor sign the financing statement.

___ 13. For individual debtors, the same debts that are dischargeable under Chapter 7 are excluded from Chapter 11 discharge.

___ 14. Preferences are not allowed under Chapter 7 bankruptcy.

__ 15. Compensatory, but not punitive, damages may be recovered for economic duress.

Multiple-Choice Questions

__ 1. Insurance companies are _____ regulated, while banks are _____ regulated.
   A.   State; state and federally.
   B.   State; federally.
   C.   Federally; state.
   D.   State and federally; state and federally.

__ 2. Funds required for a construction project are generally borrowed in the form of a _____ loan.
   A.   Term.
   B.   Revolving.
   C.   Amortization.
   D.   Insurance.

__ 3. In a _____ loan, the lender will require a commitment fee as consideration for its promise to keep the funds available on an as-needed basis.
   A.   Term.
   B.   Commitment.
   C.   Revolving.
   D.   Credit.

__ 4. A(n) _____ loan requires no collateral
   A.   Cash flow.
   B.   Asset.
   C.   Proceeds of another loan.
   D.   Signature.

__ 5. When two or more lenders together make a loan to one borrower, it is called a _____ loan.
   A.   Participation.
   B.   Syndicated.
   C.   Cartel.
   D.   *Pro rata.*

__ 6. Which of the following terms is *not* a synonymous term?
   A.   Base rate.
   B.   Prime rate.
   C.   Floating rate.
   D.   Reference rate.

__ 7.   If the basic facts upon which the lender has relied change materially after a commitment to lend has been made, the lender will need to re-evaluate the loan by

       I.   Refusing to advance the funds committed.
       II.   Refusing to disburse additional funds.
       III.   Accelerating the disbursement of the loan.

    A.   I and II.
    B.   I, II, and III.
    C.   II and III.
    D.   I and III.

__ 8.   _____ are the borrower's promises to the lender that it will take or not take specific actions during the term of the loan.
    A.   Affirmative covenants.
    B.   Covenants.
    C.   Conditions precedent.
    D.   Conditions subsequent.

__ 9.   Events of default usually include which of the following?

       I.   Failure to pay on time.
       II.   Making misrepresentations.
       III.   Failure to honor a loan covenant.

    A.   I, II, III.
    B.   II and III.
    C.   I only.
    D.   I and III.

__ 10. A _____ is any breach by the borrower under any other loan agreement that constitutes a breach in the current loan agreement.
    A.   Covenant.
    B.   Negative covenant.
    C.   Cross-default.
    D.   Trigger.

__ 11. Which of the following is a UCC security device?
    A.   Pledge.
    B.   Factor's lien.
    C.   Security interest.
    D.   Chattel mortgage.

__ 12. The proceeds from the sale of collateral must be applied in what order?

        I.   To satisfy secured obligations.
        II.   To satisfy subordinate security interests.
        III.   To satisfy reasonable foreclosure expenses.

    A.   III, I, II.
    B.   III, II, I.
    C.   I, II, III.
    D.   II, III, I.

__ 13. Which of the following security interests is automatically perfected?
    A.   Security interest in letters of credit.
    B.   Purchase-money security interest.
    C.   Security interest in negotiated documents.
    D.   Security interest in goods.

__ 14. A guaranty that covers all future obligations of the primary debtor is referred to as a(n) _____ guaranty.
    A.   unlimited
    B.   limited
    C.   restricted
    D.   continuing

__ 15. Which is a dischargeable debt under Chapter 7?
    A.   taxes
    B.   credit card debt
    C.   educational loans
    D.   child support payments

Essay Questions

1. What are affirmative and negative covenants?

2. Security interests can be perfected in what three ways?

3. Where would you file a security interest in timber?

CHAPTER 25
INTERNATIONAL LAW AND TRANSACTIONS

INTRODUCTION

International companies need to navigate international laws. In today's global economy managers must understand the risks as to take advantage of international opportunities. This chapter reviews laws of nations, international treaties, customs and relevant court decisions. The chapter also discusses NAFTA and WTO regulations. It concludes with international business transactions and questions of litigation.

CHAPTER OUTLINE

I. **NATIONAL LEGAL SYSTEMS.**

   A. **Common Law** is used in current and former lands under control of the United Kingdom. Such are governed by case law and precedent. They also use statutes to codify and or change common law rules. Courts of equity are unique to the British common law tradition. Compared to the U.S., British courts grant limited discovery, bar class-action, and make the loser pay.

   B. **Civil Law** systems, grounded in Roman law, and continued through the Napoleonic codes are prevalent in Europe. Civil law is distinct from public law. Civil law judges play a more active role often on the side of the state.

   C. **Other Families of Law.**

      1. **Islamic** law includes ideals of *Sharia* (in accord with the Koran), *Riba*, a strict prohibition on changing interest, and *Gharar* (relating to the unknown or unjust).

      2. **Socialist** legal regimes hold ideals of property held in trust by and for the public.

      3. **Hindu-based** law is primarily tied to personal or private family matters (marriage, divorce, and inheritance).

II. **SOURCES OF INTERNATIONAL LAW.** Public international law concerns interstate action, private international law touches upon non-state action.

A.   **Treaties** are proclamations of rules and agreements between at least two governments. National law usually comports with the dictates of international treaties.

POLITICAL PERSPECTIVE: THE IMPORTANCE OF FAST-TRACK AUTHORITY FOR THE PRESIDENT. Fast-track authority seeks to avoid the Constitutional provision that treaties can only be adopted with 2/3rds support of the U.S. Senate. Under Fast-Track, treaties would be presented to the Congress, and members must vote on the bill without adding amendments or deletions. A simple majority would thus ratify. NAFTA was adopted via fast-track, and supporters want FTAA passed this way as well.

> **Case 25.1--*Crosby v. National Foreign Trade Council*,** 530 U.S. 363 (2000). In 1996, Massachusetts passed a law forbidding trade with any company doing business in Myanmar. Subsequently Congress passed a law regulating trade conditions and allowances with Myanmar. The NFTC sued claiming that the Massachusetts law was pre-empted and that Massachusetts companies should be able to trade with Myanmar as Congress allowed. The Supreme Court struck the Massachusetts law.

B.   **Other Sources of International Law.**

  1.   **Customary International Law** that which is implied from customary state action related to an international matter

  2.   **Decisions of International, national, and Regional Courts**. Many international courts do not have jurisdiction, so many disputes are handled in national courts.

III. **NATIONAL LAWS**

A.   **National Laws Directed at Foreign Owned Businesses.**

  1.   Nationalization, Expropriation, Confiscation, and Privatization. Some government seize assets and nationalize property, as well, recently some countries have sold off their infrastructure. The federal government offers insurance for American businesses to invest overseas.

  2.   Constraints on Foreign Ownership. Some governments limit levels of foreign ownership and also limit wealth extraction.

B.   **National Laws Directed At International Business Activities.**

  1.   Sanctions include boycotts, embargoes and trade restrictions to control or sanction foreign governments.

2. Embargoes as defined by UN treaty are acts of war unless sponsored or ratified by the UN.

3. Export Laws seek to regulate trade and improve transparency especially in relation to weapons sales.

C. **National Laws with Extraterritorial Application.** Certain national laws are applied outside their territory, e.g. U.S. anti-trust laws, and the Foreign Corrupt Practices Act.

IV. **U.S. TRADE REGIME** is controlled by Congress and various executive agencies.

A. **Role of Government Branches and Agencies in Trade Relations.**

1. Congress has supreme authority to regulate U.S.-international trade, can impose tariffs, quotas, and grant export-import licenses.

2. The Role of the President is to enforce Congressional law, but the President can negotiate treaties.

(i) The President's Power to Restrict Trade Congress has authorized the President to use more discretion and seize assets of foreign corporations.

(ii) Trade Promotion Authority is fast-track negotiating authority.

3. Administrative Agencies deal with international economic matters, especially the U.S. Trade Representative who makes policy decisions for executive departments.

4. The Interagency Committee (which also receives corporate input) recommends policy to the President

5. Export-Import Bank finances the purchase of U.S. exports to other nations.

B. **Laws Affecting Exports.**

1. Export Administrative Act allows the Secretary of Commerce to deny certain exports as matters of national security. There is a tension between U.S. weapons exporters and national security interests.

2. Export Administration Regulations (EAR's) apply to exports of non-military and dual use goods

3. The Arms Export Control Act authorizes the Secretary of State to halt various exports. Departments of State and Commerce issue advisors opinions on what goods should or should not be exported.

4. Penalties for Violations of Export Regulations can be five times the value of the exports and five years in prison. Government may also impose civil penalties.

5. Section 301 of the Trade Act of 1974 is the primary tool of U.S. regulation of trade to retaliate against other governments. Under 301 and Super 301 the executive may impose retaliatory tariffs.

C. **Laws Affecting Imports.**

1. Tariffs are a tax on imports, usually *ad valorem*.

   (i) The Harmonized Tariff Schedule applies tariffs based on the product and their source.

   (ii) Tariff Preferences. Under the Generalize System of Preferences the President may declare some products duty-free.

2. Import Relief Laws the President has discretionary authorization to apply tariffs on specific products.

   (i) Section 201 is designed to aid American producers hurt by imports. Under the 1988 law, companies are to propose how a tariff will allow American industry to adjust to their competition.

   (ii) Relationship Between WTO Dispute Settlement Process and U.S. Trade Law. U.S. unilateral retaliation generally violates WTO rules. In one example the EU assessed a $2.2 billion fine on U.S. goods in reaction to Bush administration tariffs on steel that were not allowed under the WTO.

   (iii) The Antidumping law is the most frequently used trade penalty. Goods are dumped if sold below market value

   (iv) The Countervailing Duty Law may be invoked to respond to subsidies by foreign governments.

(v)   Section 337 is most commonly applied for trademark infringement.

(vi)   The Buy American Act. Federal agencies must give preferences for American-made products in their purchasing.

V.   **INTERNATIONAL TRADE REGIMES**. Because bilateral agreements can be limited and inefficient, international capital prefers governments to create larger agreements.

A.   **North American Free Trade Agreement** calls for a general elimination of trade barriers between the U.S., Canada, and Mexico. NAFTA divides goods into three categories and lifts restrictions on foreign investment and ownership. NAFTA has provisions for environmental concerns and allows a panel to impose fines for non-compliance. The so-called labor protections of NAFTA have not proven to be effective.

B.   **The World Trade Organization and the GATT**. The WTO is comprised of 148 nations with 30 more applying for membership. Current projects of the WTO look to reduce subsidies in various products and create uniform regimes for intellectual property, finance, and settlement dispute.

C.   **Basic Principles of the WTO**: MNF treatment, bound tariffs, and national treatment.

VIEW FROM CYBERSPACE: WTO TACKLES ELECTRONIC COMMERCE. The WTO is trying to regulate electronic commerce. There are two competing plans, the EU – trade is a service and the American idea to maximize efficiency in electronic commerce with little regulation. Currently the WTO members states have not agreed on a regime to deal with electronic commerce.

1.   Most Favored Nation Treatment. All nations in the WTO are to be treated equally.

2.   Bound Tariffs. Once tariffs are lowered they are not to be raised.

3.   National Treatment. Imports are not to be disfavored solely for their nation of origin.

D.   **Other GATT and WTO Principles.**

1.   Nontariff Barriers are not allowed, e.g. requiring that products have labels noting the use of child-labor or the use of pesticides.

2. Environmental and Health Exceptions and the SPS Agreement. Countries can enforce environmental and safety standards, but such must not be arbitrary or unjustified, e.g., GATT declared a U.S. ban on certain types of tuna fishing illegal. Similarly, U.S. regulations to promote cleaner burning gasoline were illegal.

> **Case 25.2--EC** *Measure Concerning Meat and Meat Products* **(Hormones)**, WT/DS26/AB/R. WT/DS46/ABR (Jan. 16, 1998). Europe banned the import of meat with certain hormones. U.S. firms challenged the ban. The ban was ruled illegal, and the U.S. was allowed to retaliate by laying tariffs in the amount of nearly $117 million.

E. **WTO Dispute Settlement Procedures.** The U.S. and her corporations have brought many proceedings in the WTO. Where the GATT measures allowed a party to block settlement procedures, WTO has improve the process. A panel of experts will be convened at the request of a complaining party. Panel reports will be adopted unless rejected by consensus. Losing parties can appeal.

Timetable. WTO Understanding of Rules and Procedures Governing the Settlement of Disputes sets forth a timetable of roughly 12 months to resolve a dispute.

VI. **REGIONAL ECONOMIC INTEGRATION**. Regional alliances and customs unions seek to harmonize internal trade rules and eliminate barriers to trade.

A. **The European Union** has been a long time in formation, and since 2001 has a single currency and a common customs tariff.

1. Principal EU Institutions there are five institutions responsible for governing the EU:

   (i) The European Commission is the executive branch, composed of 25 appointed leaders, it is the policy-making arm.

   (ii) The Council of Ministers is the legislative body it passes regulations, directives and decisions.

   (iii) The European Parliament offers advisory opinions on CM legislation. The parliament's rejection can be overridden.

   (iv) The European Court of Justice interprets treaties and national laws especially related to common market rules.

(v)   The European Central Bank and the EMU member states must adopt the euro and relinquish control of domestic monetary policy to the ECB.

2.   Challenges include no common European citizenship, no unitary insurance law, pension plans are not coordinated. Tax laws vary greatly especially in relation to business.

VII.   INTERNATIONAL TRANSACTIONS.

A.   **Overseas Offices and Subsidiaries**. Generally, a U.S. business establishes a local office in a foreign country to manage local activities, including acting as a liaison with the host country's officials. These offices are subject, of course, to local laws and customs and are limited in the scope of their activities.

B.   **Contracting in an International Environment**. Cross-border business contracts involve more risk and uncertainty than domestic contracts. Differences in legal systems, policies and cultures can make understanding (the "meeting of the minds") difficult and, in some cases, make provisions of the contract unenforceable.

C.   **Payment and Letters of Credit**. The preferred payment mechanism for international sales transactions is the letter of credit. Two sets of rules apply for letters of credit. Under the UCC a L/C is irrevocable unless mutually agreed. Under the UCP the rule is the opposite.

D.   **Guaranties and Standby Letters of Credit in Financing Transactions**. Under a *guaranty* arrangement, a local financial institution guarantees that the lender will be repaid if the project principals are unable to pay, as long as the project contracts have been adhered to by the parties to the project. U.S. law prohibits banks from issuing guaranties, instead they use a *standby letter of credit* which requires payment only if applicant has failed to perform obligations.

E.   **Investment Abroad**. Before investing, U.S. firms must assess goals and consider various factors.

1.   Investment Goals.

2.   Local Market Penetration. Some markets are inaccessible without some "investment" in the community such as a manufacturing facility and some countries permit only local companies to establish a retail business.

3. Regional Base. To establish credibility, U.S. companies should consider establishing manufacturing, marketing, and/or service centers in the relevant region to establish credibility with local customers.

4. Cheaper Production Costs. Developing countries typically offer cheaper labor and raw materials than more industrialized countries, but other factors such as labor efficiency, reliability of supplies, local labor-law requirements, and political stability can affect the true costs of production.

F. **Host Country Conditions**. Perspective investors must consider a number of economic, legal, and other matters.

1. Economic Conditions such as the host country's economic condition, per capita income, growth trends, readily available currency, and inflation rates.

2. Investors must look beyond the contract to political risks such as expropriation and legal risks affecting taxes and tariffs.

3. Geographic Conditions can directly affect the production and transportation costs. The ability for U.S. companies to own and manage foreign land is problematic in some countries, requiring local partners and significant capital investments. Infrastructure (utilities and police) also presents concerns.

4. Legal Conditions. Local laws and courts might be unpredictable. A reliable court or dispute resolution forum (such as an established arbitration system) is significant, without which there is little leverage to enforce contracts or invoke commercial laws. Many countries allow U.S. companies to operate as a sole proprietorship; a general, limited, or limited liability partnership; a limited liability company; or a corporation, each subject to its own set of laws, equity investment requirements, liabilities, and taxation. Licensing agreements and investment law may render intellectual property rights moot or unenforceable. Bilateral tax/investment treaties may grant special rights to U.S. businesses.

5. Labor Conditions. The true cost of labor includes labor efficiency, trainability, reliability, adherence to quality control standards and labor laws that require housing, education and food subsidies.

6. Financial Issues.

(i)   Currency Considerations. Minimal fluctuations are desired with host currency tied to another major currency such as the dollar or euro.

(ii)   Project Capitalization. Foreign projects usually require fixed capital (for construction) and flexible capital for daily operations. Local laws may not permit flexibility in capital structure.

(iii)   Taxation. Minimizing taxes should be a substantial factor in the business plan. *Gross-up* clauses require the local partner to pay all taxes other than those specifically allocated to the foreign partner. In addition, the U.S. has bilateral tax treaties with more than fifty countries to avoid double taxation of U.S.-based businesses and individuals. Tax credits may also be available to U.S. companies for doing business with particular nations.

7.   Operational Concerns. Local customs vary and make business deal difficult to navigate. Some countries may lack telecommunications, banking, or transportation services. Many U.S. firms pay their American, expatriate staff more than local employees, generating resentment.

G.   Dispute Resolution in International Business.

1.   Dispute Resolution Mechanisms. International law offers several methods to resolve disputes.

(i)   Negotiation is informal and usually the best means to handle conflicts.

(ii)   Good offices, in the event of breach of contract or material misunderstanding, parties will allow a neutral third party or panel (not a court from either country) resolve the dispute.

(iii)   Inquiry, through a commission, looks to international law to resolve matters.

(iv)   Conciliation is more formal, after a cooling off period, parties will agree to be bound by the commission's ruling.

(v)   Arbitration is the preferred method of dispute resolution because it is fast, less costly, confidential, and arbitrators are more familiar with international transactions.

2.   Choice of Law and Choice of Forum. Parties can agree which set of laws or which forum will govern a dispute. Commonly accepted terms are that disputes will be addressed by the UCC or ICISD with the process governed by international rules adopted by the United Nations Commission on International Trade Law (UNCITRAL).

3.   Enforcement of Awards is usually governed by the principle of comity. Three conditions must be met: reciprocity, notice, comportment with domestic law and treaty.

4.   Forum Non Conveniens. A defendant can claim the forum chosen by the plaintiff is not convenient and show that both public and private interests warrant the move to the defendant's jurisdiction.

5.   Suing Foreign Governments.

       (i)   Sovereign Immunity prevents the courts of one country from hearing suits against other governments.

       (ii)   *Foreign Sovereign Immunities Act of* 1976 (FSIA) grants a blanket immunity to foreign states *except* when: (i) the foreign state expressly or impliedly waives its immunity; (ii) the foreign state engages in commercial activities; (iii) the foreign state expropriates property in violation of international law; (iv) property in the United States that is immovable or was acquired by gift or succession is at issue; (v) noncommercial torts are committed by the foreign state; (vi) suit is brought to enforce a maritime lien under admiralty law; and (vii) in suit initiated by the foreign state, the defendant wishes to file a counterclaim.

       (iii)   The "commercial activity" *exception* waives sovereign immunity when the action is based upon an act outside the U.S. in connection with a commercial activity of the foreign sovereign elsewhere that causes a direct effect in the United States.

               Case 25.3--*Sosa v. Alvarez-Machain* 124 S. Ct.2739 (2004), The DEA and its agents kidnapped defendant from Mexico. Alvarez was acquitted in a criminal trial and later sued the DEA for false arrest under the Federal Tort Claims Act. The Supreme Court dismissed holding that Alvarez could not sue, given that the FTCA did not waive U.S. sovereign immunity for acts carried out in a foreign country.

6. Act-of-State Doctrine. Noncommercial acts of government that affect business. American business cannot gain relief for the acts of another sovereign.

THE RESPONSIBLE MANAGER: EXPANDING INTO INTERNATIONAL MARKETS. Before entering new markets managers should:

- Learn customs, substantive, and local laws.
- Make direct contact with local officials and merchants.
- Obtain local representatives or foreign partners.
- Review laws on investment, partnership, licensing and patents.
- Understand the intricacies of tax and corporate law in the forum.

INSIDE STORY: THE EUROPEAN UNION CONSTITUTION: UNITED IN DIVERSITY. The move toward integration of the EU has led to proposals of a constitution. At the same time, each nation wants to preserve some of its autonomy. Various matters of individual freedom and liberty need to be balanced in every nation which generally limits commercial speech, religious expressions, and connections between church and state in ways that are not practiced in the United States. If ratified, the major changes to the EU will number eight.

- EU legal authority will trump certain laws of member states.
- Division of Responsibilities – the EU will take over some powers formerly exercised by member governments.
- Qualified Voting Majority – unanimity will no longer be required, yet states will have a veto vote on decisions of war and taxation.
- President of the European Council – will serve for 30 months, with the possibility of one renewal.
- Union Minister of Foreign Affairs – a new position, that will represent the union in matters of trade and security.
- Reform of the European Commission – will consist of only 2/3rd of member states.
- Expansion of the Role of the Parliament – will become the co-equal of the Council of Ministers.
- Leaving the EU will no long be automatic through mere domestic legislation.

STUDY QUESTIONS

True-False Questions

__ 1. Common law legal systems depend more on statutes than previous court cases to guide legal decisions.

___ 2. The United States is said to be a common law country because its court system and system of law in re judges is based in that of 18th century England.

___ 3. Most European countries are civil law systems, whereby judges look to statutes as the primary source of authority.

___ 4. Banking and other types of finance may be illegal or uncommon in Muslim countries due to the dictates of the Koran and Sharia law.

___ 5. Because India was formerly in the British commonwealth, its legal traditions regarding marriage and divorce are grounded in common law rather than Hindu, or religious custom.

___ 6. Treaties can be applied unilaterally within a nation, and do not need to be in accord with international agreements.

___ 7. Fast-track trade agreements improve the efficiency of rule making and do not require standard Congressional approval for that of treaties.

___ 8. Even though there are various international law courts of varied jurisdiction, most international disputes are simply handled within the parameters of domestic law.

___ 9. The majority of American import and export policies are enforced by the legislative and branch of government..

___ 10. Countervailing duties are imposed as a response to predatory pricing schemes, not merely in reaction to unfair government subsidies.

___ 11. Under WTO rules, some U.S. tariffs may be improper and the U.S. government will have to compensate injured foreign companies or governments.

___ 12. Though the WTO seeks to harmonize trade and reduce barriers to import and export, the WTO encourages member nations to promote domestic products over foreign imports.

___ 13. The WTO restrictions on American tuna fishing that will save dolphins are either unnecessary or improper restraints on trade.

___ 14. The European Union is merely a customs union because it eliminated all duties within and between member states.

___ 15. Negotiation should be the preferred method to address and remedy international disputes and misunderstandings in business.

Multiple-Choice Questions

___ 1. American law incorporates which system of law?

A.   Case law.
B.   Statutory.
C.   International.
D.   All of the above.

__ 2.   When looking at international business dealings, the most important sources of law are:

I.   Hindu custom.
II.   English common law.
III.   Civil law.

A.   I and II.
B.   II and III.
C.   I and III.
D.   I, II, and III.

__ 3.   Which is true about fast-track trade agreements / negotiations?
A.   Congressional approval makes them treaties.
B.   Though the President does not prefer, Senators can always vote to add amendments to the proposals.
C.   They need a super majority vote in Congress to become supreme law.
D.   They are never treaties.

__ 4.   Which was an objective of NAFTA?
A.   To create a single currency among the U.S., Mexico and Canada.
B.   To eliminate all barriers to the free trade of products.
C.   To create a customs union.
D.   To ensure financiers that they could not lose investments via nationalization.

__ 5.   The U.S. Trade Representative might invoke Section 301 of the Trade Act in order to:
A.   Protect American exports.
B.   Protect foreign imports.
C.   Reward domestic producers.
D.   Punish domestic consumers.

__ 6.   When drafting international contracts one means to reduce uncertainty is:
A.   Include terms as to choose a forum for dispute resolution.
B.   Always choose a neutral third-part arbiter.
C.   Use local agents to negotiate contracts with local governments.
D.   All of the above.

__ 7.   Which is *not* a characteristic of conciliation?
A.   A cooling off period.

     B.   Binding arbitration.
     C.   International law courts.
     D.   International dispute.

__ 8.   Which of the following are the most common mechanisms applied by nations to regulate international economic and political activity?
     A.   Economic embargoes.
     B.   Retaliatory tariffs.
     C.   Most Favored Nation trade status.
     D.   None of the above.

__ 9.   The primary purpose of the U.S. Export-Import Bank is _____.
     A.   To help American banks secure loans.
     B.   To ensure that American imports do not hurt American production.
     C.   To subsidize the purchase of American exports in other nations.
     D.   All of the above.

__ 10.   The President has discretion to:
     A.   Impose *ad valorem* taxes and declare some imports as duty free.
     B.   Lift *ad valorem* taxes and impose 100% tariffs on some items.
     C.   Enforce *ad valorem* taxes and declare some imports as duty free.
     D.   Enforce *ad valorem* taxes and set duties on exports.

__ 11.   According to WTO principles, once a tariff is lowered it should:
     A.   Rise only as needed to protect local industry.
     B.   Never rise.
     C.   Never rise more than the rate of inflation.
     D.   Rise as other countries raise their standard of living.

__ 12.   In the WTO system, a domestic law that requires chemical additives be placed in gasoline as a means to reduce toxic emissions, is:
     A.   Improper because such laws raise the costs of production in exporting nations.
     B.   Improper because domestic consumers should not have to follow their own laws.
     C.   Proper because every nation has sovereignty to make its own environmental laws.
     D.   Proper because economic regulations should always touch upon the environment.

__ 13.   The European Parliament:
     A.   Give advice on the acts of the EU Council of Ministers.
     B.   Is the supreme legislative body for the EU.
     C.   Is the final body of appeal from the ECJ.
     D.   All of the above.

__ 14.   U.S. Courts will not rehear an international dispute previously adjudicated in foreign courts because:

    A.   They cannot due to international law.

    B.   It is not their custom.

    C.   Such is barred absolutely under the doctrine of comity.

    D.   American courts will hear such cases, as long as one party is tied to the U.S..

___ 15. Based on national security:

    A.   Congress can override Presdintial prohibitions on weapons exports.

    B.   The President can block weapons exports.

    C.   Weapons exporters can receive permission to export duty free.

    D.   No private company can export weapons or dual use technology.

Essay Questions

1.   Why should contracts contain a conflict of laws provision?

2.   What are the basic steps in using a letter of credit, why is it necessary, what are its advantages?

3.   What are the four most important considerations when seeking to engage in international trade or business?

ANSWERS TO THE
STUDY QUESTIONS

Chapter 1- Ethics, Value Creation, and Risk Management

True-False Questions   *Multiple-Choice Questions*

1.	F		1.	A
2.	F		2.	D
3.	T		3.	C
4.	F		4.	B
5.	F		5.	C
6.	T		6.	A
7.	F		7.	D
8.	F		8.	D
9.	F		9.	C
10.	F		10.	A
11.	T		11.	B
12.	F		12.	A
13.	F		13.	C
14.	T		14.	A
15.	F		15.	C

Essay Questions

1. **Using the Tylenol/Johnson-Johnson case as an example, discuss how a company can use ethics to increase profits.** In the Tylenol case, short-term losses were overcome by long-term profits. Johnson & Johnson showed they cared enough for public safety to endure a loss in profits when the scare was not caused by them.

2. **Discussing the Honda and Dell examples, how can a company be more proactively socially responsible?** Automaker Honda has pushed for higher fuel efficiency, created hybrid cars that have lower emissions, and redesigned factories to reduce pollution. Dell Computers has established computer recycling.

3. **Generally, what should be in a corporate code of ethics?** A code of ethics should contain clear guidelines, expectations, and principles of conduct. A code is the surest way to encourage ethical behavior and prevent a crisis before it strikes. Also, the code should incorporate a training program to implement the code, re-order corporate culture in support of the values management wishes to impart, and the manner in which employees and management consistently review and consider the code of conduct.

Chapter 2—Constitutional Bases for Business Regulation

True-False Questions　　　　　*Multiple-Choice Questions*

1.	F		1.	C
2.	F		2.	B
3.	F		3.	D
4.	F		4.	B
5.	F		5.	A
6.	F		6.	A
7.	F		7.	A
8.	F		8.	B
9.	T		9.	D
10.	T		10.	C
11.	F		11.	A
12.	F		12.	B
13.	F		13.	D
14.	F		14.	A
15.	T		15.	C

Essay Questions

1. **How did the Supreme Court use cases and the Commerce Clause to help enforce and promote the Civil Rights Act?** In the *Katzenbach v. McClung* and the *Heart of Atlanta Motel* cases in 1964, the Court linked use of food and lodging and its impact on interstate commerce.

2. **Why is the freedom of speech not unlimited in a democracy?** All speech is not worthy of protection, e.g., bribery, perjury, and solicitation are illegal. Also, tortious acts such as assault and the intentional infliction of emotional distress.

3. **How can Congress regulate speech on the internet when cyberspace includes transnational transactions?** Congress can regulate interstate commerce, particularly commerce where the ISP's are located within the jurisdiction of the United States.

Chapter 3—Courts, Sources of Law and Litigation

True-False Questions   *Multiple-Choice Questions*

1.	F		1.	B
2.	T		2.	D
3.	T		3.	C
4.	T		4.	A
5.	F		5.	B
6.	F		6.	A
7.	T		7.	D
8.	F		8.	C
9.	F		9.	C
10.	F		10.	C
11.	T		11.	B
12.	F		12.	B
13.	F		13.	A
14.	T		14.	D
15.	F		15.	C

Essay Questions

1. **Why should bias be less in federal court for diversity cases?** State judges are elected so there is a potential bias for re-election; federal judges have a lifetime tenure as a judge.

2. **Why do federal judges have lifetime tenure?** Lifetime appointments allow federal judges to do their job without political influences from parties or contributors, while not worrying about re-election or re-appointment.

3. **Why should an attorney take a deposition of a witness when the witness will be at trial?** May not be a trial, see how good or bad a witness is, impeachment, and information to possibly settle the case.

Chapter 4—Alternative Dispute Resolution

True-False Questions   *Multiple-Choice Questions*

1.	T		1.	C
2.	F		2.	A
3.	T		3.	B
4.	F		4.	D
5.	T		5.	D
6.	T		6.	C
7.	F		7.	B
8.	T		8.	A
9.	T		9.	B
10.	F		10.	D
11.	T		11.	C
12.	T		12.	D
13.	T		13.	B
14.	T		14.	A
15.	F		15.	C

Essay Questions

1. **What are the best arguments to support the idea that a mediator's decisions and work products should remain confidential?** Mediators can deal with private, confidential information during the mediation process. This secrecy should be maintained. Some states (e.g., New York) have passed statutes stating this.

2. **Why is arbitration usually binding?** Contrast to binding—consensual. Prevent going to court.

3. **Compare and contrast mediation and arbitration.** Mediation is facilitating, non-binding; arbitration has a binding decision by arbitrator.

4. **What role should the Internet have in mediating online disputes?** Online dispute resolution (ODR) can have a place in mediating and arbitrating international dispute resolutions. At the very least ODR can narrow issues prior to face-to-face meetings between the parties. See, e.g., the following websites: www.eresolution.com and www.icourthouse.com.

Chapter 5—Agency

True-False Questions   *Multiple-Choice Questions*

1.	F		1.	A
2.	T		2.	B
3.	T		3.	D
4.	F		4.	B
5.	T		5.	D
6.	F		6.	C
7.	F		7.	A
8.	T		8.	C
9.	F		9.	D
10.	F		10.	D
11.	F		11.	B
12.	T		12.	D
13.	F		13.	C
14.	T		14.	B
15.	F		15.	A

Essay Questions

1. **Why is it probably cheaper for an employer to hire an independent contractor rather than an employee for the same job?** The employer does not have to pay or withhold taxes, Social Security, or unemployment taxes for an independent contractor. Moreover, an employer may not be liable for the tortuous acts of an independent contractor.

2. **Compare and contrast actual and apparent authority.** Actual authority—express or implied from principal to agent, or conduct of the principal. Apparent authority—third party believes the agent is an agent because of the principal's words or acts.

3. **Why are principals usually not liable for the torts of independent contractors?** No control and so *respondeat superior* does not apply.

4. **What precautions should companies make to prevent liability for the conduct of an electronic agent that automatically executes a electronic contract?** Companies should amend their standard contract language that provides for the creation of a binding contract by the electronic agent, but also provides for rescission in the event of an electronic mistake.

Chapter 6—Administrative Law

True-False Questions		*Multiple-Choice Questions*	
1.	F	1.	A
2.	T	2.	C
3.	T	3.	B
4.	F	4.	D
5.	T	5.	D
6.	F	6.	A
7.	T	7.	B
8.	F	8.	D
9.	F	9.	C
10.	F	10.	D
11.	F	11.	A
12.	T	12.	B
13.	F	13.	C
14.	T	14.	A
15.	F	15.	B

Essay Questions

1. **How are administrative agencies beneficial with regards to social justice and ethics?** Administrative agencies perform acts from all three branches, and probably more efficiently than any one branch could. These acts include rule making, conducting formal adjudications, taking informal discretionary actions, and conducting investigations.

2. **Why are there no jury trials allowed in agency proceedings?** Cases have held that the 7th Amendment right to a jury trial meant the right to a trial that existed at common law, i.e., pre-enactment of the 7th Amendment. No administrative agencies then, so no right to a jury trial now.

3. **What are the benefits and limitations of the relative autonomy of administrative agencies (and the lack of judicial oversight)?** There is no judicial oversight; Congress performs this role. It is limited to the decision making process of appropriations.

Chapter 7--Contracts

True-False Questions

1.	T
2.	T
3.	F
4.	T
5.	F
6.	F
7.	F
8.	F
9.	T
10.	F
11.	F
12.	T
13.	T
14.	T
15.	F

Multiple-Choice Questions

1.	D
2.	D
3.	A
4.	D
5.	B
6.	C
7.	A
8.	D
9.	B
10.	C
11.	C
12.	D
13.	B
14.	A
15.	C

Essay Questions

1. **Why must an offer be communicated?** An offer cannot be accepted unless it is communicated to an offeree.

2. **Courts normally do not inquire about the adequacy of value of consideration in a contract. Why not?** Courts check to see that consideration is given, not how much it is or what it is. You have the right to make a bad deal. Courts are not equipped to determine the value of items.

3. **Why must an injured party mitigate his or her damages?** Because generally a court will require a party suing for damages to have mitigated their damages or injuries before a recovery from a jury.

Chapter 8—Sales

True-False Questions			*Multiple-Choice Questions*	
1.	F		1.	A
2.	F		2.	D
3.	F		3.	A
4.	T		4.	C
5.	T		5.	B
6.	T		6.	D
7.	F		7.	C
8.	T		8.	A
9.	F		9.	B
10.	T		10.	C
11.	F		11.	B
12.	F		12.	D
13.	T		13.	A
14.	F		14.	C
15.	F		15.	D

Essay Questions

1. **Why does the UCC allow a firm offer to be irrevocable without consideration?** The policy reason behind this is the movement of goods and commerce. The firm offer is not a separate money-making proposition, but rather designed to help the merchant sell the goods it has.

2. **Why are contracts for the sale of goods for $500 or more governed by the statute of frauds?** Like the other Statute of Frauds contracts, this is a type of contract worthy of protection due to the frequency of its occurrence. Proof is needed for these contracts.

3. **Distinguish FOB Seller's and FOB Buyer's place of business.** Shifts the risk of loss from buyer to seller. FOB Buyer's place of business is less risky for the buyer.

4. **Under UCITA, how would you as a manager distinguish between a good such as a computer with computer software installed on the hard drives, versus a Palm Pilot PDA? Which rules govern the sale of these different goods?** In a mixed transaction involving both tangible good and computer information, look for the primary purpose of the transaction. UCITA generally treats goods with software embedded (such as a PDA) as a good, governed by UCC 2 Sales. In other transactions, *e.g.,* sale of a computer with Windows98 install, UCC2 would govern the computer itself, and UCITA would govern the computer information.

Chapter 9--Torts

True-False Questions		Multiple-Choice Questions	
1.	F	1.	A
2.	T	2.	B
3.	T	3.	A
4.	T	4.	C
5.	F	5.	A
6.	F	6.	D
7.	F	7.	D
8.	T	8.	B
9.	F	9.	D
10.	T	10.	C
11.	T	11.	A
12.	T	12.	B
13.	F	13.	C
14.	F	14.	D
15.	T	15.	C

Essay Questions

1. **Compare and contrast assault and battery.** Assault is the intentional creation of a reasonable apprehension of an immediate harmful or offensive contact to the plaintiff's person. Battery is the harmful or offensive contact to the plaintiff's person.

2. **Compare and contrast private and public nuisances.** Public nuisance—interference with the rights of the community as a whole; suit is brought by the government. Private nuisance—a substantial and unreasonable interference with the use and enjoyment of the property.

3. **What are the requirements for *res ipsa loquitur*?** *Res ipsa loquitur* requires the exclusive control by the defendant, an accident that normally doe snot happen without negligence, and an injury not due to the plaintiff's own negligence.

4. **In what ways may a consumer have a cause of action for trespass to chattels for spam (unwanted email) that is being delivered into his or her inbox?** A consumer may allege that her own "inbox" is personal property and unwanted mailings (spam) to that inbox would be a trespass to chattels, especially after the consumer notified the spammer.

Chapter 10—Product Liability

True-False Questions

1. F
2. F
3. T
4. T
5. T
6. F
7. F
8. T
9. F
10. T
11. F
12. T
13. F
14. F
15. F

Multiple-Choice Questions

1. C
2. D
3. B
4. D
5. A
6. C
7. B
8. A
9. B
10. C
11. D
12. A
13. B
14. A
15. B

Essay Questions

1. **A hair dryer has a label on it, which states it should not be used in the shower. The same statement appears on the box the dryer came in, and in the manual for the dryer. Should this be sufficient to protect the manufacturer of the hair dryer if a purchaser uses the dryer in the shower and is injured? Explain.** Yes. Manufacturers clearly labeled the product and adequately warned of the proper use and improper use of the product.

2. **Why has market-share liability been rejected in many jurisdictions?** Market share liability has been rejected in many jurisdictions because it is a simplistic response to a complex problem; it implies that manufacturers are insurers of all of their industry's products. Further, a constitutional challenge has been made on due process grounds for failure to be able to prove individual products did not cause harm.

3. **What is the preemption defense?** The preemption defense allows immunity if a manufacturer complies with federally set minimum standards for the safety of products. The federal law preempts state law.

Chapter 11—Intellectual Property

True-False Questions   *Multiple-Choice Questions*

1.	F		1.	B
2.	F		2.	A
3.	T		3.	D
4.	T		4.	C
5.	T		5.	D
6.	F		6.	B
7.	T		7.	A
8.	F		8.	D
9.	F		9.	A
10.	T		10.	C
11.	T		11.	B
12.	F		12.	A
13.	T		13.	B
14.	F		14.	D
15.	T		15.	C

Essay Questions

1. **Why do many experts believe that the PTO is issuing business software patents too readily?** Three main reasons: 1) most software code is not published; 2) patent applications are not published unless and until a patent is issued; and 3) no opportunity for experts to introduce evidence to the PTO to prevent the issuance of the patent.

2. **Why should fair use be allowed?** For activities such as literary criticism, social comment, news reporting, education, scholarship, or research.

3. **What is the purpose of a trademark?** Four main purposes: 1) identification of goods; 2) show the single source of the trademarked goods; 3) guarantee consistent quality; and, 4) to advertise the goods.

Chapter 12—Employment Agreement

True-False Questions   *Multiple-Choice Questions*

1.	F		1.	A
2.	T		2.	B
3.	T		3.	D
4.	T		4.	C
5.	T		5.	B
6.	F		6.	C
7.	F		7.	D
8.	T		8.	B
9.	F		9.	C
10.	F		10.	D
11.	F		11.	D
12.	T		12.	D
13.	F		13.	A
14.	F		14.	C
15.	T		15.	D

Essay Questions

1. **What are some of the factors that can give rise to an implied obligation to an employee only for good cause?** The reasons are long-term employees, positive evaluations, continued employment assured if she did a good job, she was told she was doing a good job, would not be terminated except for good cause, and never warned about her conduct.

2. **What do employers accomplish with covenants not to compete?** Covenant not to compete: limit use of trade secrets. Restrict competition, and get repaid for training expenses.

3. **Why should a former employer not give an overly positive letter of recommendation about a former employee?** May be liable to the new employer and to third parties injured by employee if the employer hires him or her.

Chapter 13—Civil Rights and Employment Discrimination

True-False Questions   *Multiple-Choice Questions*

1.	F		1.	B
2.	F		2.	A
3.	T		3.	D
4.	F		4.	A
5.	T		5.	A
6.	T		6.	D
7.	T		7.	B
8.	F		8.	B
9.	F		9.	C
10.	T		10.	C
11.	T		11.	B
12.	F		12.	D
13.	T		13.	A
14.	F		14.	B
15.	F		15.	C

Essay Questions

1. **Why do some consider the ADA as the most sweeping civil rights measure since 1964?** Some consider the ADA the most sweeping civil rights legislation because it has the potential to affect so many areas, such as employment, transportation, public accommodations, and telecommunications services.

2. **How does the plaintiff prove a disparate impact claim?** The plaintiff has the burden of proof to show that an employment practice, though neutral on its face, had a disparate *impact* on a protected group. To prove the case, plaintiff must show: the specific employment practice caused, for example, a statistically significant disproportion between the racial composition of the persons holding the jobs at issue and the racial composition of the *qualified* persons in the relevant labor market. The business justification offered by the employer to justify the disparate impact must relate to job performance.

3. **In same-sex sexual harassment, must the plaintiff show the defendant was homosexual? Why or why not?** No. Same-sex means male-male and female-female harassment. The suit is not predicated on sexual desire or homosexuality.

Chapter 14—Criminal Law

True-False Questions		*Multiple-Choice Questions*	
1.	F	1.	A
2.	T	2.	B
3.	T	3.	C
4.	T	4.	D
5.	T	5.	B
6.	F	6.	A
7.	T	7.	A
8.	T	8.	A
9.	F	9.	C
10.	T	10.	C
11.	F	11.	B
12.	T	12.	D
13.	T	13.	A
14.	F	14.	C
15.	T	15.	B

Essay Questions

1. To reduce culpability under the Federal Sentencing Guidelines, what strategies must a company have in place? A company should have standards and procedures to reduce criminal conduct; high-level personnel in charge of the program; due care in delegating authority; effective communication and training; mechanisms for monitoring and reporting criminal misconduct; consistent enforcement standards; and procedure for feedback and correction.

2. Why are there different burdens of proof in civil and criminal cases? Criminal burden is beyond a reasonable doubt—the highest standard—due to the potential of loss of life or liberty in addition to a fine. The civil standard (preponderance of the evidence) is a lower standard because only money, not life or liberty, is involved.

Chapter 15—Environmental Law

True-False Questions

1. T
2. T
3. T
4. T
5. F
6. T
7. T
8. T
9. F
10. T
11. T
12. T
13. T
14. F
15. F

Multiple-Choice Questions

1. D
2. C
3. B
4. A
5. A
6. B
7. C
8. C
9. A
10. B
11. C
12. D
13. A
14. B
15. D

Essay Questions

1. **Why may congressional or administrative agency staffs be unaware of how proposed regulations may affect a particular industry?** They may not be familiar with the industry specifics for a general regulation. Industry input may produce a better way to deal with an issue than the agency had sought to implement.

2. **The EPA establishes performance standards based on the best control technology available for a category of similar sources. Why?** The sources of pollution will gradually be eliminated by this method, and similar treatment of similar sources throughout the country.

3. **In general, what is successor liability?** Successor liability is the responsibility of an acquirer of corporate assets for the liability of the corporation that sold the assets.

Chapter 16--Antitrust

True-False Questions		*Multiple-Choice Questions*	
1.	T	1.	D
2.	T	2.	A
3.	F	3.	A
4.	T	4.	B
5.	F	5.	D
6.	T	6.	D
7.	F	7.	D
8.	F	8.	C
9.	F	9.	D
10.	T	10.	B
11.	T	11.	D
12.	T	12.	B
13.	F	13.	B
14.	T	14.	C
15.	F	15.	C

Essay Questions

1. **Why does § 1 of the Sherman Act *not* penalize a manufacturer advertising suggested retail prices?** By definition, a conspiracy or concerted action required for Section 1, requires two or more persons. One person cannot violate Section 1 of the Sherman Act.

2. **Why can a franchise agreement specify that another franchise will not be awarded in the same geographic area?** To insure the success of the franchise by not competing with itself. It does not restrict competition in the general field, just within its own franchises.

3. **Briefly discuss the justifications for the defenses to an allegation of a Robinson-Patman Act violation.** Three defenses: meeting competitor's prices, cost justification (such as delivery charges), and changing conditions (such as very ripe fruit).

Chapter 17—Consumer Protection

True-False Questions		*Multiple-Choice Questions*	
1.	F	1.	C
2.	F	2.	A
3.	F	3.	D
4.	F	4.	A
5.	F	5.	D
6.	T	6.	B
7.	T	7.	B
8.	F	8.	C
9.	F	9.	D
10.	T	10.	D
11.	F	11.	A
12.	T	12.	D
13.	F	13.	C
14.	T	14.	B
15.	F	15.	B

Essay Questions

1.   **Why does the TILA provide for a right of rescission for home equity loans?** Because failure to repay the loan would lead to loss of the home. This gives the consumers more time to think it over.

2.   **What can you, as a consumer, request under the Fair Credit Reporting Act?** All information (except medical) on themselves, the source of the information, and any recent recipients of the report.

3.   **What is "bait and switch" advertising?** Bait and switch advertising is when advertiser refuses to show an item, fails to have a reasonable quantity of an advertised item, fails to promise to deliver an item, or discourages employees from selling the advertised item.

Chapter 18—Real Property and Land Use

True-False Questions   *Multiple-Choice Questions*

1.	T		1.	A
2.	F		2.	B
3.	T		3.	D
4.	F		4.	B
5.	T		5.	C
6.	T		6.	A
7.	F		7.	A
8.	T		8.	D
9.	T		9.	A
10.	T		10.	A
11.	F		11.	C
12.	T		12.	B
13.	T		13.	C
14.	F		14.	B
15.	F		15.	A

Essay Questions

1. **The modern view of tenancy** by the entirety is that it converts to a tenancy in common upon divorce. Why? A tenancy in common is durable, saleable, and inheritable, so the ex-spouses do not have to sell the property to have their children (or anyone else) inherit it.

2. **Briefly discuss the types of recording statutes.** *Race statute*—first in time wins. *Pure-notice statute*—if a person knows another person has bought the property, he or she cannot validate by recording first. *Race-notice statute*—statutes protect only good faith subsequent purchasers who record their deed before the prior purchaser records his or her deed.

3. **How does a sale and leaseback operate?** Two simultaneous transactions: a lender buys property from a corporation and then leases it back to the corporation. The lender recoups its purchase price and the lessee maintains the property.

Chapter 19—Forms of Business Organizations

True-False Questions   *Multiple-Choice Questions*

1.	T	1.	D
2.	T	2.	A
3.	F	3.	B
4.	T	4.	C
5.	T	5.	B
6.	T	6.	A
7.	F	7.	B
8.	F	8.	D
9.	T	9.	D
10.	T	10.	A
11.	F	11.	C
12.	T	12.	B
13.	T	13.	A
14.	F	14.	A
15.	F	15.	C

Essay Questions

1. **Shareholders elect the directors. Directors hire the officers. The officers run the corporation day to day. Therefore, the shareholders run the corporation day to day. Explain.** While each prefatory statement is true, the conclusion is fallacious. The shareholders are the owners, not the officers. They do not run the business day-to-day.

2. **Explain corporate double taxation.** Income earned by the corporation is first taxed at the corporate level and then in the hands of the shareholders when the profits, as dividends, are paid tot he shareholders.

3. **Why are staggered boards favorable to incumbent management?** Staggered boards mean fewer than all directors (perhaps only one director) are elected each time, so it is easier for incumbent management to win re-election tot he board. The minority shareholders need a much higher percentage of the votes to elect a director when the terms are staggered.

Chapter 20—Directors, Officers and Controlling Shareholders

True-False Questions   *Multiple-Choice Questions*

1.	F		1.	D
2.	T		2.	B
3.	F		3.	D
4.	F		4.	D
5.	T		5.	A
6.	T		6.	C
7.	T		7.	D
8.	F		8.	A
9.	F		9.	C
10.	F		10.	C
11.	T		11.	B
12.	F		12.	D
13.	T		13.	B
14.	F		14.	A
15.	F		15.	C

Essay Questions

1. **When can an officer or director rely on the company's procedures for determining what disclosure is required?** Only when he or she has a reasonable basis for believing that those procedures are effective and considers all relevant factors. Otherwise, he or she must go beyond the usual procedures.

2. **What is wrong with re-pricing executive stock options if the stock price falls?** The executive earns even more compensation even though all the shareholders have lost money.

3. **What factors will favor keeping a poison pill in place?** The factors include a tender offer only slightly higher than market price, a tender offer for less than all the shares, an active board solicitation for shares, and a tender offer in the very early stages.

Chapter 21—Executive Compensation and Employee Benefits

True-False Questions		*Multiple-Choice Questions*	
1.	T	1.	D
2.	F	2.	D
3.	T	3.	A
4.	T	4.	A
5.	T	5.	A
6.	F	6.	D
7.	T	7.	C
8.	F	8.	B
9.	F	9.	D
10.	T	10.	C
11.	T	11.	B
12.	T	12.	B
13.	T	13.	A
14.	T	14.	A
15.	T	15.	D

Essay Questions

1. **What options do directors have in lieu of stock option programs?** Directors have several options: restricted stock option plans, employee stock purchase plans, phantom stock plans and stock appreciation plans. Restricted stock plans provide employees the right to purchase a limited amount of shares, yet take possession later. ESOP's allow employee's to purchase stock as part of a benefits package but must (1) include most groups of employees; (2) receive shareholder approval; (3) not allow a transferable right to purchase. Phantom stock is a promise to pay a bonus pay a bonus in the equivalent of value of stocks or the increase in value over a period of time. Stock appreciation rights allow the employees to obtain the future appreciation in the company's stock without risking capital.

2. **What impact have tax laws had on stock options?** Companies can deduct the difference in the strike price from the fair market value of the stock when employees exercise their options, but employees are taxed whether they sell the stock or not. If the strike price is higher than the current market price, the employees may suffer a relative loss. Companies can minimize the tax impact by extending the option period, buying back the options, and lowering the strike price.

3. **What can directors do to minimize the threat of litigation regarding executive compensation?** Directors should have a truly independent compensation committee, incorporate performance-based components, avoid benchmarks that compare the company with others within the industry, use fair and proper accounting, not gimmicks, make executives hold shares to avoid pump and dump scenarios; and make executive compensation transparent to shareholders.

Chapter 22—Public and Private Offerings of Securities

True-False Questions   *Multiple-Choice Questions*

1.	T		1.	D
2.	T		2.	B
3.	T		3.	A
4.	F		4.	C
5.	T		5.	C
6.	F		6.	D
7.	F		7.	A
8.	T		8.	B
9.	F		9.	A
10.	T		10.	B
11.	F		11.	B
12.	T		12.	D
13.	F		13.	A
14.	F		14.	C
15.	F		15.	D

Essay Questions

1. **What are the tests that a court can use to determine if a general partnership is an interest in a security?** Three tests: 1) general partnership is really a limited partnership because the partners have very little power; 2) investor is so inexperienced that he or she cannot exercise their partnership powers; and, 3) investor is so dependent on the manager or promoter that he or she cannot replace them or exercise meaningful partnership powers.

2. **What is the basic managerial time line for a public securities offering?**
   Day 1-30—decide to offer and choose an underwriter.
   Day 31-60—prepare prospectus and registration statement.
   Day 61-90—file registration statement with the SEC.
   Day 91-120—quiet period—solicit offers to sell; no public disclosure of information.
   Day 121+—once the offer is declared effective, pricing amendment filed, and sales begin.

3. **What is the Rule 505 exemption?** Offerings of up to $5 million within 12 months to no more than 35 unaccredited investors is exempt.

Chapter 23—Securities Fraud and Insider Trading

True-False Questions		*Multiple-Choice Questions*	
1.	F	1.	B
2.	T	2.	D
3.	F	3.	A
4.	T	4.	B
5.	T	5.	C
6.	T	6.	B
7.	F	7.	A
8.	T	8.	C
9.	T	9.	A
10.	T	10.	C
11.	F	11.	D
12.	F	12.	A
13.	T	13.	B
14.	F	14.	C
15.	F	15.	C

Essay Questions

1. **What is an S-1 review, and why should an accountant do one?** An S-1 reviews events subsequent to the date of the certified balance sheet in the registration statement to ascertain if any material financial changes have occurred that would make the balance sheets misleading.

2. **Why is materiality judged at the time of the misstatement or omission?** Materiality is fact-specific, so when the misstatement or omission is, is critical. Some items are always material; some are not.

3. **When do courts consider a market efficient?** Courts use five factors: sufficient weekly trading, sufficient professional investment reports, presence of market makers, existence of Form S-3 short-form registrants, and a historical showing of immediate price response to unexpected events or financial releases.

Chapter 24—Debtor-Creditor Relations and Bankruptcy

True-False Questions   *Multiple-Choice Questions*

1.	T		1.	A
2.	F		2.	A
3.	T		3.	C
4.	T		4.	D
5.	T		5.	B
6.	T		6.	C
7.	T		7.	A
8.	T		8.	B
9.	F		9.	A
10.	T		10.	C
11.	F		11.	C
12.	F		12.	A
13.	F		13.	B
14.	F		14.	D
15.	F		15.	B

Essay Questions

1. **What are affirmative and negative covenants?** An affirmative covenant is something a borrower will do throughout the term of the loan (such as maintain insurance), while a negative covenant is something the borrower will not do during the loan term (such as incur additional debt).

2. **Security interests can be perfected in what three ways?** Three ways: by possession, by filing, and some are perfected automatically.

3. **Where would you file a security interest in timber?** In the county office where the mortgage on the real property is located.

Chapter 25—International Law and Transactions

True-False Questions

1.	F
2.	T
3.	T
4.	T
5.	F
6.	F
7.	F
8.	F
9.	F
10.	T
11.	T
12.	F
13.	F
14.	F
15.	F

Multiple-Choice Questions

1.	D
2.	B
3.	A
4.	B
5.	B
6.	D
7.	B
8.	D
9.	C
10.	C
11.	A
12.	A
13.	A
14.	C
15.	B

Essay Questions

1. **Why should contracts contain a conflict of laws provision?** A conflict of laws provision lessens the probabilities of a later dispute over which law applies to the contract and where a lawsuit will be held.

2. **What are the basic steps in using a letter of credit, why is it necessary, what are its advantages?** Buyer enters a contract with the issuing bank. The issuing bank issues a letter of credit in favor of the seller to be paid when stated documents are presented, such as a clean bill of lading. The issuing bank then gives the buyer the bill of lading to claim the goods from the carrier upon arrival.

3. **What are the four most important considerations when seeking to engage in international trade or business?** The Paris Convention seeks to encourage reciprocal recognition of patents, trademarks, and other forms of intellectual property among the over 80 signatory countries.